# SOCIOLINGUISTICS

**Praise for the first edition**

'Meets the need for a new coherent and developmental introduction to the subject. Provides up-to-date material, practical exercises, new first hand data and relevant questions. The whole structure and approach is satisfying to read and rewarding to use.'

*Clive Grey, Edge Hill College of Higher Education, UK*

'This textbook is enormously enabling. Not only does it comprehensively provide the basic theory and method at the right level, but beginners have the means and the models so that they can get their hands dirty with real data and real problems in doing sociolinguistics.'

*William Downes, University of East Anglia*

***Routledge English Language Introductions*** cover core areas of language study and are one-stop resources for students.

Assuming no prior knowledge, books in the series offer an accessible overview of the subject, with activities, study questions, sample analyses, commentaries and key readings – all in the same volume. The innovative and flexible 'two-dimensional' structure is built around four sections – introduction, development, exploration and extension – which offer self-contained stages for study. Each topic can be read across these sections, enabling the reader to build gradually on the knowledge gained.

*Sociolinguistics:*

- provides a comprehensive introduction to sociolinguistics
- draws on a range of texts: from an interview with Madonna to the Japanese *Asahi Evening News*
- uses real studies designed and conducted by students
- provides key readings with commentaries from works by major internationally known authors such as Norman Fairclough, Deborah Cameron, Braj Kachru, Jennifer Coates, Mark Sebba, and Malcolm Coulthard
- is accompanied by a supporting website.

Key features of the new edition include a new section on forensic linguistics and additional material on language and gender, conversation analysis, and spoken discourse. There are four new readings which investigate: the discourse practices of men; pidgins and creoles; politeness; and hidden voices in monologue. References have been updated and fresh examples and exercises have been included.

Written by an experienced teacher and author, this accessible textbook is an essential resource for all students of English language and linguistics.

**Peter Stockwell** is Professor of Literary Linguistics at the University of Nottingham. He is the author of numerous books and most recently co-edited *The Routledge Companion to Sociolinguistics*.

Series Editor: Peter Stockwell
Series Consultant: Ronald Carter

# ROUTLEDGE ENGLISH LANGUAGE INTRODUCTIONS

SERIES EDITOR: PETER STOCKWELL

**Peter Stockwell** is Professor of Literary Linguistics in the School of English Studies at the University of Nottingham, UK, where his interests include sociolinguistics, stylistics and cognitive poetics. Recent Routledge publications include *Key Concepts in Language and Linguistics* (2007), the *Routledge Companion to Sociolinguistics* (2007, edited with Carmen Llamas and Louise Mullany), *Language in Theory* (2005, with Mark Robson), and *Cognitive Poetics* (2002).

SERIES CONSULTANT: RONALD CARTER

**Ronald Carter** is Professor of Modern English Language in the School of English Studies at the University of Nottingham, UK. He is the co-series editor of the *Routledge Applied Linguistics* series, series editor of *Interface*, and was co-founder of the Routledge *Intertext* series.

## OTHER TITLES IN THE SERIES:

**Sociolinguistics**
Peter Stockwell

**Pragmatics and Discourse**
Joan Cutting

**Grammar and Vocabulary**
Howard Jackson

**Psycholinguistics**
John Field

**World Englishes**
Jennifer Jenkins

**Practical Phonetics and Phonology**
Beverley Collins & Inger Mees

**Stylistics**
Paul Simpson

**Language in Theory**
Mark Robson & Peter Stockwell

**Child Language**
Jean Stilwell Peccei

**Sociolinguistics 2nd Edition**
Peter Stockwell

**Pragmatics and Discourse 2nd Edition**
Joan Cutting

# SOCIOLINGUISTICS

A resource book for students

PETER STOCKWELL

**Second Edition**

**R** Routledge
Taylor & Francis Group

LONDON AND NEW YORK

First published 2003 by Routledge
This edition published 2007 by Routledge
2 Park Square, Milton Park, Abingdon, Oxon OX14 4RN

Simultaneously published in the USA and Canada
by Routledge
270 Madison Avenue, New York, NY 10016

*Routledge is an imprint of the Taylor & Francis Group, an informa business*

© 2007 Peter Stockwell

Transferred to Digital Printing 2008

Typeset in 10/12.5pt Minion by RefineCatch Limited, Bungay, Suffolk
Printed and bound in Great Britain by Cpod, Trowbridge, Wiltshire

*British Library Cataloguing in Publication Data*
A catalogue record for this book is available from the British Library

*Library of Congress Cataloging in Publication Data*
Stockwell, Peter.
  Sociolinguistics : a resource book for students / Peter Stockwell. — 2nd ed.
    p. cm
  Includes bibliographical references and index.
  1. Sociolinguistics.   I. Title.
  P40.S783 2008
  306.44–dc22

                                                              2007011482

ISBN10: 0–415–40126–7 (hbk)
ISBN10: 0–415–40127–5 (pbk)

ISBN13: 978–0–415–40127–2 (pbk)
ISBN13: 978–0–415–40126–5 (hbk)

# HOW TO USE THIS BOOK

The Routledge English Language Introductions are 'flexi-texts' that you can use to suit your own style of study. The books are divided into four *sections*:

**A Introduction** – sets out the key concepts for the area of study. The *units* of this section take you step-by-step through the foundational terms and ideas, carefully providing you with an initial toolkit for your own study. By the end of the section, you will have a good overview of the whole field.

**B Development** – adds to your knowledge and builds on the key ideas already introduced. Units in this section might also draw together several areas of interest. By the end of this section, you will already have a good and fairly detailed grasp of the field, and will be ready to undertake your own exploration and thinking.

**C Exploration** – provides examples of language data and guides you through your own investigation of the field. The units in this section will be more open-ended and exploratory, and you will be encouraged to try out your ideas and think for yourself, using your newly acquired knowledge.

**D Extension** – offers you the chance to compare your expertise with key readings in the area. These are taken from the work of important writers, and are provided with guidance and questions for your further thought.

You can read this book like a traditional text-book, 'vertically' straight through each unit from beginning to end. This will take you comprehensively through the broad field of study. However, the Routledge English Language Introductions have been carefully designed so that you can read them in another dimension, 'horizontally' as a *thread* across the numbered units. For example, Unit A1, corresponds with B1, C1 and D1 as a coherent thread; A2 with B2, C2 and D2, and so on. Reading across a thread will take you rapidly from the key concepts of a specific area, to a level of expertise in that precise area, all with a very close focus. You can match your way of reading with the best way that you work.

The glossary/index at the end, together with the suggestions for Further Reading, will help to keep you orientated. Each textbook has a supporting website with extra commentary, suggestions, additional material and support for teachers and students.

## SOCIOLINGUISTICS

In this book, you are provided with a map of the key areas in sociolinguistics and a toolkit for investigation in Section A. Terms and ideas are introduced quickly and clearly, so that if you read this section as a whole, you can rapidly start to link together the different areas of sociolinguistic study. In section B (Development), sociolinguistic case-studies are presented from the work of my own undergraduate students, together with my commentary. The idea behind this is to show you in as practical a way as possible that you can achieve a high degree of detailed and sophisti-cated sociolinguistic study in a fairly short space of time. If you are using this book as part of a class, the units in Sections A and B would work as good pre-reading material before the classroom discussion. Section C (Exploration) sets out some sociolinguistic data for your own investigation: you could use this material as a means of trying out the key issues in detail. Most of the questions and advice given in Section C are provided simply for suggestion. No answers, solutions or model inter-pretations are offered, because there are numerous things that a sociolinguistic exploration could produce, and I did not want to close your thinking off.

In the last section of the book (D – Extension), excerpts from professional published studies are presented. As part of a course, these units would work well as follow-up reading after the class. Alternatively, they could stand as reading for discussion in more advanced studies. Suggestions for extended investigation and projects are given, arising from the reading in Section D. Further reading for each thread is given at the end of the book, to enable you to follow particular interests in more depth. All of the sections are designed to allow you the freedom to conduct practical thinking and analysis, and present you with real examples of how to go about your own studies in sociolinguistics. If, by the end, I have encouraged you to discover more about sociolinguistics, and if you are encouraged to take issue critically with existing studies in the area, then this book will have served its purpose.

# CONTENTS

Contents cross-referenced                                         x
Figures                                                          xii
Tables                                                           xiii
Acknowledgements                                                 xiv

**A   Introduction: key concepts in sociolinguistics**            1
 1   A sociolinguistic toolkit                                     2
 2   Accent and dialect                                            4
 3   Register and style                                            8
 4   Ethnicity and multilingualism                                11
 5   Variation and change                                         13
 6   Standardisation                                              16
 7   Gender                                                       19
 8   Pidgins and creoles                                          21
 9   New, national and international Englishes                    24
10   Politeness and accommodation                                27
11   Conversation                                                 30
12   Applying sociolinguistics                                    32

**B   Development: studies in language and society**             37
 1   Undertaking a sociolinguistic study                          38
 2   Attitudes to accent variation                                41
 3   Euphemism, register and code                                 43
 4   Code-switching                                               47
 5   Social networks                                              51
 6   Shifts in prestige                                           54
 7   Genderlects                                                  59
 8   Patwa and post-creolisation                                  61
 9   Singlish and new Englishes                                   64
10   Politeness in mixed-sex conversation                         66
11   Phatics in spoken discourse                                  70
12   Language and ideology                                        72

**C   Exploration: data for investigation**                      75
 1   Collecting and exploring data                                76
 2   Dialectal variation                                          81
 3   Register                                                     86
 4   Ethnology                                                    92

 5  Perceptions of variation                                          94
 6  Prestige                                                          99
 7  Gender                                                           103
 8  Creole                                                           107
 9  New English                                                      110
10  Politeness                                                       112
11  E-discourse                                                      119
12  Critical discourse analysis                                      122

**D  Extension: sociolinguistic readings**                          125
 1  Sociolinguistics and language change (Hamer)                     126
 2  Foreign accents in America (Lippi-Green)                         133
 3  Style and ideology (Fairclough)                                  145
 4  Language contact and code-switching (Edwards)                    153
 5  The sociolinguist's responsibility (Cameron)                     159
 6  The process of standardisation (Milroy)                          163
 7  Men's language (Coates)                                          176
 8  The origins of pidgins and creoles (Sebba)                       184
 9  World Englishes and contact literature (Kachru)                  191
10  The politics of talk (Mullany)                                   202
11  Closing turns (Schegloff and Sacks)                              210
12  Linguistic detection (Coulthard)                                 219

**Further reading**                                                 227
**References**                                                      231
**Glossarial index**                                                249

# CONTENTS **CROSS-REFERENCED**

| Topic | **A** INTRODUCTION | **B** DEVELOPMENT |
|-------|---------------------|-------------------|

**1**

A sociolinguistic toolkit

2

Undertaking a sociolinguistic study

38

**2**

Accent and dialect

4

Attitudes to accent variation

41

**3**

Register and style

8

Euphemism, register and code

43

**4**

Ethnicity and multilingualism

11

Code-switching

47

**5**

Variation and change

13

Social networks

51

**6**

Standardisation

16

Shifts in prestige

54

**7**

Gender

19

Genderlects

59

**8**

Pidgins and creoles

21

Patwa and post-creolisation

61

**9**

New, national and international Englishes

24

Singlish and new Englishes

64

**10**

Politeness and accommodation

27

Politeness in mixed-sex conversation

66

**11**

Conversation

30

Phatics in spoken discourse

70

**12**

Applying sociolinguistics

32

Language and ideology

72

References

Further Reading

Glossarial

Index

**C** **EXPLORATION**

**Collecting and exploring data**
76

**Dialectal variation**
81

**Register**
86

**Ethnology**
92

**Perceptions of variation**
94

**Prestige**
99

**Gender**
103

**Creole**
107

**New English**
110

**Politeness**
112

**E-discourse**
119

**Critical discourse analysis**
122

**D** **EXTENSION**

**Sociolinguistics and language change**
**(Andrew Hamer)**
126

**Foreign accents in America**
**(Rosina Lippi-Green)**
133

**Style and ideology**
**(Norman Fairclough)**
145

**Language contact and code-switching**
**(John Edwards)**
153

**The sociolinguist's responsibility**
**(Deborah Cameron)**
159

**The process of standardisation**
**(James Milroy)**
163

**Men's language**
**(Jennifer Coates)**
176

**The origins of pidgins and creoles**
**(Mark Sebba)**
184

**World Englishes and contact literature**
**(Braj Kachru)**
191

**The politics of talk**
**(Louise Mullany)**
202

**Closing turns**
**(Emmanuel Schegloff and Harvey Sacks)**
210

**Linguistic detection**
**(Malcolm Coulthard)**
219

**Topic**

1
2
3
4
5
6
7
8
9
10
11
12

References

Further
Reading

Glossarial

Index

# LIST OF FIGURES

D1.1 Social stratification of a linguistic variable undergoing change – post-
vocalic (r) in New York City (Labov 1972b: 114)                                    130

D2.1 Persons between 18 and 65 years who claim a first language other than
English and their evaluation of their English-language skills                      136

D2.2 Breakdown of 'Asian or Pacific Islander' category in the 1990 US
census, by national origin                                                         137

D2.3 Hispanics counted in the 1990 US census                                       139

D4.1 Factors influencing language choice in Paraguay                               154

# LIST OF TABLES

D2.1 Language spoken at home by persons 5 years and older 135
D2.2 (Non-English) language spoken at home and ability to speak English, by age 136
D2.3 Hispanic origin by race 140
D2.4 Popular constructions of 'good' and 'bad' language for other countries 141

# ACKNOWLEDGEMENTS

This second edition of *Sociolinguistics* is more altered than I had intended when I started out to revise it. This is an indication of the exciting pace of change in the field, and also a consequence of the advice and comments given to me by colleagues, teachers and students: many people have used this book, found it useful, and have been generous with their thoughts.

Any book in sociolinguistics owes everything to the writing, thinking and talk of others. In this I am privileged to have worked with many people who have shaped my ideas and inspired me to think further about language and life. Paul Simpson, Andrew Hamer, and Kay Richardson first taught me the broad meaning of the word 'sociolinguistics', as represented in this book. More than any other area, I have learnt about sociolinguistics by teaching it and I am grateful to all the students who have taken my courses and especially those whose work and thinking appears directly either here or in the first edition: James Baderman, Chris Barenberg, Virginia Barnes, Vicky Bristow, Lauren Buckland, Miranda Chadwick, Li En Chong, Joel Dothie, Sharlene Goff, Matthew Hassan, Naomi Holdstock, Judith Jones, Louise Kessler, Tim Knebel, I Ching Ng, Kate Oakley, Vicki Oliver, Lynne Senior, Joanna Shirley, Hardip Singh Amarjit Kaur, Martin Stepanek, Zoe Taylor, Kathryn Tibbs, Katherine West, Sarah Wood, and Ben Woolhead.

I have benefited from discussions over the years while teaching with David Cordiner, Maureen Alam, and Rocio Montoro, and owe many of the ideas and language examples in the following pages to the conversations and hospitality of friends and colleagues around the world. I am especially grateful to Louise Mullany, Svenja Adolphs and Ron Carter, my colleagues at Nottingham, for detailed suggestions throughout. Many social conversations eventually turn into sociolinguistic discussions of accent and dialect, but for academic insight in conversation I am grateful to Michael Burke, Urszula Clark, Annette Combrink, Kathy Conklin, Szilvia Csabi, Zoltan Dornyei, Anthea Fraser-Gupta, Alex Gavins, Lucy Henderson, Howard Jackson, Lesley Jeffries, Carmen Llamas, Mike McCarthy, Iain MacGregor, John McRae, Janet Maybin, Emma Moore, Yoshifumi Saito, Norbert Schmitt, Barbara Sinclair, Violeta Sotirova, Ismail Talib, Masanori Toyota, Peter Verdonk, and Doug Yates; thanks also to the writers of the Section D readings who were interested in the book beyond the concerns of copyright. The sociolinguistic texture of life is shared with Joanna Gavins, and my daughter Ada made me aware of how much of the language development of a two-year old is sociolinguistically determined.

This book is dedicated to the men and women of Teesside, the only people in the entire history of the world who speak without an accent.

PJS
Nottingham

The author and publishers would like to thank the following for permission to reproduce copyright material:

Cambridge University Press for an extract from the Cambridge and Nottingham Corpus of Discourse in English (CANCODE) corpus, part of the Cambridge International Corpus;

Jennifer Coates and Blackwell publishers for extracts from *Men Talk* (2003);

Malcolm Coulthard for extracts from ' "... and then ..." Language description and author attribution', the final Sinclair Open Lecture (University of Birmingham, 2006);

John Edwards for extracts from *Multilingualism* (Routledge, 1995);

Norman Fairclough and Arnold Publishers for extracts from *Media Discourse* (1995);

The Guggenheim Museum, Bilbao, for extracts from the exhibition catalogue October 1999–February 2000;

Andrew Hamer for extracts from 'Early Standard English; linguistic confidence and insecurity' (English Association, 1993);

The International Phonetics Association for reproducing the IPA chart (2005);

Braj Kachru and the University of Illinois Press for extracts from 'The bilingual's creativity' in *Discourse Across Cultures* (edited by Larry Smith, 1997);

Rosina Lippi-Green for extracts from *English with an Accent* (Routledge, 1997);

*The Telegraph*, Calcutta for the article 'Sorry, no fish "n" chips for Mr John Major';

James Milroy for extracts from 'Some new perspectives on sound change', *Newcastle and Durham Working Papers in Linguistics* (Universities of Newcastle and Durham, 1993);

Louise Mullany for extracts from ' "I don't think you want me to get a word in edgeways do you John?" Re-assessing (im)politeness, language and gender in political broadcast interviews', *English Working Papers on the Web* (Sheffield Hallam University, 2002);

Harvey Sacks and Emanuel Schegloff, and Mouton de Gruyter publishers for extracts from 'Opening up closings', *Semiotica* 7 (1973);

Mark Sebba and Palgrave publishers for extracts from *Contact Languages: Pidgins and Creoles* (1997);

'Women in EFL Materials for the extract from *On Balance* (1991).

The article by Deborah Cameron, 'Respect, please', is previously unpublished and copyright remains with Deborah Cameron. Many thanks for allowing its use here.

While every effort has been made to contact copyright holders of material used in this volume, we would be happy to hear from any we have been unable to contact, and we will make the necessary amendment at the earliest opportunity.

# Section A

# INTRODUCTION:
## KEY CONCEPTS IN SOCIOLINGUISTICS

## A1    A SOCIOLINGUISTIC TOOLKIT

- ❏   All language events consist of a piece of language in a social context.
- ❏   Every different social context determines that particular form of language.
- ❏   The language used in particular situations determines the nature of that social event.

Given these three points, the potential scope of the discipline of sociolinguistics is enormous. Indeed, given such a broad definition of the field, it would be difficult to see any linguistic situation that did *not* come within the concern of sociolinguistics. Though a theoretical argument can be made along these lines, it is clearly impractical for a book on sociolinguistics to be a book on the language of everything. In fact, since there is some theoretical circularity between the three facts, we can even say that the only way of proceeding in the exploration of language is by getting on with practical investigation. So this book explores the territory and boundaries of sociolinguistics by presenting real studies and real data: the aim – as one reviewer of an earlier edition of the book observed – is to enable you to get your hands dirty with real language as soon as possible. First, though, a few precautionary words.

### Awareness of theory and method

One mistake that new students of sociolinguistics often make is to run off enthusiastically with recorder in pocket to collect some data, and then examine the transcript to see what they have caught. The problem with this 'trawling' approach is that they may not know what they have in their sociolinguistic net, may not be able to recognise it, classify it, nor know what to do with it, and they will not be able to claim anything believable about their fishing trip.

The fact is that successful explorations require a bit of planning and preparation. Fundamentally, this means knowing what you want to find out, and devising a plan of action to discover it. First, then, it is important to understand the theoretical basis of the study. Some of the following might seem obvious, but you need to be absolutely clear in your mind before the investigation how you would satisfy each requirement:

- ❏   make sure that the thing you want to investigate is a credible area for investigation;
- ❏   make sure it is a regular feature rather than an example of an individual's miscue or mistake;
- ❏   make sure the feature is available for analysis, and that you do not affect the data in the process of investigating it;
- ❏   make sure that the feature can be described systematically, so that your readers can verify that what you claim is testable, able to be replicated if possible, and able to be evaluated.

Many of these issues can be settled by reading around the area before you begin. This will also help you to resolve areas of investigation that are new or that you find unsatisfactory in previous work. Gaining a theoretical awareness will allow you to decide how far you can generalise your findings to wider social situations, and will allow you to discuss the consequences of your work for sociolinguistics, and for the understanding of language and society.

Your method of data collection will largely be determined by these theoretical issues. They will tell you where and how and what to investigate. For example, your methodology might comprise any one or a combination of the following:

- **self-report**: do you set up a questionnaire (spoken or written) and what questions do you ask; do you set up an empirical situation (a test) in which you try to elicit the feature you are interested in with the groups of people you are interested in; do you record a structured or more open-ended interview or conversation?
- **covert observation**: do you participate in the group; do you tell the informants what you are after; do you make them aware they are being recorded; do you want them in a formal or relaxed situation?
- **sampling method**: do you choose people randomly; do you select from a specified group; do you select a representative sample; do you minimise the interference by other factors by limiting yourself to one factor; how many informants do you need?

Lastly, you must also consider your **ethical** responsibilities in collecting linguistic data from people who might not be aware that they are being observed and recorded. In most cases, even where the language event is public, many linguists consider it unethical to gather data completely covertly. The problem is that in warning people they are being recorded, they are likely to alter their behaviour (this is known as the **observer's paradox**). It might be possible to avoid this by telling potential informants that they are being observed, without going into the details of what you are investigating; or by sharing your findings with them afterwards and gaining their permission; or by deciding that the observer's paradox is not a significant factor in a particular case and so the observation can be open. Whatever you decide should be considered and discussed thoroughly. (See D5 for more on this.)

## Variables in sociolinguistics

Armed with theoretical and methodological knowledge, you only need one more elementary tool. This is the notion of the **variable**.

There are two types of variable in social investigation. The **social variable** is the factor that determines a variation in language. Possible social factors include **gender**, **geography**, **age**, **occupation**, and so on, as discussed throughout section A below. The **linguistic variable** is the feature that you want to investigate. This might be a language (English, Basque, Hokkien), or a dialect (Irish Hiberno-English, Jamaican Patwa, Parisian French), or a style (formal, careful, casual), or a register (romantic novels, recipes, bank manager talk), or a syntactic pattern (passive, intransitive, verb agreement), or a word or phrase ('neb', 'you-all', 'you know') or a particular sound (/h/, /t/, /a/), for example. In particular, many sociolinguistic studies use individual sounds in pronunciation as the linguistic variable, since it is a relatively easy practical matter to either set up or come across a situation in which many of them will occur.

To investigate whether the use of a linguistic feature is *caused* by a particular social factor, you will need to collect examples of a situation in which the feature has a chance of being used. Suppose you are investigating gender-usage. You must get two groups of informants who are as alike as possible in every respect (the same age, education, social class, political viewpoint, and so on) except that one group is female and the other male. In this way, you have **controlled** for other interfering variables, and any linguistic differences you find are likely to be determined by gender alone. In effect, what you have done is focus on the **dependent** linguistic variable, and manipulated the **independent** social variable to discover social usage. If you do not have a control, for example by having not only both genders but also a range of ages, you cannot be sure which of these two social factors is actually associated with the linguistic variation that you might find.

Treating the feature as the linguistic variable, you will be faced with two circumstances of its usage. Either the feature occurs or not. For example, someone says the word 'hotel' by pronouncing the /h/ or by 'dropping' it – that is, presence or omission, written formally as: x / ∅. Alternatively, the variable is **graded** so a range of possibilities present themselves: for example, people can pronounce the middle 't' in 'butter' in five different ways: /t/, /d/, /ʔ/, /θ/ or ∅ – omitting it altogether (see A2 for an explanation of these phonetic symbols).

You can measure the occurrence or frequencies of data like this, and run statistical tests to determine the rules and principles of sociolinguistics: this is **quantitative** study. Alternatively, you can try to gain a more holistic but less precisely measurable view of language use, for example by relying more on subjective analysis of extended discourse: this sort of study is more **qualitative**. Both approaches are common in sociolinguistics.

---

## ACCENT AND DIALECT

In common perception, an **accent** is something other people have: you might hear people say things like, 'He's very broad', 'She has a lovely speaking voice', 'That's a thick accent'. Many of my students deny that they have an accent at all. These common judgements are interesting for what they tell us about people's attitudes to language, but as sociolinguists we must not share their evaluative biases. Apart from sign-language, it is as impossible to speak without an accent as it is to speak without making any sound. Since accents are so variable and universal, they are the most productive ground for sociolinguistics.

### Describing accents
**Phonology** (the study of speech-sound and articulation) provides us with a scientific and objective means of discussing accent, in the form of the **International Phonetic**

**Alphabet (IPA).** Unlike the standard spelling alphabet, the IPA sets out symbols which have a fixed value. For example, though <s> is a normal alphabetical letter (a **grapheme**, signalled by those angled brackets around it), it can sound very different in 'six', 'dogs', 'sugar' and 'leisure'. In the IPA we can distinguish these sounds: /s/, /z/, /ʃ/ and /ʒ/ (these are **phonemes**, written within slashed lines as shown). The IPA allows us to describe, compare and contrast accents in a systematic way.

## THE INTERNATIONAL PHONETIC ALPHABET (revised to 2005)

### CONSONANTS (PULMONIC)

© 2005 IPA

| | Bilabial | Labiodental | Dental | Alveolar | Postalveolar | Retroflex | Palatal | Velar | Uvular | Pharyngeal | Glottal |
|---|---|---|---|---|---|---|---|---|---|---|---|
| Plosive | p b | | | t d | | ʈ ɖ | c ɟ | k ɡ | q ɢ | | ʔ |
| Nasal | m | ɱ | | n | | ɳ | ɲ | ŋ | N | | |
| Trill | B | | | r | | | | | R | | |
| Tap or Flap | | ⱱ | | ɾ | | ɽ | | | | | |
| Fricative | ɸ β | f v | θ ð | s z | ʃ ʒ | ʂ ʐ | ç ʝ | x ɣ | χ ʁ | ħ ʕ | h ɦ |
| Lateral fricative | | | | ɬ ɮ | | | | | | | |
| Approximant | | ʋ | | ɹ | | ɻ | j | ɰ | | | |
| Lateral approximant | | | | l | | ɭ | ʎ | L | | | |

Where symbols appear in pairs, the one to the right represents a voiced consonant. Shaded areas denote articulations judged impossible.

### CONSONANTS (NON-PULMONIC)

| Clicks | | Voiced implosives | | Ejectives | |
|---|---|---|---|---|---|
| ʘ | Bilabial | ɓ | Bilabial | ' | Examples: |
| ǀ | Dental | ɗ | Dental/alveolar | p' | Bilabial |
| ǃ | (Post)alveolar | ʄ | Palatal | t' | Dental/alveolar |
| ǂ | Palatoalveolar | ɠ | Velar | k' | Velar |
| ǁ | Alveolar lateral | ʛ | Uvular | s' | Alveolar fricative |

### OTHER SYMBOLS

| | | | |
|---|---|---|---|
| ʍ | Voiceless labial-velar fricative | ɕ ʑ | Alveolo-palatal fricatives |
| w | Voiced labial-velar approximant | ɺ | Voiced alveolar lateral flap |
| ɥ | Voiced labial-palatal approximant | ɧ | Simultaneous ʃ and x |
| ʜ | Voiceless epiglottal fricative | | |
| ʢ | Voiced epiglottal fricative | Affricates and double articulations can be represented by two symbols joined by a tie bar if necessary. | k͡p t͡s |
| ʡ | Epiglottal plosive | | |

### VOWELS

Front — Central — Back

Close: i • y — ɨ • ʉ — ɯ • u
(ɪ ʏ, ʊ)
Close-mid: e • ø — ɘ • ɵ — ɤ • o
(ə)
Open-mid: ɛ • œ — ɜ • ɞ — ʌ • ɔ
(æ, ɐ)
Open: a • ɶ — ɑ • ɒ

Where symbols appear in pairs, the one to the right represents a rounded vowel.

### SUPRASEGMENTALS

| | | |
|---|---|---|
| ˈ | Primary stress | ˌfoʊnəˈtɪʃən |
| ˌ | Secondary stress | |
| ː | Long | eː |
| ˑ | Half-long | eˑ |
| ̆ | Extra-short | ĕ |
| ǀ | Minor (foot) group | |
| ǁ | Major (intonation) group | |
| . | Syllable break | ɹi.ækt |
| ‿ | Linking (absence of a break) | |

### TONES AND WORD ACCENTS

| LEVEL | | | CONTOUR | | |
|---|---|---|---|---|---|
| e̋ or | ˥ | Extra high | ě or | ˄ | Rising |
| é | ˦ | High | ê | ˅ | Falling |
| ē | ˧ | Mid | e᷄ | ˧˦ | High rising |
| è | ˨ | Low | e᷅ | ˨˩ | Low rising |
| ȅ | ˩ | Extra low | e᷈ | | Rising-falling |
| ꜜ | Downstep | | ↗ | Global rise |
| ꜛ | Upstep | | ↘ | Global fall |

### DIACRITICS

Diacritics may be placed above a symbol with a descender, e.g. ŋ̊

| | | | | | | | | | |
|---|---|---|---|---|---|---|---|---|---|
| ̥ | Voiceless | n̥ d̥ | ̤ | Breathy voiced | b̤ a̤ | ̪ | Dental | t̪ d̪ |
| ̬ | Voiced | s̬ t̬ | ̰ | Creaky voiced | b̰ a̰ | ̺ | Apical | t̺ d̺ |
| ʰ | Aspirated | tʰ dʰ | ̼ | Linguolabial | t̼ d̼ | ̻ | Laminal | t̻ d̻ |
| ̹ | More rounded | ɔ̹ | ʷ | Labialized | tʷ dʷ | ̃ | Nasalized | ẽ |
| ̜ | Less rounded | ɔ̜ | ʲ | Palatalized | tʲ dʲ | ⁿ | Nasal release | dⁿ |
| ̟ | Advanced | u̟ | ˠ | Velarized | tˠ dˠ | ˡ | Lateral release | dˡ |
| ̠ | Retracted | e̠ | ˤ | Pharyngealized | tˤ dˤ | ̚ | No audible release | d̚ |
| ̈ | Centralized | ë | ̴ | Velarized or pharyngealized | ɫ | | | |
| ̽ | Mid-centralized | e̽ | ̝ | Raised | e̝ | (ɹ̝ = voiced alveolar fricative) | | |
| ̩ | Syllabic | n̩ | ̞ | Lowered | e̞ | (β̞ = voiced bilabial approximant) | | |
| ̯ | Non-syllabic | e̯ | ̘ | Advanced Tongue Root | e̘ | | | |
| ˞ | Rhoticity | ɚ a˞ | ̙ | Retracted Tongue Root | e̙ | | | |

The IPA chart lists symbols to cover all the various sounds that can be meaning-fully produced in the world's languages. **Consonants** are described by their **place of articulation** (using the Latin words for teeth, tongue, lips and so on) and by their **manner of articulation**. For example, the four ways of pronouncing <s> given above are all fricatives: two (/s z/) are alveolar (with the tongue just behind the alveolar ridge) and two (/ʃ ʒ/) are post-alveolar (a bit behind that). In each pair, the first sound is **unvoiced** (whispered) and the second is **voiced** (with the voice-box engaged).

Vowels are described by the position of the tongue in the mouth cavity for each one: so /i/ is a high close front vowel, and /ə/ (known as 'schwa') is a mid-central vowel. These vowels are single sounds (**monophthongs**). Other vocalic sounds can be produced by sliding the tongue rapidly from one position to another: these are called **diphthongs** (for example, /aɪ/ as in 'bite' in most accents, /ɔɪ/ in 'boy', /aʊ/ in 'house', and so on).

You will see that the IPA chart gives a great many symbols and also **diacritic** marks to indicate various pronunciation effects. These subtle differences are very useful to sociolinguists; however, for ease of reference, the following is a selection of those symbols that will be useful in this book. You will notice some unusual symbols (the 'tapped' /ɾ/, for example), as well as familiar alphabetic-looking ones. In all the example words given, I assume what used to be called a 'BBC English' accent (known properly as **Received Pronunciation** – **RP**). Sometimes I have indicated a different regional accent, where RP does not use the sound.

## Selected IPA symbols

### Consonants (including glides/liquids)

| | |
|---|---|
| p – pip | ð – thy |
| b – bib | s – set |
| t – ten | z – zen |
| d – den | ʃ – ship |
| k – cat | ʒ – leisure |
| g – get | x – loch (Scots) |
| ʔ – bu'er (glottal stop) | h – hen |
| m – man | l – let ('light l', at the front of the mouth) |
| n – man | ɫ – pull ('dark l', at the back of the mouth) |
| ŋ – sing | j – yet |
| r – ride, parrot (retroflex 'r') | ʧ – church |
| ɾ – rubbish (Scots) (tapped 'r') | ʤ – judge |
| f – fish | w – wet |
| v – van | wʰ – which (aspirated, with breath) |
| θ – thigh | ʍ – which (voiceless) |

### Vowels

Accent variation is often most noticeably carried in the vocalic elements of pronunciation, and in the glides (/j/, /w/) and liquids (/r/, /l/) that are sort of

A

**Monophthongs**

ɪ – p<u>i</u>t

ɛ – p<u>e</u>t

æ – p<u>a</u>t

ɒ – p<u>o</u>t

ʌ – p<u>u</u>tt

ʊ – p<u>u</u>t

ə – p<u>a</u>tter

o – <u>eau</u> (French), <u>low</u> (Northern England)

a – c<u>a</u>lm (Scouse), f<u>a</u>rm (Teesside)

y – t<u>u</u> (French), sch<u>oo</u>l (Scouse)

ø – p<u>eu</u> (French), b<u>oa</u>t (Geordie)

iː – b<u>ea</u>n (the diacritic here lengthens the vowel)

ɜː – b<u>ur</u>n

ɑː – b<u>ar</u>n

ɔː – b<u>or</u>n

uː – b<u>oo</u>n

eː – b<u>ai</u>t (Northern England)

**Diphthongs**

aɪ – b<u>i</u>te, n<u>i</u>ght

əɪ – n<u>i</u>ght (Scots, Canadian)

ɛɪ – b<u>ai</u>t

ɔɪ – b<u>oy</u>

əʊ – r<u>oe</u>

aʊ – h<u>ou</u>se

əʊ – h<u>ou</u>se (Scots, Canadian)

ʊə – s<u>ew</u>er, p<u>oor</u>

uə – p<u>oor</u> (Northern England)

ɪə – <u>ear</u>

iə – <u>ear</u> (Northern England)

ɛə – <u>air</u>

'semi-vowels'. For example, a speaker who says [fɑːrm] rather than [fɑːm] is likely to be American or Irish rather than English: their accent is said to be **rhotic** if they pronounce this sort of **non-prevocalic** /r/ (/r/ when it is not before a vowel, as in 'farm' or 'car'). Americans and most Irish people have a 'retroflex' /r/. By contrast, if they 'tap' the 'r' (by flicking the tip of their tongue against the ridge behind their front teeth), the vowel quality is likely to change slightly and they are likely to introduce a vowel between the 'r' and 'm' to make the last two letters syllabic: [færəm]. This is more likely to be a Scottish speaker, or someone influenced by Scots, such as speakers in Ulster (and the square brackets are used to write down actual realisations in speech).

Phonetic details like these can help you pinpoint the differences between accents. The crucial factor for sociolinguistics is that accent variation tends not to happen just randomly, but in relation to observable social patterns. Accent can often tell us where someone comes from, their age, gender, level of education, social class, wealth, how well-travelled they are, and whether they are emotionally attached to their home-town, job or political party. All of these factors can also be carried in some-one's dialect.

## Dialectology

Just as everyone has an accent, so every form of English (or any language) is a **dialect**. Where *accent* refers to the sounds a speaker makes, *dialect* covers the word-choices, syntactic ordering and all the other grammatical choices a speaker could make. A **language** consists of one or many dialects, all of which are more or less mutually intelligible to other speakers of the language. The most prestigious dialect in Britain is UK Standard English (UKSE), originally a southern dialect of English which has become the form used in most print media, law and education. It can, of course, be pronounced in any accent. For example, 'It's very dirty' can be pronounced in RP ([ɪts vɛri dɜːti]), or in a northern British accent ([ɪʔs vɛri dɛːtɪ]), but the same sense can be expressed in several dialects: UKSE ('It's very dirty'); Yorkshire ('Tha's right mucky'); or Teesside ('It's hacky'), and so on.

Though, in principle, any dialect can appear in any accent, in practice some accents tend to accompany certain dialects. RP almost never appears in anything but UK Standard English, though UKSE is usually pronounced in most accents. Scouse dialect always appears in a Liverpool accent, though, Tyneside dialect in a Geordie accent, West Midlands dialect in a Birmingham or a Black Country accent, and so on. So closely are accent and dialect connected in common perception, that the word for the accent (Cockney) and the dialect (Cockney) are often the same. Different groups even have different words for other groups: thus 'Brummies' in Birmingham notice the different accent in Coventry of the 'Yam-Yams' (derived from the pronunciation of 'I am . . .').

Of course, dialects do not suddenly change from area to area. Accents and dialects that are geographically close to one another tend to be similar in form, gradually varying the further you travel away from them. We can thus talk of **dialect chains** rather than discrete dialects. This applies even across national boundaries: the dialects of northern Germany are closer in form to bordering Netherlands than to Bavarian, though the latter is usually counted as the same German language and the former is the foreign language Dutch. Political allegiances have a lot to do with this attitude, of course.

Traditionally, **dialectologists** were able to study different areas of accent and dialect use fairly easily, drawing lines on the map (**isoglosses**) to separate one form and speech community from another. This is much more difficult in an urban setting, where migration and industrialisation tend to mix up family origins. Quantitative sociolinguistic methods as outlined in A1 have enabled the study of **urban dialectology** in these situations.

## REGISTER AND STYLE

A dialect is a variety of language defined largely by its *users'* regional or socio-economic origins. However, much language variation is a result of differences in the social *situation* of use. This affects the word-choices and syntactic ordering of utterances (together, the **lexicogrammar**), and has been called **register** (or sometimes, by analogy with *dialect*, it is referred to as **diatype**). One of the recent findings of corpus linguistics (using a large computer database of actual language examples) is that there is far more variation as a result of register than as a result of dialect. Furthermore, register differences operate within and across different dialects. For example, the lexicogrammatical composition of registers such as 'playing a computer game', 'buying a coffee', or 'writing a letter to a friend' remain constant even in different dialects. People are engaged in similar communicative acts and so tend to use similar linguistic patterns.

What is surprising is that people are far more aware of dialectal differences than diatypic differences. People are readily conscious of regional words and phrases, but will only really think about the variant patterns in different registers when they are pointed out to them in a book like this. Of course, register is socially motivated and involves social negotiation among the participants in the discourse, in order to speak or write in an appropriate way. Since these decisions involve a whole range of social perceptions to do with social rank, politeness, and appropriacy, choices of register and stylistic choices are the concern of sociolinguistics.

## Register

Register can be defined either narrowly or broadly. The narrow definition sees register simply as an occupational variety of language. So, for example, teachers, computer programmers, mechanics or sociolinguists tend to have characteristic ways of speaking which involve certain particular word-choices and grammatical constructions. This is most commonly perceived as **jargon**, and most people associate it with particular word-choices. However, the syntactic ordering and patterns of larger-scale linguistic organisation are also important.

A wider definition of register sees it as a sort of social genre of linguistic usage (sometimes specified as a **sociolect** to differentiate it from *dialect*). Examples of registers under this definition would include the language of a newspaper article, the language of a conversation about the weather, academic prose, a recipe in a cookery book, and so on.

It is important that register is defined primarily by the circumstance and purpose of the communicative situation, rather than by the individual user or ethnic/social group using the variety. In other words, the definition must be a non-linguistic one, against which particular linguistic features can then be set. One way of pinpointing a register is to identify a communicative event along three dimensions:

- ❏ field
- ❏ tenor
- ❏ mode

The **field** is the social setting and purpose of the interaction. In the case of an academic article in a professional journal, for example, the field would be the subject-matter of the article, and the purpose in publishing it would be to spread the argument and ideas among academic colleagues. The **tenor** refers to the relationship between the participants in the event. The writer of the article and readers including academic colleagues and students constitute the *tenor* here. Finally, the **mode** refers to the medium of communication (as in spoken, written, or emailed). An academic article is in the written mode. Changing this last dimension to the spoken mode would alter the register from an 'article' to a 'lecture', and there would be corresponding and predictable differences in the lexicogrammar: most simply, the sentences are likely to be shorter and contain fewer embedded clauses in speech;

word-choice is likely to be slightly less formal and perhaps less technical; there might be more direct interaction with the audience and direct address in the form of 'I' and 'you'; and so on.

Clearly there are further details and sub-types within each set of three dimensions. The context of use is the crucial determinant in identifying register. In this way slight differences in linguistic style can be ascribed to close differences in social function. For example, a recipe basically has the register dimensions of (field) cookery, (tenor) professional cook to amateur cook, (mode) written, as a table of ingredients followed by the method. However, I have a French cookery reference book which clearly assumes a very knowledgeable reader: this variation in tenor makes the register very technical and mainly too difficult for me to use. I also have a cookery book with sumptuous photographs and mouth-watering lyrical prose which is clearly intended as a 'coffee table' book for reading rather than cooking anything practical, and this linguistic variation is determined by the difference in field. I have also had instructions on how to make an apple and rhubarb crumble telephoned to me by my mother, and the difference in mode here (spoken rather than written) produced a very different set of linguistic patterns.

Finally, all these register distinctions have to be matched to cultural expectations. A discussion about the weather in Britain contains a very different lexicogrammatical structure from a discussion about the weather in California (as well as the content conveyed). Similarly, I have a recipe book from the Raffles Hotel in Singapore which is clearly intended as a practical cookery manual, but since in Nottingham I cannot get ingredients like green pandan leaves, I read its register as an exotic fiction rather than a cookery book. In this case, the actual tenor has changed.

## Style

In the context of sociolinguistic study, **style** refers to variations within registers that can represent individual choices along social dimensions. One stylistic dimension within a register would be the scale of formality – casualness. 'Place the ingredients into a prepared dish' could more casually be: 'Put the mix into the bowl you've got ready'. Clearly, since the field, tenor and mode of both these utterances could be the same, *stylistic* variation can occur within a register. However, style is independent of register since the mode of the first utterance could be written and the second spoken. Very generally, the written mode tends to be more formal than the spoken mode, with email a new sort of discourse that is not so much a mid-way blend of the two as a bundle of features all of its own.

Most styles are best thought of as scales or **clines**, for example from very formal to very casual, with many relative gradations in between. People are very adept at matching their style as appropriate to the social setting. Other stylistic scales include impersonal – intimate, monologic – dialogic, formulaic – creative, and so on. All of these can be manifest in the linguistic choices of the utterance.

With both registers and styles, most people have a far greater **passive competence** than **active competence**. In other words, they can understand a great many more variations than they usually perform, and if put in unfamiliar social situations will often become highly self-conscious and misjudge the pattern they should produce. Such 'errors' are an important feature of sociolinguistic behaviour.

## ETHNICITY AND MULTILINGUALISM

Many English-speakers living in predominantly monolingual countries such as Britain, the US, or Australia, might think that it is an unusual skill to be able to speak more than one language. Indeed, English speakers in these countries have a very poor record in learning other languages, partly because the powerful influence of English world-wide makes it seem less necessary to do so. However, the ability to speak more than one language is more common in the world than monolingualism. Even in the apparently monoglot countries mentioned above, there are huge numbers of people routinely speaking not only a variety of types of English, but also many indigenous languages (Irish Gaelic, Scots Gaelic, Welsh, aboriginal languages such as Dyirbal, and native American languages) as well as community languages brought by large numbers of recent immigrants (especially Spanish in the US, Indian languages such as Punjabi, Urdu, Marathi and other south-east Asian languages in the UK and Australia, and all the European languages in all three countries).

Language use, then, though seen as a symbol of nationalism, is also the major badge of **ethnicity** – that is, racial, cultural or family origins. An individual might choose to speak in a particular language, or dialect, or register, or accent, or style (let's use the general term **code** to cover all of these varieties) on different occasions and for different purposes. The choice of code can be used to claim in-group identity with other speakers.

### Code-switching

Most individuals have a repertoire of codes available to them. Even if you only speak English, you will almost certainly be able to switch from a casual to formal style (if you employ a 'telephone voice' for example), or into different accents (as in telling a story or a joke), or even into different dialects (when moving from writing a message on a note on your fridge door to writing a letter to your bank). The main point to notice here is that these different uses of different codes are tied to different situations or **domains**. One theory of **code-switching** claims that the choice of code is determined by the domain in which speakers perceive themselves to be. This means that the choice of code itself is communicatively meaningful, as well as the actual content of what is said. For example, I recently overheard a group of three teenage boys on a bus quoting catchphrases from a popular and cultish television comedy show; in doing so, they imitated the accents of the characters when incorporating the phrases into their own speech, switching back and forth from their own voices to the 'comedy' voices. This went on for some time, but when they approached their bus stop they all switched back into their 'own' voices to make final arrangements for meeting up again that evening. It was obvious that any arrangements made in 'comedy' voices would not count as real arrangements but would be taken as a joke.

The life of one my former students illustrates the *domains theory* of code-switching very well. Melinda studied in Britain but her ethnic origins are Straits Chinese from Singapore. She speaks Cantonese with her family in Singapore, and Hokkien to traders in the small shops, markets and food halls. In larger shops, however, and especially in multinational chains, she speaks Singaporean English and can understand the popular local blend of Chinese and English known as Singlish, though as a highly educated woman she rather looks down on it. She reads the Mandarin newspaper *Lianhe Zaobao* and the Singaporean English newspaper *The Straits Times*, and she has a good knowledge of Malay and various Indian languages. In most formal correspondence in Singapore she uses Singaporean English. In Britain, of course, she reads and writes in British Standard English, though she can now switch into a Nottingham accent and dialect but only ever for comic effect. She married an Italian, Mario, and so has added Italian to her repertoire of codes to be used in different domains.

When a speaker moves from one domain into another, and changes their code as a result, this is **situational code-switching**. Sometimes, however, a speaker can deliberately change codes in the middle of a situation, in order to indicate to the hearer that they consider a new domain to be in operation. This is called **metaphorical code-switching** and can be seen in the teenage boys' usage to differentiate 'joke-time' from 'serious-time'. Conversations are often brought to a close by one participant code-switching into a different variety in order to signal that they want to get away. Metaphorical code-switching is thus a means of changing the perceived context.

Where a domain is not well defined or two domains could be seen to be operating (such as meeting a family-friend in an expensive and unfamiliar restaurant, or having a work colleague round for a family occasion), speakers can often be heard **code-mixing**, in which the switch between languages can occur within utterances. The most chaotic code-mixing I have ever experienced was with English and Scottish friends out with colleagues from their English-language school walking from bar to bar in the Basque country near the Franco-Spanish border.

### Multilingualism and diglossia

When discussing an individual's ability to speak more than one language, we usually use the terms **bilingual** or **multilingual**. A person's native language, which they learnt as a baby, is their **vernacular** (or 'mother tongue'). This is sometimes referred to as L1. Many people go on to learn another language later in life, to the point at which they become fluent in this L2 language. Such people are **compound bilinguals**, since there is a definite sequence of linguistic competence. My sister-in-law Alex is a native English speaker, but is fluent in French and Spanish which she first learnt at school, and has a passive competence in Basque.

Some people, however, are born into families in which two or more languages are spoken routinely, and they develop both languages equally as vernaculars. Such people are **co-ordinate bilinguals**. My friend Urszula was born in York to Polish parents, and is a co-ordinate bilingual in English and Polish; she has never visited Poland. Many people with this ability nevertheless associate each language with different domains (such as English with work and Polish with the children's grandparents), and will then associate each code-choice with particular situations and emotions.

An individual speaking more than one language is said to be *multilingual,* but we can also use this term to talk of whole communities in which two languages are commonly spoken by most people. Thus, Switzerland is a multilingual country with French, German and Italian the main languages, and with each language predominating in different areas; though an individual will probably have one of these as a vernacular, they are likely to have a good facility in the others. Multilingual communities include French Canadians, American Hispanics, many Welsh people, the ethnic Greek community in Sydney, English-Punjabi speakers in Birmingham, Gaelic-English speakers in Connemara, South African speakers of English, Afrikaans and Shona, and so on.

In communities in which two language varieties are used by everyone, and there is a distinct and institutionalised functional divergence in usage, this is called **diglossia**. For example, classical Arabic is the language of the Koran and is reserved for religious purposes, and a range of vernacular Arabic varieties are used for most other purposes across North Africa and the Middle East. In diglossic situations, the code which is used for writing or in prestigious or formal domains is known as the **H variety**, and the other code is the **L variety**: High German is used in books and newspapers across Germany, Switzerland and Austria, but various forms of Low German are used in regions of this area. Spoken Swiss German sounds very different from the German spoken in Dortmund, but in both areas people can read the same book or newspaper without much difficulty.

## VARIATION AND CHANGE                                                      A5

One of the most significant and also most complex determinants of linguistic variation is **social class**. This is not an easy concept to define precisely or measure accurately, and the stratification of class into different levels varies considerably across nations and cultures. Most language communities, however, have a hierarchy of wealth and power defined in relation to economics and prestige that can be covered by the term *class*.

Most sociolinguistic studies that have investigated the impact of social stratification on language use have employed the **variationist** method. That is, they have taken a linguistic variable and recorded its variations by placing it alongside a range of apparently independent factors. Variationist sociolinguistics was initially developed by William Labov's investigations of accent variation in various socially stratified situations. In the work described below, the social variables are class stratification and age, respectively, and the linguistic variables are measurable and fixed.

### Fixed variables

Perhaps the most famous sociolinguistic study of all was conducted by Labov in order to test the social stratification of rhoticity (pronunciation of /r/ when not before a vowel) in New York. This was then used as a pilot study for a much larger investigation in the city. In New York, rhoticity has been a prestige feature since the 1940s.

Labov selected three department stores each of which served as an index of social stratification. He used non-linguistic measurements to stratify the stores (location, quality of goods, size of price tags, and so on). In each shop, he stopped people and asked a question to which he knew the answer would be 'fourth floor'. He would then pretend to mishear, in order to get the informant to repeat 'fourth floor' more emphatically. In this elegant and neat way he was able to note four occurrences of /r/ pronunciation.

Labov's findings show a clear class stratification in rhoticity, confirming its prestige value: generally, more occurrences of /r/ in the higher class store than the lower class one. He also found that there was a greater /r/-stress when the speaker was emphatic and relatively self-aware. The most interesting finding was that in the middle store, the emphasis on the final /r/ in both occurrences of 'floor' was much stronger than would have been expected on a steadily rising scale from lower to higher class. This group showed a heavy emphasis on /r/-pronunciation when they were aware of their own usage.

In Labov's larger New York study, this same phenomenon occurred. This time, in order to grade the scale of self-consciousness, Labov observed informants'

**casual speech**   (in relaxed conversation)
**careful speech**  (in a more formal situation)
**reading style**   (from a set text)
**word lists**      (to focus their awareness on reading out loud)
**minimal pairs**   (to make them particularly aware of their speech by giving them closely similar words like *law/lore*).

Labov noted the same prestige variation across the socio-economic classes (a more objective measurement of class than department stores), and again the same over-emphasis by the 'lower middle class' group. He termed this over-compensation **hypercorrection**, and described it as a manifestation of the linguistic insecurity of this social group.

In a similar variationist study in Norwich, Peter Trudgill investigated 16 multiple variables including the presence or absence of /h/ in words like 'happy, home', /n/ or /ŋ/ at the end of 'singing', and the vowels in 'bad, name, path, tell, here, hair, ride, bird, top, know, boat, boot, tune'. He divided informants into five social classes, and also by gender, age and local area. Like Labov, Trudgill used a range of elicitation techniques to increase the self-awareness of informants: casual style, formal style, reading passage style and word-list style ('boot/boat, bust/burst, moon/moan', and so on).

Trudgill also found hypercorrection towards the prestige pronunciation amongst the middle class group. More specifically, he found that middle class women tended to hypercorrect the most, especially in the more self-aware styles. Most curiously, he found middle class men actually aiming for more stigmatised pronunciations when they were aware of their own speech. This sort of 'reverse hypercorrection' is called **covert prestige**, and can be explained in this case as middle class men wanting to identify with a more 'streetwise' and 'plain-speaking' lower class norm.

## Graded variables

One of Trudgill's variables was based, not on simple presence or absence (x/Ø, but on a graded scale of possibilities. He looked at variants of /t/ pronunciation, realised with lots of breath (aspirated as [tʰ]), unaspirated ([t]), glottalised (towards the back of the mouth as [tʔ]), and as a full glottal stop ([ʔ]). These four realisations are graded from the prestige standard to the stigmatised non-standard, and showed similar social stratification in the study.

Another form of gradation is apparent in Jenny Cheshire's (1978) study of schoolchildren in Reading. Focusing on verb-form agreement ('I knows, we has, they calls', and so on), she found that usage was not so much a matter of standard and non-standard as a matter of the **frequency** of use of the various possibilities. Everyday vernacular words were more likely to appear in non-standard form than verbs associated with authority and power, though it was a matter of emphasis rather than being absolutely predictable. And it wasn't that the boys used non-standard forms all the time, but they did use most of them more frequently than the girls. There was also evidence of male covert prestige: girls were quicker to switch to standard forms in formal situations but the boys maintained their non-standard usage.

Finally, then, one way of dealing with the complexity of social stratification variation is to follow Labov's 'principle of accountability': that is, we should not simply measure occurrences of a feature. Instead, we should count the number of times a feature occurs, judged against the number of times it could potentially have occurred. In this way, we can distinguish between **categorical rules** which predict usage absolutely from **variable rules** which cannot operate on individual prediction but apply more generally across groups in terms of frequencies of usage.

## Language change

Variationist sociolinguists see the business of the discipline as the investigation of language variation and change. Traditionally, the disciplines of philology and etymology have been concerned with the processes of sound and word change over time, taking a **diachronic** approach to linguistic study. However, sociolinguistics has been able to develop techniques providing insights into language change by using age variation as a social variable. Sociolinguistic studies tend to be **synchronic** in practice (like a 'freeze-frame' of society at a particular modern moment), but there has also been an interest in exploring how language is in the process of change.

Undertaking a **longitudinal** sociolinguistic study is possible over a few years but more difficult over longer periods. However, there are two ways in which sociolinguists can analyse change. One – a **real time** study – would compare older accounts and records of sociolinguistic features with modern studies. The other method is to investigate the variations in usage across the age ranges, since it is supposed that older people will manifest earlier forms of language learnt in their youth: this is known as the **apparent time hypothesis**. William Labov employed both methods in his study on the Massachusetts island of Martha's Vineyard.

Labov compared the findings of the 1930s *Linguistic Atlas of New England* with his own study, and also investigated modern usage correlated with **age** (and also geography and ideology – where on the island people lived and what their attitude was to island life). Martha's Vineyard was selected for study as a linguistically unusual place: for example, people there have rhotic accents even though the rest of New England remains non-rhotic (unusually in the US). Labov was interested in a local pronunciation that **centralised** the vowel sounds in 'night' and 'house' to the middle of the tongue; so that instead of being pronounced /naɪt/ and /haʊs/ they were closer to the Scottish and Canadian-sounding /nəit/ and /həʊs/. This centralisation was seen as a particular feature of the local island accent.

He found that the highest centralisers (that is, those who emphasised their local accent the most) were those who had the greatest loyalty to island life. This included fishermen living away from the main tourist centres (and so not dependent on it), especially men aged between 31 and 45. The most strong centralisers were those who had been away to college on the mainland and then chosen to return. Not only does this show **language loyalty**, but Labov was able to use the diachronic evidence to show that the centralisation that had been dying out in the 1930s was actually being reinforced in a modern assertion of the island's native identity.

The methods developed in these early studies continue to evolve in the hands of more recent variationist sociolinguists.

## A6     STANDARDISATION

The main social determinants of linguistic variation can be said to be:

| | |
|---|---|
| Geography | (see the thread through A2, B2, C2 and D2) |
| Gender | (see thread 7) |
| Age | (see A5) |
| Class | (see thread 5) |
| Race and ethnicity | (see threads 4, 8 and 9) |
| Occupation | (see thread 3) |
| Ideology and politics | (see thread 12) |

The last of these means that the opinions, attitudes and self-awareness of individuals and communities can affect linguistic usage. It is noticeable, for example, that in the sharply divided politics of Northern Ireland, republican and nationalist politicians adopt some of the accent features of the Irish Republic (especially the Dublin accent) and unionist and loyalist politicians emphasise particular Ulster accents, regardless of their actual regional origins (Democratic Unionist Party members have been observed moving towards the Ballymena accent of leading figure Ian Paisley, for example). Throughout history, people have altered their own language or forced others to change their language because of their own attitudes and beliefs.

Ideological beliefs (by which I mean not only explicit political opinions but also everyday attitudes) act as modifying factors in sociolinguistic usage. **Self-consciousness** changes the way people speak and write. The **formality** of the context is another important modifying factor. Two final factors act in opposite directions: the pressure of **standardisation**, usually from elsewhere in society; and the **language loyalty** of individuals to their own local usage.

### Prestige and stigmatisation

I used to teach a Finnish student who told me that there was a community on the Sweden/Finland border whose language was neither 'proper' Finnish nor 'proper' Swedish, and he said that Finns referred to these people as 'half-linguals'. Clearly this community is not without language, and it is more likely that they speak a particular non-standard dialect. However, it is equally clear that this dialect is enormously stigmatised in the eyes of Finnish speakers like my student, to the extent that they do not even regard the dialect as a form of language at all.

Such opinions of language varieties have behavioural, educational and governmental policy consequences that can have real effects on forms of language. The sociolinguist Roger Bell (1976: 147–57) has suggested several criteria by which the prestige (or stigma) in which a code is held can be measured. These are:

☐ **standardisation**    whether the variety has been approved by institutions, codified into a dictionary or grammar, or been used for prestigious texts (national newspapers, religious books, canonical literature);

☐ **vitality**    whether there is a living community of speakers who use the code or whether the language is dead or dying (like Manx, Cornish, Latin, Toccharian);

☐ **historicity**    whether speakers have a sense of the longevity of their code (compare Modern Greek with Modern Hebrew);

☐ **autonomy**    whether speakers consider their code to be substantially different from others (compare the relative status of Standard English / German with Standard English / Scots);

☐ **reduction**    whether speakers consider the code to be a sub-variety or a full code in its own right; whether it has a reduced set of social functions. For example, it might not have its own writing system (like Geordie or Scouse) or might have only a very reduced function (like a football chant accent);

☐ **mixture**    whether speakers consider their language 'pure' (as do the French) or a mixture of other languages (as are creoles);

☐ **'unofficial' norms**    whether speakers have a sense of 'good' and 'bad' varieties of the code, even if there is no 'official' codification in grammars and dictionaries.

Note that it is not always straightforward to measure these. English is a 'mongrel' language of early Germanic, Norman French, Scandinavian languages, classical Latin and Greek, and others, but instead of being stigmatised for this mixture it receives ideological spin as a 'rich' language. Similarly, institutional adoption has ensured the prestige of classical Latin and Greek, in spite of not being the living vernacular of anyone.

## Standardisation

It is common when a language community roughly corresponds with national boundaries for one dialect to be promoted above all others and attract prestige to the point at which it is regarded as the 'standard' form, even to the extent that it is seen as the 'proper' language and all other dialects 'bad' forms of the language. There are always socio-political reasons why this happens (the roots of the standardisation of UK Standard English can be seen in the domestic policy of the Tudors: see D1).

Haugen (1966) has delineated four stages in the process of standardisation:

| | |
|---|---|
| selection | of one dialect above others; |
| codification | largely through the education system; |
| elaboration | increase in functions and range of uses of the code; |
| acceptance | by the community at large of the code as the 'standard' form. |

In Britain, the dialect spoken between the East Midlands and London in the Middle Ages came to be adopted as what we now call Standard English. There was nothing inherently superior about this dialect: it is simply that it was spoken by the emerging middle class and migrants to London, so it developed as a marker of prestigious class, wealth and civilisation. With the expansion of compulsory schooling throughout the nineteenth century, culminating in mass literacy for the first time after the 1870 Education Act, the Standard English dialect came to be adopted for all print media. Spellings were fixed and 'correct' spelling became a marker of good education. The other dialects of Britain were relegated to their spoken form only, and wiped out from the education system and from prestigious texts. Through the twentieth century, a capacity for Standard English came to be regarded almost as a moral imperative.

In other parts of the world where English spread, national Standard Englishes developed, initially based on the standard in Britain at the point at which the colony made its cultural separation from the old country. American Standard English, for example, is a late eighteenth-century base with developments over the next two centuries led often by the prescriptive demands of nation-building (the demotion of other languages like Spanish, German and Dutch in the school system, the new American dictionary of Noah Webster). Australian Standard English is closer to modern British SE in several respects, but it too reveals its early nineteenth-century basis in the dialect forms of London and East Anglia, prominent areas of the early settlers. The Standard Englishes of the Indian sub-continent and other Indian Ocean and south Asian former colonies (from South Africa to Singapore and Hong Kong) retain a late nineteenth-century base, with local development over the last century. (See thread 9 for examples.)

The institutional emphasis on Standard English is so strong that it is illuminating to consider its grammatical peculiarities in relation to other varieties, as Peter Trudgill (1998) has done. British Standard English:

❑  fails to distinguish between the forms of the auxiliary verb *do* and its main verb forms (*I do it* vs. *I do think so*);

❑  has irregular present tense morphology (with the verb *go*, only the 3rd person singular is marked with -*s: he goes*);

❑  lacks multiple negation (so you ain't never able to do this);

- reflexive pronouns are irregularly formed (some are derived from possessive – *myself*, some from objective – *himself*);
- does not distinguish singular and plural pronouns in the 2nd person (*you* for both, not *tu/vous, thou/you, tha/yer, you/youse,* or *yer/yall*);
- verb *to be* is irregular in present (*am, is, are*) and past tenses (*was, were*);
- redundantly has two forms of past tense (*I saw/I have seen*);
- only has a two-way distinction in the demonstrative system (*this/that, these/those*).

To these could be added:

- redundantly adds plural *-s* to words already modified by numeral (*two dogs*);
- lacks habitual, narrative, and future tenses (unlike French or African-American English);
- currently developing confusion between subjunctive, conditional and declarative forms (*shall/will, should/would, if I was/were . . .*).

As sociolinguists, though our analysis must be as descriptive as possible, it is important that common attitudes and perceptions that might have sociolinguistic effects are taken into account. We can distinguish various degrees of awareness in common perception:

| | |
|---|---|
| **stereotypes** | the very obvious features that all speakers are aware of in their own usage (such as Scottish, Irish and American rhoticity); |
| **markers** | obvious identifiable features that are easily measurable and that speakers are aware of only when explicitly discussing their own usage (Geordie rising intonation popularly described as 'sing-song', /w/ for /l/ in a Cockney accent); |
| **indicators** | measurable features that are useful for linguists because they are below the normal level of users' awareness (/ɪn/ for /ɪŋ/ in Norwich, glottalling /t/ in London-influenced British accents). |

People commonly attach all sorts of social evaluations to variations in usage like these.

# GENDER                                                                        A7

One of the main social changes of the last 50 years, and one which has been extensively studied by sociolinguists, is the role of **gender** as a determinant of linguistic usage. We have already seen (in A5) how both Trudgill and Cheshire discovered gender differences in hypercorrection and covert prestige, even within the same social class, age and region. Trudgill also asked his informants to report what they considered to be their own usage. When compared with their actual observed behaviour, he found that women claimed to use prestige features far more than they really did, and equally that men claimed to use fewer prestige features than they actually did use. This over- and under-reporting further supports the view that women hypercorrect and men aim for covert prestige, especially among the middle class groups. However, Trudgill explains this behaviour for each gender slightly differently. Men, he says, aim for a more streetwise, 'macho' standard, whereas women are more conscious of being judged on appearance and so hypercorrect 'upwards'. Notice, though, that the scale of values and terminology here (as well as the divergent explanations) are based very much on a male-oriented value-system. It is this methodological issue that much feminist linguistic work has addressed.

Early feminist commentators on language suggested that English was inherently sexist and structured and fixed to reflect a male world-view. Sociolinguists have more recently taken the view that it is linguistic practices that are often sexist and communities who use language in a sexist way, rather than the language itself being controlled by men (largely since, it is argued, meanings are a matter of social negotiation and cannot be fixed by anyone). There is certainly enough evidence that we can use the term **genderlect** to refer to the different lexical and grammatical choices that are characteristically made by men and women. In an early study, Robin Lakoff pointed to certain features she identified as 'women's talk' in the 1970s US, such as the frequency of particular colour terms (*mauve*); frequency of certain evaluative adjectives (*lovely, sweet*); hesitant intonation; pitch associated with surprise and questions; tag-phrases (*you know, kind of, sort of*); and superpoliteness (including euphemism, less swearing, more indirectness and hedging).

Many of these claims have since been investigated and criticised, and it is certainly true to say that society has also changed a great deal in the intervening time. For example, a linguist could note even in the 1990s that 'Admiring one another's clothes is far more acceptable among women: a woman can say *Julia, what an absolutely divine tunic!*, but it would be decidedly unusual (in most circles, anyway) for a man to remark *Those are great jeans you're wearing, Ted*' (Trask 1999: 275). My male students today have no qualms in discoursing on fashion, even without the hint here that to do so is a bit effeminate.

These early accounts rest on an assumption that women's language is deficient in some way relative to the **norm** of men's language. Such a **deficit** view typically expresses the features of women's language as lacking certain elements, being weak in certain respects, having less semantic or logical content, and so on. An approach that focuses on **dominance** rather than deficit is only marginally better: regarding male discourse as oppressive and women's language as subordinated to it moves on from the notion of the masculine as norm and the feminine as marked, but it offers no possibility for variation or the sort of linguistic creativity and shift that does evidently exist.

More recently, sociolinguists like Deborah Cameron, Jennifer Coates and Deborah Tannen have shown that it is features at the level of discourse and interaction that mainly realise the underlying variation in the socialisation of men and women. For example, men seem to see the purpose of conversation as information-gathering, whereas women see it as a support-mechanism, and both groups act accordingly. All of this translates into different linguistic behaviour: in mixed groups, men tend to dominate the time and turn-taking; women tend to support and reply; men explain things to women; women ask more questions, use more 'backchannel noise' (*uh-huh, yeah, yes, hmm, hmm . . .*) and invite participation; women regard forcefulness as personal aggression; men see it as normal conversational organisation, and so on.

Of course, it could be that these are all features associated directly with **power** and only indirectly an index of *gender*, correlated by the still unequal power balance in most societies. What is termed 'women's talk' with the features suggested above, has also been observed in the language of powerless men, and 'male' features in the practices of powerful women. Modern sociolinguistic analysis of genderlects focuses on the **social construction** that is accomplished by language. In other words, gender is negotiated and performed culturally and socially in the operation of discourse. Furthermore, it has become clear that there is not one rigid set of language features that are characteristic of women and another set for men. Degrees of masculinity and femininity overlap and are expressed in relation to each other, so we can talk of **masculinities** and **femininities** being performed in every language event, constructing our gender (here a graded notion) in a variety of ever-changing ways. For example, four paragraphs above I observed that the discourse of gender even of the fairly recent past assumed a simple cline from male to female, such that 'girlie-talk' amongst men would serve to 'effeminise' the speaker. This is simplistic, of course. Sexuality and biological sex are major factors in gender but are not the only influences: gender is a socio-cultural phenomenon.

Questions about the sociolinguistic method (especially variationism (see A5) and qualitative analyses) from a broadly feminist perspective have led to gender studies taking a generally qualitative and holistic character in sociolinguistics. Researchers are likely to spend an extended period of time with the speech community under investigation, and the categories for analysis are more likely to be suggested by the group's view of their own usage rather than being imposed from linguistic theory.

## PIDGINS AND CREOLES                                              **A8**

New languages are continually being born to language families. All natural languages develop from and alongside other languages to which they are closely related. English was originally a West Germanic language, which developed directly from the Anglo-Frisian dialects of invaders, and was subsequently heavily **lexicalised** by words borrowed from Norman French, then by French, Latin and Greek, with a few loan-words from the Celtic languages, from Spanish and Italian, and from every language in contact with the British Empire (including Persian, Hindi, Bengali and various African languages). In short, English has achieved its globalisation by allowing itself to become greatly **hybridised**.

Though the origins of English, and most long-established languages, are lost in time and have to be reconstructed from old documents, sound-change rules and partial evidence, the process of language-birth and maturation can be observed at first hand through modern **pidgin** and **creole** languages.

This thread can be summarised by the following diagram:

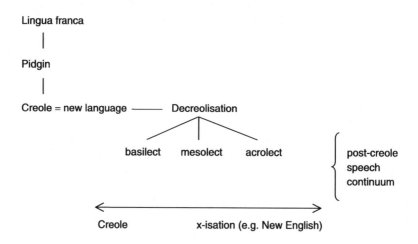

### The evolution of pidgin languages

In situations in which two speech communities come into prolonged contact, a **lingua franca** (common language) usually develops. This can take one of four forms: a **contact language**; an **auxiliary language**; an **international language**; or a **trade language**.

Ancient Greek around the Mediterranean basin, or later Latin throughout the Roman Empire, were both **contact languages**. Such languages tend to vary in use in different local contexts, and there is often a great deal of local language interference. Latin, for example, later developed many local dialectal forms which eventually became French, Italian, Spanish, Portuguese, and so on. The contact language usually dominates in situations in which the speakers of that language have military or economic power over other language users.

By contrast, a **trade language** such as Swahili on the east coast of Africa often indicates a more equal relationship. This coastal Swahili is only used in commercial contexts, whereas further west into the interior of Africa, Reconstructed Swahili serves as a fully-functional language, and consequently is much more developed in complexity. Where a language is functioning as a trade language, usually only the lexicogrammatical patterns associated with commerce, negotiation, finance and exchange are fully realised and practised.

An **international language**, such as English, is often used as a neutral form, as in India after independence in 1947. Indian English did not privilege any of the native-speaker communities, and also gave India a linguistic access to the western world.

Other international languages have included French (especially amongst the ruling class in the eighteenth and nineteenth centuries, Spanish across large areas of south, central and north America, Chinese in both China and the headlands and islands round east Asia, and Arabic across the Middle East, North Africa and in Islamic countries. More recently, English has ridden on the back of American economic and political influence. Most tellingly, 80 per cent of global internet traffic is in English. In fact, English is so widely spoken and has such global dominance that it can even be regarded as a separate category of language in its own right.

**Auxiliary languages** include the artificial languages such as Esperanto (largely composed of European elements), Business English, Maritime English (Sea-Speak), and Air-Traffic Control English (as well, coincidentally, as other artificial languages such as those produced by philosophers, fantasy writers and other hobbyists). Such **Englishes for Special Purposes (ESP)** tend to have a highly restricted and technical vocabulary, and exist in a frozen, regulated form. It would be highly danger-ous, for example, for airline pilots suddenly to develop dialectal innovation in their expressions while requesting permission to land!

When the contact between groups of people is prolonged, a hybrid language can develop known as a **pidgin**. These tend to occur in situations where one language dominates, and there are two or more other languages at hand. Elements of the syntax and lexis of each language are simplified and combined as speakers struggle to make themselves understood by accommodating towards each speech community; one language (the **lexifier**) tends to provide most of the words in the new pidgin. Though the pidgin might have recognisable elements of existing languages, it is not simply a 'broken' form of one of the languages: pidgins have rule-systems and have to be learnt. Nevertheless, pidgin languages tend to be restricted in vocabulary, are usually syntactically simple, and have a limited range of functions (trade, local com-merce, marriage negotiations, land disputes, for example). Anyone who uses the pidgin will always have their own native vernacular language, and will switch into the pidgin only when necessary.

Pidgins tend to be found in coastal areas, generally around the equatorial belt in former colonial locations, and have arisen typically in times of imperialism, slavery, plantation-labour migration, war and refugee situations, and around trading ports. For these reasons, pidgins tend to be lexified from the languages of the European imperial powers: French (in Louisiana, Haiti, Seychelles); Dutch (Afrikaans); Spanish (Papiamentu); Portuguese (Guine Crioule, Macau); and English (Melanesian Tok Pisin, West African Krio, Jamaican Patwa). Around a quarter of all pidgins and creoles have English as an element.

### Creolisation

A pidgin becomes a **creole** as soon as it is learnt as the first language of a new generation. In these circumstances, pidgins rapidly develop a wider range of phonemes, a larger vocabulary, more complex syntax and a greater range of stylistic options to the point at which the creole can be used in every context and to express every requirement of the speaker. However, not every pidgin becomes a creole, and sometimes a pidgin and a creole can co-exist in urban and rural locations.

Some creoles rapidly undergo **standardisation**: pronunciations and spellings are judged 'correct' or 'incorrect'; law and government administration are conducted and recorded in the creole; newspapers, books and prestigious texts are produced in it; and the creole becomes the language in which education is delivered (see A6).

Creoles can develop into fully-fledged languages in their own right, like Afrikaans, with little interference from either the European parent (Dutch) or local African Bantu languages. However, many English-based creoles come under pressure from locally-powerful English-speaking standards (America, Australia, or British textbooks). In these circumstances, a **post-creole speech continuum** can develop. Different forms of the creole become socially stratified: the fully-fledged creole is spoken by illiterate manual workers (the **basilectal** variety), and a variety (the **acrolect**) closer to standard English is spoken by the social elites, with a range of varieties (**mesolects**) in between. As described in unit A9 below, the acrolect can evolve into a **New English**, such as Singlish or Jamaican English, for example. This is part of the wider process known as **x-isation** (for example, 'indianisation, sinicisation, americanisation' and so on).

If the pressure from the powerful local standard is sufficiently strong, the creole can become **decreolised**, and the basilectal and mesolectal varieties become stigmatised and associated with illiteracy and ignorance. In such situations, local governments often proscribe the use of the creole as 'improper', and the schools and newspapers teach against it. Unless language loyalty or covert prestige sustains it, the creole can disappear and eventually lose all its speakers and die.

## NEW, NATIONAL AND INTERNATIONAL ENGLISHES

The English language was developed by Germanic invaders into the south and east of Britain, and spread west and north into Ireland, Wales and Scotland. From the Renaissance to the eighteenth century it was spread by the English navy and emigrants to north America and Australasia. At the height of the British Empire in the nineteenth century, English became the administrative language of large parts of Africa, the Indian subcontinent, and strategic trading outposts like Hong Kong and Singapore. The number of **extraterritorial** English speakers means that the language no longer belongs to any one nation, and that we must speak not of English but of *Englishes*.

### The standard Englishes

In those countries in which English is the official, main or dominant language, we can talk of **standard Englishes**. Braj Kachru (1988) differentiates 'the inner circle' of standard English-speaking territories from 'the outer circle' where English is very important but does not dominate to the same extent. At the beginning of the twenty-first century, a variety of standard Englishes are spoken in:

| The British Isles | (around 65 million people) |
| USA and Caribbean | (around 300 million people) |
| Canada | (around 27 million people) |
| Australia | (around 18 million people) |
| New Zealand | (around 4 million people) |

Thus just under half a billion people use English as their first or main language in the world.

The characteristic accents and standardised dialects of these areas derive from the time at which the main settlement from Britain occurred, and they are all founded on southern British speech variants. North American speech derives from the seventeenth and eighteenth centuries and shows an especial East Anglian influence. Australasian accents come mainly from the south-east of England and London in the eighteenth and nineteenth centuries – at which time parts of South Africa were also settled. The rest of the Commonwealth (across Africa, India and south-east Asia) takes its English norms from the late nineteenth and early twentieth centuries. Former British colonies were garrisoned and ruled by an army largely recruited from southern England, led by public-school educated officers who were upper middle class or even aristocracy, speaking RP. Caribbean accents derive from the west African origins of slave ancestors.

Later local variations entered as a result of later settlement and evolution. For example, the influx of eastern European refugees, Irish and Jews from famine and war in the late nineteenth and early twentieth centuries gave the arrival point of New York its characteristic accent. Large numbers of Scots and Irish emigrants to Canada produced Canadian English, and the Scots dialect similarly influenced New Zealand speech.

Historically, the population of English L1 speakers has been larger than the number of English L2 users in the world, with a shift of influence to the USA over the twentieth century. However, the populations of the 'outer circle' are increasing at a faster rate, and the estimate is that the number of L2 users is now in the process of overtaking the number of L1 users in the world.

## The standardising Englishes
Kachru's 'outer circle' includes:

| African territories (Ghana, Kenya, Nigeria, Tanzania, Zambia) | (300 million) |
| Indian subcontinent (India, Pakistan, Bangladesh, Sri Lanka) | (1.2 billion) |
| Pacific rim (Malaysia, Singapore, Philippines) | (80 million) |

In total, a population of 1.5 billion live in these areas in which English has a special importance – though of course not everyone speaks English either as a vernacular or fluently.

English in these areas co-exists with many other indigenous languages. Inevitably, there is **interference** between the codes, with lexical copying and grammatical structures repositioning the English variety. We can thus talk of the **x-isation** of English, and *x-ised* forms include the Indianisation of English, the Africanisation of English, and so on, to produce **New Englishes** with their own lexicogrammars and rules. In effect, they are in the process of standardising.

The Americanisation of English, for example, has been documented for many years, with many eighteenth-century British features (rhoticity and other variant pronunciations, verb-forms like *do you got,* older meanings of words like 'mad', 'guess' and 'fag', among many others), as well as subsequent independent developments. American English has a noticeably developed spelling system, thanks to lexicographer Noah Webster and his efforts to establish 'an American language'.

The Indianisation of English is also a global force. Written Indian English uses many features which would be considered very polite, formal or conservative in a British or American setting. Features of spoken Indian English include:

| | |
|---|---|
| omission of articles | 'I borrowed book from library' |
| Subject-Object-Verb word-order | 'I door open' |
| prepositional variation | 'I my aunt to visited' |
| comparative/superlative | 'good, more good, most good/good of all' |
| itself/only | 'Can I meet with you tomorrow itself' |
| adverbial for dummy 'there' | 'Meat is there, vegetables are there' |
| politeness markers | 'These mistakes may please be corrected' |
| tense and aspect | 'I am having a cold' |
| question non-inversion | 'Who you have come to see?' |
| undifferentiated tag-question | 'You are going home soon, isn't it?' |
| lexical variation | bandh (regional labour strike) |
| | crore (10 million) |
| | lathi (bamboo iron-clad police truncheon) |
| | biodata (CV) |
| | co-brother (wife's sister's husband) |

Other New Englishes show similar interference patterns and characteristic features.

Finally, English is an increasingly important L2 in the rest of the world, which Kachru calls 'the expanding circle':

| | |
|---|---|
| Far East (China, Indonesia, Japan, Korea, Nepal, Taiwan) | (1.7 billion) |
| Middle East (Egypt, Israel, Saudi Arabia) | (70 million) |
| Africa (Zimbabwe) | (10 million) |

Thus, around 20 per cent of the world's population have English as L1 or L2, and a further 45 per cent have English as an important language in their lives: this amounts in total to nearly two-thirds of the human race.

## POLITENESS AND ACCOMMODATION

Much of this section has focused on 'macro-sociolinguistic' dimensions of language. However, social negotiation also has an individual, micro-sociolinguistic aspect. Language choice is motivated by **recipient design** – that is, users aim for an effective communicative purpose, bearing in mind the target of the utterance. All languages have a range of features available that encode very subtle social and individual relationships, and many areas of sociolinguistics are concerned with encoding **power**. This suggests perhaps that power is a super-determinant in sociolinguistics.

### Name and address

Many languages, including some varieties of English, differentiate singular and plural second person. This is known as the T/V system:

| | |
|---|---|
| French | tu/vous |
| Latin | tu/vos |
| Russian | ty/vy |
| Italian | tu/Lei |
| German | du/Sie |
| Greek | esi/esis |
| Swedish | du/ni |
| Old English | þe/ge |
| Middle English | thou/you |
| Yorkshire English | tha/you |
| Liverpool and Dublin English | you/youse |
| Appalachian English | you/yall |

These forms can have a variety of functions:

❑ **number**      differentiating singular (T) and plural (V)
❑ **politeness**   to mark intimate and familiar (T) or respect (V)
❑ **social rank**  V used to superiors, T used to inferiors
❑ **solidarity**   V used outside the group, T used as an in-group marker

English developed its T/V through number to include politeness by the early Middle Ages. It developed as a marker of social rank during the Renaissance, but then became non-differentiated in many dialects (including the dialect that was to become Standard English) beginning around the time of the English civil war (the seventeenth century). In modern times, a T/V distinction is only heard in some dialects (Yorkshire 'thee/you', Liverpool 'you/youse'), and in frozen utterances such as the traditional wedding service, prayers from the Authorised Version of the Bible, Quaker language, and in productions of Shakespeare plays.

   In other languages, speakers are aware of the choice to be made: French signals it with the verbs *vousvoyer* and *tutoyer*; German with *duzen* and *siezen* and a little ceremony to mark the shift in the relationship. Speakers have the choice of:

❑   **reciprocal T usage** to show equality and familiarity (used by French revolutionaries in 1789 and modern communists)

- ❑ **reciprocal V usage** to show mutual respect or formality (French aristocrats such as former president Valéry Giscard d'Estaing used V to everyone, including, it is reported, to voters, ministers, his wife and passing dogs. Apparently Jean-Paul Sartre and Simone de Beauvoir addressed each other using V.)
- ❑ **asymmetrical T/V usage** to show power difference (based on age and youth, serving staff and customers, boss and worker, professor and student, for example).

There are cultural variations within this, of course. The rigid asymmetrical T/V usage is loosening, especially amongst young French speakers. French and Italian speakers are more likely to use T to friends than Germans, but Germans are more likely than them to use T to distant relatives. Norwegian schoolchildren can use T to teachers, but German and Dutch tend not to do so. Male Italian students are likely to use T to female students, but then in general Italians use more T than French or Germans. Speakers who are politically conservative tend also to be linguistically conservative and preserve the T/V asymmetry.

This system is echoed in the title and address options which are also available to all English speakers without a T/V system. Politeness is encoded by use of Title, First Name, Last Name, by combinations of these (TLN, TFN, FNLN), or by avoidance (Ø). Again, asymmetrical usage indicates a power inequality, and a switch from a more polite to less polite form must always be initiated by the most powerful person ('Professor Stockwell?' 'Please, call me Peter'). Breaking these norms generates certain social effects: consider, on meeting the Queen of England, 'Alright Betty!'

English has to use title and address options very subtly, since it lacks the complex verb-ending system of, for example, Korean:

| | |
|---|---|
| intimate | *-na* |
| familiar | *-e* |
| plain | *-ta* |
| polite | *-e yo* |
| deferential | *-supnita* |
| authoritative | *-so* |

The pragmatics of politeness affects all linguistic choices, including accent and intonation selection and choice of register: consider the real 'Customers are reminded that New Street is a no smoking station. Please extinguish all smoking materials', with a possible alternative, 'Oi you, stop bloody smoking – get that fag out'.

One influential model of politeness (Brown and Levinson 1987) is based on the notion of **face**. This is the social role that you present to the world. **Negative face** is your desire to be unimpeded in your actions; **positive face** is your desire for identification with the community. Any interpersonal event is potentially a **face threatening act (FTA)** which needs to be negotiated with particular politeness strategies:

**positive politeness**     appealing to positive face ('you look fit and healthy – any chance you could help me push the car?')

| negative politeness | hedge ('could I, er, just, sort of do this . . .') |
|---|---|
| | indicate pessimism ('I don't suppose you have the time on you?') |
| | minimise the imposition ('do you mind if I borrow it for a second?') |
| | indicate deference ('I'm an idiot – forgotten my keys again! Any chance of borrowing yours?') |
| | apologise ('sorry about this, but could I . . .') |
| | impersonalise ('the management reserve the right to refuse admission') |
| | use politeness tag ('please', 'cheers') |

Of course, it is important to match the politeness strategy to the force of the imposition: you would not require much politeness to ask the time, but you would need a lot to borrow a car. Mismatching the expected norm will be seen as rudeness, over-familiarity, aggression, or over-formality, obsequiousness or sarcasm. Of course, you always have the option of just asking, plainly and baldly, without any redressive politeness, for the thing you want, but usually only those with either extreme power or extreme intimacy can get away with this.

## Accommodation

All of these linguistic facilities are available for social negotiation. Participants also evolve their strategies and choices in the process of interaction. The most interesting is the phenomenon of **accommodation**, in which participants **converge** their speech styles. This can mean that people with different accents alter their vowel quality towards each other, or begin to echo certain words or phrases used by the other person, or adopt similar discourse and politeness strategies over time. (Incidentally, accommodation causes problems associated with the **observer's paradox** for socio-linguistics, since informants are likely to drift towards the interviewer's speech style in an extended interview: see A1).

As always, there are cultural differences here of course. For example, in mixed sex conversations, men and women tend to use fewer features of their genderlects and tend to move towards a common norm. In Britain, however, men tend to accommodate more towards women, whereas in the US, women tend to move further towards the male norm.

Just about every conversation anyone ever has exhibits some element of accom-modation at this interpersonal level (the term also encompasses wilful or resistant accommodation which is manifested as **divergence** in accent or register mirroring). There is obviously a **power** dimension to take into account with interpersonal accommodation, with the most powerful individual likely to be the focus of any convergence. Power can be measured here not just in terms of wealth, class or con-ventional prestige, but also in terms of the individual's centrality to a **social network**, for example (see B5).

Such interpersonal accommodation tends to be temporary. However, it is also possible to observe accommodation between entire speech communities, where the dialects of each group become merged or one group converges to a greater proportional extent. Such **dialect contact** can be a factor in language change.

**CONVERSATION**

Conversations are comprised not of sentences (which are units of written language) but of utterances – which are the equivalent of sentences taken in their social context, and including a sense of the situation of the speaker and hearer, the purpose of the utterance, and the effect of the utterance. The unit of analysis in other linguistic disciplines such as syntax or semantics is usually taken to be the clause; in sociolinguistics, the organising unit of conversation is the **turn**.

### Organising conversation

Different cultures perceive the norms of conversation differently, of course, but in most English-speaking societies there is only a very short tolerance of silence. Some cultures (North American Indian, Japanese, and even Quaker communities in Britain) regard long pauses in conversation as normal and polite. In other cultures, silence can be taken as hostile, rude or submissive. In British, American and Australian English, for example, conversations often consist of pairs of turns in which a direct question or elicitation is expected to be answered immediately by a response turn. Such an elicitation-response pattern is known as an **adjacency pair**, and the pair is rarely divided by a long pause.

Since conversation (even argumentative or obstructive speech) is organised to produce conventional responses in the interlocutor, it can be said to be characterised by **recipient design**. In the elicitation turn of an adjacency pair, then, there is often an implicit **preferred response**: giving a dispreferred response has a social effect. Here, for example, is a real example from one of my more obstructive friends:

A:  What time is it?
B:  What? Now?

Clearly, the preferred response to my (A's) question is a turn which – in preferred order – either gives the time directly ('two-thirty'), gives an indirect but relevant answer ('the shops have just shut'), gives an indication that B doesn't know ('no idea, I haven't got a watch on'), or even answers in some other relevant way ('you're so uptight always wanting to know the time'). However, B's actual answer above is not only perturbing because it is dispreferred, it also breaks the adjacency pair by initiating another pair by asking a (absurdly obvious) question.

Ordinary adjacency pairs consisting of an elicitation and a preferred response are often followed by the first speaker providing **feedback** on the response:

A:   Can you give me a hand?
B:   Sure.
A:   Thanks.

This sequence was followed by another initiated by B:

B:   What do I do?
A:   If you could just push, I'll be able to jump-start it.
B:   OK.

In real conversations, however, patterns are often more complex. Here is the example given in full:

A:   Can you give me a hand?
[Before B answers, A shouts across the road to C:] BOB! Any chance of a hand here?
C:   Yeah, be there in a minute.
B:   Well, will it take long – it's just that I'm in a rush and
A:   No, a couple of seconds. Can you?
B:   Sure. I've got to be at the station soon.
A:   Thanks.
B:   What do I do?
A:   If you could just push, I'll be able to jump-start it.
B:   OK.

The adjacency pairs and feedback have been interrupted with other turns. The first interruption occurs when A 'leaves' the current conversational trajectory to call across the road to Bob (C): 'Any chance of a hand here? and Bob replies. This 'external' adjacency pair is a **side-sequence**: it is independent of the first pair of turns. There is a second interruption when B stalls his answer in order to ask 'Well, will it take long . . .' and this creates its own response ('No, a couple of seconds') – this 'internal' adjacency pair is an **insertion-sequence** dependent on the main conversation. Once it is completed, A repeats the original elicitation ('Can you?') and B answers it ('Sure'). This final answer was dependent, for B, on the answer to the insertion sequence pair. There is also an example in this conversation of **skip-connecting**, where B started to explain 'it's just that I'm in a rush', and returns to the topic later on: 'I've got to be at the station soon'.

Even this example is relatively 'clean' in its orderly structure. Most extended conversations involve interruptions, sound effects (laughing, coughing, intonation patterns), questions which are not answered, topics which are skipped back to over very long sequences, insertions that become the topic such that the original topic is lost, and so on. People often are observed **latching**, where a hearer will complete a speaker's turn, talking simultaneously, or producing **backchannel** noise ('aha', 'hmm', 'yeah', and nodding) to maintain the conversation.

## Turn-taking

Turns are utterances produced by a speaker, and a conversation consists of two or more turns produced by different speakers. **Turn-taking** in conversation is a linguistic variable that is determined very considerably by social factors, especially *power*. The conventions of turn-taking are so strongly embedded within any given speech community that power can be asserted, maintained or relinquished by the organisation of turn-taking in conversation.

Taking a turn in a conversation is often simply a matter of speaking first in a silence. However, anticipating silences is an incredibly precise ability, and hearers can be observed drawing breath as the syntax of the current speaker winds towards a clause-boundary. Where the conversation is non-competitive, speakers might keep their turns short, signal the end of their turn by slowing down their speech or using syntactic forms which signal completion. They might even invite another turn by asking a direct question, by naming the next speaker, nominating them with an open facial expression, direct gaze or indicative hand-gesture.

In competitive conversation, where speakers are vying for the chance to 'take the floor', hearers can exploit some of these patterns to take the turn from the current speaker. So catching his eye, anticipating a clause boundary and jumping in, inserting your hand into the social space of the conversation, or simply beginning to talk simultaneously but faster or louder will often prove successful in taking your turn from him. Other common strategies include making backchannel noise or latching but speeding it up and converting it into substantive content so that you take the turn.

Where a speaker does not want to give up the floor, he might avoid eye-contact, avoid direct questions, avoid naming names; he might carefully plan his breath so that he breathes in the middle of a syntactic constituent rather than at a boundary, might speed up near clause boundaries, might talk louder, or might preface a turn with a statement such as 'I have three points to make . . .'. He might pause after an **utterance incompletor** such as 'but . . .' or 'meanwhile . . .' Sometimes he might even produce some **metalanguage** that draws attention to the interruption itself ('If you could just let me finish'). Politicians are very adept (and are often trained) in these techniques. Social judgements of politeness, rudeness, arrogance, emotional state, power and timidity are made on the basis of an individual's turn-taking style relative to the conventions of the speech community involved.

---

**A12**          **APPLYING SOCIOLINGUISTICS**

All sociolinguistic studies are examples of **applied linguistics** in the broad sense: that is, they deal with examples of natural language in their original social settings, rather than theorising aspects of language without any empirical data. However, sociolinguistics as the broad field represented in this book demonstrates a concern for politics, ideology and engagement that applies itself to the world more directly than many other disciplines within linguistic study. Sociolinguists who become interested in accent and dialect are often reacting to earlier work which takes a disparaging view of a particular accent feature and its users. I have often been struck by how many sociolinguists themselves speak with non-standard and often stigmatised accents. Many sociolinguists begin their studies as graduate students by researching their home town, or a feature of language that correlates with a social variable that is personally significant for them. Many sociolinguists are involved in advisory capacities for their governments or local councils, bringing their expertise to bear on issues that they care about and that they wish to influence. In short, sociolinguistics is strikingly a *humane* discipline within the social and human sciences, both in its method and in its practitioners.

Taking a broad and socially engaged view of the discipline is characteristic of many (though by no means all) of those who regard themselves as sociolinguists. Where the field ends and other disciplines begin is a debatable matter. There are clear overlaps in sociolinguistics with areas in pragmatics such as politeness, or stylistics in register, or discourse analysis in conversation, and so on. In this final unit of section A, I would like briefly to sketch a few of the many fields that sit across the boundaries of sociolinguistics, or have strong connections with sociolinguistic concerns or practices. In placing these here, I have not avoided political assertions or contentious claims: these too, for me, are part of sociolinguistic debate.

### Critical discourse analysis

The field of **critical linguistics** developed in the 1970s as linguists looked above the level of the clause and connected their approach with work being produced in anthropology and cultural studies. Simple grammatical analyses of transitivity (*who did what to whom* with *what* and *how*), or the semantics of naming strategies, or the commitment to truth shown in modal choices ('might', 'could', 'will', 'ought to'), for example, all revealed how linguistic patterns encoded a socially and ideologically motivated view of the world. Critical linguists argued that as members of the society in which they worked, they had an ethical responsibility to use their expert linguistic knowledge in socially useful and just ways.

However, critical linguistics came under attack for two related reasons. First, most critical linguistic work was explicitly left-wing and progressive in orientation, leaving the discourse of the left itself relatively unexamined. Second and more importantly, critical linguists often talked as if the discourses of the media were a *distortion* of a true version of events. Of course, this simply places one discourse in a prestigious position and in many ways was regarded as an outdated view of language, based on the idea that some meanings were fixed and determinate.

In response, the discipline has become a **critical discourse analysis (CDA)**, drawing in sociolinguistic methodology and rigour, and a greater philosophical sophistication from social theory. Critical discourse analysts treat all linguistic representations as motivated ideological choices, with no pre-linguistic truth that is thinkable. See B12 for more.

### Language and education

Much work that is concerned with literacy, with school standards, with strategies for teaching and with government educational policy is strongly informed by sociolinguistics. Sociolinguists have been interested in how the linguistic practices of both students and teachers are affected and determined by social factors such as gender, family wealth, class, second language fluency, and so on. Sociolinguistic studies have been conducted in classrooms across the world with an objective of discovering how students' language relates to the discourse expected by teachers and the examination system. Sociolinguistic evidence has been deployed by politicians to demonstrate the need for reform in raising standards of schooling, and has been produced also by critics of those initiatives in order to show why the policy was faulty or misplaced.

Sociolinguistics, then, has played a part in both national educational policy and in the training given to teachers. The ideological sensibility brought to socio-linguistics by CDA has resulted in studies of the classroom in which language is central, and the variety of language used is related to its social factors outside the boundaries of the school. The richness that a sociolinguistic account brings to our understanding of how schooling works has assisted in the increasing politicisation of education, which has had its positive and negative effects.

From being regarded as an individual psychological skill, **literacy** has come to be sociolinguistically defined as a social and functional skill. We can place a child in relation to different discourse environments (newspaper print, fiction, playground, home, sport, internet, phone texting, magazine, advertising) and talk about their different **literacies**. We can account for the ideological motivations behind these discourses, and can offer ways of enabling students to read the world around them critically and powerfully. See A3 and C3 for more.

## Identity and community

Like *literacy*, identity is usually regarded as a purely psychological notion, but socio-linguistic work has demonstrated precisely how individual identity is socially bound up and mutually determined. Judy Dyer (2007) points out three phases in socio-linguistic treatments of identity. Early sociolinguistic studies focusing on **quantita-tive** methods addressed the accent and dialect usage of individuals defined in relation to large social categories (age, class, gender). Later, more **ethnographic** research emphasised the place of individual identity within speech communities. Lately, sociolinguistics has focused on the **social meaning** of language usage, where identity is constructed from linguistic features and the individual is performed through language, socially.

Throughout the history of sociolinguistics, the social importance of individual identity has been central. Without becoming simply a branch of social psychology, sociolinguistics has explored the continuities of accents, dialects and languages across geographical boundaries. The ways that politeness norms have become established, or how speakers accommodate towards each other in extended conversation, or how political, gendered, ethnic or age groupings are built and maintained have all been the fruitful ground of sociolinguistics. **Identity** is pivotal in all this, such that the notion is increasingly regarded as being as much a social factor as a psychological one. See B4, A7 and B7, A9 and B9, and A10 for more.

**A**

## Language planning

Since sociolinguistics encompasses both society and the individual's place in that social whole, it is not surprising that macro-economic views of the world have drawn on sociolinguistics in the form of national and international language policy. Governments throughout history have seen the political value and significance of language planning, whether that has involved suppressing the language of rebellious groups or encouraging ideological standards in discourse conventions. The former is usually effected through legislation and policing, the latter through the education and qualifications system.

**Language planning** involves surveying the state of the language across large social groups, and then taking interventionist measures to shift usage in desired directions. There are positive and negative consequences of this. Nationalism usually encourages a national language, with standardisation as the main process. This produces mutual intelligibility among peoples, but also often serves to wipe out the richness of dialectal variation. Standardisation of the language and its codification in the education system creates an equal ground for any with access to schooling, but sociolinguistics has shown how the language background of students can influence their performance in this system.

Almost all administrative, legislative and political arms of government anywhere in the world have a language policy, whether explicit or implicit, drawn from a combination of actual research, folk-mythology and shared intuitions about the state of the language of the state. Sociolinguistic research can differentiate between these perspectives, can provide a systematic account of the language as it really is, and can suggest effective means of implementing policies for social justice rather than inequality.

# Section B

# DEVELOPMENT:
## STUDIES IN LANGUAGE AND SOCIETY

## UNDERTAKING A SOCIOLINGUISTIC STUDY

The key concepts set out so far in this book are the product of many discussions by many researchers in sociolinguistics. Some of these professional studies are represented in section D. Students setting out to investigate language and society use the published work and concepts to structure their own explorations, and to provide a disciplined framework within which to conduct and present their study. In this section, I will outline the work of my own recent undergraduate students in sociolinguistics. The intention in doing this is to encourage you, if you are new to the area, to have confidence in your own skills and thinking.

Each study is linked to the corresponding numbered area in section A. The students who conducted each study also read theoretical work and case studies in their area of investigation. In contextualising their work for this book, I have added my own comments. You will find further reading in the area at the end of the book. Some of the data for your own analysis in section C also comes from fieldwork studies collected by my students.

### Finding an area for study

The most successful studies tend to be those that are done by students with a direct interest in the area of investigation. This can arise in two different ways: **theory-driven** or **data-driven**.

In a theory-driven investigation, students are introduced to key ideas and debates within an area, and are led to further reading of published material. As they read and engage with the subject, I encourage them to 'read with a pencil', to think critically about their reading. A useful way of doing this is to assume a sceptical attitude towards every claim made in a book or article, unless direct evidence or reasoning is provided. Students are encouraged to examine closely every detail of the presentation, and also to think in general about what theoretical assumptions and positions underpin the writing. Often, what might at first glance appear to be minor details of difference between different studies can turn out to be examples where the writer 'buys into' a set of associated frameworks and positions that are highly contentious. Encouraging students to seek out these frameworks and discuss them directly is often a successful way of getting them to the heart of a discussion, and to engage seriously with the research. Theory-driven work is often the only practical way a British-based student can investigate, for example, African or Pacific pidgins and creoles, or diglossia, or cross-cultural politeness norms, and so on.

The contrary way of approaching an area of sociolinguistics is to discover the personal sociolinguistics in a student's life and develop that in a systematic way within the discipline. For example, many of my international students choose to investigate community multilingualism, personal bilingualism and code-switching, or examples of language loyalty towards new Englishes, and so on. By far the most popular area for study amongst English students at the moment is language and gender. The danger in exploring a familiar area, of course, is that the work becomes anecdotal and over-subjective. The way of avoiding this is to send students off to read published material in the area, and to develop very rigorous and transparent empirical procedures. They should also be encouraged to apply the same sort of sceptical rigour to their own draft work as they would apply to published studies.

It should be clear by now that the decision as to whether a study is theoretically led or practically led is a matter of emphasis rather than exclusiveness. Theoretical discussions tend to be poor if they have no data for evidence, and presentations of data are often rather meaningless unless you know what you are doing with the information.

## Planning the study

Once you have decided on an area for study, it is important that you spend some time planning the investigation. At this point, practical considerations will come into play: how long have you got to complete the fieldwork; do you have any resources, such as friends to help with interviewing, or cash to pay informants; how easy is it for you to get at the data you are interested in; is this the only research work you are engaged in, or are you splitting your time with other subjects? A key question often asked with a fieldwork sample is: how many people should I involve? This is not straightforward. Sociolinguistic studies tend to operate with larger numbers than, say, psycholinguistic studies, but that is partly because the nature of the fieldwork requires more depth typically in other areas. It also depends on the efficiency of your fieldwork design: you can stop people on the street and ask them a simple question, and easily get hundreds of informants in a day; alternatively, you might want to elicit an extended personal narrative from informants, and might end up with only five examples. The crucial factor to bear in mind is to make sure that the claims you make arising from the data that was available to you are neither immodest nor overblown. If it's any comfort, there are plenty of professional and published sociolingustic studies that are guilty of one or the other of these faults.

Given the practical parameters of your circumstances, the design of your field-work should be entirely directed at answering a research question. This should be framed in your own mind as precisely as possible. Ideally, you should set down exactly what you are trying to discover as a **hypothesis** – your educated guess as to what exactly you expect to find. Your study will then be designed to prove or disprove this hypothesis. If the factors you are interested in are not amenable to a 'yes/no' hypothesis, you should at least have as precise a **research question** as possible. If you have the luxury of time, you can conduct a **pilot-study**, a small-scale version of your eventual study, that will help you to refine your hypothesis and might even bring to light some flaws in your fieldwork plan that you did not anticipate. Your full study design after this can then be improved.

## Writing the study

It is also part of the learning process in sociolinguistics that you develop your skills in academic writing. Though it is possible to set out the linguistics of academic prose and teach it, selecting the most appropriate conventional register is best learnt by reading lots of professional sociolinguistic studies. The key to ensuring both this and a high level of rigour in evidence is to insist upon accurate and thorough referencing of all material read for the study. The model for setting this out is used in this book. I refer simply to the author's name and date of publication in the text, and all references are collected together efficiently at the end. Irritating footnotes and other scrappy asides are thus avoided.

Though there are many different ways of setting out a sociolinguistic report, the basic pattern follows the classical scientific format:

| | |
|---|---|
| Introduction | This sets up the parameters for research, and explains why the study needs to be done. |
| Review of published work | In which you collect the existing state of knowledge, commenting on it, evaluating it for the rigour of its procedure, and identifying the gap which you are about to fill with your own work. |
| Fieldwork design | Here you set out the terms of the study, your method of collecting the data, the nature of the population you are investigating, the linguistic feature under analysis, and the procedure you adopted. |
| Results/discussion | If you have complex results, it is better to present them separately from your discussion, and summarise them graphically or in tabular form. Alternatively, you can thread your results through a discussion of the significance of your findings, informed by your knowledge of the field as already indicated in your Review section. |
| Conclusion | Here you circle back to pick up the frame of reference of your Introduction, to show that your study did what you said it would do. You summarise the key findings, and point to further work that might be done in the area. Sometimes you might want to indicate some of the potential flaws in your own study, but it is obviously a bad tactic to dwell on these too much! Make sure you have planned your investigation so well that any problems that arise will have been ironed out long before this point. |
| References | This should be a list *only* of those citations that appear in the text, rather than a list of books (a 'Bibliography') of stuff you vaguely might have used. You should set this section out very precisely (see the References at the end of this book for a model). Accuracy and fullness of referencing is your best firewall against any suspicion of plagiarism. |

Obviously you write the Introduction and Conclusion last, and you probably write the Review section first. If you think it's important to include all your raw data, then you can attach an Appendix. Your tutor, assessor or editor will tell you whether this is possible. Even if you cut material or don't include some information, it is likely that you will be able to use what you have learnt or even the material itself in some future form. Never throw anything away.

## ATTITUDES TO ACCENT VARIATION

The reason why accent variation is so important in sociolinguistics is because of the significance people attach to different accents. The case-study below is partly a **replication study** of original work in informants' subjective evaluations of accent. Replications are a key element in scientific discovery: they test out whether an original investigation is still valid; they can indicate a change over time; and they are good places to start your own sociolinguistic study.

### Evaluative reactions to accents

As part of my sociolinguistics course, Sarah Wood researched original work done by Giles and Powesland (1975) and others which used a method of data elicitation known as the **matched-guise** technique. Briefly, this involves playing a recording of the same speaker imitating a variety of different accents, and then asking listeners to rate each 'speaker' on a range of different dimensions. These might include their sense of the attractiveness of the speaker, how communicative they were, what their social status seems to be, and so on. In this way, a pattern of common stereotypical associations in attitude to accents is built up. The original studies used a range of British accents (northern, southern, rural, urban and RP) and some foreign-accented English (American, Italian, Indian, German, French, and so on), and used informants from south Wales and the south-west of England.

The findings were that, for many people, standard accents (such as RP) were more likely to be considered as belonging to prestigious, aesthetically pleasing and intelligible articulate speakers. The 'broadest' accents and those associated with urban and industrial areas, by contrast, were considered to be used by low-status speakers and were regarded as unattractive. Rural accents were considered aesthetically pleasing, but subordinate to RP on the dimensions of social status and intelligibility.

Much of this work was conducted in the 1970s, and Sarah Wood was concerned with discovering the current situation. In general, she replicated Giles' (1970) study but made a few adjustments to improve the analysis. She restricted the recordings to eight native British accents (RP, west London, Norwich, north-east England, Nottingham, Cheshire, Burnley, and Sheffield), and she used genuine native speakers of these accents in the recordings. All speakers read a passage which was specially written to contain many accent-variant features (this 'Goldilocks' passage appears in C2). All speakers and informants were female students in their early twenties, to control for gender, age and some class variation, and the informants included two northern speakers, two southern speakers, and a Midlands speaker.

Sarah ensured an easy comparability of data by setting a written, multiple-choice questionnaire, as follows:

Q1  Please name the accent you have just heard.
Q2  Please circle the description you most agree with based on your view of the pleasantness/unpleasantness of this accent:

1 extremely pleasant        2 pleasant            3 neutral
4 unpleasant                5 extremely unpleasant

Q3  Please circle the prestige rating you would give this accent:

1  very prestigious        2  prestigious        3  neutral
4  unprestigious           5  very unprestigious

Q4  Please circle the intelligence rating you would give this speaker:

1  very intelligent        2  intelligent        3  neutral
4  unintelligent           5  very unintelligent

Q5  Please circle the type of house you would expect this person to live in:

1  homeless
2  council/housing association rented
3  council/housing association owner-occupied
4  rented private housing
5  terraced owner-occupied
6  average-sized owner-occupied
7  large owner-occupied
8  'mansion'-size owner-occupied

Q6  Please circle the type of job you would expect this speaker to have (examples are simply guidelines):

1  unemployed
2  unskilled manual (rubbish collector)
3  semi-skilled manual (factory worker)
4  skilled manual (engineer)
5  routine non-manual (clerical, sales)
6  low professional (civil servant)
7  self-employed (own business)
8  management
9  higher professional (doctor, lawyer).

Sarah presented her detailed results as a table, and then contrasted her findings with those of 30 years previously. She found that the 'southern' accents (RP, west London and Norwich) attracted the highest and most prestigious overall ratings in most categories, across all informants. Though the RP speaker was judged more intelligent than the others, they were judged equal in social status, and the RP accent was judged as being less pleasing. The northern accents came out worst in the prestige judgements, with the urban accents more stigmatised than the rural ones.

It is interesting that there was largely a consensus across informants, which suggests that language loyalty was only a small factor in this study (though the northern informants did rate the northern accents slightly higher). Furthermore, judgements tended to parallel each other across the dimensions: so an accent tended to be judged consistently either prestigious or stigmatised across all the questions. Sarah also conjectured that the status of RP was changing so that it was becoming seen as 'too posh' and thus untrustworthy, and she discussed other reading which supported this view. Finally, she discussed the consequences of such accent-stereotypes for non-standard speakers in relation to their social-standing, job opportunities and educational access.

There are all sorts of connections to be made from Sarah's study. First of all, replication studies are a very useful means of investigating **language change**: in this case, changes in attitude to accents. It is largely as a consequence of such attitudinal changes that the use of RP seems to be diminishing in Britain (it is certainly less commonly heard in universities and on the BBC), and in many cases is being 'toned down' by being casualised in the direction of local urban vernaculars like Mancunian, Geordie and Cockney. This process produces the sort of hybrid 'posh Geordie', and so on, that can be heard on regional television news programmes, and has been characterised in relation to Cockney as 'Estuary English'.

Second, Sarah's study could lead into a discussion of the prestige and stigmatisation of accents and dialects in general. When people are aware of their own accent and its prestige-value, they will often adjust it either towards a more standardised form (this is **hypercorrection** if it is over-done) or even towards a more stigmatised form (if they want to sound 'less posh', this is **covert prestige**).

Finally, Sarah's study offers a refinement of sociolinguistic methodology along the lines of using naturalistic elicitation procedures to generate naturalistic and reliable data. It is thus a contribution to the methodological discussion of the field.

## EUPHEMISM, REGISTER AND CODE                                   **B3**

Register and style are both means of marking out social groups and establishing solidarity. In general, the sort of lexicogrammatical choices made at this level are based on the selection of words and sequencing them in particular ways. Selection can be seen as a sort of metaphorical system, since one word is chosen to fill a linguistic slot in place of another word. **Idioms** (the individual words and phrases peculiar to a language variety – see B12) often rely for their meaning on metaphorical interpretations. 'Kick the bucket', for example, has a metaphorical meaning of 'to die' (rather gruesomely originating in the method of hanging criminals by kicking an upturned bucket away from their feet). Conversely, **euphemism** can be seen not so much as a lexical replacement by a dissimilar word as a replacement by a closely associated word (a **metonymy** rather than a metaphor). 'The rest-room' is not a metaphor; rather it conveys slightly different, more pleasant associations than other possibilities ('bog, crapper, thunderbox, shithouse', and many others). Many terms take polite cover under foreign languages ('toilet, lavatory, netty' all mean 'washroom' in French, Latin and Italian, and the French 'loo' – the place – is the most vague of all). Euphemisms for taboo areas (still sex, death, war, defecation, and all manner of social unpleasantnesses) are a useful area for the sociolinguist to map social relationships and attitudes.

### Euphemism and death

One of my students, Vicki Oliver examined ways of presenting death in 100 obituaries from the British newspapers *The Times* and *The Daily Telegraph* on the same day. She noted that *Roget's Thesaurus* lists 115 terms for the verb 'to die', and a further 65 noun-phrases for the word 'dead'. Not surprisingly, the newspaper obituaries only used a tiny proportion of these (excluding, for example, 'croaked, snuffed it, bit the dust' and so on). The main linguistic strategy was *euphemism* – 'the saying of something innocuous that either hints at, or establishes a precondition of some previous offensive intended act' (Ortony 1993: 43). Otherwise, the only conceptual metaphor used was the notion that LIFE IS A BATTLE, as in the baby who 'bravely fought but sadly lost her battle', and the cancer patient who 'died suddenly after a courageous fight'. This was only applied in the case of illnesses, however, and not in the case of old people who have 'had a good innings', relying on a different conceptual metaphor, LIFE IS A GAME OF CRICKET.

What was immediately noticeable in this small corpus of data was that the word for death was often omitted entirely (omission is itself a form of euphemism). Only 25 of the 100 obituaries used the word 'died' at all, and of these, 12 were qualified by the adverbs 'peacefully' or 'quietly'. In fact, many obituaries simple began with the adverb, omitting the verbal element: 'Mitchell, Eric James, peacefully at Bognor War Memorial hospital'. These elliptical forms are not simply the result of space-saving in newspapers; the 'Forthcoming Marriages' section nearby often begins, 'The engagement is announced between . . .'. Vicki points out that it would be unthinkable to begin an obituary, 'The death is announced of . . .'.

The standard form, then, is: '*Name > adverb > prepositional phrase denoting location > details of funeral service time and place*'. Variations on the adverb include 'joins Arthur after a long illness,' and 'reunited with Vic'. Deviations from this pattern are thus foregrounded: only one obituary used the word 'killed', in relation to a 19-year old student who 'died tragically after a fall at university'.

Vicki discusses her data using work done by Paul Chilton (1986), in which he identifies in the ideological field a point similar to the notion of a **face threatening act** (see A10). He calls such moments, when the dominant ideology is potentially transparent, a **critical discourse moment (CDM)**. Talking about death is a CDM, a taboo area that needs to be linguistically negotiated. Euphemism, argues Vicki Oliver, is a form of verbal avoidance designed to preserve negative face, or the reader's right to be ideologically unperturbed.

Chilton (1986: 15) defines two 'functional poles of ideological discourse', as follows:

| | | |
|---|---|---|
| Twin poles of ideological discourse: | *metaphor* | *euphemism* |
| Methods: | *coercive* | *suppressive* |
| | *legitimising* | *dissimulating* |
| Typical linguistic strategies: | *replacement* | *omission* |
| | *framing* | *passivisation* |
| | *modalisation* | *nominalisation* |
| | *narrative . . .* | *lexical replacement . . .* |

In these ways, ideologically problematic areas can be negotiated and fitted into the speaker's (or, more typically, the writer's) worldview. Chilton analyses the discourses of war and the nuclear arms race ('Nukespeak') in order to illustrate how governments use metaphor to coerce people into thinking in a particular way, and euphemism to avoid facing up to the harsh realities of war. In Vicki Oliver's study of death notices (and notice how 'obituary' is itself a euphemistic shift into a word from Latin), euphemism as opposed to metaphor is the preferred approach, because the intent is to repress rather than broaden the meaning. The result, claims Vicki, is a prototypical form of discourse (a naturalised register for announcing deaths in newspapers) that is designed to comfort rather than confront social concepts of death. She asserts that the obituaries simultaneously evade its reality, respect its significance, and conform to an accepted but implicit social format.

## Register and code

One of the reasons sociolinguistic study is so important is that thinking about the link between language and society is also the ground for language planning by governments largely through the education system. Performance in linguistic skills (literacy in reading and writing, oracy in listening and speaking) is taken as an indicator of educational level and intelligence, and provides access to the whole range of education in the first place. The way that the links between language, education, social class, wealth, family background and gender are made involve theoretical and ideological frameworks that can be made explicit by sociolinguists. The discipline is inescapably bound up with political thinking in this respect. I also believe it is our ethical responsibility to use this special training and knowledge to influence current thinking and policy.

Some of the most influential work in the area of educational linguistics has been done by Basil Bernstein and his colleagues. Observing the difference in educational attainment by middle class and lower working class schoolchildren, Bernstein set out to establish a connection between their school experience and their characteristic language usage. He distinguished two types of linguistic patterns used by schoolchildren: **restricted code** and **elaborated code**.

| Restricted code features | Elaborated code features |
|---|---|
| unfinished and short sentences | accurate grammatical order |
| simple clauses | complex sentences: coordinacy/ superordinacy |
| commands and questions | frequent use of prepositions |
| categoric statements | impersonal pronouns |
| repetition of conjunctions | passive constructions |
| hesitancy | unusual adjectives and adverbs |
| confusion of reasons and conclusions | |
| rigid and limited use of adjectives/adverbs | |
| sympathetic circularity ('you know') | |
| language of implicit meaning | |

Elaborated code is explicit and can be communicated without gesturing to the immediate context: it is thus **universalistic**. Restricted code is implicit and requires participants who share assumptions and a local context: it is **particularistic**. Bernstein claimed that middle class children have access to both codes, whereas lower working class children only had access to restricted code. Since school life and education generally is 'predicated upon elaborated code', Bernstein asserted that exclusive users of restricted code are likely to do less well at school.

Bernstein's work is primarily sociological rather than sociolinguistic, as you might guess from some of the impressionistic and evaluative terms in the lists above. Nevertheless, his approach presents a linguistic explanation for educational attainment and failure. Though Bernstein has denied the label, his approach is clearly a **deprivation theory** in that it claims to offer a linguistic indicator for cognitive ability. This would need to be balanced by 'compensatory' education schemes such as special literacy programmes, teaching the prestige-value of standardisation, and so on.

There have been many criticisms both of Bernstein's experimental methodology and his theoretical reasoning. However, the linguistic choices characterised by 'restricted' and 'elaborated' codes do seem to represent the reality of some children's performance. (In fact, the patterns typical of restricted code are common in the discourse of any closeknit group with their own norms of jargon, register and style: airline pilots, lawyers, drinking buddies and football teams all use their restricted codes.) The features of restricted and elaborated code look very like the difference between spoken and written discourse, and it may well be that middle class children are socialised more readily into literacy and understanding the rules and conventions of the middle class school system. Bernstein has gone on to suggest that these respective linguistic choices are dependent on family background. He differentiates **positional** family types (in which everyone has a distinct and fixed role) and **person-oriented** family types (in which familial roles are shared and individual characteristics are more prominent), and connects them respectively to restricted and elaborated codes.

A student of mine, Vicky Bristow devised a classroom-based experiment with two groups of 10-year-old boys, one from a fee-paying school (F) and one from a state school (S), in neighbouring areas of Nottingham. She used the sensitivity to social status and readiness and ability to pay for education as an index of social class. In the experiment, she discussed a moral beast fable with the two groups, and transcribed the discussion. Her aim was twofold: to determine whether the features characterised as restricted and elaborated code could be differentiated in the data; and to evaluate whether there was any perceivable cognitive or communicative difference between the groups.

Along most of the code dimensions listed above, there was very little difference between the groups. Noticeable differences were in self-aware references and pronoun usage. In order to compare similar functions, Vicky examined all the utterances which were concerned explicitly with the indication of turn-taking (including nominations of who was to talk next, reference to the speaker's own talk, and explicit instructions such as 'shut up you'). She found that group F produced this sort of 'meta-talk' on 33 occasions, compared with the 20 occurrences of group S. Furthermore, group F used only 28 pronouns, compared with the 40 pronouns used by group S. In the work of Bernstein and his colleagues, pronominalisation represents limited possibilities for modification, since pronouns unlike nouns cannot take adjectives. High pronoun usage, then, is treated as part of the implicit, context-bound restricted code, with an implication that it is also cognitively limiting.

However, in Vicky's data, group S also used proper names 16 times, compared with only 1 direct nomination by group F. This would seem to be a universalistic feature more associated with elaborated code. Vicky points out that all these linguistic performances could simply represent different ways of negotiating the context. After all (as Stubbs 1983 also points out), in a face-to-face interactive discussion, the use of implicit and particularistic meaning is entirely appropriate, and elaborated code is rather redundant. One explanation could be that group F saw the task as a test-situation and group S as a simple discussion, and each acted accordingly.

Finally, to illustrate the complexities of trying to equate form with function too inflexibly, compare the following two utterances from Vicky's data in which children summarise the moral of the fable:

**Group F**
Child 2: follow your destinies whatever whatever it takes try. and because if you if you try and do something and finally – you got this chance. take it. and no matter what happens try try and achieve it

**Group S**
Child 6: try – I'd try because if you try you never knew. if you try you could do it

The first example is syntactically more complex and indeed is longer, but the propositional content is simply a repetition of the injunction to 'try'. The second example, though shorter, completes the conditional clause and gives a reason for the proposition. The problem, as Vicky ends by pointing out, is that qualitative evaluations of this type cannot measure cognitive ability simply by a surface linguistic analysis. Studies in educational linguistics need to be theoretically aware and sophisticated if the consequences in educational policy and pedagogic practice are to have any value.

## CODE-SWITCHING

B4

There are many permanent multilingual communities around me in Nottingham. The university sits in a park with Polish and Ukrainian bilinguals on one side, and bilingual speakers of Punjabi and English, and Patwa and English on the other, living alongside the main student areas in the city. Within the campus there are many more temporary multilingual communities, as international and exchange students form their own groups. In the city and university, then, there are many opportunities for my own students to investigate multilingualism.

**Types of switching**

Christopher Barenberg was chatting in English outside the library to a German friend who suddenly said: 'I think the essay will be alright, aber Du weisst ja wie das ist' (*but you know what it's like*). This is code-switching as defined by Gumperz (1982: 59): 'the juxtaposition within the same speech exchange of passages belonging to two different grammatical systems or subsystems'. The essay in question would have been written in English, and the two Germans were standing in a British university. This domain is shifted onto the level of intimacy and familiarity: both speakers are German exchange students facing the uncertainty of submitting an essay in a different university culture.

Since Chris is a part of the speech community under investigation, the method employed is one of **participant observation** (see B5). He recorded several exchanges within the German student community – previously all living in monolingual Germany or Austria but now living as a bilingual minority in a predominantly English-speaking culture. Only he was aware that the conversations were being recorded for a sociolinguistic study.

Using Romaine's (1989: 112) descriptive terms, he provides examples of the different types of code-switching used within his speech community, and he discusses the motivations behind each usage in the light of the domains underlying the utterances:

❑ **tag-switching**
'I'm pleased to see you're getting a Bewegungsmelder, ja' (*security light, yes*). Chris surmises this tag-switch might simply be because the speaker lacked the necessary vocabulary in English for the previous word.

❑ **intersentential switch**
'We're going to Nicki's house at nine and maybe to the Bomb [a nightclub] afterwards. (Short pause). Kristina bleibt allerdings zu Hause sie muss noch arbeiten' (*Unfortunately Kristina is staying at home because she still has to do some work*). This telephone conversation switches at a sentence boundary, marked with a short pause, at the point where the topic changes to refer to the speaker's German housemate.

❑ **intrasentential switch**
Though there were many examples of the first two types recorded, the only example of a shift within a sentence was the conversation outside the library given above. Even this occurs at a clause boundary rather than mid-clause. Chris points out that this sort of switch is the most 'risky', requiring the greatest degree of mutual bilingual proficiency which might not have existed in this temporary speech community.

The German students manifested the use of German as an 'in-group' marker, using it in the domains of 'home' and 'socialising', and illustrated their **code-loyalty** by greeting each other in German while on campus. However, they also showed their sensitivity to both the domain and to the 'out-group' by switching back into English whenever the domain became 'academic work' or when monolingual English-speakers were to be included.

### Du and Sie

Martin Stepanek used a questionnaire to determine the domains in which a German speaker today would use the familiar 'Du' and the plural, respectful 'Sie' (see A10). He found that the published studies did not match up to his intuitions as a native German speaker, and he suggests that the sociolinguistic situation in this area is changing very rapidly.

He talked through 18 questionnaires with German-speaking students studying in Britain. All were 19–25 years old, 13 from Germany (including five from the eastern part of the country), four Austrians and one of Swiss origin but living in Germany. On the age dimension, this 19–25 year old group are at the boundary of asymmetrical T/V usage, and are thus most likely to show up changes in progress. The questionnaire (in German) firstly established the social background of the informants' age, gender, origins, vernacular, education and attitude. Informants were encouraged to give details and examples in addition to their 'yes/no' answers.

The questionnaire asked a series of open-ended questions such as:

❑ Can you think of situations in which you aren't sure which form to use?
❑ Has there ever been a situation in which you felt uncomfortable being addressed with 'Du' or with 'Sie'?
❑ Do you ever address someone with 'Sie', being addressed by this person with 'Du' in return?

Then a series of 'yes/no' questions, with boxes to tick (I include the results here too):

❑ Do you find it OK to be addressed with 'Du'?

| | |
|---|---|
| in a furniture shop | 11 yes, 7 no, 0 don't know |
| in advertisements | 14y, 3n, 1dk |
| on national election posters | 6y, 12n |
| on student union election posters | 18y |
| by professors | 7y, 7n, 4dk |
| by students | 18y |
| in a student magazine | 18y |
| in a newspaper/weekly magazine | 4y, 14n |

❑ Do you find it OK to be addressed with 'Sie'?

| | |
|---|---|
| by professors | 14y, 1n, 3dk |
| by younger people (−18) | 1y, 14n, 3dk |
| by older students (40+) | 2y, 15n, 1dk |
| by students of the same age | 1y, 17n |
| by an acquaintance of your parents | 3y,14n, 1dk |
| by a former teacher | 6y, 9n, 3dk |

❑ With which form are you normally addressed?

| | |
|---|---|
| by parents | 18 Du |
| by grandparents | 17 Du, 1 Sie |
| in primary school | 18 Du |
| in lower school (10–14) | 15 Du, 1 Sie, 2 both |
| in upper school (15–19) | 11 Du, 3 Sie, 4 both |

| | |
|---|---|
| by professors | 14 Sie, 4 both |
| by students | 18 Du |
| by people over 50 | 3 Du, 11 Sie, 4 both |
| by unfamiliar children | 4 Du, 9 Sie, 5 both |
| by youngsters | 9 Du, 3 Sie, 6 both |
| on the street | 12 Sie, 6 both |
| in a pub (i.e. bar) | 13 Du, 2 Sie, 2 both |
| in a café | 7 Du, 9 Sie, 2 both |
| in a club | 7 Du, 9 Sie, 2 both |

❑ Which form do (did) you normally use?

| | |
|---|---|
| as a primary school pupil to teachers | 1 Du, 17 Sie |
| in lower school to teachers | 18 Sie |
| to university professors | 17 Sie, 1 both |
| to students over 40 | 10 Du, 5 Sie, 3 both |
| to youngsters | 18 Du |
| to a former teacher who has not explicitly offered you 'Du' | 18 Sie |

Having heightened the informants' self-awareness, the questionnaire then asks some more open-ended questions designed to elicit anecdotes and opinions. It ends by asking whether the informants find it acceptable that the questionnaire uses 'Du' throughout! All 18 approved.

In both these quantitative findings, as well as in the qualitative data from his discussions, Martin found that although younger Germans use mutual 'Du' more with each other, it seems that these young adults are moving towards 'Sie' as a neutral option, especially in traditionally asymmetric T/V domains. They do not like the use of 'Du' when it denotes disrespect, in a service setting where it shows undue deference, or when used by older people to frame them as having child-status.

Martin discusses his findings in relation to the published literature, identifying the dimensions of power and solidarity, especially in terms of age, in his data. He also uses the background information to speculate on possible differences between these informants' reports of their usage with their actual observed usage. Finally, he also considers the situation within his own dialect of Vorarlberg in Austria. Here, an additional pronoun 'Ihr' is used. Originally a second person plural, Martin notes how his 75-year-old grandmother's generation use it as the neutral option to refer to people singularly without the deference and formality of 'Sie': 'She only uses "Sie" with people she doesn't know (and probably does not like), and to people who she thinks are to be highly respected, like architects, and people who studied at university'. 'Du' is then reserved for very close family and children.

However, Martin notes that neither he nor his parents' generation seem to use 'Ihr' in this way, and he claims that the standardisation pressure of High German in schools and the media is causing it to die out.

## Diglossia
My student, Tim Knebel re-examined the situation in the Middle Ages using a modern sociolinguistic framework. Adapting Ferguson's (1964) classic study of diglossia (see A4), he discussed the linguistic situation of Middle English with French as the H

variety and native English as the L variety. The following characteristics of diglossia from Ferguson were applied convincingly to medieval society:

- ❏ H is written;
- ❏ H is the medium of education;
- ❏ diglossia is a socially stable pattern;
- ❏ H has greater prestige than L;
- ❏ H vocabulary is often copied into L;
- ❏ repeated vocabulary ('doublets') often diverge in meaning and connotation.

French was the dominant written and literary form in the twelfth and thirteenth centuries, and was taught alongside Latin and Greek. This situation lasted almost 500 years, with Francified English maintaining its prestige in parliament, government, law, administration, ecclesiastical and culinary domains. Many French words passed into English, with divergences between, for example, 'lamb/mutton', 'beef/cow', 'pig/pork', and so on.

Tim pointed out that modern diglossic situations have been shown to come to an end in the same way as did medieval diglossia. Ferguson (1964: 436) gives the following reasons:

- ❏ the expansion of literacy;
- ❏ broader communication and social mobility;
- ❏ standardisation as a mark of national sovereignty.

All three of these can be discerned in fourteenth- and fifteenth-century English life. Furthermore, Tim used the model of the late medieval collapse of diglossia in order to make surmises about a similar H/L assimilation in modern Arabic. A strong factor against such a collapse, however, is the prestige attached to the H form of classical Arabic in religious form (it is the language of the Koran).

## SOCIAL NETWORKS                                              B5

Not all sociolinguistic situations are amenable to careful control of the variables to link specific linguistic features with specific social determinants (this is the **variationist** method – see A5). Alternative methods of accessing and eliciting sociolinguistic data have been developed which place an emphasis on more complex causes and effects. One of the first and most famous examples of this is Lesley Milroy's (1978a, 1987b, 1987c) study of **social networks** in Belfast.

### Networks in Belfast
Recognising problems in the application of a social stratification model (see A5) to local communities, Lesley Milroy applied the notion of social networks to the study

of three inner-city speech communities in Belfast. The advantages of a social network approach are: it is a useful tool for studying small, self-contained groups in detail; it is useful in situations (such as immigrant communities, or amongst schoolchildren) where the concept of social class is either irrelevant or not clear-cut; and it is based on the relationships between individuals rather than subsuming individuals into group averages, and so it is fundamentally inter-subjective.

Milroy developed a **network strength score** based on the nature of social network connections within a group of people. This had two main dimensions:

- ❑ a **dense** social network results when all the people in a group are linked to each other, so that everyone knows everyone else;
- ❑ a **multiplex** social network results when individuals in the group are related to each other in a number of different ways (such as being neighbours, drinking in the pub together, working together, having children at the same school, and so on).

A very close-knit community will be both dense and multiplex and thus have a high network strength score.

Milroy was interested in how stigmatised vernacular norms (mainly accent variants) were maintained in local communities. She collected her data by being introduced to the communities as 'the friend of a friend', a method known as **participant observation**. She found that the highest incidence of the vernacular norms occurred in those communities with the highest network strength scores (in the Belfast communities studied, this was among Protestant men in Ballymacarrett who both worked together and lived in the same neighbourhood, and young Catholic women in the Clonard whose partners were mainly unemployed, isolating the community even more).

It seems that a close-knit social network operates as a 'norm reinforcement mechanism' – encouraging innovative linguistic features and helping to maintain them and diffuse them into wider society. Furthermore, close-knit networks are very common in low-status communities, and this partly offers an explanation for language-loyalty as resistance to the pressure from standardisation.

## The sociolinguistics of football crowds

My student, James Baderman applied a range of sociolinguistic methods, including Milroy's study of social networks, in his analysis of football crowd discourse. His participant observation technique involved attending Tottenham Hotspur games and making covert recordings amongst the crowd at both home and away matches. His findings and analysis are as follows.

'Spurs' are a football club based in London, and James found that when inside the ground the supporters used songs and chants that accentuated the most covertly prestigious elements of the Cockney accent. This meant that particularly stereo-typical accent features were adopted, even by speakers who were observed outside the ground with more standardised accents. For example, the cry, 'Come on you lily whites', aside from displaying a close cultural knowledge of an antiquated nickname for the team, was always uttered in an exaggerated, even cartoonised Cockney accent: [kam ɔn juː lɪliwɔɪtsɑ], with a forceful final vowel added for extra emphasis.

James suggests that many of the most familiar chants were deliberately phrased or owed their success to the fact that they used stereotypical Cockney features. Furthermore, it seems that the language loyalty effect was even more emphatic when the team were playing away, with even more emphasis placed on the Cockney stereotype. Most surprisingly, the emphasis was most strong when playing Spurs' close London rivals Arsenal, whose stadium, then barely two miles away, is nevertheless perceived as being in 'south London' and their supporters thus as an 'out-group'.

In relation to the segregation of rival supporters that is a characteristic of the policing of British football crowds, the aisles and lines of stewards can be seen as **isoglosses** marking out different areas on a dialect map. These areas are also linguistically maintained to preserve group-identification. Rival fans' chants, in other, perfectly clear accents, are likely to be met by feigned misunderstanding: 'You what, you what, you what you what you what?' Where a linguistic structure crosses these boundaries (as in certain songs that are common in tune and general lyrics), it will undergo assimilation and **x-isation** in the new speech community (such as the insertion of the local team name and nickname into generic songs in order to make them the fans' own).

Entering the highly-specified domain of a football ground renders many registers inappropriate, and limits the sociolect of the crowd. James adopts Platt and Platt's (1975: 35–6) distinction between the group's **speech repertoire** and an individual's **verbal repertoire**. Unusually, the crowd repertoire is smaller than the repertoire of individual people. James notes that unlike in society at large, there is no prestige to be gained by exhibiting a large repertoire; prestige lies in conformity to and knowledge of the group codes. All lexicogrammatical choices must reflect the register of 'football-talk'.

Furthermore, the 'football' code is reserved exclusively for the domain inside the stadium, or closely related domains such as pubs on match days and the area immediately around the ground. The accent features of football chants, for example, are never considered appropriate in any other context. Equally, a register which in any other domain would be perceived as aggressive and hostile is downgraded to the level of normative discourse in the ritualised code of the stadium.

James notes that, in Milroy's (1987b: 35–6) social network application, vernacular norms 'are perceived as symbolising values of solidarity and reciprocity rather than status'. This applies to football fans though, curiously, the crowd could well be composed of non-dense and uniplex social network groups: people whose only relationship is attendance at the game. It seems that a further dimension is needed to add to density and complexity in social network texture, and this is the **perceived value** of the network link. Although football fans' links are loose and simplex, the passionate value they place on their support serves to make the norm reinforcement function operate in any case. This is a strong consequence of solidarity and reciprocity.

Applying Brown and Levinson's (1979) notion of **segmentary structure** to account for the different identifications felt by supporters relative to other groups, James points out that someone is a Spurs fan in relation to an Arsenal fan, but an England supporter (even when England includes Arsenal players) in relation to an Italian supporter, and a football fan in contrast with a rugby fan. All of these social roles are linguistically encoded. Not only this, but the detailed communicative competence diminishes upwards on this scale. That is, there are fewer linguistic discontinuities at the national level, whereas the sub-cultures of different clubs are marked with very specific chants. A smaller number and variety of chants are heard at national games. And at a recent international tournament, all nationalities were observed singing the same 'official' song.

All of these findings illustrate that even an apparently highly codified speech community can reveal sociolinguistic complexities on closer examination.

---

**SHIFTS IN PRESTIGE**

Prestige values attaching to dialectal or accent variation are subject to shifts over time. These perceptions can emerge from the ground up, or they can be affected by a top-down imposition from government and institutions. In this unit shifts in the perception of Received Pronunciation and the effects of prescriptivism are explored.

### Changes in RP

The prestige dialect Standard English is spoken by around 15 per cent of the population of Britain; the prestige accent **Received Pronunciation** is spoken by no more than 5 per cent of the population (Holmes 2001: 144). This means that many people are speaking Standard English using a regional accent, and also that there is a different perception in status between the standardised and codified dialectal form and the accent that is still popularly known as 'BBC English'.

Two studies by my students show the prestige value of RP today. Judith Jones took a random sample of 64 television advertisements and analysed them along Hymes (1974) dimensions of a communicative event (he uses the acronym 'SPEAKING'):

❏ **Setting:**        daytime 81 per cent; evening 11 per cent; night-time 8 per cent;

❏ **Scene:**          home 34 per cent; countryside 30 per cent; office 8 per cent; shop 9 per cent; bar/restaurant 5 per cent; other 6 per cent;

❏ **Participants:**   monologue/voice-over 61 per cent; dialogue 30 per cent; multiple people 9 per cent;

❏ **Ends:**           the framing purpose or objective was, of course, to sell the product, but most ads drew mainly on narrative structures and 'mini-soap' formats;

❏ **Act sequence:**   (the actual linguistic content, register and style used) this was always appropriate to the setting – formal in the office, casual in the bar, for example;

- ❑ **Key**:                    (the tone of the event) 75 per cent light-hearted; 23 per cent serious; 2 per cent (i.e. 1 ad) mock-pompous;
- ❑ **Instrumentalities**:   (choice of speech-style) RP 70 per cent; other accents 20 per cent; music only 10 per cent;
- ❑ **Norms**:                all choice of language was non-deviant and appropriate to the setting;
- ❑ **Genre**:                advertising.

Analysing the accents in the adverts, Judith found that RP was generally used to advertise expensive products, electrical goods and financial services, and regional accents were used for natural products, especially food. Furthermore, 63 per cent of voices were male, against 37 per cent female; and women tended to have RP accents, with men showing the regional variation.

A similar analysis of seven hours of television advertisements over one week, conducted by Lynne Senior, also revealed a bias towards RP usage. RP was used in 60 per cent of the adverts, with Scottish, Irish, Yorkshire, American and Cockney accounting in almost equal part for another 25 per cent. These are also mainly prestigious accents. The remaining 15 per cent consisted of other accents such as Mancunian, Scouse, Lancashire, Black English and 'cartoon' French, all used in humorous contexts. Lynne discussed the claims made by Wilkinson (1965) and Giles and Powesland (1975) that there are three bands of prestige in British accents: first RP; second the rural regional accents and educated Irish, Welsh and Scottish; and finally the modern urban accents.

The prestige of the Oxford/Cambridge, educated middle class London and home counties accent that became RP owes much to its recommendation by phonetician Daniel Jones and its adoption by Lord Reith as the appropriate 'voice' of the early BBC on radio in the 1920s and 1930s. Since then, like every other linguistic code, RP has changed along with changes in the social environment of its speakers. We can track historical change by looking across the age ranges (see A5) to see an older form of **conservative RP** retained from the 1930s by older people: markers of this accent include the pronunciation of 'off' and 'lost' as /ɔːf/ and /lɔːst/ rather than /ɒf/ and /lɒst/, for example. RP users between age 35 and 65 tend to speak **general RP**, while younger users speak a more casualised **advanced RP**. This last change (recorded by Trudgill and Hannah 1982) has since then developed even further.

It seems that by the early twenty-first century, general RP has come to be seen by many people as being 'too posh'. Trudgill (1974, 1988) found that as early as the 1970s, middle class men tended to aim for the covert prestige of a non-RP form (see A5), seeing the RP usage as being somehow unmanly. More recently, advanced RP forms have been heard more often on nationally-broadcast media, with conservative RP almost never heard now except in historical archive material or in comic situations.

Many younger adults in the greater London area whose social and educational background might traditionally have meant that they used RP have begun using an accent called **Estuary English** or the **New London Voice**. First observed by David Rosewarne (1994) around the Thames estuary, east of London, Estuary English is described as being 'mid-way' between RP and Cockney. It manifests some Cockney features such as /w/ for word-final and medial /l/ (in 'real' and 'always', though not the first /l/ in 'little), use of /d/ and fronting of /t/ in words like 'little', 'gateway,' 'Gatwick,' and 'seatbelt,' and 'yod-dropping' (/j/ loss) in words like 'tune' and 'news'. What makes EE a mid-way accent is that speakers will sometimes pronounce the Cockney variant of these features and sometimes the RP variant. They will also code-shift from RP to EE when they are sensitive to and aware of their own usage.

Rosewarne claims that EE has spread across the south-east of England and can now be heard from the river Avon to the Wash, and is spreading north and west to become, in effect, the new RP. It is perceived as a classless, regionless accent that has prestige value, especially among younger men in their twenties and thirties. Of course, EE can be seen as a local manifestation of a global trend in the post-standardisation process: **x-isation** (see A8). EE is an example of the **casualisation** of RP towards the local vernacular – in this case, Cockney. While there are some Cockney elements observable in northern English (such as /t/ fronting), other regions of Britain have manifested their own casualisations of RP towards the local vernaculars. So people talk of 'posh Geordie,' 'posh Brummy,' 'posh Scouse,' 'posh Leeds' and so on.

Kathryn Tibbs studied regional BBC news programmes with local presenters to identify this casualisation process across the country. In all cases, newsreaders from Manchester, Nottingham, and Newcastle all displayed a blend of RP and local accent features. This is the new BBC English.

A corresponding change is rapidly affecting the pronunciation of younger women. If you are female, middle class, under age 35 and live in the south or east of England, you will probably use a rising intonation (which has traditionally marked questions) even on declarative sentences. This **uptalk** or **upspeak** (more technically, a **high-rising terminal**) spread rapidly during the 1990s amongst young women in London enjoying high-earning careers in media and public-relations. It is rapidly spreading, geographically so that it can now be heard being used by women in the north and west, by age as its original users move into their thirties and forties, and even by gender as the male middle class partners of uptalking women adopt their speech patterns.

Traditionally associated with a questioning or uncertain tone, uptalk is now so common that it seems to represent a default norm of female discourse, corresponding better with the greater use women make of backchannel noise and cooperative feedback in conversation (see A7). Perhaps this too can be seen as a new, gendered response to the casualisation of RP?

Meanwhile, Kathryn Tibbs argues, RP maintains its status mainly outside the British Isles. Through the BBC World Service and old textbooks, wherever English is not taught with an American or Australian accent, it is learnt in an RP accent. In Japan, Indonesia, Saudi Arabia, Argentina, Chile, and many other places, general RP retains a prestige value that it is rapidly losing in Britain.

### Dialect standardisation

Ancient commentators on language change assumed that languages only changed when a country was invaded by foreign speakers, and so change was associated with degeneracy or mongrelisation. Of course, though invasion often affects language, specific changes reflect existing trends or newly required features. For example, the loss of inflectional suffixes in Old English words was an existing process that was accelerated by both Viking and Norman French invasions in the tenth and eleventh centuries. As an international language, with many cultural varieties, English as a whole is now uninvadable. Changes in World English can be said to fall into two areas: a general realignment to reflect social and technological evolution (this largely involves creation and innovation in language); and a local realignment in contact with other languages (this involves borrowing or **copying**). Aitchison (1991: 120–3) has codified the principles of copying:

- ❑ Detachable elements are most easily copied
  (for example, Middle English copied words from French but not its future-tense inflectional system.)
- ❑ Copied elements are x-ised
  (Russian or Japanese copies from English are rendered into Russian or Japanese phonology; English copies from Spanish, French, Latin or Greek are anglicised.)
- ❑ Copied elements have an existing superficial similarity
  (for example, words which already 'fit' the English phonological system are copied.)
- ❑ Changes happen a small step at a time – the principle of 'minimal adjustment'
  (for example, the loss of rhoticity in most English accents has taken over 500 years and is still ongoing).

Labov (1994: 21) points out that long-term stability is in fact more puzzling than linguistic change. He claims a continuity between the past and current sociolinguistic study by quoting Christy's (1983) **uniformitarian principle**: 'knowledge of processes that operated in the past can be inferred by observing ongoing processes in the present'. This notion of a continuity of linguistic principles is fundamental to socio-linguistics, which must not treat language as a 'random fluctuation system' (that is, as simply being at the whim of fashion) but as a system governed by discoverable patterns and conventions.

The difficulty of studying language change is a consequence of the complexity of the past, and the fact that evidence and data are always incomplete. This is the **historical paradox**: studying the past demonstrates the extent to which it is not absolutely recoverable. Labov's solution is a sort of 'triangulation' method:

> Solutions to the Historical Paradox must be analogous to solutions to the Observer's Paradox. Particular problems must be approached from several different directions, by different methods with complementary sources of error. The solution to the problem can then be located somewhere between the answers given by the different methods. In this way, we can know the limits of the errors introduced by the Historical Paradox, even if we cannot eliminate them entirely.
>
> (Labov 1994: 25)

Claiming a uniformitarian link with the past does not entail a commitment to seeing history either as a series of catastrophes nor gradualness. Labov points out that catastrophic changes (large political and population disjunctions) tend to generate external change that is properly sociolinguistic; gradual change tends to generate change internal to the language system (strictly linguistic). Language change, then, seems to happen in both rapid shifts interspersed with gradual adjustments, analagous to 'punctuated equilibrium' in evolutionary science (sudden change between long periods of stability).

In the popular view, a sort of 'Golden Age-ism' persists. Even in ancient Athens, writers looked back to a previous age when their language was more 'pure' and 'elegant' than their own. This nostalgic delusion occurs throughout the ages: fifteenth- and sixteenth-century English writers looked to ancient Latin as having more prestige than English; seventeenth- and eighteenth-century English writers compared their own 'corrupt' English with the language of Chaucer, Shakespeare and Milton; in the nineteenth century they looked back to the previous 'Augustan' age; and politicians in the twentieth century longed for Victorian values. In all of these, there is often a linkage made between linguistic 'purity' and national 'purity', and it is then a short step from merely describing language to setting out **prescriptive** rules by which you would like it to change.

The notion of 'correctness' emerged in the late sixteenth century, and this golden age notion was applied to produce **standardisation**. In the late seventeenth and eighteenth centuries, it was taken up by influential people including Dryden, Swift, Addison, Johnson, Priestley, Sheridan and especially Bishop Lowth, whose *Short Introduction to English Grammar* (1762) pontificated the following, mainly by (false) analogy with Latin:

- ❏ he condemned 'had rather', 'had better' for 'would rather';
- ❏ condemned the use of the double negative, previously perfectly respectable;
- ❏ condemned ending a sentence with a preposition;
- ❏ condemned splitting an infinitive;
- ❏ condemned 'between you and I' and 'it is me', on the basis of Old English grammar;
- ❏ arbitrarily preferred 'different from' to 'different to';
- ❏ preferred 'larger' when the comparison was only for two items (not 'largest');
- ❏ preferred 'you were' not 'you was', even when the 'you' was singular;
- ❏ distinguished 'shall/will' and 'should/would' though there had been little agreed distinction across the country for 500 years.

These prescriptions from the great age of dictionary and grammar writing still find their counterparts in modern prescriptivism. Applying a descriptive but analytical sociolinguistics to these attitudes in the past can also provide critical insight into the ignorance of the present.

## GENDERLECTS

Linguistic studies in this area tend to be concerned either with the reality/mythology of genderlect, or the sexist use of language in general. One particular issue is the notion of **common gender**: words which might be assumed to be sex-neutral turn out to be used in very specific and exclusive ways. Examples from Cameron (1992) and Coates (1993) include: 'fourteen <u>survivors</u>, three of them women . . .,' '<u>people</u> are much more likely to be influenced by their wives than by opinion polls', where the underlined element is clearly not gender-neutral in the succeeding context. In a similar way, women are often named in newspaper articles only in relation to men ('wife,' 'sister') or in evaluative ways ('Mrs Hall, a blonde 45-year old') that are almost never used for men.

Corresponding with this is the feature of **semantic non-equivalence** between gendered pairs of words. Consider the differences in connotation and the register where you are likely to find the following pairs used: 'waiter – waitress,' 'master – mistress,' 'bachelor – spinster,' 'patron – matron,' and try other collocations such as 'head waiter' or 'old master.' Similarly, if a man has a 'client', he is a businessman, but if a woman has a 'client' (especially in inverted commas), she is a prostitute. A man who is a 'pro' is highly competent or a golfer, a woman is a prostitute. A 'tramp' is a homeless scruff if a man, but not (at least in American English) if a woman. These distinctions also show up in collocations such as the comparison between: 'She's John's widow'; ?'He's Sally's widower'. Many terms of abuse are female-based, and there are still no real male equivalents for 'tart,' 'harlot,' 'slut,' and so on, when spoken seriously.

English has a long tradition of differentiating roles or jobs on the basis of a male norm and a marked female form (a 'baxter' is a female 'baker', for example). Suffixes such as *-ess -ette, -ienne, -ine, -ix*, and *-euse* denote not only femaleness but also have strong connotations of diminution or triviality. Consider, for example, *actress, poetess, jewess, authoress, sculptress, stewardess, waitress, governess, comedienne, heroine, masseuse, usherette, brunette, aviatrix* and the marked forms for *confidante, blonde, divorcée*, and *starlet*.

### The semantics of gender

Lauren Buckland conducted a study to discover whether men and women instinctively preferred to express themselves in characteristic semantic domains. She asked five men and five women to write down the first 50 words that occurred to them as fast as possible on a piece of paper. Folding over the name on each sheet (thus 'marking' them without reference to gender) she then analysed the lists to see whether there were any discernible semantic trains of thought characterising each informant.

This economical and neat study showed that words tended to cluster along the features of: rhyming, alliteration, abstract, particular/response to surroundings, and swearing/innuendo.

Cross-referencing the lists for gender revealed the following frequencies of words:

| rhyming | women 1 | men 14 |
| alliteration | women 13 | men 25 |
| abstract | women 10 | men 13 |
| particular/response to surroundings | women 90 | men 24 |
| swearing/innuendo | women 4 | men 20 |

Most noticeably, the women overwhelmingly tended to produce words that referred to their immediate concrete surroundings ('table, chair, carpet, badge, laundry basket'). Men tended to favour abstract words ('speed, music, fellowship') and were much more likely to produce sequences by word-play ('night, fright, kite', 'bin, brown, blue') than women. Far more men relied on sexual swearwords to fill out their 50 words. Lauren used this analysis to discuss the published work in the area and argue that many stereotypes were based on real usage.

### Colour terms and evaluation

Louise Kessler wanted to test the ability of two groups of men and women to give verbal descriptions of pictorial stimuli. Since it is still the case that there is a gender imbalance in subject areas at university, she chose three male and three female physicists, and three male and three female art historians as her informants. She gave them a series of photographs taken from magazines and the university promotional material: all in full colour, realistic and not explicitly 'artistic'. Each person was invited to 'describe and discuss the images, spending no longer than one minute on each'. The responses were recorded and transcribed.

The proportions of the total number of words used was interesting:

| Male Art students: | 33 per cent of the total |
| Female Art students: | 30 per cent |
| Male Physicists: | 24 per cent |
| Female Physicists: | 13 per cent |

Louise pointed out that this supports Coates' (1993) claim that men are more verbose than women, though it is women who 'chatter', in stereotypical mythology.

She also found that the men, of both groups, used the most colour terms (see A7 for contrast). However, a closer analysis revealed that men tended to use modifiers with their colour terms: 'very green, unusually green, rather green, slightly green'. The women tended to use adjectives as intensifiers instead: 'bold reds', 'vibrant colour'. Furthermore, women used far more evaluative adjectives ('nice, beautiful, rather bizarre') in general than men; even the female physicists used these more than the male art historians. It seems that genderlect considerations outweighed academic discipline in this respect.

### Men, women and prestige

One problem in using a variationist method to pin down gender as a linguistic determinant is that so many other factors interfere. Matthew Hassan tried to control for these by setting up a microsociolinguistic qualitative study of the language of a brother and sister (thus assuring parity of geography, age, class, education and social background). In order to minimise non-verbal factors, he recorded a telephone conversation between the two, and analysed the transcript for the phonetic variables /h/-dropping and use of the glottal stop for medial /t/ – both stigmatised features. After the conversation, Matthew revealed the purpose of the study, and got the brother and sister separately to read out a list of words: 'better, getting, butter, water, have, horse, has, horn'.

Matthew found a marked difference between the sister's higher use of the prestige variant, both in casual conversation and in continual usage in the word list, and the brother's speech. By contrast, he always glottalised the /t/ in conversation and dropped the /h/ in the majority of cases. In the word-list, he glottalised 'getting' and 'water', but not 'better' or 'butter', and he pronounced the /h/ in 'horse' and 'horn' but omitted it in the grammatical words 'have' and 'has'.

Having reproduced the findings of Trudgill and others, Matthew discussed possible reasons for the disparity. He dismissed as sexist the notions that women are intuitively more concerned with prestige or being conservative or with social status or ambition, and instead focused on the speech patterns as examples of solidarity. He noted that the brother had a more close-knit social network and thus was more likely to have his vernacular norms reinforced. Moreover, the sister tended only to use the stigmatised features when talking about the 'male' domain of football and hooligans, so it seems that a semantic field element is also pertinent. Even in such a carefully controlled study, there are problems of interference.

## PATWA AND POST-CREOLISATION                                    B8

One of the most influential and wide-spread creoles is Jamaican Patwa. It is obvious from the history of the slave trade why it shares many of the features of West African creoles and the African-American vernacular English (AAVE) spoken across the United States. The third point of the slave-trade triangle first brought the language to Britain, and twentieth-century immigration to the UK consolidated the Caribbean roots of British Black English.

### Jamaican Patwa and Jamaican English
Patwa and Jamaican English stand in a post-creole continuum relationship with each other, as basilect and acrolect respectively. The following is a brief description of the basilectal form; Jamaican English features some of the pronunciation patterns and lexical choices, but is otherwise closer to UK Standard English.

Jamaican Patwa has a distinctive phonology. The following vowel sounds appear in the words given:

| | | | | | |
|---|---|---|---|---|---|
| /ɪ/ | pit | /ɛ/ | pet | /a/ | pat, pot, one, father |
| /ʊ/ | put | /o/ | putt, run | /iː/ | bee |
| /uː/ | boot | /aː/ | bard, law | /oː/ | board, bird |

(the last two words are pronounced without the /r/ – Jamaican English, unlike some other Caribbean Englishes, is non-rhotic).

/ie/ bay, beer, bear      /ai/ buy, boy

These sets of words are all pronounced the same. In order to make some distinctions not allowed by vocalic variation, Patwa introduces glides to distinguish

/kjat/ cat          /bwail/ boil
/kat/ cot           /bail/ boil

There tends to be no /t – θ/ or /d – ð/ distinction, making /wɪt/ ('with') and /dɪs/ ('this').

As in AAVE, final consonant clusters tend to be devoiced (/d/ becomes /t/), reduced, or deleted altogether. So 'child', 'tact', 'wind' are pronounced /tʃaɪl/, /tak/, /wɪn/.

Most difficult of all for non-native speakers is the fact that Patwa is not stress-timed (as General American English and most native British accents), but is syllable-timed. In the following words, for example, each syllable receives almost equal emphasis: /dʒamieka/ ('Jamaica'), /daːta/ ('daughter'), /wandaful/ ('wonderful').

At the lexicogrammatical level, there are also distinctive features in relation to other Englishes.
Variant plurality marker on nouns – 'five dog', 'all di cat'.
Variant possessive marker on nouns – 'dis man son' (this man's son).
Variant pronouns – 'me' (I), 'im' (he), 'dem' (they, their).
Variant 3rd person verb concord – 'im like it' (he likes it).
Copula deletion/variation – 'di boy sad' (the boy is sad), 'im a come' (he is coming).
Variant negative formation – 'di woman no see dat' (the woman does not see that).
Tense is marked lexically rather than morphologically:

　　'he walk home last night'
　　'he did walk home last night'
　　'he bin walk home last night'.

Many lexical items are specific to Patwa, and have been codified in the *Dictionary of Jamaican English* (Cassidy and Le Page 1980).

**Patwa and its influence in the UK**
One of my students, Virginia Barnes designed a study to investigate early claims by Hewitt (1986) that Patwa was becoming highly influential in Britain beyond the traditional base of its native speaker community. Specifically, Hewitt noticed that elements of Patwa were being borrowed by young white and Asian people in east London youth clubs at the time. Virginia was surprised that, as a white woman a couple of decades later, she was able to recognise and even used some features of Patwa herself. These features tended to be lexical items rather than grammatical or pronunciation patterns.

She based her study on Hewitt's written test, and chose subjects at random but who were in their early twenties and thus had grown up in the years since the original observations. These subjects were divided into a northern, midlands and southern group, in order to provide some guide as to the degree of diffusion of the linguistic features geographically. Using Hewitt's work, and the contemporaneous glossary from Sutcliffe's (1982) *British Black English*, Virginia compiled a lexical list of 20 words. She printed these in a questionnaire with two possible meanings for each item, and invited the informants to tick what they thought the word meant. (Correct answers, *a* or *b*, are marked here on the right.)

| | |
|---|---|
| bad-mouth ((*a*) to insult; (*b*) ear-hole; don't know) | a |
| bahty (exclamation of annoyance; buttocks; don't know) | b |
| chip (to take one's leave; to enrage; don't know) | a |
| cruff (untidy, rough, ugly; yapping dog; don't know) | a |
| cuss (tin can; mock aggressive use of language; don't know) | b |
| go deh/there (disbelief; exclamation of encouragement; don't know) | b |
| hard (excellent, admirable; very bad; don't know) | a |
| juba (unflattering term for a woman, busybody; extravagance; don't know) | a |
| kenge (puny; shed; don't know) | a |
| labrish (gossip, relaxed lively talk amongst friends; laziness; don't know) | a |
| renk (superior; impudent, cheeky, wild; don't know) | b |
| ress (stop; untidy; don't know) | a |
| sad (sorrowful; pathetic; don't know) | b |
| soff (clumsy; weak, ineffective; don't know) | b |
| stylin (showing good style; wrapping in paper; don't know) | a |
| star (annoyance; close friend; don't know) | b |
| sweet (complete; pleasing, satisfying; don't know) | b |
| tracing match (quarrel; fire-lighter; don't know) | a |
| wicked (excellent; old-fashioned; don't know) | a |
| wickedness (mischief; excellence; don't know) | a |

In her findings, Virginia discovered a marked increase overall in the correct scores for the group. She suggested that many of these terms, originally Patwa words, had diffused into general British youth usage and were even beginning to lose their sense as markers of Caribbean ethnicity. Many of her informants were unaware of the origins of the words. More strikingly, the midlands group scored highest, followed by the southern group, with the northern group least accurate of all. If generalisable, this could suggest two possibilities. It could be that the words were innovative borrowings into young white speech in London in the 1980s, and have since spread out across the country. They have then become less used (or replaced by other words) in London. The study is thus a 'snapshot' of geographical diffusion away from London. Alternatively, Virginia suggests that the high numbers and integration of multi-ethnic communities in the Midlands compared with both London and the north have made the terms more current and longer-lasting amongst young people in the Midlands than elsewhere. She optimistically suggests that this indicates the potential for the development of a modern vernacular that borrows freely from different ethnic origins and better reflects the multi-racial nature of Britain.

**SINGLISH AND NEW ENGLISHES**

New Englishes have developed all over the world, but just as with indigenous Englishes in Britain, the US, Canada, and Australia, for example, these codes also show sociolinguistic variation. Many of the New Englishes have similar features in terms of accent and grammar, as a result of similar conditions of origin (typically having made contact with English through colonialism and trade). Most are distinguishable from each other at these levels and especially at the level of lexis, as a result of interference patterns in contact with the indigenous languages. Patterns of intonation, 'straight' translations of local language syntactic ordering, and lots of copied words in each case create a blended New English with its own form and sound.

### Singaporean English and Singlish

Singapore has a population of just over 3½ million, of which 76 per cent are Chinese, 15 per cent Malay, 7 per cent Indian, and 2 per cent other. There are four official languages: Chinese, Malay, Tamil and English, and a 92 per cent literacy rate. Because the island is so small, there is no regional variation in Singaporean English. Sociolinguistic variation occurs solely along the scale of education, which confers social status. So, using the terms of Fraser-Gupta (1991) and Pakir (1994), it is possible to talk of an acrolectal *Singaporean English* that is close to the standard Englishes of Britain, America and Australia; a *Singapore Dialect English* that forms a mesolectal continuum; and an x-ised version of English that is popularly known as *Singlish*, as a basilect (see A8 for definitions of these terms). The process of x-isation in the last of these can be divided further into indianised, sinicised and malayanised influences.

Singaporean English speakers tend to reduce final consonant clusters, so that 'next' becomes /nɛks/, 'just' becomes /jʌs/, 'recent' becomes /risən/, and so on. This feature is also found in various Caribbean New Englishes, African-American English, and the Patwa spoken in English cities; in Singapore it is further distinguished by word-final stops being glottalised and unreleased. So, for example, 'rope', 'dog', and 'pick' become /rəʊpʔ/, /dɒkʔ/ and /pɪkʔ/. In basilectal varieties of 'Singlish', all word-final clusters are reduced to the unreleased glottal: /rəʊʔ/, /dɒʔ/ and /pɪʔ/.

Acrolectal Singaporean English speakers tend to aim for a general RP accent on the British model, and the emphasis across an utterance is 'stress-timed': that is, contrastive emphasis falls on different parts of the word (every poly-syllabic word in this sentence would take its stress – underlined – on the first syllable in an RP voice). However, most Singaporean speakers' accents are rather 'syllable-timed', with a much more even emphasis in intonation. Where there is a contrastive stress, it tends to occur later in the word than in RP: 'associated, educated, expert, literature, opportunity, academic, individual, distributor,' and so on.

All of these phonological features produce a 'staccato' effect, which is further reinforced by the fact that Singaporeans tend not to *elide* words together. In fluent RP, for example, there is no break across the underlined words in, 'I'll have an apple'. Singaporean speakers tend to insert a very brief break between these words.

At the grammatical level, there are further distinctive features. For example, 'got' is used very commonly for possessive 'have' and existential 'there are':

*I got very good cabinets here*
*Here got many restaurants*
*Got very good beach on Sentosa.*

'Can or not' is often used as an interrogative tag, as is 'isn't it':

*You will come, can or not?*
*They'll hit him, isn't it?*

The indefinite article is used less frequently than in other Englishes:

*She is computer programmer.*

'Would' is used for 'will', perceived as being more polite (in general, Singaporean English uses register that would be considered formal or polite by British or American speakers):

*We hope you would return to teach us next year.*

Aspectual variation reveals most interference from other languages:
Completive 'already':
*My son was born already two years* (i.e. two years ago).

Habitual 'use to':
*She use to shop in Takashimaya* (i.e. and still does today).

Many Singaporean words are copied from the indigenous and neighbouring languages. A stereotypical feature is the insertion of 'la' as a marker of informality and solidarity, deriving from Hokkien Chinese (it also corresponds to the Malay 'lah', and the Chinese has its origin in the Liverpool dialect back in the UK). Similarly, the Chinese 'ah' is used as an intimacy marker by inserting it between the two parts of a Chinese name. In Singapore, this is also used around forenames. Other Singlish words include:

| | |
|---|---|
| *hepch* | often used by sales assistants as 'help', showing a variant of the cluster /lp/. |
| *kena* | Malay for 'receive' or 'get'. |
| *chope* | 'reserve', also used in the children's game of 'tag' in Singapore to denote the player who has been 'got' or 'tagged'. In Malay, 'cap' is a stamp or seal trademark, deriving from Chinese printing in which a 'chop' was a seal or stamp (also, in Hindi, 'chhap'). |
| *chin chye* | Hokkien, 'it doesn't matter'. |
| *dowan* | a common form reduced from 'I don't want'. |
| *botak* | Malay, 'bald', also used to refer to a 'crew-cut' hairstyle. |
| *keen* | Hokkien, 'quick', often repeated (or *reduplicated*) for emphasis or intensification. |
| *alamak* | an exclamation, from the mild Malay curse 'Mother of Allah'. |
| *kiasu* | someone who does not want to lose out, from a popular comic strip character, Mr Kiasu. |

*hup-ply*         'half price'
*kenna ketok*   Malay, 'to get a knock', metaphor for 'being cheated'.

All of these words can be used to translate the passage below.

### A Singlish haircut

In times past, foreign visitors with long hair would be asked to have a haircut at the airport before being allowed into Singapore. These days, immigration is more tolerant of scruffy westerners. The following exchange is reproduced from the work of Li En Chong, one of my Singaporean students, from a barber's in the Takashimaya department store on Singapore's Orchard Road. The store has been renamed in Singlish from the original Japanese (in English spelling) 'Takashimaya' into the English spelling rendering of the Mandarin 'Da Jia Qu Mai Ya'.

Hairdresser:   hello ah-John-ah long time no see. how can I hepch you?
John:          okay I want to cut my hair
Hairdresser:   sorry lah cannot sit here. after I kena scolding. another client chope the seat already. so how do you wan me to cut your hair?
John:          chin chye but dowan botak okay? also keen keen I got a meeting soon
Hairdresser:   so long never see you. you frequent another hairdressers ah?
John:          yah lah you so expensive since you move here to Da Jia Qu Mai Ya
Hairdresser:   alamak don so kiasu lah. I give you hup-ply discoun. you go to another stylist sure kenna ketok

Both Li En Chong and another student, Hardip Singh Amarjit Kaur, discussed the features of Singaporean English and Singlish, and related the variants to the government policy of promoting a standardised Singaporean English. Their essays focused on the formation of New Englishes and on language planning respectively.

---

**POLITENESS IN MIXED-SEX CONVERSATION**

In many sociolinguistic studies, the language of men and women is observably different. Whether this is a result of innate 'hard-wiring', different processes of gendered socialisation or merely men and women acting to their domain roles and expectations is a matter of ongoing debate. Gender certainly seems to affect every different level, from accent variation to lexical choice and syntactic preference. One of the most interesting areas of research has been in studying gender differences at the level of discursive strategies: how men and women perceive spoken discourse differently and so behave differently in conversation. This is most apparent in the discursive politeness markers used by the different genders.

## The difference between men and women

In a range of studies, the following characteristics have been observed:

- ❑ men are more likely to interrupt others;
- ❑ when they interrupt, men are more likely not to wait for a pause or clause boundary;
- ❑ women are more likely to make backchannel noise and support;
- ❑ men are more likely to use backchannel noise as a means of entering the conversation;
- ❑ women are more likely to frame their turns as questions;
- ❑ men speak more than women, both in terms of word-total and number of turns;
- ❑ men's turns tend to last longer than women's turns;
- ❑ men keep their turn by avoiding pauses at clause-boundaries, by using 'utterance incompletors ('firstly . . .,' 'but . . .,' 'and so . . .'), by fillers ('mmm,' 'er'), by raising their voices, speeding up, and avoiding 'nominating' eye contact;
- ❑ women pass on their turns by nominating by name, by eye-contact, by open-hand gesture, and by signalling their turn is over (by falling intonation and pausing);
- ❑ women reply to men;
- ❑ men make jokes and women laugh at them;
- ❑ men and women accommodate through a conversation towards each other's norms;
- ❑ women are more likely to use polite forms of register and indirectness;
- ❑ women use more hedges ('kind of,' 'sort of,' 'I think . . .,' 'maybe');
- ❑ women use more hedges and fillers as embarrassment markers before using technical or over-fluent words or phrases;
- ❑ women perceive men's conversation as aggressive and unsubtle;
- ❑ women are more likely to repair the conversation after a silence;
- ❑ women are more likely to personalise, using a range of personal pronouns;
- ❑ men are more likely to generalise, only using 'I' and using nominalised and passive verb forms;
- ❑ men tend to end a conversation by summarising its content or end-point;
- ❑ women are less likely to initiate the close of a conversation.

Of course, the reality of all of these has been hotly debated, as well as the complexities arising in single-sex or mixed-sex groups, and because of age differences, social class and education differences, and topic differences.

## A gender-comparison study

Sharlene Goff recorded different groups in conversation:

> mixed conversation between 4 friends (see C7);
> single-sex conversation between two male friends;
> single-sex conversation between two female friends;
> mixed conversation between 4 people unfamiliar with each other.

She minimised the awareness of the recording equipment by using the Labovian technique of getting the informants emotionally involved in the topic, setting them questions that she knew they cared about: fox-hunting, the abolition of the monarchy, and genetic experimentation. Using some of the features she had studied in the published research, she examined her transcripts for evidence of gender-polarisation at the level of politeness strategies. Her conclusion was that there does seem to be a 'dominant' style of discourse, but this could not necessarily be equated with gender. She argued that factors such as familiarity seemed to exert a strong modifying influence on gender as a factor in discursive behaviour.

### Single-sex conversation between male friends

Q:   what are your opinions on the monarchy – are they still important to society?

M1: absolutely. mmm – I think history's a terribly important thing and the monarchy's been around for a long time and there's something – they're a body and an institution and. they might not have as much meaning as they used to. as much power or authority but – nevertheless they're a figurehead and they symbolise our nation and therefore they should stay put

M2: well I fully concur – well it's easy to be an idealist and say there's no place for a monarchy in a truly democratic society but. looking at it objectively what can the monarchy offer us right? it's unreasonable to expect them to be perfect fucking citizens but – what we can say is what can they bring to this country and they bring millions upon millions of tourists into this country – okay. get all the monarchy's money and give it to everybody in the country and everyone will have a mars bar – millions and millions of pounds in like. revenue in the tourist industry

M1: people think of England they think of the Queen

M2: exactly –

M1: keep the Queen.

M2: keep the Queen.

### Single-sex conversation between female friends

Q:   what are your opinions on the monarchy – do you think they should be perfect role models for society?
     (2.5)

F1:  it's a very difficult thing – but. personally. I think that. mmm. that. they should be allowed to do whatever they want – they're just people. I mean –

F2:  yeah. you can't expect people to be perfect – and its quite rare for royal families to even exist at all so=

F1:  but then they are – mmm – in the public eye all the time – so if they're [–     ]

F2:                                                                                              [yeah]

F1:  if they're giving a bad impression then. it's surely going to reflect on the rest of society

F2:  I think as well that we have to bear in mind that the Queen's head of the church – and having affairs is going against the ten commandments
     [–          ]

F1:  [yeah – sure]

F2:                          so I'm not sure they should be having – if they have that sort of responsibility. they should take it seriously –

F1:    but then do you think that Charles should be allowed to remarry?

F2:    mmm well. I think I agree – I mean it's only fair enough cos they're people – but I think its. mmm. contradictory of their roles to claim to be head of one thing and not of the other. but I guess that shows that they're just normal people

F1:    yeah definitely


### Mixed-sex conversation between people unfamiliar with each other

Q:    what are your opinions on choosing your own baby – selecting attractive genes for engineering?

M1:    I've got opinions – mmm – I mean. based on what I know. I don't know a great deal but – mmm. I sort of learnt a little bit and I reckon that – mmm – that although they've – well. they're trying to put ethical stops on it – mmm. but I still don't see how – mmm – they're gonna stop scientists doing whatever cos they'll pursue it to the limit won't they=

F1:    yeah

M1:    they'll try and get as far as they can. mmm – and. yeah I think it's bad wrong to. to. mmm. have the choice of the perfect baby and stuff

F2:    I think there are some cases where it's acceptable. for instance – mmm – there's lots of – mmm – hereditary diseases which can be avoided if they just look at the embryo and test it and find one that doesn't have a certain – disease that's going to be fatal to [them then]

F1:                                [mmm    ]

F2:               I think it's acceptable – I mean. do you agree?

M1:    yeah yeah I mean. I know they're doing stuff with – mmm. cystic fibrosis you know? having inhalers with – mmm. like. genetic inhalers – but at the same time they could stop it completely [–           ]

F1:                                   [mmm    ]

M1:                                            by looking. like you say. at the [embryos   ]=

F2:        [yeah      ]=

F1:    haven't they got some kind of law though stopping it?

M1:    yeah they're not allowed to stop it before it's born

F1:    no but I mean. not allowed to use it for like. choosing hair colour

F2:    yeah

F1:    mmm

F2:    there's obviously going to be some kind of black market. I mean – I should think=

F1:    yeah

F2:    that there's a black market being set up [where   ]

F1:                                     [yeah    ]

F2:                                      I mean – it's probably already happening we just don't know about it

M1: mmm

F2: I think it's sort of in theory but they're definitely thinking about it and sort of bidding for the best genes and=

M1: what happens to all the ugly babies?

F2: I don't know

((laughter))

M2: I mean – what – mmm=

F2: it's like the film Gattaca. has anyone seen it?

All: no

F2: it's all about that

F1: really?

F2: and the sort of reality – its. like. a futuristic. sort of – science fiction all about the reality of that sort of situation

F1: yeah

F2: it's quite interesting

F1: it's scary isn't it

**PHATICS IN SPOKEN DISCOURSE**

**Phatic tokens** are the parts of conversation whose primary function is social rather than content-bearing. They are used typically at the beginning and end of exchanges, and to repair a conversation when it collapses. Examples include 'Good morning', 'How are you?' 'Nice weather we're having', and so on. According to Laver (1975), phatic tokens normatively:

> are emotionally uncontroversial
> expect a positive response
> expect a non-committal response.

So, the normative response to 'Nice weather we're having' would be 'Hmm, lovely isn't it'. It would be very strange to reply with 'Rubbish. Any fool can see it's going to rain. What are you, an idiot?' Again, non-normative choices will generate particular sociolinguistic effects.

Laver distinguishes three types of token:

❑ **neutral token** – refers to the context of situation (the weather, the view, the news)
❑ **self-oriented token** – is personal to the speaker ('my, I'm hot today')
❑ **other-oriented token** – is personal to the addressee ('How are you?').

He claims that the normative pattern is that when a superior (his example is a passing baron) initiates a conversation with an inferior (a peasant building a wall), he will use an other-oriented token ('That looks like hard work'). When an inferior begins the conversation, he will use a self-oriented token ('Hard work, this'). Though this example is extreme, the same pattern can be observed where the 'superior' is socially more powerful, chairing a meeting, in authority in a situation, seated physically higher than the other, sitting in their room and interrupted, answering the door or phone in 'their' territory, and so on. Phatic and politeness mitigation is also required when a person in motion encounters a stationary person – since they have intruded on their personal space (an FTA, in effect; see A10).

## A study of conversational endings

Joanna Shirley wanted to investigate how conversations were closed and how the participants 'escaped' from the exchange. She noticed that conversations often ended with phatic tokens, farewells, and idiomatic expressions, and set up an experiment to focus on the last of these: idioms.

**Idioms** are 'ready-made phrases that communicate a clear, agreed meaning' (Carter 1997: 99). They are fixed and cannot be replaced in part by a synonym: thus 'over the moon' but not 'over the satellite' (Wood and Hill 1989). Makkai (1972) claims that idioms can work even with two lexemes, as in phrasal verbs such as 'give in', 'run up (a bill)', or as in 'take-away (food)'.

With a colleague, Joanna covertly recorded (in a notebook) the ends of 30 conversations held in public places (because she was not interested in the content, and the informants were not identifiable, she did not regard this as an ethical problem), in a variety of randomly chosen locations. They noted the gender and rough age of the participants.

Joanna distinguished between **escapable** and **non-escapable** conversations. The first is when both participants are free to signal the end of the talk and move away physically without breaking any social norm. A non-escapable conversation is when neither is free to move away (because of being 'trapped' on a bus or train journey, in a lecture, and so on). Of course, this distinction only works prototypically where the power relations are symmetrical. In an asymmetrical exchange, the conversation is more escapable for the powerful participant (who has 'licence' to end the exchange) than for the less powerful person (who has to remain there until 'released'). Disruption of these norms constitutes rudeness.

The results revealed that escapable conversations ended with phatics and a farewell (such as 'bye,' 'see you later'). However, the signal for the ending occurred just previously in the conversation. These idiomatic signals fell into four types:

- ❏ *the excuse* ('better go', 'I've gotta go to the shops', 'I'd better be going now')
- ❏ *the single-word signal* ('well', 'so', 'anyway', 'right')
- ❏ *the future-phatic* ('have a nice evening', 'hope it goes well')
- ❏ *the rendezvous strategy* ('meet you outside the shop at 6').

These were often also combined, especially the 'single-word signal' with the others. The 'single-word' was used in 65 per cent of escapable conversations.

By contrast, non-escapable conversations ended with silence. Where escapable conversations are oriented towards the end of the interaction (and thus require social markers such as phatics and farewells), non-escapable conversations end when the topic ends. The silence signals the end of topic, and is broken only by the resumption of a new topic. Alternatively, the conversation can be moved by one of the participants into an escapable mode. An example concerned two people on a bus who had not spoken for a minute, but who got off the bus together, and had an escapable closing conversation on the pavement before going their separate ways.

---

## B12    LANGUAGE AND IDEOLOGY

It will have become clear by now that sociolinguistics has come a long way from being a straightforwardly descriptive discipline. Sociolinguists do not live outside society but are an integral and even privileged part of it. Developing sociolinguistic theory has demonstrated that people's attitudes and perceptions towards language help to shape their usage, and these perceptions shape governmental and educational policy and language planning. All studies are undertaken, not in a vacuum, but for a social and individual purpose: methods of data collection, deciding what even counts as data, as well as the analytical approach to take, all rely on an ideological awareness. **Ideology** here does not just mean political ideology, but the particular system of beliefs and assumptions that underlies every linguistic analysis and every social event. The only way of investigating these assumptions and understanding their workings is by an exploration of the language that represents them. Ideology, then, is also a sociolinguistic matter.

### The linguistics of ideology

The sub-disciplines of **critical linguistics** and **critical discourse analysis** (CDA) have emerged with a specific concern for the ideological investigation of linguistic representation. Central to their approach is the notion that language is only meaningful in its social setting. The method of analysis, however, is different from traditional sociolinguistic studies. CDA uses close linguistic analysis mainly of written texts such as newspaper reports, political speeches, institutional regulations, advertising, contracts, romantic fiction, graffiti, and other public announcements. Its objective is to reveal, through analysis rather than experimentation, the underlying ideological **discursive practices** involved in the production of the text. In the work of Norman Fairclough, CDA has relied on the **systemic-functional grammar** of Halliday as its main linguistic framework. This is an approach to the analysis of language that categorises the parts of language in terms of their function in the world. Halliday differentiates three dimensions of language:

❑   **textual** the actual organisation of language features to appear grammatical
❑   **interpersonal** the relations between the participants in a communicative event
❑   **ideational** the content and belief-system involved.

These dimensions are all involved in any single text or utterance. The classic example of the relation of linguistic form and function lies in the two alternative headlines:

*Demonstrators are shot*
*Police shoot demonstrators*

The second of these places the agents of the action ('police') in the prime position and the active verb attributes the action clearly. In the first example, the agents have been deleted by the passivisation of the verb-form. Here, it is the 'demonstrators' who are the focus and appear almost to be responsible for events.

At the centre of CDA is a treatment of language as **discourse**: that is, as a social process involving participants in a specific social situation with particular aims and objectives and beliefs. Practitioners of CDA claim to be **interventionist**; they want to create an explicit awareness of the linguistic forces of social control and manipulation, in order to resist these forces. This is very different from the **descriptivist** paradigm that dominates in most other areas of linguistics, to the extent that some other linguists deny that CDA can be included within the field at all.

The area of metaphor and euphemism (see B3) can be seen as an example of CDA interest in the linguistics of coercion in media representation. Fairclough has argued:

> Metaphor is a means of representing one aspect of experience in terms of another, and is by no means restricted to the sort of discourse it tends to be stereotypically associated with – poetry and literary discourse. But any aspect of experience can be represented in any number of metaphors, and it is the relationship between alternative metaphors that is of particular interest here, for different metaphors have different ideological attachments.
>
> (Fairclough 2001: 119)

For example, in newspaper reports he distinguishes between **metaphorical** and **congruent** orders of discourse. The latter consists of the register you would ordinarily expect: medical register for a medical story; formal style for a parliamentary story; less formal style for a political sketch, and so on. Metaphorical orders of discourse are often used to 'spin' a controversial or sensational story, such as a war report. For example, where a broadsheet newspaper might report an air-strike using journalistic attribution and citing evidence of eye-witnesses, a tabloid newspaper might blend the lexicogrammatical choices usually associated with playground bullying, sport, sensational war fiction, fairy tales and fables, and so on. Fairclough points out that when such blends are habitually used, they become **naturalised** forms of discourse: we no longer see them as ideological 'spin' but as the natural way of talking about war and conflict.

## Studying the news

Katherine West recorded and transcribed two radio news reports from the upmarket, serious BBC Radio 4 and the youth music-oriented BBC Radio 1. She was particularly interested in Fairclough's notion of the **conversationalisation** of news, by which informal features of style and register are adopted. This forces a political story into the evaluation of an everyday conversation. While this may appear to appropriate politicians' discourse in favour of ordinary people, Katherine argues that it makes it much more difficult to disentangle the reporter's opinions from those of the other participants (in this case, politicians). Having two news reports of the same story allowed her to see what had been edited out from each story. She focused on several different linguistic features, including the representation of the politicians and public through naming strategies and direct address, the framing of the story of an election as a fairy-tale with a hero and villain, and the placing of the participants in grammatically foregrounded or backgrounded positions.

Ben Woolhead investigated television news, focusing on how the **identities** and **relations** of participants are linguistically represented. He recorded six different channels' news programmes on the same day, and examined the transcripts for the same story, looking particularly at the lexical and syntactic levels. His aim was to construct a scale of apparent 'authority', in terms of the claims to truth and certainty and rejection of arguability in the news discourse. Specific linguistic choices which encode these different points of view can be seen in a selection from Ben's data:

> *The battle of Seattle* (BBC Nine O'clock News)
> *siege conditions* (ITN News)
> *thugs invaded the city* (BBC News)
> *protestors hijacked the agenda* (BBC News)
> *rentamob* (Channel 5 News)
> *Protesters without gas masks fell victim to police pepper spray* (Channel 4 News)
> *Police used tear gas against protesters* (Channel 4 News)
> *The police used tear gas, pepper spray and rubber bullets to try and keep the crowd under
> control* (BBC Newsround – news programme for children).

All of these represent different versions of the story.

It is important to remember that none of the versions can be the 'true' form, against which all the others are 'distortions' or are 'biased'. *All* representations encode a viewpoint and an ideology, even if their linguistic patterns claim an apparent certainty, truth-value or neutrality. To return to a sociolinguistic principle: it is as impossible to say anything without an ideological dimension as it is to say anything without an accent.

# Section C
# EXPLORATION:
## DATA FOR INVESTIGATION

## COLLECTING AND EXPLORING DATA

The units in this section present real examples of language that have been collected for the purpose of sociolinguistic analysis. For each, I provide some details of the original naturally-occurring social context. Some of the data are from students' fieldwork and some are from my own notes and files. Of course, no piece of language is one-dimensional, and although each passage appears under a heading, there are often insights to be gained by examining the data with a different concern in mind.

Each area corresponds roughly with the similarly numbered units in sections A and B in the book. For each, I have suggested some analytical questions, discussion points, and issues to consider, though of course the whole point of engaging with data like this is to apply your own analytical methods and thinking and develop your own ideas and conclusions.

### Transcription conventions

If you are collecting spoken data, you might need to use a systematic set of notational conventions when transcribing speech, as set out below. The level of detail depends on what you are investigating: you will need the IPA for accent variation (see A2); you will need to note pause lengths and overlaps to study politeness and conversational 'turns' (see A10 and A11); you might only need the barest annotation if you are investigating features such as a word or idiom occurrence, or discoursal features across the whole transcript, for example.

You should bear in mind that transcription will take you a lot longer than you will imagine, and certainly a lot longer than the recording took to make. You should be selective and only transcribe those parts of the discourse that you need to examine closely.

| | |
|---|---|
| → | utterance continues without a break onto the next line of text |
| ← | line of text is a continued utterance from the last arrow |
| = | next speaker's turn begins with no break after current speaker |
| ↑ | point at which heavy emphasis by rise in pitch begins |
| ↓ | point at which lowering of pitch begins |
| ? | intonation marking a question |
| *word* | indicates heavy contrastive emphasis on a single word |
| WORD | indicates shouting |
| ( ) | indecipherable word |
| (word) | indecipherable word, containing best guess as to what was said |
| ((smiles)) | contains note on non-verbal interaction |
| (2.3) | indicates pause, with length in seconds |
| . | indicates significant pause below measurable length |
| – | indicates very brief pause |
| [ | point at which overlap between speakers begins |
| ] | point at which overlap between speakers ends |

You might also want to develop your own notes to signal features you are particularly interested in.

### An example

S1:   ↑WHAT do you think you're doing. look at the *mess*
      (0.7)
S2:   it wasn't me – ↓it was (Clare)=
S1:   *don't* lie to me. you clear it up ↑right now ((points)). she's not even here –
      I just saw her in the garden [and she could hardly be      ] in two places at
      once→
S2:                                [but it was her ((starts to cry))  ]
S1:   ←now could she
      (2.0)
S2:   ((continuous crying))
      ((S3 comes into room))
S3:   what's all this noise then. shush shush ↓shush ok that's alright (0.5) ↑what
      have you said to her=
S1:   *look* at the mess she's made – and. and *I'll* be the one who has to clear it up
      ((begins to clear up))
S3:   look. you go and find Clare and we'll all (      ) together. that's a good girl
      ((S2 leaves))
      (7.0)
S1:   give me a hand then
S3:   here. let me do it. go and have a coffee
      ((S1 leaves room))

This passage represents about 45 seconds of recording, but it would take anything up
to half an hour to transcribe. There is no punctuation or capitalisation in the passage,
since these are features of written language. The dots and dashes have a fixed value.
This passage could be used for various investigative purposes, such as turn-taking
between child–adult or between mother–father. It could not be used for accent
investigation – for this you would need a closer phonetic transcription. Similarly, the
passage is useless if you are investigating inter-language code-switching, creolisation,
dialectal markers, metaphoric usage, and so on. The point here is that you need to
decide in advance what you are studying, in order to go somewhere that you are likely
to find it. Data is never just data – all data-collection is theory-driven. You should
take this into account when planning your project.

## Statistics, logic and correlations

As a way into thinking about practical methodology, consider some of the following.
(Comments follow, but try to think about each one before turning to them.) Though
the fields of statistics and logical reasoning are beyond the scope of this book, sociolinguists need to be able to reason and present their conclusions logically, and you
will often have to rely on some statistical understanding and methods in examining
the data that you collect.

### a Chickens and eggs and Mozart

According to *The Farmer's Guardian*, chickens lay more eggs when they listen
to Mozart. Researchers suggest it is the intricate modulation of the notes which

stimulates the hens and makes them less stressed. It has also been suggested that the same applies to children, whose learning shows an improvement if they are played classical music both pre-birth and in the first couple of years. Can you explain why stories such as these are nonsense?

### b Sofa: so good

In one advertising campaign, the furniture shop Ikea used the results of a survey that said: people with green sofas are more likely to be adventurous in bed; people with flowery wallpaper were more likely to gossip about their friends and neighbours; people who kept cacti as domestic plants were likely to be cold and unemotional. What conceptual step has been leapt over in the logic of these findings?

### c Shooting the milkman

A few years ago in Belfast, a French TV news crew filming an item on the 'troubles' persuaded a gang of children to throw some stones and a few petrol bombs for the cameras. When the trouble escalated, a local milkman was killed in the rioting. Which rule of social science had the film-crew broken?

### d Not being beastly to fascists

Especially during general election campaigns, the BBC tries to abide by its regulations for equal coverage given to the political parties. In 1997, there was an outcry at the right-wing British National Party being allowed a party political broadcast. Similarly, Conservative politicians – then virtually extinct as a political force in Scotland – were allowed equal TV time as Labour, Liberal Democrat and Scottish Nationalist politicians. What sort of sampling method is being used here?

### e Test-drive your date

'Test-drive your date. Behind the wheel, does your prospective partner regularly . . .

- ❑  jump red lights?
- ❑  clip kerbs?
- ❑  cut up other cars?
- ❑  use his horn?

If you answered "yes" to more than one, he could be a bad lover. A report by Cris Burgess, for the AA, says so-called "wilful offenders" are selfish lovers as well as being a menace on the roads. "If they don't get what they want, they're not interested and won't make an effort," explains Burgess. "They tend to have poor sex lives because they find it hard to maintain close relationships. They won't give – they only take" ' (*Cosmopolitan*, Sept. 1998, p.81). What do you think of the linkages between cause and effect going on here?

### f The message is the medium

In order to have a discussion on whether seances work, the researchers of a BBC TV daytime talk show placed an ad in newspapers asking for people to participate in the programme. Is this alright as a sampling method?

### g Is there anybody out there?

In the mid-West of the US, there are many reported cases of unidentified flying objects, lights in the sky, electricity power cuts, mutilated cattle, and crop circles. These have been attributed to the activities of extra-terrestrial intelligences. Why is this feeble-minded?

### h Who you gonna call?

A recent TV advert for an insurance company features a man walking past a burnt out building, with the line: 'You'd go to the fire service to put out the fire, but they can't arrange your insurance for you.' What is the false logic involved here?

### i Hey kids, just say no

A recent billboard 'drugs awareness' campaign featured the line: '80 per cent of children will try drugs,' over the large image of a hypodermic needle. Why is this ad unnecessarily alarmist in its statistical claims?

### j The one about the taxi driver

An urban myth: if the Sultan of Brunei took a taxi through London, the average wealth of the two occupants of the taxi would be several billion pounds. Why is this true fact of little comfort to the taxi-driver?

### k Dead good

The town with the highest mortality rate in the UK is not in inner city Manchester, London or Birmingham but the warm and prosperous seaside resort of Torquay. Why is it so unhealthy there?

### l Cats/dogs

When it's raining, will you be drier if you run through the rain or if you walk? What are the variables to consider?

## Comments

### a

There is a problem here with uncontrolled independent variables. That is, there could be a whole range of other factors that explain why hens lay more eggs: perhaps farmers who play their chickens Mozart also feed their stock better? So Mozart is not a causal factor but is an **index** of the cause. Furthermore, the explanation presented means there is no reason why any intricate sound should not work, but no one has yet claimed that productivity goes up with the music of Jimi Hendrix.

### b

*Ikea* are deliberately missing an intermediate step here. These examples present $x$ as causing $y$, whereas actually both factors are *independently* caused by another factor $z$. A comparison would be trying to decide whether working class children tend to fail at school because their language is different, or whether both these phenomena are caused by a different attitude to the middle class codes in which schools tend to operate. Whenever there is an apparent correlation between two factors for a group of people, you also have to ask what else is common for that group.

### c

Interfering with the data you are there to record is the **observer's paradox**, which the film-crew have seriously misjudged. Sociolinguists have tried to minimise the observer's paradox with a range of elicitation methods to collect naturalistic data. While the film-crew are not social scientists, thair actions were certainly unethical (and arguably even a criminal incitement to riot).

### d

The sample represents all opinion equally but it doesn't weight the relative popularity of the parties. Of course, doing this would then preserve either the results of the previous election or the *status quo*. All of these options thus represent an ideological choice, and this illustrates that 'balance' is impossible and even statistics have an ideological dimension.

### e

This is similar to the *Ikea* ad (*b* above). Factor *x* (bad driving) does not cause *y* (being a bad lover); instead both are results of factor *z* (selfishness). Notice also how the ambiguous word-choices reinforce the suggestion ('jump', 'red lights', 'use his horn') and how the syntactic form moves from possibility ('if . . . could') to assertion. You should look out for such rhetorical sleight-of-hand when statistical evidence is presented.

### f

This is **circularity**. The sampling method is set up to produce a self-selecting group of people who will already have extreme views. In sociolinguistics, circularity would be involved if a linguistic means were used to select a group for a linguistic analysis: for example, investigating the accent of working class people, but using the presence or absence of non-standard verb agreement partly to determine whether they are working class or not.

### g

The explanation selected here is possible but the least likely. Of the range of possible causes of *a*, such as *b* (military test-flights), *c* (weather patterns), *d* (psychotic local people), you decide that factor *z* (slobbery beings from planet Zog) *must* be to blame. In sociolinguistics, there is usually a range of possibilities that can be ordered into a sequence of probable to improbable, and it is useful to do this in discussion, in order to keep your conclusions in touch with the rest of the discipline.

### h

Chronological cause and effect are reversed here. Many people find this sentence acceptable until they think about it. The reason might be that both clauses in the sentence are stylistically connected ('but') and both belong to a similar semantic domain (fire and insurance). However, the two parts of the sentence do not logically follow: this is a *non-sequitur*.

## i

'Drugs' might mean anything from heroin, to cannabis, to ecstasy, to alcohol or caffeine, though the image strongly suggests 'hard' drugs. More misleadingly, the assertion is an (unproven) prediction ('will') that also hides the less emotive fact that '100 per cent of children will die' (eventually), and *all* drug-users were once children.

## j

This illustrates the problem with **group means** in statistics. Taking a mean average when the population (that is, the elements) of the group are very disparate mis-represents the reality. The taxi-driver's income has not actually risen (unless he gets a good tip). A calculation of **standard deviation** (how far most elements are away from the mean average) would help here.

## k

Be careful with terms. The measure of environmental healthiness is *infant* mortality rate. Torquay is a popular retirement resort for older people.

## l

This raises all the complexity of controlling for possible relevant factors: distance, speed, rate of rainfall, balance of water on your head or chest, what clothes you are wearing, what sort of rain it is, what sort of haircut is optimal, and so on. Think of an experiment to decide the matter, and how you would control for all of these factors.

---

## DIALECTAL VARIATION                                        C2

### An accent-elicitation reading passage

The following passage has been specially written to contain many of the linguistic features that have multiple variants in different accents of English. It is, of course, one of the advantages of having a standardised written dialect (Standard English) and a frozen medieval spelling system that written English can be read and written by anyone in their own accent.

> Once upon a time there were three bears: a Daddy bear, a Mummy bear and a little baby bear. They lived in a cottage deep in the woods. One morning, Mummy bear had made some porridge for breakfast, but it was too hot to eat at once. 'Let's go for a walk while it cools down,' said Daddy bear. 'What a good idea!' exclaimed Mummy bear,

and, with their bear coats and bear shoes on, they all set off for a short walk in the woods.

That morning a little girl called Goldilocks was also walking in the woods. She was picking flowers and had wandered deeper in among the trees than her parents allowed her to go. After a while of being completely lost, she came into a clearing and saw the pretty little cottage. 'I wonder who lives there?' she thought to herself, and walked up to the door. When she knocked, there was no answer, so she pushed the door. It swung open, and she went in.

Can you identify some of the particular items (letters, words or links between words) in this passage that are likely to elicit a range of variant phonetic features when read aloud in different accents? It might help if you try out different accents while reading the passage: New York, Glasgow, Dublin, Birmingham; or think of ways that men, women, boys, girls, bus-drivers, mechanics, professors, sales assistants and others might pronounce the text.

### Word-pairs and variant pronunciations

You could use the Goldilocks passage to elicit informants' speech patterns. The familiarity of the story and the ease of its vocabulary will minimise disfluency and hesitancy, and it is likely to produce a natural accent. Of course, it is still a reading passage. You can get even more relaxed data with casual conversation, informal interview, covert recording, and so on. You can increase informants' self-consciousness and 'carefulness' by openly recording them, interviewing them formally, telling them you are interested in their speech, or by using minimal pairs or groups of words like these:

| | | | | | | |
|---|---|---|---|---|---|---|
| bear | beer | bier | bare | | | |
| oil | air | ear | moor | poor | pore | paw |
| bag | beg | big | | | | |
| bad | bard | board | bored | bawd | | |
| cot | caught | cat | | | | |
| blue | blew | | | | | |
| moan | mown | moan | moon | | | |
| plaster | master | grass | laugh | | | |
| which | witch | weather | whether | whither | wither | |
| butter | mother | brother | parrot | Paris | | |
| farm | bird | lore | law | law and order | | |
| lamp-post | pen-knife | bread-tin | crisp packet | | | |
| Cuba | news | Tuesday | tissue | sexual | | |
| missile | tile | leisure | tomato | either | | |
| spear | actually | constitution | | | | |
| bath | run | put | putt | pot | pat | pet |
| hotel | happy | house | | | | |
| Mary | merry | marry | Murray | | | |
| letter 'a' | letter 'i' | | | | | |

How do you pronounce these words? Do you think you pronounce them the same in these small groups as you would in normal conversation? Which accents would make differentiations between some of the words in ways that you do not? Try saying each of these words in the accents of America, northern England, southern England, Birmingham, Norfolk, Wales, Jamaica, Belfast, white South Africa, black South Africa, Glasgow, Australia, and any others you can manage. Can you outline the differences using the phonetic notation of the IPA?

## Regional variation

In different parts of Britain, these words are all used to refer to more or less the same thing:

| | | | |
|------|--------|-------|-------|
| bun  | bap    | barm  | batch |
| cob  | roll   | cake  | flat  |
| loaf | fadgie | stotty | |

Do you recognise all of these? Do you use any of them? Do you have a different word? Can you think of any other items which have a similarly rich set of dialectal lexical variants? For example, which words do you use to refer to:

- the soft cheap black or dark blue shoe that children often use for gym activity?
- someone who is left-handed?
- your ears?
- your nose?
- spectacles for correcting vision?
- giving a ride to a friend on your bicycle?
- the action of touching a player in the children's game which involves passing on the 'touch'?
- being cold?
- being hungry?
- being annoyed or irritated?
- truanting from school?
- informing on friends to someone in authority?
- and so on.

Consider the dialectal differences in these sentences:

I haven't spoken to him
I've not spoken to him

Is John at home?
Is John home?

I live in Nottingham, on Lenton Boulevard, at number 23
She lives on our street
She lives in our street
On the street where you live
They play in the street

Give me it
Give it me
Give it to me
Give us it
Give it

I should like to thank you
I would like to thank you
I'd like to thank you

I'll be here while 10
I'll be here 'til 10

Is that you?
Are you through?
Have you finished?
Are you done?

Could I have a ham sandwich?
Can I get a ham sandwich?

Drive-through
Drive-in
Drive-by
Drive-way

Lie-in
Over-lay
Sleep-over
Over-sleep

Off-licence
Off-sales
Offie
Beer-off
Liquor store
Bottle store
Bottle bank

Who would use each of these? What contexts would they be used in?

## Literary dialect

Here is a song that my mother sang to me in a mock-Cockney accent when I was a baby. I have used the **nonce-spelling** form rather than a strict IPA transcription:

> A muvver was barfin' 'er biby one night,
> The youngest of ten and a tiny young mite,
> The muvver was pore and the biby was fin,
> Only a skellington covered in skin;
> The muvver turned rahnd for the soap orf the rack,

She was but a moment, but when she turned back,
The biby was gorn; and in anguish she cried,
'Oh, where is my biby?' – the Angels replied:
'Your biby 'as fell dahn the plug'ole,
Your biby 'as gorn dahn the plug;
The poor little fing was so skinny and fin
'E oughter been barfed in a jug;
Your biby is perfectly 'appy,
'E shan't need a barf any more,
Your biby 'appy as fell dahn the plug'ole,
Not lorst, but gorn before!'

(Traditional; written version adapted from *The Rattle Bag*, eds Seamus Heaney and Ted Hughes (1982), Faber and Faber).

Clearly, this picks up on many of the stereotypical features of the Cockney accent as well as some dialect features. As a piece of popular (oral) 'literature' rather than sociolinguistics it can present such a cartoon-like version of Cockney. Note the elements that this common written form attempts to capture (like 'fin' for 'thin') and those that it doesn't (not 'toiny' for 'tiny' for example). Why is it not consistent or thorough? How could you identify the features (using a phonetically-informed technical description) of the Cockney accent based only on this data?

There are many examples of literary uses of non-standard accent and dialect which you could investigate as a means of exploring prestige/stigmatisation and the attitudes and stereotypes which are popularly held. Some examples include:

- the speech of Joseph in Emily Brontë's *Wuthering Heights*
- the speech of Stephen Blackpool in Charles Dickens' *Hard Times*
- Mrs Durbeyfield in Thomas Hardy's *Tess of the d'Urbevilles*
- the speech of Morel in D.H. Lawrence's *Sons and Lovers*
- Scots in the poetry of Hugh McDiarmid
- the poetry of Barnsley poet Ian McMillan
- the poetry of Glasgow poet Tom Leonard
- the narrative style of Irvine Welsh's *Trainspotting*
- Irish English in the novels of Roddy Doyle
- Indian English in Salman Rushdie's fiction

and many others. You could measure these versions against an actual sociolinguistic account of the variety, in order to understand what is being foregrounded in the literature and how the traits of the accents and dialects are used to build the characterisation.

**C3** **REGISTER**

### The art of writing

Here is an extract from the exhibition catalogue from the Guggenheim museum in Bilbao (English version), part of the International Currents in Contemporary Art exhibition:

> Gallery 303 and corridor:
>
> **Gillian Wearing** (Birmingham, United Kingdom, 1963), **Pipilotti Rist** (Rheintal, Switzerland, 1962), **Andreas Slominski** (Meppen, Germany, 1959)
>
> British artist Gillian Wearing is particularly interested in the fears, fantasies, and secrets of ordinary people and in the processes of identification set up with the viewer. In *Sacha and Mum*, 1996, Wearing attempts to unmask the ambivalent emotions surrounding the complex personal relationships between a mother and her daughter. The warmth of an embrace becomes transformed into a confrontation bordering on violence. The palpable tension in Wearing's work is in sharp contrast to the sensual celebration of the body in Swiss-artist Pipilotti Rist's video installation *Sip My Ocean*, 1996. Rist has created a magic submarine dream world in this video, which was filmed almost entirely under water and is accompanied by her own cover of Chris Isaak's love song 'Wicked Games.' Her entire aesthetic borrows from pop music and the vast area of mass culture. Double screens and spectacular effects suggest an ideal region of unadulterated pre-Oedipal pleasure. The work is Rist's personal invitation to take part in the eternal dance of desire and satisfaction. For more than fifteen years, German conceptual artist Andreas Slominski has been reinterpreting the concept of the trap. Slominski, who designs his own functional traps for all kinds of animals (foxes, marder, birds, insects), has found a perfect metaphor for art: like art, the trap seduces and deceives. Hermetic and humorous, the work lures its viewers, asking them to ponder the very limits of what constitutes the absurd and, hence, to contemplate the boundaries of art.

What is it that linguistically characterises this as an art exhibition catalogue? You might look particularly at the syntactic arrangement of the sentences, and especially at the complexity of noun-phrases. Try to write the 'rules' of this genre of language as precisely as you can.

Could you rewrite this for a different audience: for children on a school-trip, for a group of people on their first ever visit to an art gallery, for the use of people whose first language is not English? Could you reframe it as speech? In each case, decide exactly what you would need to change in order to switch registers.

### A registered nurse

My student Kate Oakley was interested in shifts in register amongst nursing staff in a large city hospital, in order to identify their occupational language code.

The following is from the operation notes to treat a 'slipped disc':

> PR Exploration Of L. Spine. – Operative procedure.
> Patient prone on Toronto frame.
> Previous incision used and extended.

L3 to S1 Vertebrae exposed.
L3 Laminectomy performed.
Normal Dura was identified at that level and traced Caudally, by careful dissection, all
the scar tissue was dissected off.
The Dura was exposed fully at all the levels from L3 to S1.
Laminectomy widened to effect better decompression.
No obvious Dural tear seen.
At the end of the procedure, standard closure in layers with Vicryl. Continuous
Prolene to skin.

Make a systematic list of the stylistic features that identify this as, respectively: a piece
of writing rather than speech, a report rather than a narrative fiction, a medical
report rather than a report of a football match.

Here is a conversational exchange from Kate's data:

*(Consultant, senior nurse and junior doctor, away from the bed of a patient with
tuberculosis and another long-term chest complaint)*

Consultant: we'll stop Mrs Pxxxx's A[drug's pharmaceutical name] – it's done
bugger all to help her. just made her more vulnerable to infection
*(moving to the patient's bedside and addressing her)*
Consultant: well it is TB – as long as you take the tablets to fight the infection
there will be no problem – we are going to stop your breathing tablets as it's just
not helping
*(she turns to the junior doctor)*
Consultant:  it should show up on microexamination. we need to inform the P.H.D.
– forms are in the office
*(moving back to the ward station away from the patient)*
Consultant:  unfortunately her emphysema masked the underlying tuberculosis –
I've actually seen at PM widespread milliary infection that was not picked up by
either CT scan or PA view on x-ray

Identify the code-switching points here, and compare the different linguistic choices
of the different codes in operation.

The following written nursing notes also show a marked code-switch:

R. Leg no movement. NBM. from midnight. S/B Mr G.
For IV. Dexamethasone. T.= 37.4C. IVI. in progress.
Unable to PU. catheterised. 10mls. H20 in balloon.
CBD. good volumes. Vital signs normal. PA's intact.
Apyrexial. Feeling really fed up.
Ensure TED's are in situ.

Here is a written 'ward report' list of patients with notes for the nursing staff on
duty:

Mrs S:  Not coping. TIA's. # of R.Radius. G.I. bleed.
Mrs F:  Not for 2's. Ascites, tapped. Ca. of pancreas. I.V. down. T.L.C.
Mrs J:  MI.

Mrs P:  Ca. Colostomy. Oromorph given.
Mr T:   SOB. A/F. Digoxin. 02 PRN.
Mr G:   NIDDM. Actrapid if over 27. 6 hrly. BM stix.
Mr P:   COAD. Cont. 02. Nebs. 4 hrly.
Mr G:   Haematuria. R.B.K.A. and CVA. Multi-infarct dementia.
Mrs N:  For FOB.

If you can understand all of the terms used in these, you are probably a nurse, and the 'face' you present to the world as a nurse is in a large part a result of this sort of linguistic competence and performance. Can you decide which other occupations and professions have a similarly exclusive register (or **jargon**)? For each, either list some of the characteristic features, or you could go and collect some real data like that used above, and analyse it. Comparing the registers of closely associated groups is illuminating: teachers and lecturers, checkout operators at different supermarkets, bar staff in different types of bar, decorative designers and decorators, professional engineers and mechanics, journalists and reporters, senior managers and middle managers, and so on.

Here are two letters written by a consultant surgeon. This first one was sent to the patient's General Practitioner:

> Dear Dr H,
> As you know I sent M.R.I. scans and clinical details of Mr L to a very good friend of mine, Mr Q in Cardiff, who recommended a Thoracic Spine M.R.I. scan to be performed and this has shown a very significant lower Thoracic spinal stenosis especially at TH/12. Changes do extend to higher up but it is the lower three Thoracic levels which are most significant. His Cervical spine M.R.I. scan is really not too bad and I think consideration for a lower Thoracic Laminectomy is worthwhile. He could walk 4 miles just over a year ago, but now his performance is considerably less.
> Mr L is going to think about it and let me know.
>                    Yours sincerely,
>                    Mr N. FRCS.

The second letter was sent to the patient:

> Dear Mr L,
> There is one part of your spine that does not show up on the M.R.I. scan and that is at the low Thoracic level. My colleague Mr Q in Cardiff has recommended we do an M.R.I. scan at this level, and if you are agreeable we will do this as soon as possible and then I will see you again.
>                    Yours sincerely,
>                    Mr N.

Identify and list the differences between these. Can you imagine the same information expressed in a conversation between the consultant Mr N and the GP Dr H, or between Mr N and the patient Mr L, or how Mr L might recount what has happened to his friend in the pub who enquires about his health?

## Some medical acronyms and terms

| | |
|---|---|
| # | fracture |
| 02 | oxygen |
| *Actrapid* | a quick-acting insulin |
| *A/F* | atrial fibrillation |
| *Apyrexial* | not feverish |
| *Ascites* | fluid accumulation in the peritoneal cavity |
| *BM stix* | trade name for blood glucose monitoring |
| *B/P* | blood pressure |
| *Ca.* | cancer |
| *CBD* | catheter bag drainage |
| *COAD* | chronic obstructive airways disease |
| *Colostomy* | surgery to bring bowel out to body surface |
| *cont.* | continuous |
| *CT* | computerised tomography |
| *CVA* | cerebral vascular accident (stroke) |
| *CXR* | chest x-ray |
| *dexamethasone* | a steroid |
| *Digoxin* | heart medication |
| *emphysema* | a lung disease |
| *FOB* | faecal occult blood – a test for blood in the stools |
| *GI* | gastro-intestinal |
| *H20 in balloon* | catheter is kept in bladder by a water-filled balloon |
| *haematuria* | blood in urine |
| *IV(I)* | intra-venous (injection) |
| *MI* | myocardial infarction (heart attack) |
| *microexamination* | microbiological investigation of tissue samples |
| *NBM* | nil by mouth |
| *Nebs* | nebuliser |
| *NIDDM* | non-insulin dependent diabetic |
| *not for 2s* | 222 is the telephone number of the heart resuscitation team. So 'not for 222' means 'not for resuscitation' |
| *OE* | on examination |
| *Oromorph* | form of morphine |
| *PA* | posterior anterior |
| *PHD* | public health department |
| *PM* | post-mortem / autopsy |
| *PMH* | previous medical history |
| *PU* | pass urine |
| *PRN* | pro re nata – as required |
| *S/B* | seen by |
| *SOB* | shortness of breath |
| *T* | temperature |
| *TB* | tuberculosis |
| *TED* | thrombo-embolic disease stocking |

| TIA | trans-ischaemic attacks – small strokes |
| TLC | tender loving care |

## Children's written register

My student Zoe Taylor undertook a detailed study of writing produced by fifty 14–15 year old boys at a state comprehensive school in Stockport near Manchester. Although the school is mixed, English is taught in single-sex groups. She identified those boys from a working class background using the following criteria for the area in which they lived:

- ❑ high unemployment
- ❑ large numbers of local council-owned houses
- ❑ high proportion of lone parents
- ❑ large number of households with no car
- ❑ large proportion of houses with no central heating

Replicating the elicitation method of Lawton's (1968) study, Zoe asked the boys to write a short essay on the topic, 'Life ten years from now'. The essays were produced by three classes: Set 1 (the group rated by the teacher as top ability); Set 5 (the least able group); and SEN (a group with 'special educational needs' in terms of behavioural problems and low ability). All essays were thus produced on the same topic by boys from a similar class and family background. She analysed four essays randomly selected from each group using Bernstein's criteria for restricted and elaborated code (see B3).

Here are six of the essays, two from each group; all essays were originally handwritten.

### Set 1 essays (top ability)

1

In 2009 I dont think that life will be much different. There wont be any robots cooking cleaning and doing other household jobs. Cars wont be flying and huge skyrise buildings. Not many inventions will have been made either but one that will be made will be small not very important ones. People still wont be living in space, on the moon or on any other planet and aliens wont be living on earth.

The environment will be better due to cars and other pollutants letting out much less dangerous gases into the air, but the polar ice caps will Probably have melted that would mean the low lying flat countries such as Holland would no longer exist. Weapons will be more advanced and dangerous so more people will be killed in wars. The crime rate will have raised because its always increasing. In home entertainment will be a lot better because of digital TV where you can watch films whenever you want. You can also watch some sporting events on iteractive tv so you can watch the sport anyway you like.

2

I think life in 10 years will not be that different from now. I think small things will have changed but on the larger scale things will be very similar e.g. Homes, food and Pubs will stay the same, but music, clothes and appearances will have changed.

10 years ago in 1990 people would have thought that it will have been different by now but again only small things have (music, cars, clothes). Some people think that everything will change, like flying cars and learning off computers but I disagree, and think that things will stay similar.

## Set 5 essays (low ability)

1

In the year 2009 everybody will start thinking about things like kids drinking on the street and they will put an end to it, the same with violence they will try to stop it but I don't think alot of the violence will stop some of it will but not a lot things like (etc) kid fighting in the street older men when there drunk in a pub will fight over something stupid. I don't think there will be many drugs in the year 2009 than there is know. I think fags will be band because there is to many kids smoking and its there parent fault because they see them smoke so they think that it is alright for them to smoke.

In britain I think they will make new money like bringing new coins and notes out. There won't be as many cars with fumes coming out of them they will run of bactery or the sun.

2

I think that life would be very different because every thing would of changed, new people around you, go to better places with other friends. I think transport would be different. I wish Stockport County will go in the premiership. There will be lots of new buildings.

## SEN essays (special educational needs)

1

In the future I recon We are going to live in space and the moon and hovering car's. I said that because most of the planet might be mostly covered in water and we would be friends with alien beings.

Dinosaurs may rule the earth like tyrannosaurus rex and smilodons (this is a big cat) and new animals may be created or transported to earth. I thingk the earth it self would be hoter because of Global warming.

I recon there we be able to have a teleporter on the internet shopping.

2

  1.) fossile fules bured out.
  2.) space ships hovering everywhere in the shape of cars.
  3.) ground which was groud would be under water.
  4.) all cars eletrik.
  5.) live on the moon in ecow buble.
  6.) could all die of world war 3.
  7.) more space like clothes.
  8.) more cloning.
  9.) all paper would run out.
10.) so that leads to computer work.
11.) By your owr engergy electicity boxes.

Can you identify any features characteristic of elaborated or restricted code here (see B3)? Alternatively, can you set up a systematic linguistic account of the differences between these essays? Are the variations necessarily evidence of cognitive differences, indexes of social class background, or supportive families?

---

## ETHNOLOGY

### East Asian languages and prestige

The following article formed part of a special debate in *The Straits Times* 'Life!' supplement (Saturday June 12th, 1999), published in Singapore. The newspaper was discussing the relative statuses of British and American English, Singaporean English, Singlish, and the different views of Chinese languages.

> *Actually, Chinese May Not Be The Mother Tongue by Sunny Goh*
>
> [. . .] Does mandarin deserve such an unqualified position?
>
> Two other translators, Larry Teo and Dai Shiyan, both steeped in the understanding of the Chinese language, offer contrasting views.
>
> In my explanation on the differences between Chinese language (*huawen*) and Mandarin (*huayu*), I had made the point that in Singapore, Mandarin is deemed the only exclusive spoken form, as Teochew, Cantonese, etc are referred to as dialects (*fangyan*).
>
> That is why in Singapore, we refer to the Chinese language as *huawen* and Mandarin exclusively and interchangeably as *huayu*. This is not exactly correct, as *huayu* is defined, strictly in most international Chinese dictionaries, as spoken Chinese. It may or may not be Mandarin.
>
> To the global Chinese community, Mandarin, which is equivalent to *putonghua*, is 'a common or standard spoken form of the Chinese language'.
>
> In short, Mandarin is *huayu* but *huayu* is more than just Mandarin.
>
> Dai disagreed with me, saying that Mandarin can be used interchangeably with *huayu* because it has been recognised internationally as the standard spoken form.
>
> Shanghainese, Ningbo and the southern dialects such as Hokkien and Teochew are all sub-standard representations of the Chinese language.
>
> 'Mandarin is the pure form and should be regarded as such,' he said, just as Received Pronunciation in Britain has been regarded as the standard spoken form of the English language. (Linguists are more diplomatic when they refer to English variants such as Cockney English, by using the neutral term 'non-standard form' rather than the emotional term 'sub-standard form' to refer to them).
>
> Teo disagreed with Dai, saying that Mandarin is not the natural acquisition of Singapore students, who are required to learn to speak a tongue that has always been

considered 'alien' by many Chinese in China itself, especially those from the south, where the ancestors of most Chinese-Singaporeans hailed from.

In the final analysis, it is evident that where a language is used, and by whom, plays a vital role in determining how it is being defined.

The communists in China called Mandarin *putonghua*, which fits in well with their idea that it should be the language of the masses.

Interestingly, the Hong-kongers call it *zhongwen*, which means Chinese language, while the Taiwanese call it *guo-yu*, meaning national language.

Only South-east Asians, including Singaporeans, call it *huayu*, which might have stemmed from the emphasis that they are *huaqiao*, meaning Overseas Chinese.

*Huaren* (Chinese people) is another, more significant, derivative of *huawen/huayu* to describe Singaporeans.

'Singaporeans who are *huaren*' is certainly a more detached term to describe Chinese-Singaporeans in a multi-racial country, as it gives the connotations that we are Singaporeans first, Chinese second.

*Huaren* is also not as politically-charged as some older terms which had been used to describe overseas Chinese, such as *tongbao* (Chinese compatriots) or, worse, *zhongguo ren* (people from China).

So if you think about it, *huawen*, *huayu* and *huaren* do make sense for Singaporeans after all.

Try to discern the different language loyalties in evidence here. You will also be able to use your knowledge of sociolinguistics to take issue with the comparison with RP. Applying a knowledge of the socio-political alignments of east Asian nations will also help here: you might research comparable newspaper items by searching online amongst Malaysian publications, for example.

### Hong Kong chat: 'Mix'

This is an extract from I Ching Ng's data, used as part of her investigation into 'Mix', the blend of English and Cantonese heard in Hong Kong. The script is from an internet chatroom run by a local radio station. In the original, the text in square brackets was entered in Chinese characters; I Ching provides a translation here.

| Occupants: | little kit – popcorn – pp – smiling – [sara] – [granny number 8] |
|---|---|
| smiling: | [wrong spelling. shit] |
| granny no. 8: | i am super 8 |
| little kit: | logged on. |
| pp: | logged off. |
| smiling: | HAHAHA ................ SERA, [so you make fun of him]! |
| granny no.8: | smile~ |
| popcorn: | smiling, [you want to spoil the whole thing]? [Ha] |
| smiling: | not too GER? [So, must be pretty cool]???[You're pretty confident No.8] |
| [sara]: | popcorn, u too ar! don't play me next time!! |
| popcorn: | [sara], bye bye! take care! |
| pp: | logged on. |
| smiling: | [I'm no good. So, you are good] |

| | |
|---|---|
| [sara]: | But i go la! bye all again!!!! |
| popcorn: | little kit, hello! |
| popcorn: | [grin]:[You think I can't] put u in invisible? [You idiot]! |
| smiling: | [Oh]!!!!!![How dare you]!!!![Put me in invisible]!!!!!!!! |
| little kit: | hello~~~~~~~~~~~~~~~~~ |
| granny no.8: | go lar ~~ bye bye |
| granny no.8: | i am boring ar |
| granny no.8: | logged off. |
| smiling: | [yes obviously so stupid ............ .don't know where to escape] |
| smiling: | kitkit [did somebody] kick [you]??? [Because you didn't] online for ages [of course don't see you, you idiot] |
| popcorn: | smiling, u shooting arrows? |

There is obviously a great deal of code-switching here, and the electronic medium makes the blending even more fluid and non-standard (to 'put in invisible' is to wipe a speaker from the screen, thus freezing them out). Exchanges are initiated in English: 'popcorn' uses mainly English with 'sara' who uses English Mix all the time, but 'popcorn' uses Chinese for 'smiling' who uses Chinese entirely. These uses (supported by the friendly 'la/lar') are also marked for solidarity by the text being posted in a purple colour. There are some direct interferences from Chinese: 'granny number 8' denotes a 'nosy' person, as '8' and 'nosy' are homophones in Chinese; 'shooting arrows' is a Chinese idiom for a personal attack; and 'GER' is an English spelling of the Chinese word for 'only'.

The common grammatical 'errors' are frequent in fast electronic posting, but also reflect the fact that only about 30 per cent of people in Hong Kong speak English – and then, most of them as an L2. English is only used in public domains: high-status financial jobs, media and entertainment. Thus, English and Cantonese in Hong Kong can be regarded as being on a cline of bilingualism, with 'Mix' being a stigmatised form gaining in popularity among young people.

You might take some samples from other online activity and compare the linguistic patterns involved. How far can you decide whether electronic discourse such as this is representative of different international forms of English, or can it in fact be described as a dialectal form in its own right? How could you categorise other forms of electronically-mediated discourse (such as phone texting, email, instant messaging, and so on) in sociolinguistic terms?

---

## C5    PERCEPTIONS OF VARIATION

All sociolinguistic variation is accompanied by the perceptions and attitudes of speakers and hearers, whether these perspectives are sub-conscious or explicit. People have strong feelings about the value of particular codes, and often these feelings are taken to such an extreme that the usage of a perceived 'low' form is regarded as a moral issue and a sign of poor character and ill cultivation. Particular features which are regarded as indicators of 'correct' usage are called **shibboleths**, from the biblical story of the war between the Gileadites and the Ephraimites. The word *shibboleth*, in ancient Hebrew, means an 'ear of grain', but the Ephraimites did not have the initial /ʃ/ in their phonological system. In order to root out refugees, the Gileadites stopped people trying to cross the river Jordan and made them say the word. Those who could not pronounce it as a Gileadite instantly became one of the 40,000 killed as enemies (Judges 12: 5–6).

Most modern languages have shibboleths that arouse irrationally strong reactions in many people. Though a sociolinguist knows better than to participate in these prejudices, the fact that people act upon their feelings has a sociolinguistic impact in its own right, and this phenomenon then becomes of interest.

## Some non-standard usages

The following are all examples I have recently collected. Every one of these features is regularly denounced in newspaper letters pages for being 'incorrect' English. Can you decide what people see as being 'wrong' in each case?

a   10 items or less (Marks & Spencer)
b   We was just doing us job (Nottingham Council worker on local TV news)
c   We have much to thank the government for (Prof. Ron Carter in an article on Standard English)
d   CVs should be included with application forms (university job application rubric)
e   Just along on the left you will pass a dilapidated wooden shed (North Yorkshire Moors walking guide)
f   Just meet with him and talk with him and try to resolve it (Agony aunt on *This Morning* TV magazine programme)
g   To boldly go where no one has gone before (*Star Trek*)
h   The data is presented in tabular form (student's sociolinguistics essay)
i   Hopefully the box office will be open when we get there (overheard on London bus)
j   Look at it's tail! (sign on exhibit, Nottingham Castle museum)
k   The Color Purple (UCI cinema, Preston)
l   Come on down! (Chris Tarrant, *Who Wants to be a Millionaire?* TV programme)
m   I ain't never done it, Miss (Sheffield schoolchild)
n   If I was rich, I'd still do the lottery (old man in Birmingham newsagent)
o   Donuts (sign at Goose Fair, Nottingham)
p   The crowd are literally glued to their seats (John Motson, football commentator)
q   Six cours'es for £5 (Yorkshire pub sign)
r   FRESH HEN EEGS (notice by a farm next-door to the pub in *q*).

## Some observations

a   So many people complained to the shop that this should read '10 items or fewer' (since 'items' is a count noun) that M&S changed all their signs.

b   This verb agreement and possessive pronoun are non-standard, but are certainly grammatically correct Nottingham dialect, and it would be odd for the man to express himself in Standard English in context.

c   This is the last line of the article, and it ends a sentence with a preposition, something Bishop Lowth prohibited in the eighteenth century by analogy with Latin. Of course, Professor Carter knows this and is being deliberately mischievous. Winston Churchill lampooned the syntactic knots the rule could cause in declaring, 'This is the sort of pedantry up with which we will not put!'

d   Strictly speaking, CV abbreviates the Latin 'curriculum vitae', and so it should not take the plural '-s' suffix which is part of the English morphological system. Applicants could only hope that the pedant who pointed this out was not on the interview panel. Many foreign-language loan-words are anglicised in their plural form: 'schemas', 'agendas', 'hippos', 'corpuses', and (as the same Prof. Carter in *c* insists) computer 'mouses'.

e   The Latin root of 'dilapidated' comes from *lapis* for 'stone', so, strictly, a *wooden* shed cannot be dilapidated. Similarly, 'companion' (*com panis*) should only be someone with whom you share bread. And you should only 'consider' (*con sideris*) if you are astrologically-minded 'with the planets'. There comes a point, of course, when etymologies are so buried that only an etymologist should be interested in them.

f   The preposition 'with' used twice here is often seen as an 'Americanism'. The speaker is actually a British woman from County Durham. However, the added preposition conveys a greater sense of sharing and participation than is appropriate in this context. This idiomatic phrase is rapidly becoming more popular.

g   This is the most famous 'split infinitive' in history (another of Bishop Lowth's prohibitions, on the grounds that infinitives cannot be split in Latin). However, the alternatives ('Boldly to go . . .', 'To go boldly . . .') sound much more clumsy and destroy the powerful rhythm of the iambic pentameter.

h   The word 'data' is the plural of 'datum' so the verb-agreement does not match. However, 'data is . . .' sounds perfectly fine to a lot of people, and it seems likely that this will become the standard 'correct' usage.

i   Within an old-fashioned view of sentence grammar, the adverb 'hopefully' cannot attach to 'the box-office' since box-offices cannot be hopeful. Of course, what the speaker is doing is using 'hopefully' as a sort of pragmatic adverb to attach to her own hopes. The sentence means 'I am hopeful that . . .'

j   The possessive apostrophe is not used with 'it', since it is a remnant of the Anglo-Saxon genitive (possessive) case ending and 'it' only appeared in English much later. There are more mis-uses of the possessive apostrophe than any other part of the language, and correct usage is now so confused that we would all be better off if no one used it at all. In fact, possession is usually very clear in context and the feature is largely redundant.

k   This, of course, is the American spelling of the American film from the American novel. Noah Webster was largely responsible for adjusting many American spellings ('plow, ax, thru, nite, tire, humor, defense', and so on) – which are denounced as 'Americanisms' in certain conservative British newspapers. Many American forms, though, are becoming standard in Britain ('jail' rather than 'gaol'; 'spark-plug' for 'sparking plug'; and a computer 'program' routinely uses the US spelling).

l   Another American prepositional variant, instead of the more traditional British 'Come down', though appropriate in the context of a glitzy quiz show.

m   The child uses his vernacular non-standard verb 'to be' and employs grammatically correct negative concord. The latter is disparaged as illogical (by ridiculous analogy with maths where 'two negatives make a positive') rather than being emphatic. 'Aint' (pronounced /ænt/) was the standard negative form of the copula ('to be') and verb 'to have' until it was argued away by ignorant schoolteachers in the 1890s.

n   Since an unrealised speculation is involved, the verb form should be in the **subjunctive mood**: 'If I were rich'. Nowadays, so few people understand or require the subjunctive in English that it only remains in frozen forms such as 'If I were you . . .'. It seems to me highly likely that it will disappear entirely in British English.

o   This American spelling is fast becoming the standard form instead of 'doughnut'. An examination of national British newspapers suggests similar shifts are happening to 'swap/swop', 'jewellery/jewelry' and 'judgement/judgment', to add to those listed in k above.

p   This non-literal use of the word 'literally' is often lampooned. However, Motson is following common usage in using the adverb as an emphatic marker of a figurative idiom, in order to enliven a dead metaphor. The sentence means roughly the same as, 'The crowd are really glued to their seats here!'

q   Another example of confusion of the historical usage of the possessive apostrophe. The writer obviously knows that it should be used somewhere near an 's', but would be better overall if they just stopped using it altogether.

r   This is the most spectacular example of non-standard spelling I have seen. I know it was not a one-off error, since it was repeated on another hand-drawn notice further down the road. Even so, there is no communicative problem here, though I never called in to see if they really were selling eegs.


## Working like a canine in translation

The following interview with Madonna was conducted in English while she was in Hungary filming *Evita*. It was then translated into Hungarian and published in the magazine *Blikk*, and then translated back into English. This version appeared in *The Daily Mail* (Thursday May 16th, 1996):

Blikk:      Madonna, Budapest says hello with arms that are spread-eagled. Are you in good odour? You are the biggest fan of our young people who hear your musical productions and like to move their bodies in response.

Madonna:  Thank you for saying these compliments. Stop with taking sensationalist photographs until I have removed my garments for all to see. This is a joke I have made.

Blikk:      Let's cut towards the hunt. Are you a bold hussy woman that feasts on men who are tops?

Madonna:    This is certainly something which brings to the surface my longings. In America it is not considered to be mentally ill when a woman advances on her prey in a disco setting with hardy cocktails present. And there is a more normal attitude towards leather play toys that also makes my day.

Blikk:      Is this how you met Carlos, your love servant who is reputed? Did you know he was heaven sent right off the stick? Or were you dating many other people in your bed at the same time?

Madonna:    No, he was the only one in my bed then so it is a scientific fact that the baby was made in my womb using him. But as regards these questions, enough. I am a woman not a test mouse. Carlos is an everyday person who is in the orbit of a star who is being muscle-trained by him, not a sex machine.

Blikk:      May we talk about your other 'baby', your movie. Do not be denying the similarities between you and the real Evita are grounded in basis. Power, money, tasty food and Grammys – all these elements are afoot.

Madonna:    What is up in the air with you? Evita was never winning a Grammy.

Blikk:      Perhaps not. But as to your film, in trying to bring your reputation along a rocky road, can you make people forget the bad explosions of Who's That Girl and Shanghai Surprise?

Madonna:    I am a tip-top starlet. That is something I am paid to do.

Blikk:      OK. Here is a question from left space. What was your book Slut about?

Madonna:    It was called Sex.

Blikk:      Not in Hungary. Here it was called Slut. How did it come to publish? Were you lovemaking with a man-about-town printer? Do you prefer making suggestive literature to fast selling CDs?

Madonna:    These are different facets to my career highway. I am preferring to become respected all over the map as a 100 per cent artist.

Blikk:      How many Hungarian men have you dated in bed. How are they comparing to Argentine men who are famous for being tip-top?

Madonna:    To avoid aggravated global tension, I would say it is a tie. See here, I am working like a canine all the way around my clock. I have been too busy even to try the goulash that makes your country one for the record books.

Most of the miscues that give this text its special flavour are a result of mismatched idioms and register, as well as direct translations of Hungarian grammar. Try to translate it back into the fluent English that Madonna might recognise as her own words. Can you work out for each alteration what has gone wrong and what difference the shift in choice of register would make? The passage illustrates how much of our everyday talk consists of idioms and formulaic phrases. Though some journalists bemoan the use of clichés in everyday speech, in fact genuinely creative and innovative speech would mark out the speaker as being very odd indeed.

## PRESTIGE

As a result of their colonial history, the main European languages have influenced the speech of millions of people around the world. English, Spanish, Portuguese, French, Dutch, Italian and German exist in a range of varieties. The histories of the native countries of these languages have largely been ones of suppressing the other indigenous languages, either by official prohibition (Basque in Spain and France) or by official indifference and lack of support (Scots/Lallans and Cornish/Kernewek in the UK). The status of these languages is a consequence of their history of stigmatisation. In this section, several brief case-studies of minority European languages are given (using data from *Contact*, the journal of the European Bureau for Lesser Used Languages). You could investigate these further, and evaluate their prestige value and the language loyalty felt by their speakers, using Bell's criteria (set out in detail in A6):

❑  standardisation
❑  vitality
❑  historicity
❑  autonomy
❑  reduction
❑  mixture
❑  'unofficial' norms.

### Some European linguistic minorities

#### Scots/Lallans

Scots is the modern English descendant of the Old English Northumbrian dialect, now spoken in southern Scotland. About 80 per cent of Scotland's 6 million population have access to it, and it is a vernacular for many. It is under extreme pressure of standardisation from Standard English, though there is a Scottish National Dictionary and a version of the New Testament of the Bible in Scots. It is mostly encountered in written form in the poetry of Robbie Burns, Hugh McDiarmid and Tom Leonard. The migration of Scots speakers to the province of Ulster in Northern Ireland was the basis for the local variant of Ulster Scots, now recognised as a dialect in its own right and sometimes by analogy called 'Ullans'.

Scots, unsurprisingly, has a number of loan-words from Gaelic (see below). The legal and education systems have remained distinct from the conventions in England and Wales, and many Scots words from these domains have moved into British

English in general. Scots itself can be decomposed into several broad dialects. Ulster Scots is one; 'the Doric', spoken towards the north of the country; a central dialect; the 'Border Tongue' in the south; and 'Insular Scots' in the Western islands when Gaelic is not being spoken, in the Orkneys and Shetland.

### Cornish/Kernewek

Cornish is a Celtic language with no surviving native speakers (the last died 200 years ago), though there were 40,000 speakers at the time of the Norman Conquest in the eleventh century. The Cornish Language Fellowship claims that 400 people speak the language fluently, with a further 5,000 having a working knowledge. However, it is evident mainly only in written form in place-names and geographical features, and it survives only as a learnt second language. It is possible to take school examinations in Cornish, and although there is no regional Cornish-language newspaper, a learner's magazine *An Gannas* is circulated. The language has no legal or official status in Britain, though the European Union recognised it formally in 2002. This recognition and financial support has meant that written Cornish has become very visible in the last few years: signage, leaflets, radio broadcasts and columns in local English-language newspapers can now be seen in Cornish. Numerous committees, boards and panels promote the language.

Cornish is related to the Gaelic languages of Welsh and Breton (separate from the other branch of Scottish, Irish Gaelic and Manx), and it shares four-fifths of its vocabulary with them. Several attempts at codification were made throughout the twentieth century, largely by Cornish linguists; all of them were based on an extra-polation of a particular historical moment of Cornish development and placed an emphasis on establishing a written standard for spellings. Sometimes people speak of the dialects of Cornish, but there is little regional variation: instead, these dialects refer to the different revised forms promoted by linguists.

### Welsh/Cymraeg

Around 20 per cent of Wales' 3 million population speak the Celtic language of Welsh, almost all of them as bilingual Welsh/English speakers. Welsh was largely kept alive against encroaching English from the east by its non-conformist religious tradition, a version of the Bible in Welsh, and the success of the Circulating Schools. After centuries of suppression and prohibition, the Welsh Courts Act (1942) and the Welsh Language Acts (1967 and 1993) provided for official recognition of Welsh. Some local councils operate a policy of bilingualism in administration, and all official documents and public notices are produced bilingually. Since 1998, the new Welsh Assembly recognises both English and Welsh as official languages. A predominantly Welsh television channel (Sianel Pedwar Cymru), radio station (Radio Cymru), a strong nationalist political party (Plaid Cymru), several newspapers and magazines and community newspapers (papurau bro) have supported the language recently. School examinations can be taken in Welsh as a subject, and in other subjects through the medium of Welsh. The language is now compulsory for all schoolchildren in Wales.

There are broad dialectal differences between the Welsh language spoken in the north of the country (*Gog*, from the word *gogledd*, meaning 'north') and in the south

(*Hwntw*, 'those over there'), though there are many more local pronunciation variations. There is also a broad division between rural areas (where Welsh-speaking is most concentrated) and the larger urban centres (where the highest number of monolingual English speakers can be found). There is a small Welsh-speaking community in Patagonia in southern Argentina.

### Scottish Gaelic/Gaidhlig

This Celtic language is spoken by up to 80 per cent of the population of the Outer Hebrides, with fewer speakers in the islands of the Inner Hebrides and nearby mainland, as well as an exile community in the Glasgow area. In total, around 2 per cent of the Scottish population speak Gaelic fluently. It is not used officially either in the Scottish Parliament nor in routine government publications, and is not exclusively associated with Scottish nationalist politics. However, a sort of semi-official status has been conferred by the Gaelic Language (Scotland) Act 2005, which was passed unanimously by the new Scottish Parliament, and the language is used commonly in the local government proceedings of the western isles. In the Gaelic-speaking areas, bilingual school provision exists, and there are also bilingual schools in Glasgow and Inverness. A variety of radio stations broadcast mainly to the islands and highlands in Gaelic, and there is a children's language programme, 'Ceredigion', but no large circulation newspaper.

Scottish Gaelic and Irish Gaelic (see below) used to be linked through a dialect continuum across the narrow strip of sea separating Argyll and Ulster: the coastal communities on each side speaking a similar variety of the language. However, with Scots Gaelic pushed out of the south of Scotland and both Standard English and Scots English (Lallans – see above) pushing Irish Gaelic out of Ulster, this dialect mixing no longer exists.

### Irish/Gaeilge

Around a third of the population of the Republic of Ireland can speak Gaelic, with a further 60,000 Gaelic speakers reported in Northern Ireland. However, for many of these people, Gaelic is a poor L2 or an aspiration. Vernacular Gaelic speakers are mainly restricted to the Gaeltacht areas of the north-west and west, and a part of County Louth in the east. There are probably around 70,000 fluent speakers of Gaelic as a vernacular. (There is also a Gaelic-speaking community in Cape Breton Island in eastern Canada.) Officially, Irish Gaelic is the 'national language' and 'first official language', with English being the 'second official language'. In practice, most administration and publication is conducted in English and subsequently translated into Irish, though a facility in Irish is an advantage for civil servants and university staff. and regional radio. Irish Gaelic is a treaty language of the European Union, and so all executive and parliamentary documents appear in it.

The Bord na Gaeilge promotes Irish across Ireland, but especially in the west. Only about 2 per cent of the state television (RTE) output is regularly in Irish, though there is an Irish-language channel. Broadly there are three dialect areas: Munster, Connacht and Ulster (the last of which includes County Donegal in the Irish Republic as well as the counties making up the province of Northern Ireland. In the Gaeltacht areas of the west, a government order in 2004 dictated that all place-name signs must be in Gaelic, which has caused controversy since these areas are the most popular tourist destinations in the country.

### Basque/Euskara

The territory of the 'Basque Country' is defined largely by the presence of Basque speakers: Euskal Herria. It straddles the border of Spain and France. In the Spanish-governed area, Basque is now an official language, with 700,000 speakers. All of these are bi- or multilingual in Basque, Spanish and French. The language is pre-Indo-European and is not related to any other European language. Basque has only been allowed to be taught for the last 20 years. Prior to that it was suppressed under General Franco, with schoolteachers punishing children caught speaking their vernacular. Regional radio, television, and a daily newspaper *Gara*, as well as a number of both parliamentary and extremist political parties support the use of Basque as part of a campaign for independence from Spain (and France).

Basque is now a co-official language in the Basque country. There are six identifiable dialects, two of which cross the Pyrenees into France, though the fragmented geology of the area has led to micro-dialectal variations between valleys that were relatively isolated until modern communications. 'Batua' (meaning 'unified') has been adopted as a standard in practice, based on the Guipuzkoan dialect.

### Galician

The area of Galicia in north-west Spain contains a population with 80 per cent speakers of Galician. This is a Latin language closer to Portuguese than Spanish. Up until the 1930s, there was a strong development of Galician literature, but the language was suppressed under Franco and Spanish imposed on administration, education, the media and the Church. More recently it has again become the permitted common language of the area.

### Catalan

Spoken by 60 per cent of the population of Catalonia along the eastern coast and Balearic islands of Spain, Catalan is also understood by a further 20 per cent of the people. After suppression under Franco, it has since been recognised as an official language of the region alongside Spanish, in line with the political process of 'linguistic normalisation'. This has meant that administration in the region is bilingual. There is a Catalan television channel, and several local radio stations and newspapers, though Spanish remains the dominant force in the mass media and in schools.

### Luxembourgeois

This variety of German – Moselle Frankish or Luxembourgeois – is the vernacular language of the independent Grand Duchy of Luxembourg (population just under 400,000), as well as of the area around Arlon/Arel in Belgium, the Germanic part of the French Moselle, and areas in Germany around Bitburg and Plum (totalling a further 40,000 speakers). In Luxembourg itself, the language is encouraged though French is the official language of written administration, and German dominates in newspapers and magazines. Most of the population is therefore trilingual.

### Frisian

Spoken as a vernacular by 60 per cent of the 600,000 population of Friesland, Frisian is the official second language of the Netherlands. After centuries of standardisation pressure from Dutch, it is now compulsorily taught in primary schools. It is not broadcast on television except as a curiosity, though there are Frisian 'slots' on local radio and news bulletins given hourly in the language. Only about 5 per cent of the content of the two regional newspapers is in Frisian. The scientific journal of the Frisian Academy has half its articles in the language.

There are many other minority languages and dialects in Europe: Friuli, Ladin, Occitan, Sardinian, Franco-Provençal, Slovene and Romany just within the borders of Italy, for example. Try to apply a measurement of prestige and status to these and to local dialects that you know. Notice, too, that the sense of prestige and value of a code varies depending on which group is making the evaluation.

You could try to find out as much as you can about these languages, their structure and origins, as well as their sociolinguistic situation. Modern communication technology and international infrastructure are reducing the number of languages in the world. Using the evidence from European minority languages, you could discuss the processes involved in **language death** and decide what you might do if you wanted to preserve a language.

## GENDER

C7

### Writing gender

The following is taken from the leaflet *On Balance: Guidelines for the Representation of Women and Men in English Language Teaching Materials*, produced by the group 'Women in EFL Materials' in 1991:

These guidelines have been compiled as a reminder to people involved in all aspects of ELT publishing to be aware of discriminatory language and stereotypical images and, wherever possible, to use inclusive language and images which reflect a more balanced and accurate view of the world and of the present state of English [. . .]

*Avoiding stereotypes*
Much can be done to *avoid* presenting people in a stereotyped way. [. . .]

*Character*
Are both women and men shown in texts, dialogues, recordings and illustrations:

– being bold and assertive?
– being weak, vulnerable or scared?
– instructing, leading, rescuing?
– being instructed, led, rescued?

- displaying self-control?
- responding emotionally?
- being strong, capable and logical?
- being uncertain and in need of reassurance?
- being powerful and able to deal with problems?
- being inept and defeated by problems?
- belonging to a range of emotional types?
- starting dialogues?
- making arrangements?

[. . .]

*Women in language*

As with stereotypes, language which excludes women can be dealt with 1) by avoiding its use and 2) by dealing sensitively with exclusive language that comes up in, for example, authentic recordings. In the second case it is often enough to suggest that teachers point out that a particular usage may offend many women, and to ensure that other authentic recordings demonstrate inclusive language.

*False generics*

Studies of native English-speaking college students and school children have shown that the generic use of words like *man* (ostensibly to include all humans), does not elicit mental images of both sexes. [. . .]

*Avoiding false generic 'man'*

| *Instead of* | *Use* |
| --- | --- |
| mankind | people, humans, humanity |
| manpower | work force, staff |
| man-made | artificial, synthetic, manufactured |
| man-to-man | person-to-person |
| prehistoric man | prehistoric people |
| manned by | staffed by |

[. . .]

*Instead of generic* *Use*

| businessman | executive |
| --- | --- |
| cameraman | camera operator |
| chairman | chairperson, chair |
| fireman | fire fighter |
| foreman | supervisor |
| policeman | police officer |
| statesman | leader, politician |

The leaflet goes on to give guidelines on how to avoid the false generic 'he', advises not using female diminutives in job titles ('actress, manageress, poetess'), and suggests appropriate situations for using 'girl' and 'lady'.

You will probably not have to look too far in newspaper and magazine articles, and especially in advertising language to find examples of such non-PC language. (Note that PC – 'political correctness' – was a term originally coined by right-wing commentators in America to refer scornfully to the efforts of some people to avoid being racist and sexist). Do you think that such prescriptivist interventions in language are justified? Is gender stereotyping more prevalent in certain texts and discourse situations?

## A mixed-sex argument

The following transcript is taken from Sharlene Goff's data (see B10). It records a discussion between two men and two women who are all friends:

Q:    do you have strong opinions on fox-hunting?

F1:   yeah I do. I'm for it – but you all know that anyway

Q:    why?

F1:   why? because – the foxes need – to be killed because they destroy other animals
     [and   ]

F2:   [but.  ] can they not be killed in a more humane way?=

F1:   like=

F2:   than by chasing them and making a sport of it

F1:   but –  [yeah  ]

M1:          [no    ]

F1:   I can see that point that they're making  [a sport  ] of it – I *can* see your point but→

F2:                              [yeah    ]

F1:   ←otherwise it's not – mmm – you've *still* got to kill them – it's statistically proven that fox-hunting is the best way to kill them. I mean – shooting – how can they ever find them?

M1:   poisoning them you kill the wildlife as well

F1:   yeah. gassing is just hideous=

F2:   I know but – I can't understand how you can go and think I'm gonna enjoy [myself –      ] I can see the whole sport of it and I see can the – mmm→

M1:   [yeah definitely]

F2:   ←dragging thing=

F1:   drag hunting. yeah=

F2:   yeah I can see that and I know that's different but – I just can't see how you can enjoy going out and doing something you *know* is going to hurt something so much

F1:   yeah definitely – and I understand that but what *I'm* saying is that it is a [necessity –      ] it's like shooting fishing. anything→

M1:   [it is a necessity but=]

F1:   ←like that

M1:   yeah but basically you're saying they're vermin and you need to get rid of them like rats you don't glamourise rat-hunting [and get out your    ] poncy red coats→

F1:                                             [no of course you don't]

M1:   ←and black hats to do it – so I think it's a necessity but they go about it in entirely the wrong way. glamourising it

F2:   [yeah  ]

F1:   [mmm   ] but it has been a tradition for hundreds and hundreds of years

F2:   tradition can't be kept up just because it's tradition
when.  [when it's – like                        ] inhumane

M2:              [it can be kept up just for tradition's sake  ]

M1:   [what. like the monarchy?   ]

M2:   [of course it can           ]

F1:   yeah. like the monarchy

M2:   yeah

M1   yeah but like a monarchy that rules everything cos traditions are there to be changed for the better=

F2:   yeah

M1:   you know what I mean. we=

F2:   we're trying to change society to make it better

M2:   it's people like you who live in towns that come in  [and you just don't know  ] you→

M1:                                                  [no no no
        ]

M2:   ←you just  [don't understand   ]

M1:               [no I'm an *advoc*    ]ate of fox-hunting I'm an *advocate* of it=

F1:   and also=

M1:   I honestly am but I. think they go about it the wrong way=

F1:   and also. if you take away the whole sport around it which I can see is wrong. you're also taking away a lot of employment=

F2:   I don't agree with that=

M1:   okay okay okay. people are from. you know. going to watch bear-fighting cock-fighting. shit like that. pitbull-fighting. shit like that. you don't glamourise stuff and say come and see this do you know what I mean – you don't say come and see hounds tearing apart a fox you shouldn't need to do that. you shouldn't need to glamourise=

M2:   it shouldn't be glamourised=

M1:   they shouldn't glamourise it

M2:   it shouldn't. no

Can you characterise the language and discourse strategies of these participants along gender lines? You might like to compare this transcript with those reproduced in B10, and any of your own recorded discussions, to see if you can come to any conclusions about gendered discourse in spoken language.

You could set up your own recording of gendered discourse and try to identify different discourse patterns practised by women and men. Do you find any evidence of **accommodation** between the participants? Could you devise a study that aimed to discover whether gender difference varies with age?

Can you apply the recommendations from the *On Balance* guidelines above to the style in which this book is written? Have I avoided gender-stereotyping? Do the transcripts of real language use in this book present men and women along the lines set out under 'character' in the guidelines? Can you find examples of other texts which break these aspirations? It is easy to find newspaper and advertising language that presents a cartoon-like image of men and women, but what about recipes, car manuals, computer manuals, nightclub flyers, music lyrics and reviews, and other texts?

## CREOLE

Collecting examples of pidgin and creole if you do not live in an area where it is used is not necessarily as difficult as you might think. There is a mass of published resources on the internet, and of course you can find communities who use Patwa, creolised African-American English, or pidginised aboriginal languages in Britain, America and Australia too. For example, my student Hamish Crombie was able to investigate the identification of Afro-Caribbean teenagers in Nottingham with Patwa-based song lyrics played in his local club. He noticed the code-switch by his local kebab-seller, which he transcribes as follows (non-phonetically):

| | |
|---|---|
| To Hamish: | would y'like some chilli sauce wit' dat. it's pretty dry |
| To a black customer: | WILLY – wan sam sauce onit or ya wantit drai |

Joel Dothie revisited Labov's studies into African-American English and used Milroy's notion of social networks to re-interpret his data. Hannah Neale used the published work on Jamaican Creole and Tok Pisin, a creole used in Papua New Guinea, to try to identify common processes of lexical formation. All of these are examples of secondary analysis: they take a published study and explore its data using a different perspective.

### A crash course in Tok Pisin

Papua New Guinea contains over 800 languages, with three forms of common contact:

- English – used in writing and for international business communication
- Hiri Motu (Police Motu) – used around Port Moresby, a pidgin spread by Sir William MacGregor's police force in the late nineteenth century
- Tok Pisin (Neo-Melanesian) – a creolised language used in speech and writing, in the process of standardisation and codification.

The features of Tok Pisin include:

- ❑ consonant assimilation: so no distinction is made between /p/f/, /g/k/, or /s/ʃ/tʃ/.
- ❑ simplified consonant clusters ('sol' = salt, 'kol' = cold, 'sikis' = six)
- ❑ few vowel categories: Tok Pisin uses /a, e, i, o, u/ for all vowel sounds
- ❑ reduplication for emphasis ('look' = look, 'looklook' = stare)

- ❑ two forms of 'we': 'mipela' = I and others not here, 'yumi' = I and others here
- ❑ plural suffix '-pela'
- ❑ English-based lexicon ('bagarap' = break/destroy, 'hangre' = hungry)
- ❑ Local borrowings in lexicon (Polynesian 'kaikai' = food, Malay 'susu' = milk)
- ❑ compounding in word-formation ('plantihan' = plenty hands: centipede, 'pikinini pik' = piglet)
- ❑ metaphor in word-formation ('haus pepa' = house paper: office, 'haus bilong spaida' = spider's house: web)
- ❑ circumlocution ('singsing bilong haus lotu' (worship) = hymn)
- ❑ three basic prepositions: 'long' (to, for, from), 'bilong' (of), 'wantaim' (with)
- ❑ tense markers by auxiliary: 'bin' (past), 'baimbai' or 'bai' (future)

## A short story

This is a story for children (which has drawings accompanying the original) in Tok Pisin. Try to translate it into Standard English without looking at the gloss below it.

> *I am a crocodile*
> by Steve Simpson
>
> Mi wanpela pukpuk.
> Mi hangre nogut tru.
> Ooo, mi laik kaikai pis. Swit moa!
>
> Mi laik kaikai kuka.
> Em tu swit moa.
>
> Narapela samting mi laik kaikai, em pik!
> Mi laik gris bilong pik tumas. Em swit moa!
>
> Rokrok, i namba wan! Mi laik kaikai rokrok nau tasol.
> Na em swit moa yet!
>
> Olaman! Mi laik kaikai trausel ya! I gutpela tumas. Na em swit moa yet!
>
> Dok tu em i gutpela tru. Mi laik kaikai dok tude! Swit moa ya!
>
> Na, wanem samting moa mi laik kaikai?
>
> YU YET!
>
> *(British English version)*
> I am a crocodile.
> I am very, very hungry.
>
> I like to eat fish. Mmm . . . good (very sweet)!
>
> I like crabs.
> They are yummy (very sweet)!
>
> Another thing I like eating is pig!
> I like the flavour (grease) a lot. It is very sweet!

Frogs are excellent! I like eating frogs right now!
They are even sweeter!

Wow! I like eating turtles! They are wonderful. They are even sweeter!

Dogs are good too. I would like to eat a dog today! Mmmm . . .!

And what else would I like to eat?

YOU!

## The mountain burns

The following are the lyrics of a song by Panim Wok Band, composed just before a volcanic eruption destroyed the town of Rabaul in Papua New Guinea in 1994.

*Mounten ipaiya*

Hey yumi no save bai yumi go we
Sapos-mountain paiya bai ipairap
Hey yumi no sawe bai yumi laip yet,
Sapos-maunten paiya bai ipairap

Mi no laik lusim peles bilong mi
Mi no laik stap long narapela hap
Mi laik stap yee et long Rabaul

Mi no laik lusim peles bilong mi
Mi no laik stap long narapela hap
Mi laik stap yee et long Rabaul

(Chorus)

Mi no laik Rabaul taun bai ibagarap
Mi no laik stap long narapela hap
Mi laik stap yee et long Rabaul (twice)

(Chorus)

Mi no laik lusim peles bilong mi
Mi laik stap long narapela hap
Mi laik kam bek long Rabaul

Mi no laik Rabaul taun bai ibagarap
Mi no laik stap long narapela hap
Mi laik kam bek long Rabaul
Mi laik stap yee et long Rabaul
Mi laik stap yee et long Rabaul

From the examples of Tok Pisin given above, try to discern features of the creole that you know. You could search for further examples of the language by visiting Melanesian newspaper and company webpages online.

## C9    NEW ENGLISH

### Indian English news

The following is a report from the front page of the Calcutta *Telegraph* (Wednesday 8th January, 1997). It covers the visit of the then UK Prime Minister John Major to India. The visit was a target for various Indian protestors, including the Naxalites, a socialist movement associated with violent protest across the country.

*Sorry, no fish 'n chips for Mr John Major*
by Meher Murshed and Shona Bagai

Calcutta, Jan. 7: Mr John Major may have to do without his fish and chips, for chefs at Taj Bengal firmly believe that made-in-India *kebabs* are better than those grilled in the UK.

And they feel the British Prime Minister's visit will not be complete unless he tastes the roasted delicacy.

Mr Major will be staying at the Taj during his brief visit to the city.

He, however, will not dine at the hotel. He will be lunching with the Prime Minister, Mr H.D. Deve Gowda, at Raj Bhavan, while dinner will be hosted in his honour at Tollygunge Club.

But chefs at the Taj cannot breathe easy. They only have a day to sharpen their skills. For, the hotel will be catering at Raj Bhavan and Tolly.

Mr Major shall have one meal at the hotel – breakfast.

The general manager of Taj Bengal, Ms Shireen Batlivala, said, 'We have not decided on a specific menu for him in the morning. He shall be served what he asks for.'

Ms Batlivala said the focus at the Raj Bhavan lunch would be on Indian curries. Curry powder, obviously, is a big no-no with the chefs.

But there is bad news for those whose palates do not fancy a spicy meal. There will be no continental dishes, no bland fare for people with delicate alimentary canals.

'The Prime Minister's Office in New Delhi has approved of the menu for lunch. There is no going back now,' Ms Batlivala pointed out. [. . .]

Delegates and the British Prime Minister could choose from three kinds of cuisine during dinner at Tollygunge Club. Taj officials said there would be French, Italian and Indian dishes. And, this time, some would be bland too.

The managing member of Tolly Club, Mr Bob Wright, said the meal would be grand, but did not give further details.

'We promise to look after him well,' he said. But would there be fish and chips? Mr Wright just guffawed.

*Security beefed up for visit*

Calcutta, Jan. 7: The state law enforcement machinery slipped into high gear today in the face of sporadic protests against the British Prime Minister, Mr John Major's visit to the city, beginning on Thursday, says our staff reporter.

The city police were on their toes today with Naxalites burning Mr Major's effigy and hawkers demonstrating outside the British Deputy High Commission.

[A photograph of the demonstrators appeared here, holding the burning effigy with the sign 'John Major Go Back' attached].

In general, written Indian English is characterised by:

❑ particular words that have local reference and specific cultural meaning
❑ specific idiomatic phrases that are not commonly used in other English varieties
❑ a choice of register that would seem very formal or conservative in a British or American context
❑ a form of address that might appear more polite than in the UK/USA.

*The Telegraph* is a serious, quality broadsheet, and includes this gently humorous report alongside other national and international political news. Perhaps because of the intended tone, the features of Indian English which appear are more prominent than with these other reports. Try to identify all the features of the article that you would not find in a British, American, or Australian press report. Look especially for constructions that would seem to be register-mixing in these other cultures, but which are acceptable in Indian English.

### Japanese English news
The following is a collection of headlines and story-extracts from the English-language *Asahi Evening News* (Monday 22nd May, 2000), published in Tokyo:

A former gardener confessed to lacing a soft drink with an agricultural pesticide in a revenge attack for being fired, police said Sunday.

Kunitake Ando, who will become president of Sony Corp., says Nobuyuki Idei will remain the top leader.

Emperor, empress tour Geneva suburb.

9 hurt by schoolyard twister.

Love is in the air for soon-free Keiko [the killer whale].

Sherpa slams Everest record [in the sense of 'breaking' or 'smashing' it].

Chen offers China big door to talks.

Labor and the China vote.

School-police links aim to nip problems in the bud.

Cops and teachers used to rarely cross tracks. Now, though, with children's behavior a mounting concern, that gulf is being bridged in a variety of constructive ways.

Airline cargo hold absolutely no place for an much-loved pet.

TV & Radio/Comics [meaning 'cartoons']

'We expected them to own the ball more. The Marinos have many talented players' [. . .] 'It's a good thing (Yoo) Sang Chul wasn't playing. Otherwise they would have figured us out.'

Miyabiyama's rise to ozeki in 12 tourneys since first stepping into the dohyo as a professional equals the fastest promotion since the start of the Showa Era in 1926.

Arden Yamanaka Beauty Salon. US Licensed Beauty Operator. Personalized hair-styling, haircoloring, frosting, permanent waving, manicuring, pedicuring, electrolysis, waxing, etc. Please call Hibiya Park Bldg.

Hiroo: 1 bedroom apartment, ¥220.000, 2 bedroom apartment with washing modern, dryer, refrigerator.

Seijo: Near station, residencile area, 4 bedroom house, 2 bathrooms, power room, living room, dining room, parking, ¥470,000.

Eda (Oimachi Line): 4 bedrooms, German School convenience, few steps to station, large living room, tatami room, greenery area, ¥550,000.

In collecting these, I have excluded items reprinted from international news agencies; nevertheless, even in calling these 'wire reports', the newspaper further illustrates the high level of influence from American English in its usage. Every example above seems to me (a native British English speaker) to be idiomatically non-British English. Many examples (such as narrating an event and adding 'Sunday' rather than 'on Sunday', listing participants in a headline 'Emperor, empress' without adding 'and', and American spelling forms) are common to those used by American reporters and television news presenters. Other examples simply seem to represent interference from the local indigenous language, Japanese. Try to identify all of these features. Out of your list, can you generalise some of the features of Japanese English, or at least the register of newspapers in this L2 English?

---

**POLITENESS**

### (Im)politeness

In order to illustrate the reality of very subtle phatic norms, I sent out some of my sociolinguistics students one week with instructions to break the expected conversational norms in specific ways. Some of these follow, with the actual consequences. For each, decide which social expectation of politeness or phatics has been deviated from, and explain the consequence.

*(At a bus stop)*
Stranger:  beautiful day
Student:   well no – actually. I think you'll find that there is an approaching cold front bringing heavy precipitation from the north-west. followed by high winds tonight.
Stranger:  mmm *(says nothing more, turns to face the oncoming traffic as if searching for the bus)*

*(In passing along the corridor)*
Friend:     alright?
Student:    no I've just got out of hospital. had a terrible time of it. the old problem
            playing me up again. still – mustn't grumble I suppose. I'll tell you all
            about it . . . *(and so on, and on)*
*(Friend stands for several minutes listening, nodding and making sympathetic backchannel noise.)*

*(At a supermarket checkout queue a student would pull up with a full basket and ask to go in front of people in the queue. Even though she had more items than them, on eight out of ten occasions, other people allowed her to push in. The two other occasions went as follows:)*
Person A:   what? oh. no I'm sorry I'm in a bit of rush myself and *(shrugs apologetically)*
Person B:   ey? you're joking aren't you? you've got a full basket you cheeky sod – piss off

*(Students did not make any backchannel noises during any of their telephone calls for a week. Consistently, after around 10 seconds, the other person would stop what they were saying to check whether the student was still there, and would also often ask if there was anything wrong, which the student would repeatedly deny.)*

*(Similarly, students would ask strangers for directions on the street and then listen without nodding or making any utterance or backchannel noise. The person would repeat the information unprompted several times and then ask if the student understood.)*

*(Students were able to categorise their close friends and acquaintances by asking, without any politeness tags:* 'Lend me your bike', *to see who would simply say,* 'OK'.*)*

What is non-normative, in terms of Laver's model of phatic tokens, in each of these (invented) situations? What is the effect that is consequently generated?

*(Backstage at the Royal Variety Performance I)*
Actor: By God, your Majesty, that's a terrible boil on your neck there!

*(Backstage at the Royal Variety Performance II)*
Queen: I'm completely knackered after that!

*(Someone rings your doorbell, you open the door, and the person standing there says,* 'Yes?'.*)*

*(Your bank manager begins a meeting with you by saying that his cat has just died.)*

*(Held at gunpoint by terrorists, you comment to your fellow hostage on how good the weather has been recently.)*

## Face and address

How would you appropriately ask for the following?

❑ to borrow a pen from a friend
❑ to borrow a pen from a stranger in the street
❑ to climb on to someone's roof to fetch a football
❑ to get in front of someone in a supermarket queue
❑ to borrow someone's phone on a train
❑ to borrow £10,000 from a mafia godfather.

For each, also write out the script of how *not* to do this.

How are you addressed by the following?

| | | |
|---|---|---|
| parents | brother/sister | housemate |
| lover | shopkeepers | waiters |
| train guards | bus drivers | university lecturer |
| bank statements | checkout operator | advert for a mail-order firm |
| personal computer | hospital doctor | priest |
| television chef | Radio DJs | street newspaper seller |

For each, consider the 'face' that each is trying to present, and how this is encoded by naming conventions, politeness strategies, and register. Which social factors determine the form? Consider also how you would address each of these in turn.

How would the following conversations begin? Imagine a setting and write short (2–3 line) scripts for each. Try also reversing the order of who initiates the conversation to see if this would make a difference.

❑ Teacher – pupil
❑ Teacher – person sitting next to them at a football game
❑ Teacher – referee after a bad decision
❑ Japanese businessman in Britain – woman on street giving out leaflets for a club
❑ Student – landlord/lady
❑ Beggar – passing office worker in suit
❑ Beggar – passing scruffy student
❑ Drug dealer – drug dependent
❑ Drug dealer – his dog
❑ Driver – broken down car
❑ Gardener – tomato plants
❑ Medieval baron – peasant building a wall
❑ Autograph hunter – you, falsely assumed to be someone famous
❑ Armed bank robber – you

For each, identify the pragmatic rules that are followed (or not).

### Some intimate conversations

For obvious reasons, it is very difficult to obtain naturalistic recordings of intimate style. The observer's paradox is likely to alter the speakers' language significantly, and of course there are ethical problems involved in recording – even non-covertly – intimate and private conversation. However, the following transcript appeared in many non-UK newspapers in the form set out below; it was alleged that the recording had been made by the British security services' electronic monitoring station in 1993. Examine the forms of address, and also track the phatic strategies used to try (and several times fail) to close the conversation.

Charles:  What time do they come in?
Camilla:  Well usually Tom never wakes up at all, but as it's his birthday tomorrow he might just stagger out of bed. It won't be before half-past eight (pause). Night, night my darling.
Charles:  Darling.
Camilla:  I do love you.
Charles:  (sleepily) before?
Camilla:  Before about half-past eight.
Charles:  Try and ring?
Camilla:  Yeah, if you can. Love you darling.
Charles:  Night darling.
Camilla:  I love you.
Charles:  Love you too. I don't want to say goodbye.
Camilla:  Well done for doing that. You're a clever old thing. An awfully good brain lurking there, isn't there? Oh darling. I think you ought to give the brain a rest now. Night night.
Charles:  Night darling. God bless.
Camilla:  I do love you and I'm so proud of you.
Charles:  Oh, I'm so proud of you.
Camilla:  Don't be silly, I've never achieved anything.
Charles:  Yes you have.
Camilla:  No I haven't.
Charles:  Your great achievement is to love me.
Camilla:  Oh darling. Easier than falling off a chair.
Charles:  You suffer all these indignities and tortures and calumnies.
Camilla:  Oh, darling, don't be so silly. I'd suffer anything for you. That's love. It's the strength of love. Night night.
Charles:  Night, darling. Sounds as though you're dragging an enormous piece of string behind you, with hundreds of tin pots and cans attached to it. I think it must be your telephone. Night night, before the battery goes (blows kiss). Night.
Camilla:  Love you.
Charles:  Don't want to say goodbye.
Camilla:  Neither do I, but you must get some sleep. Bye.
Charles:  Bye, darling.
Camilla:  Love you.
Charles:  Bye.
Camilla:  Hopefully talk to you in the morning.
Charles:  Please.
Camilla:  Bye, I do love you.
Charles:  Night.
Camilla:  Night.

Charles:   Night.

Camilla:   Love you for ever.

Charles:   Night.

Camilla:   G'bye. Bye my darling.

Charles:   Night.

Camilla:   Night night.

Charles:   Night.

Camilla:   Bye bye

Charles:   Going

Camilla:   Bye.

Charles:   Going.

Camilla:   Gone.

Charles:   Night.

Camilla:   Bye. Press the button.

Charles:   Going to press the tit.

Camilla:   All right darling, I wish you were pressing mine.

Charles:   God, I wish I was. Harder and harder.

Camilla:   Oh darling.

Charles:   Night.

Camilla:   Night.

Charles:   Love you.

Camilla:   (yawning) Love you. Press the tit.

Charles:   Adore you. Night.

Camilla:   Night.

Charles:   Night.

Camilla:   (blows a kiss).

Charles:   Night.

Camilla:   G'night my darling. Love you.

(Charles hangs up).

You could also use the framework set out by Schegloff and Sacks in D11 to analyse this passage.

The following transcript, adapted from the Cambridge and Nottingham Corpus of Discourse in English (CANCODE), features a student couple chatting at home while cooking.

A:   well would you like to go to the castle on Friday afternoon?

B:   mm. okay

A:   cos it's free during the week

B:   yeah. yeah. cos I li – I keep on walking by it

A:   I know. I wanna go. Elizabeth went with. thing

B:   Gerry

A:   Ge- Eli- yeah.

B:   Gerry?

A:   Elizabeth went with her mum and dad

B:   yeah?

A:   erm. because you know they're staying in=

B: is it burning?

A: =a cottage somewhere. it's just something that must be on the ring. no let it boil

B: it doesn't doesn't need to be boiled. boiling

A: oh. but it says put into boiling water

B: no. does it?

A: mhm.

B: oh I don't do it that way. [singing] on top of old smoky all covered in grass a bald headed eagle

A: yeah. so. yeah she went with her mum and dad and sister

B: mm.

A: she said it's quite good but it's not like an old castle. it's not like a castle castle

B: no it's not like a castle at all

A: she said it's like a stately home or something

B: did you want any more money?

A: no. do I? no

B: thought it was twenty three.

A: was it? oh. that's a shame isn't it?

B: what?

A: just give us twenty. or are you giving us twenty?

B: mm. oh that means you've got a part share in my T Y Beanie Baby. mm. no I erm

A: your T Y Beanie Baby? this is the present that you bought for me

B: I looked at the T Y Beanie Baby website today

A: mm.

B: I might become a member of the T Y Beanie Baby group or something

A: can I not be a member?

B: yeah but it costs money. so we could join together. we could be Mr and Mrs T Y Beanie Baby – things are a cooking at the K F C – ooh look what I picked up the other day. you might be intrigued by this one. that's if I can bloody find it. now er

A: how are you feeling?

B: eh?

A: about your vitiligo. Cos I know it's you know scars peoples lives. I thought that was the thing you were going to show us. is that not the

B: eh? what are you gibbering on about?

A: you said your vitiligo you know that you picked up a leaflet about it the other day?

B: yeah

A: and you said I'm mentally and you know physically scarred

B: I just didn't say I didn't say vitiligo

A: what is it? is I'm completely wrong? what is it?

B: yeah. I said. here's something I picked up the other day. that's if I can find it

A: no I. oh never mind. I thought you were going to show me that leaflet again

B: oh right

A: because you thought you hadn't showed us it but you have showed us it. so

B:  you're tryi- now you're trying to read my mind ahead of me
A:  yeah
B:  I'm trying to show you this
A:  ooh.
B:  the best restaurants in your area as chosen by Observer readers
A:  let me guess. the Japanese restaurant
B:  is not in here
A:  is it not?
B:  no. that's because er Nottingham people obviously don't know good taste. no
    what was (   )
A:  we're going there for our Christmas meal
B:  who?
A:  the house.
B:  ohh. you see n- because as soon as I invite you, you know take you to these er
    swish places you know everyone has to copy me
A:  oh I'm sorry. did you not want me to take anyone else?
B:  no.
A:  did you want it to be special?
B:  yeah.
A:  did you really?
B:  yes
A:  I'm sorry
B:  erm right
A:  are you annoyed?
B:  no. right
A:  why not? it's meant to be a special place
B:  I know. twelve XXX road. okay?
A:  Mm
B:  is a restaurant called XXX and it is no – ((reading)) a very small intimate and
    exceptionally friendly local favourite where chef XXX XXX offers a varied menu
    with good vegetarian options from which everything is done to a turn. ((End of
    reading)) erm you can bring your own wine. sample dishes deep fried goats
    cheese which is gorgeous. (      ) of black pudding and mustard sauce. never
    had. white chocolate cheesecake. er five minutes from the Town Hall

Identify all the features that signal that this is a conversation between people who
know each other very well. The politeness and phatic features are particularly
interesting.

# E-DISCOURSE

Technological changes alter the forms that language takes. The word 'hello' did not exist as a greeting before the invention of the telephone made an 'announcing' phatic tag necessary (the word was previously only used as a hunting cry: 'halloo'). Similarly, the last couple of decades have seen a huge growth in computer-mediated communication (CMC) in the form of email, instant messaging, chatrooms, online discussion boards, and phone texting. Each of these forms has developed its own characteristic grammatical and graphological features, neither spoken nor written but partly a blend of these and partly with some new features. There is some evidence that CMC is also influencing traditional written forms of language use.

Both Miranda Chadwick and Naomi Holdstock produced detailed analyses of electronic chatroom discourse on the internet. Neither the normal patterns of writing nor the characteristic features of speech apply perfectly to this mode of discourse, leading them to the conclusion that email, electronic chat and telephone texting all represent not a 'mid-point' between speech and writing but a new, third mode of discourse.

The samples from internet discourse come from Miranda and Naomi's data, and some of my own. I now communicate with colleagues around the world far more by email than by any other form, and it is clear that I have started using a sort of 'World Standard Electronic English'. This is mainly a code of avoidance of idiomatic or culturally specific British features that I know colleagues in Japan or America would not understand. Electronic discourse operates within well-defined domains (academic discussion, teenage chat, student bulletin board, and so on); the fact that the participants share common assumptions means that it is often characterised by restricted code features (see B3, C3). My emails to British colleagues are characterised far more by a sort of restricted code, with implicit gestures to local popular culture and in-group linguistic and literary references.

## Chatroom discourse

This is a 'webcast' discussion with founder of the Cyber Angels Internet Safety Organisation, Colin Gabriel Hatcher. It is easy for you to find current chatroom language on the internet; this passage is interesting as an early (1990s) example of the form:

| Colin Gabriel Hatcher: | hi folks :) |
|---|---|
| Petal262: | err gabrielca |
| Colin Gabriel Hatcher: | lol |
| Petal262: | dang . . . can't type today . . . sorry |
| Colin Gabriel Hatcher: | I am loggin by telnet . . . ugh : / |
| Petal262: | oh . . . |
| Colin Gabriel Hatcher: | my new puter just broke down . . . power supply . . . |

| | |
|---|---|
| Petal262: | I hope you don't mind that I forwarded my invitation to Cheron . . . she is trying to connect up now. |
| Colin Gabriel Hatcher: | telnet was not made for fast chat!! |
| Colin Gabriel Hatcher: | she should have got one too |
| Petal262: | she said no . . . so I forwarded mine to her |
| Colin Gabriel Hatcher: | hmmm well she is on the list |
| Petal262: | maybe something she overlooked . . . |
| Jady: | gabriel :) |
| Colin Gabriel Hatcher: | jave/telnet reminds me why I like irc ;) |
| Petal262: | :))) |
| Petal262: | Hello Commander Morg |
| Commander Morg: | hey, just checking out what 'electronic Fronties' is . . . |
| Colin Gabriel Hatcher: | hi morg |
| Commander Morg: | oops, just realized I put another space in my name, must remember to stop doing that . . . |
| Colin Gabriel Hatcher: | its a discussion forum morg |
| Jady: | hi morg :) |
| Commander Morg: | oh, ok |
| Colin Gabriel Hatcher: | starting I believe in 10 mins |
| Commander Morg: | sorry to interrupt, where you discussing something? |
| Jady: | just waiting for it to start : 0 |
| Colin Gabriel Hatcher: | nope morg :) I was just whining about telnet |
| Petal262: | there were a couple here earlier that said they missed it by about 2 hours . . . |
| Commander Morg: | oh |
| Jady: | I saw that . . . had to figure my time stuff again |
| Commander Morg: | I'm in the Java client, works pretty well |
| Colin Gabriel Hatcher: | 2 hours?? |
| Petal262: | Hi BypsyRogue |
| Petal262: | GypsyRogue |
| Jady: | hi Gypsy :) |
| GypsyRogue: | thanx for the correction |
| Colin Gabriel Hatcher: | lol petal . . . i c you r having a b-g prob today :) |
| GypsyRogue: | sound like some teeny bop w/ a b |
| Jady: | hehehe |
| Colin Gabriel Hatcher: | morg my netscape is down so I am stuck with telnet :) |
| Colin Gabriel Hatcher: | lol jady |
| Commander Morg: | oh, bummer |
| Colin Gabriel Hatcher: | : D |
| Commander Morg: | try to the new Netscape |
| Commander Morg: | Netscape Java was really bad, I think the programmers were on crack |
| Commander Morg: | :) |
| Colin Gabriel Hatcher: | lol . . . |
| GypsyRogue: | comp talk – how dull |

Notice how the usual turn-taking mechanisms from speech do not apply here. Other 'voices' appear while a user is typing, so it seems as though there is a lot of 'skip-connecting' back to previous topics. This means that participants have to keep track of several threads of chat, only one or two of which will be developed. You will see by comparing this with other chatrooms that there is a great deal of variation in linguistic usage, with different registers and dialects in the process of emerging. It seems that the main determinant of sociolinguistic stratification and variation in e-discourse is the level of technical expertise of the user.

## Glossary of emoticons and net acronyms

There are very many internet catalogues of 'emoticons' (graphic keyboard tricks to encode tone of voice, irony, sarcasm, gesture, and so on). However, many of these are simply clever jokes and are almost never used:

| | |
|---|---|
| :^) | user has a broken nose |
| :-# | user wears braces |
| :-Q | smoking cigarette |

However, Miranda discovered a chatroom for experienced users with the following:

> *room*:    #weed
> Thunder: :-Q :/ :/  :/sssss  :-)

Here, 'Thunder' has renamed the room and smokes a virtual joint with the other chatters.

More common emoticons include:

| | |
|---|---|
| :-) | the basic smiley |
| ;-) | wink, used to mark a joke |
| :-( | unhappy or frowning |
| :-l | indifferent |
| {{{you}}} | hugging 'you' |
| :-@ | screams |
| :-D | laughing |
| :-s | confused or unsure |
| : 0 | yawn, tired |
| :-x | user's lips are sealed, confidential |

and the acronyms

| | |
|---|---|
| BTW | by the way |
| HH | holding hands |
| r | are |
| u | you |
| c | see |
| lol | laughing out loud |
| a/s/l | age, sex, location |

For example:

| | |
|---|---|
| Kt1_red: | a/s/l??? |
| Spunky2000_uk: | gloucester, and u |
| Juicyjess: | scotland, 19 |
| Dr_rich3: | call me stoopid, but i dunno what a/s/l means |
| Kt1_red: | stoopid |
| Jamieton99: | stupid |
| Dr_rich3: | 24, bloke manchester   :-s ?? |
| Kt1_red: | cool thats ur a/s/l ☹☺☺ |
| Dr_rich3: | I've learnt somethin. What's your a/s/l? |

It is an easy matter to 'lurk' in a chatroom and print out some discourse data. What are the naming and address conventions in email and electronic discourse? What other means are used to maintain 'netiquette'? Is e-discourse a third mode of communication, or is it mainly a blend of speech and writing? Is there such a thing as an emergent World Standard Electronic English? What do you think will be the impact of improved voice-recognition software on world accents, when the computer keyboard finally becomes a quaint relic of the past?

---

**C12**     **CRITICAL DISCOURSE ANALYSIS**

Here are two texts which come from roughly the same source. The first is a letter confirming an offer of a job at a British university. It is a standard letter that was sent in this form to all newly contracted staff. The second text is from the same office, sent to all staff in post at the university, to warn them of procedures in the event of a planned demonstration by students. In both cases, names and locations have been changed or obviously disguised.

### Contract

| | | |
|---|---|---|
| *Our ref* | P/JDM/MSC/MPA | Personnel Department |
| *Your ref* | | Bigcity University |
| *Date* | 22 April | [Address details] |

John D Bossman
BA(hons)
Personnel Manager

Dear Mr Newboy

I am delighted to be able to offer you the post of Lecturer in English at Bigcity University. The post is offered with effect from 1 September subject to medical clearance.

I enclose with this letter two copies of the University's contract of employment. I should be grateful if you would indicate your acceptance of this offer by signing and returning the top copy. The second copy is for you to retain.

As a result of recent changes under the Education Reform Act 1988, the University is revising its procedures. Therefore new arrangements covering such matter as grievance procedures, disciplinary procedures and other provisions are included in the staff handbook which will be issued to you in due course.

I should be grateful if you could come to the Personnel Office on the 4th floor of Labov Building at the Nice View site at 9.00 am on your first day of employment. You should bring your P45, birth certificate and qualifications.

I look forward to meeting you.

Yours sincerely

J D Minion
Director of Resources

## *Memo*

| | | |
|---|---|---|
| *To* | All Staff | Bigcity University |
| *Our ref* | KCB/SJK | Memorandum |
| *Your ref* | | |
| *From* | Dr K.C. Bigcheese | |
| *Centre* | Labov Building | |
| *Telephone* | 5555 | |
| *Date* | 16th January | |

*Demonstration*
To minimise any consequences of the demonstration, the following action will be taken:

1. Between 12.30 p.m. and 2.30 p.m. all lights will be extinguished in offices on the fourth floor of Labov Building facing the quadrangle.
2. When unoccupied, all offices are to be kept locked and all papers to be kept locked in drawers if possible.
3. People are not to look out of the window; it will only encourage the rabble.
4. The entrance doors to the Directorate are to be shut and not held open on the magnetic locks.
5. Someone is to test the button.
6. Finance, Personnel and Payroll are also to keep their offices locked when unoccupied.
7. Occasionally in these events, idiots press fire alarms. If the fire alarm sounds, the building is to be evacuated in an orderly manner and if time allows offices are to be locked.
8. If staff are nervous about the effects of a demonstration, they are to take a long lunch hour.

9.  I will not be on site, I will be at the Cityview site. In the event of a crisis, I am
    available on the mobile phone.

    Sylvia
pp. Dr Keith C. Bigcheese
    Director

Both texts encode an ideological view of the event and the participants in particular
ways. Try to draw up a systematic linguistic analysis to uncover the ideological
viewpoints realised by these two texts. Categories you might focus on could include,
for example:

❑   how layout signals the text-type
❑   naming strategies including titles, job-titles, forms of address and nouns used for
    reference to people
❑   formality expressed through lexical choice and syntactic pattern
❑   assignment of blame, or delineation of inclusive and exclusive participants
    ('us' and 'them') by naming, lexical choice, or verb-form.

Both texts are, at a fundamental level, instructional, but how do they each go about
encoding their viewpoints of different participants and groups?

    You probably work or study within an institutional setting. How is your
behaviour regulated linguistically by your institution? How is your identity and 'face'
delineated by the institution, and how far do you conform to this when you are in the
institutional setting? Do you code-switch into a different register when you leave for
other parts of your life?

# Section D

# EXTENSION:
# SOCIOLINGUISTIC
# READINGS

Throughout this book I have been at pains to emphasise the importance of reading in the area of sociolinguistics. Extensive reading of books and articles has several benefits:

❑ it provides you with the necessary background of the history of the discipline;
❑ it familiarises you with the main current research areas;
❑ it allows you to see the sorts of methods and approaches that are used by different sociolinguists;
❑ it gives you a model for how to express yourself in appropriate academic and scholarly language.

Reading with a critical awareness (that is, reading and thinking rather than simply being a passive reader) allows you to see that different writers come to different conclusions and interpretations. This sort of critical engagement will spark your own ideas and allow you to see areas that need further investigation. The journey from being introduced to sociolinguistics to being a serious researcher doing valuable and innovative work is a short one, and by this point in the book you are already well on the way.

The twelve readings in this section have been selected to give you a useful resource across the field of sociolinguistics. They range from surveys to specific details of research studies; they include classic articles as well as extracts that are more difficult to find; and they cover material which is accessible as well as writing that can give you a taste of complex analysis and argument. After each reading, some suggestions for thinking and critical engagement are offered. It is often useful if you make brief notes and ideas either in the margins (if this book is yours) or in a notebook. If you get into the habit of 'reading with a pencil' you will find you are never short of ideas.

The numbered sections roughly correspond with the corresponding unit earlier in this book, though sometimes the readings combine several areas of interest. The first reading, below, uses many of the terms introduced in A1, though Hamer also discusses issues of standardisation (thread 6) in relation to language change (B5, C5), and refers to Labov's work (A5) in order to make a point about language and education (B3, C3).

---

**D1**    **SOCIOLINGUISTICS AND LANGUAGE CHANGE**

**Early Standard English: linguistic confidence and insecurity**

**Andrew Hamer** (reprinted from *Proceedings of the English Association North* Vol.VII (1993), Liverpool: Liverpool University English Department, pp. 31–42.)

The advantage claimed for studying developments in the history of English has traditionally been the insight these provide into trends in the modern language. This is a view which may be attractive to teachers faced with presenting unfamiliar material to students they fear may find it irrelevant, but which relegates language history to the status of a discipline not worth studying for itself. Less commonly appreciated is the fact that diachronic developments in English can be studied using linguistic insights gained from examining the modern speech community. In this way, the past ceases to be relevant only as an aid to understanding what is *really* important, the modern period, and becomes an exciting challenge, a laboratory where students can apply the analytic techniques they have learnt elsewhere in their course.

In what follows, I intend to look at the consequences for the speech community of the establishment of a written standard form of English during the late fifteenth and sixteenth centuries. One might reasonably expect to be able to apply sociolinguistic insights here. After all, defining the sociolinguistic situation in modern Britain is made possible largely by the existence of a prestigious dialect (Standard English) and accent (Received Pronunciation – RP). The speech patterns of groups of individuals, whether these be social classes, or regional or gender groupings, can be shown to vary systematically in terms of the percentage of occurrence within them of prestigious forms.

One should probably *a priori* expect the linguistic situation during the century after c.1470 to have differed from that of our own time in one important respect, however: there might well exist a great variety of competing forms in texts written in a transitional period, during which a standard dialect was becoming established. Since this has been shown indeed to be the case (see Dobson 1968), it follows that there must at that time have been some confusion about the relative status of linguistic variants, confusion that can only have aggravated any linguistic insecurity a vulnerable social group might have felt. It is the evidence for this nervousness about language which interests me here.

Texts from this period show evidence of two sorts of linguistic anxiety: a speaker's insecurity about his own dialect; and a nervousness about the ability of English to serve as a vehicle for all kinds of written communication. The view normally taken is that the second type of insecurity disappeared 'quite suddenly between 1575 and 1580. Before 1575, nearly everybody agrees that English is barbarous; after 1580 there is a whole chorus of voices proclaiming that English is eloquent' (Barber 1976: 76–7). Such a sudden change may well strike the reader as unusual, to say the least. In this essay, I hope to show that scholars have taken too uncritically expressions of the second type of insecurity, and that in fact from c.1500, members of elite groups had considerable confidence in their own articulatory powers in English.

Between the time of the Norman Conquest and the first half of the fourteenth century, the sociolinguistic situation in England could roughly be characterised as follows: there existed a set of English dialects, none of which enjoyed any more prestige than the others; the functions which are now the domain of Standard English were then largely carried out by dialects of Latin and French. This situation changed from the late fourteenth century, when a number of standardised forms of English started to appear in texts, a trend which culminated in the widespread appearance, by 1470, of 'Chancery Standard,' which provided the ancestor of the later standard dialect.

The use of Chancery Standard, though widespread by 1470, was by no means universal. Caxton, in the famous Preface to his *Eneydos* (published in 1490), complains that the lack of an agreed standard causes particular problems for the printer. Baugh and Cable (1978:195) quote the complaint with no more comment than: 'it was not easy for a writer at the end of the fifteenth century to choose his words so that his language would find favor with all people.' Attempts to assess Caxton's motives in more recent histories than theirs are clearly influenced by Sociolinguistics: Dick Leith (1997: 40) notes that Caxton's complaint that English has changed much since he was young has been followed by 'a good many people since'; more interestingly, Barbara Strang (1970: 157, 197) urges Caxton's modern readers not 'to take too much at face-value his observations on variation', since 'he does seem to be picking an example to labour a point.' In the light of these comments, it is worth looking again at this Preface to see whether anything more can be gleaned from it that might add to our knowledge of the sociolinguistic situation in the late ME period.

> And that comyn englysshe that is spoken
> in one shyre varyeth from a nother. In so
> moche that in my dayes happened that certayn
> marchauntes were in a shippe in tamyse, for
> to have sayled over the see into zelande, and
> for lacke of wynde, thei taryed atte forlond,
> and wente to lande for to refreshe them. And
> one of theym named Sheffelde, a mercer, cam
> in-to an hows and axed for mete; and specyally
> he axyd after eggys. And the goode wyf answerde,
> that she coude speke no frenshe. And the
> marchaunt was angry, for he also coude speke
> no frenshe, but wolde have hadde egges, and
> she understode hym not. And thenne at laste
> a nother sayd that he wolde have eyren. Then
> the good wyf sayd that she understod hym wel.
> Loo, what sholde a man in thyse dayes now wryte,
> egges or eyren? Certaynly it is harde to playse
> every man by cause of dyversite & chaunge of
> langage.

We must ask ourselves at the outset, who were the likely readers of Caxton's *Eneydos*? This text is an English translation of a French prose version of Virgil's *Æneid*, and must therefore have been aimed at literate, monolingual English speakers. In other words, Caxton's intended audience did not include either of the two elite groups: those who were educated to the level where they could read Latin with any fluency would not be interested in this text, as they would certainly have read Virgil's epic in the original, while the French-favouring social elite would naturally read the French version.

It is also clear that during the early printing period the very wealthy were not interested in buying printed books. They continued to be attracted by manuscripts, in part because these represented sound investments, being individual and exclusive. It is more likely, therefore, that Caxton would have to find his readers among sections of the community which traditionally had wielded little power, but which now, for the first time, had a little spare money and some leisure. Significant numbers of this group were by now literate also, and this combination of factors meant that conditions were ripe for some of these people to want to improve themselves, through an acquaintance, however indirect, with the classics. A shrewd entrepreneur, Caxton catered for the emerging lower middle class, those beneficiaries of the collapse of the old economic system.

What evidence is there in the text to support this view? It seems to me that a lower middle class audience is precisely the group that will identify with the predicament of Sheffelde the mercer. By the time that Caxton wrote this Preface, southerners had for more than a century been poking fun at Norse-influenced Northern dialects. Writing in 1385, John of Trevisa (in Cornwall) claims that:

> Al þe longage of þe Norþhumbres, and
> specialyche at ʒork, ys so scharp,
> slyttyng, and unschape, þat we
> Souþeron men may þat longage unneþe ('scarcely')
> undurstonde.

Little wonder if Sheffelde (note the name) felt sensitive about his dialect when in the South-east. (His word comes from the Norse 'egg' /ɛg/ while the good wyf's is from Old English 'æg' /æj/). His anger at the woman's response, that she couldn't understand him because she couldn't speak French, is understandable when seen against the background of this long tradition of southern superiority. Of little education himself ('for he also coude speke no frenshe'), he assumes that the woman is pretending he is French in order to mock his uncouth dialect. To the monolinguals to whom Caxton addressed his translations, Sheffelde's predicament may well have been embarrassingly familiar.

To suggest in this way that Caxton's intended readership was a lower middle class one which would empathise with Sheffelde fits well with what is known about the sensitivity to linguistic variation of today's lower middle class. In a famous study, William Labov (1972b) examined a series of phonological variables in the speech of a random sample of New Yorkers. Among the variables studied was /r/ in such words as *guard, floors, certain* (ie. when not before a vowel). The results of his findings were summarised in the following diagram [Fig. D1.1].

In New York city, the presence of /r/ in words such as these can be shown to be prestigious by the fact that for all social groups, there is a correlation between increasing frequency of pronunciation of /r/ and increasing formality of speech styles. As Labov (1972b:115) says: 'at the level of casual, everyday speech, only the upper middle class shows a significant degree of r-pronunciation. But in more formal styles, the amount of r-pronunciation for other groups rises rapidly. The lower middle class, in particular, shows an extremely rapid increase, surpassing the upper-middle-class level in the two most formal styles.' This 'crossover pattern' for the lower middle class is found 'for all those linguistic variables which are involved in a process of linguistic change under social pressure,' and may therefore be taken as an 'indicator of linguistic change in progress.'

The only explanation possible for this regular hypercorrecting among the lower middle class appears to be this group's linguistic insecurity, which 'is shown by the very

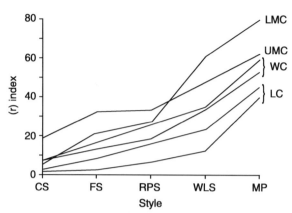

*Figure D1.1* Social stratification of a linguistic variable undergoing change – post-vocalic (r) in New York City (Labov 1972b: 114)

wide range of stylistic variation used by lower-middle-class speakers; by their great fluctuation within a given stylistic context; by their conscious striving for correctness; and by their strongly negative attitudes towards their native speech pattern' (Labov 1972b: 117). If the interpretation given above of Caxton's account of Sheffelde the mercer is correct, the linguistic insecurity of the lower middle class has a history in this country of five hundred years.

The linguistic insecurity typical of the modern lower middle class is a largely unconscious response to social pressures on the part of a group that is peculiarly susceptible to social change. We do not find indicators of this insecurity in the speech patterns of today's upper middle class, and would certainly not expect to find them in the writings of those among Caxton's contemporaries who enjoyed a privileged social status. Oddly enough, at least at first glance, this is exactly what we do appear to find, in a number of statements about English from the first half of the sixteenth century.

[. . .]

It would appear [. . .] that the speech community of Tudor England shared some sociolinguistic characteristics with that of the modern period: a linguistically insecure lower middle class; and a social-cultural elite, confident about their own articulacy. Any tendency among the latter group to feel linguistically, as well as socially, financially and educationally, superior to others could only be reinforced by the former group's attempts to imitate the speech patterns, as well as the life-styles, of those who they believed enjoyed social prestige.

Whether the complementary attitudes to language of these two social groups were the reflection or cause of the belief that some forms of English were 'better' than others is not clear, but certainly, two significant attitudes to language variation developed during this period. These attitudes, which were both destined to have a long, and some would say still unfinished history, can be summarised as follows: (i) some speakers, through their own fault, lack the ability to express themselves as well, eloquently, elegantly as they ought; and (ii) things were better in the past.

Caxton prefaces his simple observation that 'that comyn englysshe that is spoken in one shyre varyeth from a nother' with a hint that he sees language change through time as the result of a fault in the speakers: And certainly our 'langage now used varyeth ferre from that whiche was used and spoken whan I was borne. For we englysshe men ben borne under the domynacyon of the mone, whiche is never stedfaste, but ever waverynge, wexynge one season, and waneth & dyscreaseth another season'. Such blame as Caxton does apportion here, he does so indiscriminately to the whole nation.

Sixty years later, Richard Sherry's writing shares Caxton's nostalgia for a better past, but coupled with it is a confidence that certain of the author's (socially prestigious) contemporaries are fully the equals in articulacy of even their most famous predecessors. Any failure of articulacy in an Englishman, moreover, can only be the result of his not availing himself of the opportunities that the language offers him. For Sherry, this involves actively seeking out eloquence, something which the lazy will not do:

> It is not vnknowen that oure language for the barbarousnes and lacke of eloquence hathe bene complayned of, and yet not trewely, for anye defaut in the toungue it selfe, but rather for slackenes of our countrimen, which haue alwayes set lyght by searchyng out the elegance and proper speaches that be ful many in it: as plainly doth appere not only by the most excellent monumentes of our auncient forewriters, Gower, Chawcer and Lydgate, but also by the famous workes of many other later: inespeciall of the ryght worshipful knyght syr Thomas Eliot.
>
> (Sherry, reproduced in Hildebrandt 1977:4–5)

Linguistic performance is now plainly considered the reflection of moral worth. Coincidentally, this period sees the emergence of an educational attitude which will be familiar to many modern readers: those concerned with the education of the young must teach the standard dialect, and those determined to improve themselves must learn it. Peter Levins's English rhyming dictionary (*Manipulus Vocabulorum*, 1570) offers an opportunity to learn something of 'the chiefe grace and facilitie of our Englishe tong', whereby 'children and ruder schoolers, as also the Barbarous countries and ruder writers, may not a little (if they wil enioy the offered occasion) well and easely correct and amend, both their pen and speache' (in Dobson 1968: 20).

Levins's own dialect, though 'plentifully sprinkled with Northernisms, . . . was certainly accommodated in many ways to the language of the South' (Dobson 1968: 20). This was probably the safest course for an educator at that time: the inspectors who made the first visitation of Merchant Taylors' School (16th August, 1562) under the headmastership of Richard Mulcaster, reported only one fault in the teachers: 'that being northern men born, they had not taught the children to speak distinctly, or to pronounce their words as well as they aught' (quoted in Dobson 1968: 125).

Mulcaster's *Elementarie* was planned as a text book on the whole range of elementary education, including, as far as English is concerned, reading, writing and grammar. Indeed, the study of orthography which forms most of the work as published was intended as a background to the teaching of reading and writing, and not as a guide to 'better' pronunciation. Four hundred years ago, Mulcaster's concern to improve the literacy skills of his pupils contrasted with the inspectors' concerns that those pupils were not being taught 'to pronounce their words as well as they aught'. The comments of these inspectors, whether they were reacting to their own prejudices or to real or perceived pressure on the part of parents or governors, show that linguistic insecurity was a real force at this time. Indicative of this insecurity is the refuge sought in rules: 'as well as they aught'.

The English-teaching aims, no doubt only slightly different, of Mulcaster and the inspectors may be compared with a shift in emphasis between the Kingman Report (1988) and the National Curriculum Council's (1993) revision of the English Order. Both reports recognise the need to teach written and spoken Standard English, and both also accept that the standard dialect can be spoken 'in a variety of regional and social accents'. But whereas in the Kingman Report the Standard is an indispensable, though not intrinsically superior, variety, those who have revised the English Order are certain (p.9 para. 6) that 'Standard English is characterised by the correct *(sic)* use of vocabulary and grammar'. The concept of correctness in language does not tolerate the existence of variation, since a form is either 'correct' or not. It would appear therefore that, if implemented, the revised English Order may well prove a fertile breeding ground for future linguistic insecurity.

### Issues to consider

The 'English Order' referred to at the end was the UK government's curriculum for English teaching in England and Wales. The 1993 proposed revision to the curriculum for English met with a great deal of criticism from teachers and academics, centring round the question of standardisation. The proposal in its 1993 form was quietly dropped. Shortly afterwards the National Curriculum Council was replaced by a body with a wider authority for maintaining standards in the curriculum and assessment.

The intersection of sociolinguistics and politics is an interesting area of investigation, touching upon issues of language planning, and notions of standardisation, codification, prescriptivism and linguistic authority. Any government around the world has to decide how language skills and literacy are to be taught in their education systems, and decisions are often made on the basis of politics, ideology, history and economics, as well as on the state of linguistic understanding. The places to begin to explore these matters are newspapers (especially educational supplements), political manifestos, and the documents that schools in your area will have received from their authorities. You could compare the view of language practice embodied in these official documents with the reality around you. Alternatively, you could use your sociolinguistic knowledge to explore issues of historical language change in the past, and see connections and continuities with the present, as Hamer has done. Practical investigations might include:

❑  analysing official documents to discover which dialect(s) of your national language is/are privileged, and then investigating the consequences for students who do not use that dialect;

❑  using your reading and skills as a sociolinguist to evaluate the pronouncements of politicians, journalists and other commentators when they discuss issues of language policy, linking the issues to published work in the field;

❑  using data such as school-children's written work to explore differences in class or other social background, or to see whether important local dialects affect their writing, and what attitude teachers take to these effects in assessing the work;

❑  focusing on a specific feature of a change in language in the past, and using your knowledge of sociolinguistics to re-evaluate it;

❑   speculating on one main historical difference in the past (e.g. the Norman Con-
    quest of England did not happen in 1066; a Spanish empire was maintained in
    North America; steam computers and the internet were perfected in the early
    nineteenth century; Germany and Japan won the Second World War, and so on)
    and using your sociolinguistic knowledge to discuss what the differences in
    language use might be, based on real principles from your reading;
❑   imagining how language might change in the near future, based on what you
    observe around you and what you know about the sociolinguistic principles of
    language change.


## FOREIGN ACCENTS IN AMERICA                                              **D2**

In those countries of the world in which English is the official language (see A9),
monolingualism can often seem to be the global norm. Not only is this a delusion
across the world, it is also often a distortion of the multilingual and multi-ethnic
composition even within those countries. In the following chapter from her book,
Rosina Lippi-Green provides a well-argued antidote to such views. She takes a macro-
sociolinguistic approach, using historical and census data to discuss the importance
of recognising all of the accents of American speech. She emphasises in the rest of the
book the importance of attitudes to accent differences in relation to educational
performance and ethnic discrimination.

You will recognise connections here with the terms we covered in A2, B2 and C2.
Notions of prestige (thread 6) are central to Lippi-Green's approach, as well as the
linguistic effects and markers of ethnicity (thread 4). Her book is concerned with
exposing the educational consequences of prescriptive linguistic attitudes (B3, C).

### The stranger within the gates

**Rosina Lippi-Green** (reprinted from *English with an Accent: Language, Ideology and
Discrimination in the United States*, London: Routledge, 1997: 217–39.)

The 1990 census established that the United States is a nation of some 248 million
persons, of whom 2,015,143 are Native American and 205,501 Hawai'ian. Thus it is an
obvious and inescapable truth that the majority of people residing in the US are immigrants, or the descendents of immigrants, the greatest portion of whom came of their
own will, while others came in chains. We are a nation of immigrants, but having made
the transition and established ourselves, we have a strong urge to be protective of what
is here; we talk at great length about closing the door behind us. At times, we have acted
on this impulse:

❑   In the 1840s during a depression, mobs hostile to immigrant Irish Catholics burned down
    a convent in Boston.

❑   Congress passed the Chinese Exclusion Act in 1882, one of our first immigration laws, to
    exclude all people of Chinese origin.
❑   In 1942, 120,000 Americans of Japanese descent had their homes and other property
    confiscated, and were interned in camps until the end of the Second World War. At the
    same time, many Jews fleeing Nazi Germany during that war were excluded under
    regulations enacted in the 1920s.

                                                      (American Civil Liberties Union 1996)

Language often becomes the focus of debate when these complex issues of nationality,
responsibility, and privilege are raised. English, held up as the symbol of the successfully
assimilated immigrant, is promoted as the one and only possible language of a unified
and healthy nation. Using rhetoric which is uncomfortably reminiscent of discussions of
race in fascist regimes, a California Assemblyman notes the multilingual commerce in
his home town with considerable trepidation: 'you can go down and apply for a driver's
license test entirely in Chinese. You can apply for welfare today entirely in Spanish. The
supremacy of the English language is under attack' (report on pending English Only
legislation in California, CBS Evening News, October 1986).

    In considering the history of multilingualism and public fears around it, Ferguson
and Heath noted that 'whenever speakers [of other languages] have been viewed as
politically, socially, or economically threatening, their language has become a focus for
arguments in favor of both restrictions of their use and imposition of Standard English'
(1981: 10). This is illustrated by the history of German use in the US, a language (and
people) which particularly irritated Benjamin Franklin.

    [. . .]

### Who has a foreign accent?

The census bureau estimates that 22,568,000 persons or 8.7 percent of the population
of the United States was foreign-born in 1994, a figure which is nearly double the
number of foreign-born in 1970 (4.8 percent). A total of 31,844,979 persons – many
of these not foreign-born – reported that they spoke a language other than English in
the home, as is seen in Table D2.1. We note that this list does not specify a single
language from the continent of Africa beyond the Arabic languages of the north. It must
be assumed that as immigration from the mid and southern African nations is limited,
speakers of languages such as Swahili and Zulu are subsumed under the category 'Other
and unspecified languages.'

    If the purpose is to come to an approximation of who speaks English with a foreign
accent, it is useful to have some accounting of proficiency in English. The census bureau
attempts to access this information by simply asking the question. The published results
are conflated into four groups: native English speakers who have no other language in
the home (this would include, for example, people who have limited second-language
ability through schooling) and then three universes, as seen in Table D2.2: speakers of
Spanish, speakers of Asian and Pacific Rim languages, and speakers of other languages
which do not fall into any of the previous groups. This last group must include a great
variety of languages, from those spoken in Africa to Scandinavia and middle and eastern
European.

    A graphic representation of the 18–65-year-old group from this table is given in
Figure D2.1. Here we see that there is in fact a differential in the individual's assessment

*Table D2.1*  Language spoken at home by persons 5 years and older

| Language | No. of people |
| --- | --- |
| English only | 198,600,798 |
| Spanish or Spanish Creole | 17,345,064 |
| French or French Creole | 1,930,404 |
| German | 1,547,987 |
| Chinese | 1,319,462 |
| Italian | 1,308,648 |
| Other and unspecified languages | 1,023,614 |
| Tagalog | 843,251 |
| Polish | 723,483 |
| Korean | 626,478 |
| Other Indo-European language | 578,076 |
| Indic | 555,126 |
| Vietnamese | 507,069 |
| Portuguese or Portuguese Creole | 430,610 |
| Japanese | 427,657 |
| Greek | 388,260 |
| Arabic | 355,150 |
| Native North American languages | 331,758 |
| Other Slavic language | 270,863 |
| Russian | 241,798 |
| Other West Germanic language | 232,461 |
| Yiddish | 213,064 |
| Scandinavian | 198,904 |
| South Slavic | 170,449 |
| Hungarian | 147,902 |
| Mon-Khmer | 127,441 |

*Source:* 1990 US census data. Database: C90STF3C1

of ability to speak English according to national-origin subgrouping. In all three groups, the majority of non-native English speakers claim a very good command of their second language. The differential between 'very good' and 'not well at all' is smallest for the Asian-languages group, which is in turn the smallest of the three groups overall.

We note especially that there are four million people in the 'Other language' category who call their own English 'very good' and another million or so of this same group who find their English not very good at all. This mysterious 'Other language' group is in fact larger than the Asian-languages group. While this profusion of numbers still does not provide an exact count of how many people speak English with a foreign accent, it does raise two crucial points.

First, millions of people resident in the US are not native speakers of English, and use a language other than English in their homes and personal lives. Any individual who

*Table D2.2* (Non-English) language spoken at home and ability to speak English, by age

| Age | Language spoken | Evaluation of English-language skills: census count | | |
|---|---|---|---|---|
| | | 'Very well' | 'Well' | 'Not well' or 'Not well at all' |
| 5–17 | Spanish | 2,530,779 | 993,417 | 643,457 |
| | Asian or Pacific Island | 455,339 | 224,821 | 135,430 |
| | Other | 948,573 | 262,442 | 128,676 |
| 18–64 | Spanish | 6,105,722 | 2,589,195 | 3,425,937 |
| | Asian or Pacific Island | 1,496,466 | 1,048,835 | 755,324 |
| | Other | 4,312,500 | 1,315,685 | 658,210 |
| 65+ | Spanish | 398,568 | 223,350 | 434,639 |
| | Asian or Pacific Island | 99,461 | 82,351 | 173,594 |
| | Other | 1,515,069 | 570,205 | 316,934 |

*Source:* 1990 US census data. Database: C90STF3C1

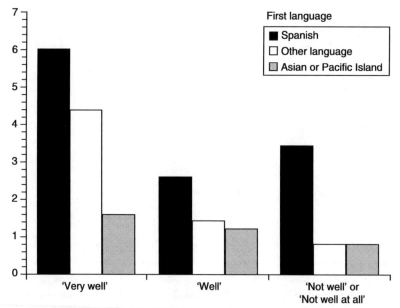

*Figure D2.1* Persons between 18 and 65 years who claim a first language other than English and their evaluation of their English-language skills
*Source:* 1990 census

takes on the task of learning a second or third language in adulthood will have some degree of L2 accent, a degree which is not readily predictable and will not correlate, overall, to education, intelligence, or motivation. Thus there is a large population of US residents who speak with an L2 accent.

**D**

Second, there are preconceived notions about non-native speakers of English which have repercussions even in the way we count their numbers and talk about them. The US Census Bureau distinguishes between Spanish, Asian, and other languages. It is from this departure point that we look at the way foreign-language groups and the language stereotypes associated with those groups are used to classify – and often to dismiss – individual needs and rights.

### From Bali Hai to New Delhi: what it means to be Asian

[. . .]

The Census Bureau lists a figure of almost 7.3 million Asians in the US population. Figure D2.2 breaks down this figure, according to census data, into more specific national origins. In examining this chart, it immediately becomes apparent that even in its more specific form, the subgrouping 'Asian' is internally immensely complex and diverse. It might be argued that generalizations are necessary when dealing with this kind of data, for the nations of Asia and the Pacific are numerous. In linguistic terms, even this breakdown is deceiving.

We take for example India, a nation of 844 million persons which recognizes fifteen official national languages each with a large number of dialects. India is linguistically complex, especially when viewed in comparison to the US, but it is not the exception to the rule. It is not even extreme in the larger global view. We consider China (population 1.1 billion), with fifty-five official minority nationalities and eight major languages in addition to literally hundreds of other languages from Mongolian to Hmong; or Fiji with a mere 740,000 residents spread out over 7,000 square miles of islands on which fifteen languages (in addition to Fijian) are spoken.

While it would be an unreasonable burden on the Census Bureau to make note of each and every world language spoken in the US, the great disparity between how we make official note – what we see when we look outward at the majority of the world's population – and the *reality* of those nations, bears some consideration. What are the

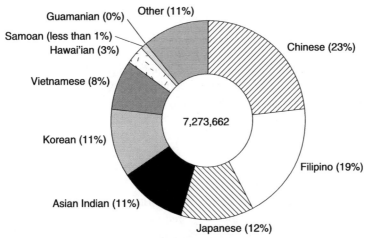

*Figure D2.2* Breakdown of 'Asian or Pacific Islander' category in the 1990 US census, by national origin

repercussions of the fact that we group together persons as different as the native people of Hawai'i – US citizens with a history which should be very familiar to us – with Cambodians who sought political asylum in the US and middle-class exchange students from New Delhi? How can policies which do not distinguish between the immigration patterns and educational and language backgrounds of such disparate peoples be functional?

And why do we do this? Is expediency the single most viable answer? Or is it simply that when it comes to language, we hear a single 'Asian' accent? An obvious but disturbing answer is that we feel justified to group so many distinct nations and peoples and languages together because they all look alike to 'real' Americans, to European Americans. *Asian* evokes an association not to national origin, but to race.

[. . .]

The issue is not so much accent as 'otherness,' as illustrated in a series of court cases involving Asian American English:

> Managerial level employee [LS] told Xieng he was not being promoted because he could not speak 'American.'
>
> (Xieng 1991: Appeal Court Opinion: 5)

> the complainant's supervisor had removed her because of concern about the effect of her accent on the 'image' of the IRS, not any lack in either communication or technical abilities.
>
> (Park: EEOC press release, June 8, 1988)

Our relationship to the Far East and Pacific is shaped to a great degree by the facts of nineteenth-century colonialism, in which the US, young in comparative terms, followed the European model in the way that smaller nations were overcome and dominated politically, economically, and socially. We have a history of dealing with the Asian world as a warehouse of persons and goods available to suit our own purpose and fill our own needs, a practice justified by the supposition that those people are inherently weaker. Because they are also cast as manipulative and wont to use natural wiles and treacherous means to achieve their own ends, we are able to rationalize aggressions toward them. Thus the primary male Asian stereotype is of an intelligent, clever, but crafty and unreliable person. A secondary stereotype grows out of the mystification of Asia, the mysterious 'Orient' where hardworking but simple people ply their crafts and study arcane philosophies, attaining wisdom and a spirituality specific to their race. We are uncomfortable with Asians unless they correspond to the stereotypes we have created for them.

[. . .]

Like African Americans, Asian Americans have more and more difficult hurdles to leap before they can transcend stereotype and be accepted as individuals. Accent, when it acts in part as a marker of race, takes on special power and significance. For many in the African American community there is little resistance to the language subordination process, in part because the implied promises of linguistic assimilation – while obviously overstated – are nevertheless seductive, *precisely because the threats are very real*. The seduction of perfect English, of belonging absolutely to the mainstream culture of choice, is one that is hard to resist for Asian Americans as well.

It is easy to establish that language variation is linked to race, and more specifically that foreign-language accent is linked to national origin. But once accomplished, what is to be done with such a collection of facts? Perhaps the only realistic thing is to ask harder questions of ourselves. Discrimination against Asian Americans which centers on language, but which has more in actual terms to do with race, is an established practice. How is it that in a nation so proud of its civil rights legislation and democratic ideals, people can so easily use accent to exclude, to limit discourse, and to discredit other – very specific – voices, because they simply do not sound white enough?

It is necessary and important at this point to look at another large group, composed in large part of non-native speakers of English. The Spanish-speaking people of this country comprise nations within the nation. As speakers of languages other than English, they are also subject to the process of homogenization which has been seen for other groups.

### *Chiquitafication*

The group of peoples which the Census Bureau calls 'Hispanic' included some 22 million US residents in the 1990 census. As was the case for the Asian population, this overarching term hides a great deal of ethnic variety, in this case compounding the racial diversity, as seen in Figure D2.3 and Table D2.3.

As might be predicted, Mexican Americans account for most of the Latino population, with a much smaller Puerto Rican population and a Cuban population of just over one million, or about 5 percent of the whole. Almost a quarter of Latino is made up of 'Other,' in this case comprising primarily Central and South Americans (just over a million residents each) and half a million Spaniards. About half a million persons could or would not be specific in identifying their national origins.

It is important to note that the racial classifications do not include mestizo, and thus persons of mixed European and Native American ancestry – a large portion of the population of Mexico and Central America – must choose between allegiances (a fact which probably accounts for the large number of persons who identified themselves as 'other race'). This oversight is compounded by the assumption of an overarching

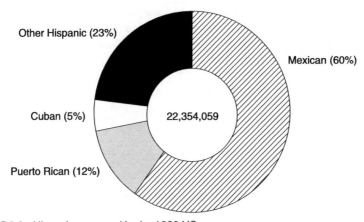

*Figure D2.3*  Hispanics counted in the 1990 US census

*Table D2.3*   Hispanic origin by race

| Race | Non-Hispanic | % | Hispanic | % |
|------|--------------|-----|----------|-----|
| White | 188,424,773 | 83.1 | 11,402,291 | 52.1 |
| Black | 29,284,596 | 12.9 | 645,928 | 2.9 |
| American Indian, Eskimo, or Aleut | 1,866,807 | 0.8 | 148,336 | 0.7 |
| Asian or Pacific Islander | 6,994,302 | 3.1 | 232,684 | 1.1 |
| Other race | 239,306 | 0.1 | 9,470,850 | 43.2 |
| Total | 226,809,784 | 100 | 21,900,089 | 100 |

*Source:* 1990 US census data. Database: C9OSTF3C1

Spanish monolingualism which spans more than ten countries in three continents. The Mexican population of more than 88 million includes more than 5 million speakers of indigenous Indian languages (about 8 percent of Mexico's total population), of whom almost half a million are monolingual and speak no Spanish at all (Grimes 1992). Guatemala's population of 9.3 million is approximately 55 percent Indian and 44 percent mestizo. The Indian population includes some 20,000 speakers of Kanjobal, 5,000 of whom are reported to be in Los Angeles [Grimes 1992].

In addition to racial and ethnic diversity, 'Latino' subsumes persons from all economic groups, political and religious backgrounds, and does not recognize a residency status differential. It overlooks the fact that many ethnically Spanish speaking persons live here on land their families have owned for many generations, and predate European settlement. In addition to this group, which cannot logically be called 'immigrant,' there are populations of more recent arrivals, short-term residents, cyclical immigrants made up primarily of farmworkers, and individuals who seek asylum in the US to escape political persecution, in addition to undocumented workers.

The use of language as a preliminary qualifier in the construction of ethnicity is an established custom, but it is nevertheless a troublesome one, as the scope and depth of 'Hispanic' has made clear. Zentella (1996) speaks and writes of what it was like for her as a child to have had a singing and dancing Chiquita Banana as a solitary Latina figure in the public eye. Thus she uses the term *chiquitafication* to speak of public policies and practices which homogenize Latino cultures and languages into a tidy and digestible package for the rest of the nation. Three areas which concern her greatly are

❑   the construction of a homogenous 'Hispanic community' that refuses to learn English;
❑   the belittling of non-Castilian varieties of Spanish;
❑   and the labeling of second-generation bilinguals as semi- or a-linguals.

(Zentella 1996: 1)

The second of these concerns points to an issue which has not been raised much in this discussion, and that is that language ideologies are not restricted to the English-speaking world. Discourse around 'good' and 'lesser' language, 'appropriate' and 'inappropriate' varieties can be found wherever people care to look. For each nation, there is a

*Table D2.4*  Popular constructions of 'good' and 'bad' language for other countries

| Country | 'Good' 'Proper' 'Cultured' 'High' | 'Low' 'Bad' 'Inappropriate' |
| --- | --- | --- |
| Italy | Florence | Sicily Calabria |
| Spain | Burgos Valladolid | Huelva |
| England | Oxford Cambridge | Liverpool Birmingham |
| Turkey | Istanbul | Black Sea Southeast Anatolia |
| Northern India (Hindi) | Delhi | Bombay Calcutta |
| Northern India/Pakistan (Urdu) | Lucknow | Hyderabad |

supra-cultural awareness of which are the 'right' varieties, although there will also be competing constructions of social acceptability – for without those who find the 'right' language unacceptable in social terms, stigmatized language would not flourish as it does. Table D2.4 presents the simplest answers one would be likely to get in asking an average person on the street 'Where is the best [language] spoken?' and 'Where is the worst [language] spoken?'

For Spanish, with a much greater geographic coverage than any of the other European languages with the exception of English, standard language ideology has established Castilian Spanish and, following therefrom, Castilian literature and culture as inherently superior and more worthy of study than New World language or language artifacts, as Zentella notes. Within Central and South American nations, there are similarly constructed ideologies, so that in Mexico there is a conception of three *normas* or levels of speaking: *la norma culta*, which Valdés (1988: 119) calls 'educated standard,' *la norma popular* ('a less elaborate and cultivated style'), and *la norma rural* ('This style of speaking generally sounds rustic to city people and is normally associated with rural lifestyles and backgrounds'), as well as a conception of good and bad varieties over space, so that the Spanish spoken in the Yucatan is stigmatized. Overarching the national constructions of 'good' and 'bad' language, however, is a very persistent idea that Castilian is the only real, original language. This functions much in the same way as it does in the US, when popular belief may point to Ohio as 'Standard US English' but then defer to that mythical beast 'the King's English,' or a British norm.

As interesting as it would be to compare the way language subordination tactics function across language and cultural boundaries, here I would like to concentrate instead on the first and third of Zentella's concerns. Together they summarize some conflicts about the process of language subordination which are instructive and important.

Zentella states that there is a troublesome, contrary-to-fact 'construction of a homogeneous "Hispanic community" that refuses to learn English' in the US, and she goes on to demonstrate how dangerous such homogenization can be. This is a wilful policy which

> encourages wholesale demonizing of the type reflected in a memo written by John Tanton when he was Chair of US English, the group that has been lobbying to make English the official language of the United States since 1981. Tanton portrayed Hispanic Catholicism as a national threat to the separation of church and state, and declared that a Latin American tradition of bribery imperiled US democracy. His most outrageous insult was a vulgar reference to 'the Hispanic birthrate,' charging that 'perhaps this is the first instance in which those with their pants up are going to get caught with their pants down.'
>
> (Zentella 1996: 9)

Zentella's analysis of US English and other English Only movements as xenophobic, hostile, and threatening to more than just language rights is clear and convincing (see also Crawford 1992 for a lengthy discussion). When she sets out to counter their arguments with hard data, she does so carefully:

> Despite the continued influx of monolingual immigrants, Veltman (1983) found that Hispanics are undergoing language loss similar to, and even exceeding that of other groups in US history. Language shift is most advanced among the US born, who constituted the majority (64 per cent) of the US Latino population in 1990; immigrants shift to English within 15 years . . .
>
> (Zentella 1996: 10)

But somewhere an issue has gone missing.

Tanton and his colleagues construct not only a *homogenous* 'Hispanic' community, but a resistant one. Zentella attacks both premises: it is not true, she asserts, that Hispanic immigrants are resistant to, and reject, the importance of English or the necessity of learning it. She claims that this is not true because the numbers show us that they do indeed learn it. But does the result preclude resistance to the process, or resentment of the necessity? Further, if this kind of resistance does exist, is it necessarily bad? Would the existence of a Spanish-speaking community in Florida or Texas or New Mexico which does not use and manages to function without English render Tanton's claims credible? Would asserting the right not to be bilingual (a right which would bring along with it many great difficulties) be tantamount to an attack on American democracy? It is clear that Zentella does not mean to make this claim, and that she is constructing 'resistance' in a purposefully narrow way.

However, the third concern (*the labelling of second-generation bilinguals as semi- or a-linguals*) does demand a wider conception of resistance. This question moves beyond the issue of whether or not bilingualism is necessary and reasonable (something she, and most others, take for granted) to the issue of *Which English?*

Some immigrants live in communities of monolingual English speakers, where a Spanish accent stands out. Others live in communities where multiple varieties of English coexist in relative harmony, in which Spanish, English, and Chicano or another variety of Latino English each have a sphere. Chicano English, Puerto Rican English and Cuban English in Los Angeles, New York, and Miami are individual varieties of English, distinct in certain syntactical, morphological, and discourse markers from one another and from other varieties of English (Penfield and Ornstein-Galicia 1985; Zentella 1988; Valdés 1988). There is a recognized Chicano American and Latino American literature which is taken as a serious object of study.

When Zentella protests the labeling of second-generation Spanish-language immigrants as semil-ingual or a-lingual, she is discussing a related phenomenon, that of code switching. Code switching is the orderly (rule-based) alternation between two or more languages, a subject of great interest to linguists and one which is widely studied. This complicates the picture of the Spanish-speaking universe considerably. We have distinct languages, each with its own stylistic repertoires: Spanish and English. To these we add more recently developed but distinct varieties of English, for example Chicano English as it is spoken in Texas. Now we have also the phenomenon of living and working with three languages, and switching among them as determined by language-internal (syntactical and morphological) rules as well as social and stylistic ones. The criticism Zentella discusses is aimed at switching, which may seem to an unsympathetic outsider nothing more than a language hodge-podge, and is often labelled *Spanglish*.

In fact, I would argue that whether the object of subordination is the act of style switching, or pressure to use a specific language, the ultimate goal of language subordination remains the same: to devalue and suppress *everything Spanish*.

To call code-switching *Spanglish* in a dismissive way is just another subordination method with a long history: to deny a language and its people a distinct name is to refuse to acknowledge them. There is a shorthand at work here, and that is, there is only one acceptable choice: it is not enough for Spanish speakers to become bilingual; they must learn the *right* English – and following from that, the right US culture, into which they must assimilate completely.

[. . .]

Stereotypes around Chicano and Latino Americans are almost exclusively negative, in all forms of popular culture. Penfield and Ornstein-Galicia identify the exception to this, the Californian *Don* or the New Mexican *Rico* who as 'symbols of the aristocratic class . . . were both linked more to Spain than Mexico' (1985: 78). These characters in film (*The Mark of Zorro*) or popular fiction speak an English which is accented, but elegant and archaic. Both men and women speak this kind of 'noble Spaniard' English:

'Come out,' she said.

'Ay! They have me fast. But when they do let me out, *niña*, I will take thee in my arms; and whosoever tries to tear thee away again will have a dagger in his heart. *Dios de mi vida!*' . . .

'But thou lovest me, Carlos?'

(Gertrude Atherton (1901) *The Doomswoman: An historical romance of old California*, as cited in Simmen 1971: 40)

More usually the stereotypes for Mexican Americans depart from the *greaser*, a classification subdivided into three types: 'a Mexican *paisano* – poor rural inhabitant; as a *mojado* – "wetback" or illegal alien; and as a *bandido* – a robber wearing "huge sombreros . . . tobacco-stained fingers and teeth, and grotesque dialect and curses" ' (Penfield and

Ornstein-Galicia 1985: 78). These characters are portrayed as speaking English with extreme dialect features; the more stereotypical the role, the more extreme the features:

> Billee the Keed. Ah, you have heard of heem? He was one gran' boy, senor. All Mexican pepul his friend. You nevair hear a Mexican say one word against Billee the Keed . . . so kind-hearted, so generaous, so brave. And so 'andsome. Nombre de Dios! Every leetle senorita was crazy about heem . . .
>
> (Walter Noble Burns, *The Saga of Billy the Kid*, as cited in Pettit 1980: 162)

Recent stereotypes in film and television, note Penfield and Ornstein-Galicia, have one thing in common: Mexican Americans are almost always portrayed as violent; they are drug-pushers, gang-members, pimps. A particularly extreme example of a trivialized character was Frito Bandito, a 1980s counterpart and mirror image of the wholesome Chiquita Banana. In the 1980s, however, the Latino community was vocal and persuasive enough to convince the Frito-Lay company to drop that negative character (1985: 84).

The Spanish-speaking population of the US is very large, and has more resources and expertise with US law and the legal system than other groups. Latino resistance to all kinds of discriminatory practices is well organized, and extends to language matters, especially when education is at issue. Unlike a smaller and more fragmented Asian population, many Spanish speakers are ready and willing to speak out on these issues. Unfortunately, they continue to have to battle, because as the San Diego businessman makes clear, equal opportunity and equal standing are not always forthcoming.

## Summary

[. . .]

It is crucial to remember that it is not *all* foreign accents, but only accent linked to skin that isn't white, or which signals a third-world homeland, that evokes such negative reactions. There are no documented cases of native speakers of Swedish or Dutch or Gaelic being turned away from jobs because of communicative difficulties, although these adult speakers face the same challenge as native speakers of Spanish, Rumanian, and Urdu.

Immigrants from the British Isles who speak varieties of English which cause significant communication problems are not stigmatized: the differences are noted with great interest, and sometimes with laughter.

[. . .]

But most do not have these resources. People have always come to the United States because in the mind of the world it is a place of real opportunity. The hidden costs of democracy, of assimilation, are not spelled out in the papers they must file to live here, but in the stories of people like Henry Park. The narrator of *Native Speaker* draws a vivid picture of himself and all immigrants: 'They speak . . . not simply in new accents or notes but in the ancient untold music of a newcomer's heart, sonorous with longing and hope' (Lee 1995).

What the newcomer must learn for him or herself is the grim reality of limitations imposed by a standard language ideology.

## Issues to consider

The approach demonstrated in this reading shows that sociolinguistic data is not necessarily 'raw' data: processed data such as census information, and interpreted data such as film and television representations can be used in sociolinguistic explorations. This latter sort of mediated information can be used to investigate attitudes to different forms of language. Cartoons, film, television, literature, newspapers and magazines have all been used to gather sociolinguistic data in recent years. As long as you remember that mediated data must be treated differently from 'raw' data, there is a lot of useful material that can come to you in this way.

Some practical investigations might include the following.

❑ Make a list of all the different linguistic codes available within a particular boundary: accents, dialects, registers, languages. You could define the boundary in different ways: the people in your classroom, the people in your extended family, the people near where you live, your town or city, your region, your nation, and so on. You could also make decisions on the level of competence of each code for each person. Who has a large repertoire of codes available to them, and what difference does this make to their lives? Are some codes more socially valued than others?

❑ You could investigate the history of what dictionary compiler Noah Webster called 'the American language'. What were the language-planning motivations of American politicians and thinkers in promoting an American style of English? How did they go about codifying this and encouraging its use in the United States?

❑ The influence of American forms of English on the other Englishes around the world has been immense. Take one local area (in the UK, Australia, Singapore, or non-English places like Japan, Thailand, France, Germany, and so on) and explore the influence of American English. This could have effects at the level of accent, or particular word-usage and spelling, or at a dialectal level. See if you can find examples of local resistance to 'Americanisms', such as in the letters pages of conservative newspapers.

❑ How does the English spoken by ethnic minorities in general English-speaking environments show interference patterns? You will need to compare real examples of the community speech in English with what you know or can discover about the grammar of the influencing language.

❑ How are attitudes to particular linguistic codes represented by the media? You should focus on one aspect of the media (such as television news, newspaper cartoons, magazine advertisements, the representation of African-Americans by Hollywood, and so on) and draw out the attitude to the language involved. Is the representation consistent across your data, or are there shifts in attitude over time or between different texts?

## STYLE AND IDEOLOGY

In the article by Norman Fairclough below, the notion of metaphor is used as a means of describing two different sorts of ideological representation in newspaper reporting.

Elsewhere in the book from which this extract is taken, Fairclough uses a linguistic analysis to draw out many different aspects of media respresentation, linking the form of expression with the ideological motivations underlying the discourses.

In discussing forms of register, metaphor and euphemism, this reading complements issues discussed in thread 3. Language and ideology are also treated in B12 and C12.

## Analysis of discourses in newspaper texts

**Norman Fairclough** (reprinted from *Media Discourse*, London: Edward Arnold, 1995b: 94–102.)

Discourses are [. . .] constructions or significations of some domain of social practice from a particular perspective. It is useful to identify discourses with names which specify both domain and perspective – for instance, one might contrast a Marxist political discourse with a liberal political discourse, or a progressive educational discourse with a conservative educational discourse. I shall illustrate the analysis of texts in terms of discourses using press coverage of an air attack on Iraq by the USA, Britain and France on 13 January 1993 (two years after the Gulf War), referring to 14 January editions of five British newspapers: the *Daily Mirror*, the *Sun*, the *Daily Mail*, the *Daily Telegraph* and the *Guardian*, and the *Guardian Weekly* for the week ending 24 January 1993. I focus upon two issues: the 'congruent' as opposed to 'metaphorical' selection of discourses for formulating who did what to whom and why within the attack; and the role of *configurations* of discourses in the construction of these events.

The distinction between congruent and metaphorical discourses is the extension of a terminology used by Halliday (2003). A congruent application is the use of a discourse to signify those sorts of experience it most usually signifies; a metaphorical application is the extension of a discourse to signify a sort of experience other than that which it most usually signifies. The distinction is a rough one, but a useful one. Metaphorical applications of discourses are socially motivated, different metaphors may correspond to different interests and perspectives, and may have different ideological loadings. The following examples (headlines and lead paragraphs) illustrate how congruent and metaphorical discourses combine in the coverage of the attack.

*Spank You And Goodnight*
*Bombers Humble Saddam in 30 Minutes*
More than 100 Allied jets yesterday gave tyrant Saddam Hussein a spanking – blasting missile sites in a raid that took just 30 minutes.

*(Sun)*

*Saddam's UN Envoy Promises Good Behaviour After Raid by US, British and French Aircraft*
*Gulf Allies Attack Iraqi Missiles*
More than 100 aircraft blasted Iraqi missile sites last night after the allies' patience with Saddam Hussein's defiance finally snapped.

*(Daily Telegraph)*

In the examples I looked at, it is a discourse of military attack that is congruently applied (e.g. *jets* or *aircraft blasting missile sites* and *Gulf Allies Attack Iraqi Missiles* in the examples above). Not surprisingly, we find such formulations in all the reports, along with expressions like 'retaliate' and 'hit back' (e.g. *Iraq To Hit Back*, in the *Sun*) which represent these events as a contest between two military powers. But there are distinctions to be drawn. Whereas the *Guardian*, the *Daily Mail* and the *Daily Telegraph* use what one might call an 'official' discourse of military attack – that is, they use the sort of language that might be used in official and military accounts – the *Sun* and the *Daily Mirror* (and exceptionally the *Daily Telegraph* in the example above: *more than 100 aircraft blasted Iraqi missile sites*) use a fictional discourse of military attack, the discourse of stories about war (whether purely fictional, or fictionalized versions of fact), which highlights physical violence. The *Daily Mirror* is particularly rich in expressions for processes of attack which link to this discourse: *blitz, blast, hammer, pound, blaze into action,* (warplanes) *scream in*. While the attacks are mainly formulated as action by aircraft or 'the allies' against 'Iraq' or specific targets (e.g. 'missile sites' or 'control centres'), both the *Daily Mirror* and the *Sun* also formulate them in a personalized way as directed at Saddam Hussein (*The Gulf allies struck hard at Saddam Hussein*, '*Spot Raids Give Saddam Pasting*', *allied warplanes have bombed the hell out of Saddam Hussein*).

The main headline and lead paragraph from the *Sun* above show that formulations of the attack do not by any means draw only upon military discourse: *Spank You And Goodnight* (notice the play on 'Thank you and goodnight' which makes a joke even of this serious event) and *More than 100 Allied jets . . . gave tyrant Saddam Hussein a spanking*. This is a metaphorical application of an authoritarian discourse of family discipline which is a prominent element in representations of the attack – Saddam as the naughty child punished by his exasperated parents. The *Guardian* editorial sums it up as *an act of punishment against a very bad boy who thumbed his nose several times too often* – also notice *the allies' patience . . . finally snapped* and *good behaviour* in the *Daily Telegraph* example, both consistent with this disciplinary discourse. (One might also be tempted to read 'spanking' in terms of a discourse of sexual 'correction'.) The attack is formulated several times in the reports as 'teaching Saddam a lesson' (for instance, *The allies launched 114 war planes to teach defiant Saddam a lesson* in the *Daily Mirror*, and *Let's hope he's learnt his lesson*, attributed to a US official in the *Sun*). This is again consistent with the discourse of family discipline, or disciplinary discourses more generally. So too with *Toe The Line Or . . . We'll Be Back!*, the main page-one headline in the *Daily Mirror*. Such conditional threats ('do x or we'll do y', 'if you do x – or don't do x – we'll do y') occur several times in the report.

A related but rather more specific metaphorical discourse that is evoked is that of the disciplining of young offenders, juveniles found guilty of crimes (with the focus on crimes of particular sorts, such as 'joy-riding'). A British government official is quoted in most reports as saying that the attack was *a short, sharp and telling lesson* for Saddam. This evokes the expression used by the British Conservative government in the 1980s, when it tried to develop the policy of delivering a 'short, sharp shock' (in the form of incarceration in highly disciplined quasi-military institutions) to juvenile offenders. The same group of discourses is indicated in reasons given for the attack. The headline for a report on pages 2–3 of the *Sun* is *He Had It Coming*, and the lead paragraph refers to the *pasting* that Saddam Hussein *has been asking for*. According to the *Daily Mirror*, Saddam had *pushed his luck too far*. These formulations evoke a conversational or 'lifeworld' version of an authority-based discourse of discipline, referring to what is elsewhere frequently formulated in the reports as the 'provocations' of the subordinate party in this disciplinary relationship, i.e. Saddam (note also formulations such as Saddam 'goading' or 'taunting the West'). Disciplinary formulations such as 'provocations' alternate with legalistic formulations such as 'breaches' and 'infringements' (of the UN ceasefire conditions).

The metaphorical application of such discourses is a very prominent feature of these reports, and in assessing that application one might wonder whether such a disciplinary relationship applies or ought to apply in relations between nations, or indeed whether the relations between nations ought to be personalized as they con-sistently are here: the target of discipline is Saddam, not Iraq or the Iraqi government – whereas its source is mainly 'the (Gulf) allies' or 'the West', and rarely George Bush (the American president at the time).

Other discourses are metaphorically applied, though they are less prominent in the reports. One is evident in the *Sun* headline *Bombers Humble Saddam in 30 Minutes* as well as the *Daily Mail* headlines *Allies Humble Saddam* and *Retribution in the Gulf*. I think these can be read in terms of a (Christian) religious discourse, though 'retribution' also evokes a legal discourse. Another discourse which features only once here – attributed to a Whitehall official by the *Daily Mirror* – but was quite common in coverage of hostilities in the Gulf at the time, is a discourse of communication exchange, of 'signals' sent through military actions. (In the words of the Whitehall official, *If Saddam does not get this message . . . he knows there will be more to come.*) Again, both the *Sun* and the *Daily Mirror* draw upon a discourse of dangerous-animal control in their editorials: the air strikes are intended to 'curb' Saddam, and if *he doesn't learn this time, he will have to be put down for good like the mad dog he is* (*Daily Mirror*), *the tragedy is that we did not finish him off last time* (the *Sun*).

An important distinction within a report, which takes us back to the discussion of discourse representation earlier in this chapter, is between discourses which occur in represented discourse attributed to the 'voices' of others in quotations or summaries, as opposed to discourses which are unattributed and are drawn upon by the 'voice' of the report itself. However, a key question (which requires historical research and research on production processes) is where the discourses of reporters come from. By com-paring attributed and unattributed formulations within and across reports, one can often see the same discourses being drawn upon by reporters and official sources. For example, the discourse of correction (in *Spank You And Goodnight*, also in the *Daily Mirror* inside-page headline *A Spanking Not A Beating* and in the headline of the *Guardian* editorial *More A Smack Than A Strike*) may have originated in a statement by a US official: *It's just a spanking for Saddam, not a real beating*. Similarly the *Sun* headline *He Had It Coming* and more generally 'teach-Saddam-a-lesson' formulations apparently echo official sources – the *Sun* quotes a White House statement: *Saddam had this coming. Let's hope he has learnt his lesson.*

Official influence upon media formulations is built up over the longer term rather than just on a day-by-day basis; 'teach-Saddam-a-lesson' formulations had been widely used officially and by the press for a period before the attack, and similarly official sources including President Bush had spoken of 'patience running out' in the weeks before the attack. (Also, this relatively minor Iraq crisis was intertextually linked to earlier ones including the Gulf War, and fed discoursally from them. See the discussion of 'discourse-historical' method of analysis in Wodak 1990.) The *Guardian*, the *Daily Telegraph* and the *Daily Mail* are more likely generally to use such formulations only as attributions. There is a constant flow between official sources and the media: the latter may take up the discourses of the former, but the former also design their statements and press releases to harmonize with discourses favoured by the media. Bruck (1989) points out that the influence of official discourses on media discourse depends upon the discourse type – it is, for instance, likely to be greater in news reports than in editorials or features.

While the discourses and specific formulations of certain favoured sources are massively present and foregrounded, those of other – and especially oppositional – sources are either omitted altogether from some reports, or backgrounded. For example, the Labour Party leftwinger Tony Benn described the attack as the *last piece of gunboat diplomacy* of a *lame-duck US president* according to the *Guardian*, but that was the only report of Benn's comment, and it was backgrounded (positioned in a single paragraph in the middle of a report in the bottom left-hand corner of a centre page). Formulations of the attack attributed to the Kuwaiti government, which draw upon a discourse of disease and surgical intervention (*bursting the abscess of the Baghdad govern-ment* according to the *Sun*, *removing the Iraqi cancer* according to the *Daily Telegraph*), were quite widely reported though backgrounded. By contrast, only the *Guardian* reports formulations of Saddam's actions prior to the attack as 'acrobatics' and 'mere fireworks' (from the newspaper *al-Ahram*, Cairo), and 'clownish' behaviour (*al-Thaurah*, Damas-cus), constructing Saddam in the less threatening role of a clown/performer (clowns don't generally merit bombing). Significantly, the same reports highlight the 'double standards' applied by the West, in not reacting as vigorously to the plight of Muslims under attack by Serbians in Bosnia, or of the 400 Palestinians extradited by Israel and isolated in No Man's Land between Israel and Lebanon at that time, in defiance of a United Nations resolution. Why no air attacks on Israel?

If selection between alternative congruent and metaphorical discourses is one issue, another is configurations of discourses, how discourses are articulated together within discourse types. Bruck (1989), for instance, suggests that five main discourses were drawn upon by the Canadian media in the mid–1980s in their coverage of dis-armament, peace and security issues, which he calls: the discourse of state leaders, bureaucratic-technical discourse, scientific-technical discourse, the discourse of victims, and the discourse of survival. The first three are dominant discourses, the last two oppositional discourses. The analysis of news output is concerned with both the selec-tions made between these discourses, and the ways in which they are articulated together, which between them allow the analyst to describe the range of discursive practice in the coverage of these issues.

The following report was inset in a double-page spread in the *Daily Mirror* of 14 January, dealing with the attack in Iraq. (Major reports are often made up in this way of combinations of smaller reports, and the relationship between articles on a page in such cases is worth attending to.)

### The Mother Of All Rantings

Evil dictator Saddam Hussein promised Iraq last night they were winning a new great victory – just like they had in the 'Mother of All Battles' in Kuwait. His pledge came three hours after allied aircraft pounded his missile sites.

In a ranting, confused speech, he told his nation on television that a new jihad – holy war – had begun. He urged the Iraqis to fight 'in the name of God' . . . and he promised them they would humiliate the allies.

Saddam called the allies 'the infidels' and said they were 'under the influence of Satan'. And he raged: 'Every aeroplane of the aggressors in the Iraq sky shall be a target for us and we shall fight in the name of God and down their aircraft. The aggressors will be defeated.'

Reading stiffly from hand-held notes, he said: 'The criminals have come back. But tonight they came back without any cover, not even a transparent one.

'They came back for the purpose they never spoke about the first time in their evil aggression, namely to impose colonialism.'

This report includes a new and clearly oppositional configuration of discourses for formulating the attack, attributed to Saddam himself: an Islamic religious discourse (*infidels, under the influence of Satan*), and political discourses of aggression and colonialism. The reference to the absence of any 'cover' obliquely cues also a legal discourse – the attacks were condemned as 'illegal' by those who opposed them. Notice also that the allies are referred to here as *criminals*.

However, this oppositional configuration of discourses is framed within a larger configuration by the dominant discourses I have discussed above. Saddam's speech is firstly formulated and summed up in the headline in an ironic play upon his own (in)famous description of the Gulf War as 'the mother of all battles', with *rantings* evoking discourses of madness and political fanaticism. In the lead paragraph, Saddam is referred to as an *evil dictator*, deploying the religious and political discourses I referred to earlier as part of the anti-Saddam armoury. The summary of Saddam's speech in the second paragraph is framed by the initial thematized phrase in a ranting, *confused speech*, and similar framing devices are used where Saddam is directly quoted – notice the choice of *raged* as a reporting verb, and *reading stiffly*. In the first two of these cases there is again an evocation of the discourse of madness. The net effect of the framing of Saddam's oppositional discourses with the dominant ones is to undermine and ridicule the former.

Diverse discourses are articulated together in the naming and identification of both the protagonists and the antagonists, though to quite different effects. The identification of the protagonists caused some difficulty in that the USA, Britain and France were claiming to act to enforce a United Nations resolution, but neither the 'no-fly' zone they had imposed on southern Iraq nor the attack had been endorsed by the UN. The attackers are referred to in the reports as 'the Gulf allies', 'the West', and most frequently 'the allies'. 'The Gulf allies' is problematic in that the alliance which fought Iraq in the Gulf War was actually divided on this later attack, and none of the Arab members of the alliance was involved. 'The West' is problematic because a number of members of 'the West' were also critical. 'The allies', with its reassuring evocation of the Second World War, seems to have been the least problematic label. The *Guardian* also refers 'correctly' to 'the United States, Britain and France'. A number of other identifications were used elsewhere: in the *Guardian Weekly* 'the coalition' and 'the US and its allies' were used, and President Clinton was quoted as supporting *the international community's actions*. The variety of these formulations, the range of discourses they draw upon, and the instability of naming practices here, are indicative of the difficulty in constructing an identity for the protagonists.

By contrast, the considerable range of expressions used to refer to Saddam Hussein shows a number of discourses working together to discredit him, as in the following editorial from the *Sun* on 14 January:

### Wipe Out The Mad Menace

At long last, Allied warplanes have bombed the hell out of Saddam Hussein.

The Iraqi madman has pushed the West too far.

He has played a dangerous game and now he must pay the price.

Four times Saddam has sent raiding parties over the border into Kuwait.

### Menace

His boast that Iraq planned to 'recover' Kuwait was the last straw.

The tinpot tyrant could not be allowed to cling onto power a moment longer.

He is an international terrorist, a constant menace to peace.

The tragedy is that we did not finish him off last time.

Go get him, boys!

This is discoursal overkill: a remarkable range of discourses are articulated together in the verbal annihilation of Saddam Hussein. The density of the assembled discourses is no doubt attributable to the fact that the genre is editorial rather than news report: this is an apologia for the attack, based upon a thorough discrediting of Saddam Hussein. He is referred to as a *madman*, a *menace to peace*, a *tyrant*, a *terrorist*, a *blusterer* (cf. *his boast*), and a figure of ridicule (the implication of *tinpot*), yet at the same time a calculating politician (who has *pushed the West too far*, and *played a dangerous game*), and actions against him are formulated in terms of discourses of legal retribution (*he must pay the price*), war fiction (*bombed the hell out of*) and even westerns (*wipe out, finish off, go get him, boys*). We find the range of discourses extending further elsewhere – he is referred to, for instance, in the terms of religious and ethical discourses as 'evil' and a 'coward'.

A configuration of discourses is put to different effect in the editorial in the *Guardian Weekly*, where evaluation of competing discourses is itself a topic. The editorial is a critique of the attack, under the headline *What Signal Will He Read?* The editorial is a dialogue with opposing positions represented by different discourses. Thus it refers to – and distances itself from – *headmasterly talk of Teaching Saddam a Lesson*, and attributes the discourse of *delivering a signal* to Saddam to what it calls *the tough-minded* (this discourse generates the expression 'coercive bombing' in another report in the same edition). It does, however, in its own voice draw upon some of the dominant discourses for formulating Saddam and his actions (he is *evilly brutal Saddam*, with a *record of provocation* – though perhaps *deliberate*). The editorial also formulates the attack, tentatively, in a different discourse: *Mr Bush's likely desire to settle accounts before leaving office*.

Other terms which are roughly equivalent to 'discourses', but derive from different theoretical frameworks and traditions, are quite widely used, including schemata, frames, and scripts (from cognitive psychology), metaphors, and vocabularies. I have discussed metaphorical applications of discourses, and for the most part the discourses I have referred to are realized in the vocabulary of texts. Aspects of grammar may also be involved in the realization of discourses. For instance, I noted earlier that conditional threats (e.g. *Toe The Line . . . Or We'll Be Back*) are a feature of disciplinary discourse, and these are realized in particular syntactic constructions (in this example, imperative clause *or* declarative clause).

Analysis of *collocations* in texts (patterns of co-occurrence between words) is a way of linking analysis of discourses to the linguistic analysis of texts (Sinclair 1992). Configurations of discourses identified in the analysis of discourses may be realized in – condensed into – collocational relations in phrases or clauses (Fairclough 1991). Collocations are often a good place to look for contradictions in texts. For example, in the editorial from the *Sun* above, the following collocations occur: *mad menace, tinpot tyrant, the Iraqi madman has pushed the West too far. Mad* evokes the discourse of madness whereas *menace* evokes the discourse of political extremism, and the collocation bonds the two discourses together in a detail of the text. Similarly, *the Iraqi madman has pushed the West too far* compacts together the discourse of madness and the discourse of political calculation.

Both selections amongst available discourses and selection of particular ways of articulating them together are likely to be ideologically significant choices. There may, for instance, be various ways of rationalizing the decision to construct relations between 'the West' and a 'Third World' country like Iraq as relations between a teacher and a recalcitrant child, but such a construction implicitly evokes an imperialist and indeed racist ideology of relations between nations, which contributes to the continuity of imperialist and neo-colonialist relations in practice. Of course, [. . .] one cannot assume ideological effects consequent upon selections of discourses, merely that the question of potential ideological effects is always worth raising.

### Issues to consider

Exploring ideology or metaphor or euphemism are fruitful dimensions of study. Sociolinguistics students, however, must be careful that work in these areas has a social dimension as well as a purely grammatical analysis. The key is to engage in both social theory and linguistics, and relate the two. Many students' essays in ideology remain general and simply opinionated; the way of avoiding this is to ensure you return constantly to examples of the actual language used, and apply a linguistic analysis to it.

Some practical suggestions follow.

❑   As a means of achieving a focus in analysis, restrict your data to one story on one day across a selection of newspapers, or one story over two weeks, or just the front pages of a day's newspapers. Ask yourself questions such as: how are different groups represented in language? Are different grammatical constructions used consistently for different groups of people? Are words from certain semantic fields used consistently for particular groups? Which groups tend to appear as the subjects of sentences and which as the objects? What evaluative adjectives and adverbs are used? Is there a semantic pattern in the verb choices associated with particular groups?

❑ Most news reports concern people (such as politicians, judges, representatives and commentators) saying things, making speeches, issuing statements, and then debating the utterances made by others. How is all this speech reported? When is speech quoted directly, when is it paraphrased, and when is it summarised? How does the ideological stance of the reporter, newspaper or TV programme have an effect on the choice of representation?

❑ Take Fairclough's notions of metaphorical and congruent configurations of discourse and track their use and sources in other news stories. If metaphorical configurations are discovered, identify the source domains of the metaphors and consider, like Fairclough, how these choices affect the ideology of the text.

❑ What metaphorical configurations are used to represent America and Europe, or your own government and politicians, or countries in the developing world, or democracy, or even sports reports or natural or human disasters? Do the media represent particular relationships in consistent ways?

## LANGUAGE CONTACT AND CODE-SWITCHING

In the reading which follows, John Edwards draws the connections between borrowing (or 'copying') and how this contact between languages often results in interference patterns in the target language. Code-switching is often the specific mechanism through which the borrowing of words and constructions happens.

The terms used here were introduced in A4, B4 and C4. The influence of the processes discussed, especially on newer forms of English, was also mentioned in A9, B9 and C9.

### Borrowing, interference and code-switching

**John Edwards** (reprinted from *Multilingualism*, Harmondsworth: Penguin, 1995: 72–8.)

Outright language choice is obviously available to bilingual individuals, and an illustrative example is found in Paraguay. Here, more than 90 per cent are bilingual in Guaraní and Spanish. Language choice is non-random, and heavily influenced by external constraints, as Figure D4.1 shows.

It is also common to find linguistic alteration occurring within one unit of speech directed to one listener. In his classic volume on the subject, Weinreich (1966) stated that all such 'deviation from the norms of either language' may be referred to as *interference*. It seems evident, however, that not every switch from one language to another results from the unwelcome intrusion which the term *interference* suggests; speakers may often switch for emphasis, because they feel that the *mot juste* is found more readily in one of their languages than in another, or because of their perceptions of the speech situation, changes in content, the linguistic skills of their interlocutors,

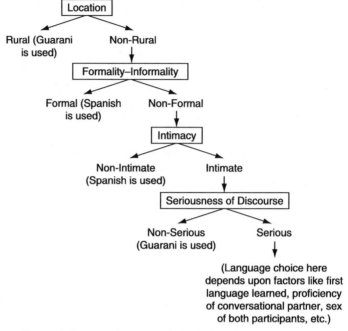

*Figure D4.1*   Factors influencing language choice in Paraguay
*Source:* after Rubin 1968

degrees of intimacy and so on. Some writers have thus opted for the more neutral term *transference* which implies, among other things, a greater element of volition. There is certainly a wide range of possibilities, as the following examples suggest:

(1)   The proceedings went smoothly, ba? (Tagalog)

(2)   This morning I hanter my baby tu dekat babysitter tu lah ('This morning I took my baby to the babysitter'). (Malay–English)

(3)   De pompier militaire van de staat . . . loop partout me ne vitesse zoo rapide as de chemin de fer ('The state military fireman . . . runs everywhere with the speed of a railway'). (French–Dutch)

(4)   Sano että tulla tänna että I'm very sick ('Tell them to come here that I'm very sick'). (Finnish–English)

(5)   Sometimes I'll start a sentence in English y termino en español ('Sometimes I'll start a sentence in English and end it in Spanish').

These examples of code-switching (some refer to it as code-*mixing*; these and other terms have yet to reach agreed-upon definition) illustrate changes of various types. Example (1) shows 'tag-switching', where a stock element in one language (often interrogatory or exclamatory) is joined to an utterance in another. A common related event is when speakers of German French, for whom the tags *nicht wahr* and *n'est-ce pas* are all-purpose say, in English, something like *She's a nice person, isn't it?* This is plainly a matter of interference. Examples (2) and (3) show *intrasentential* mixing; indeed, (3) is particularly interesting. Is this mainly lexical interference, since the basic structure is Dutch, or is it better seen as repeated switching? Finally, examples (4) and (5) show *intersentential* mixing/switching, where the change occurs at a clause or sentence boundary.

A considerable amount of research has been devoted to the understanding of the linguistic factors which may account for various types of code changing, the constraints which make one form more likely or common than another, and so on. Obviously this has a great deal to do with the grammar and syntax of each of the languages involved.

Different *types* of language transfer can be easily understood. For example, if a Brussels French speaker uses the Dutch *vogelpik* for a game of darts, rather than the standard French *flèchettes*, this is an example of *lexical* transfer. Further, *vogelpik* in this context constitutes a *loanword* since it is an 'intrusion' regularly used in unchanged form. It may, however, be given a French pronunciation, which indicates another type of 'change', an attempt to bring the foreign element into the maternal fold (another familiar example is the French adoption of the English *pullover*, pronounced 'poolovaire').

Sometimes loanwords become very widely used and, if we go far enough, we reach the level of permanent interlanguage borrowing. Here are some 'English' words showing eastern influence:

> ALCOHOL (Arabic *al-koh'l*): powdered antimony, then any quintessence (e.g., 'alcohol of wine' via distillation), then just the intoxicating ingredient.
> ALGEBRA (Arabic *al-jebr*): the reuniting of broken parts, first used in English to refer to the setting of bones.
> ASSASSIN (*hash-shashin*): hashish-eaters, a sect who killed under the influence of cannabis.
> BUCKRAM: first meant a high-quality fabric from Bokhara then, later, coarse cloth.
> EUNUCH (Greek *eunoukhos*): 'bed-guard'.
> GAZETTE (Italian *gazeta* or *gazzetta*): name of a small Venetian copper coin.
> ONYX (Greek *onux*): 'claw, fingernail'(pink, with white streaks).
> PUNCH (Hindi *panch*, Sanskrit *panchan*): 'five'(i.e., the five basic ingredients: wine/spirit, water/milk, sugar, lemon and spice).
> TABBY: from *Al-'at-tabiya*, a suburb of Baghdad named for Prince Attab where a cloth was made known as *attabi*; this was usually striped. Later applied to cats.

A modern example of words beginning to enter a foreign vocabulary is found in the English of Quebec, where a speaker might now say something like:

> I took the autoroute to the dépanneur [convenience store], stopped at the caisse populaire [credit union] . . . crossed [met] the representative of my syndicate [union], who has been seized with [informed of] my dossier.

It is interesting to note, though, that not all languages can incorporate borrowed elements equally easily. The grammatical constraints may be such – say, between two languages widely removed from one another typologically – that borrowing may be less frequent than it is between closely-related languages. More simply, borrowings from language A may not fit as easily into B as into C. This may have important consequences for B and C if A, for example, is the variety of a 'developed' society and they are not.

Another variety of lexical transfer occurs when loan *translation* occurs: for example, the adoption of the English *skyscraper* into Dutch (as *wolkenkrabber*), German (*wolkenkratzer*), French (*gratte-ciel*) and Spanish (*rascacielos*). Such words are called *calques* (literally, 'copies'). *Morphological* transfers occur when a word in language A is more fully embraced by language B: the Dutch *kluts* (dollop) becomes, in Brussels French, *une clouche*, and *heilbot* (halibut) becomes *un elbot*. *Syntactic* transfer occurs in such examples as *Tu prends ton plus haut chiffre* ('You take your highest figure') – said by a native Dutch speaker, who makes his adjectives precede the noun, as they would in Dutch (*Je neemt je hoogste cijfer*) but not as they would in French. *Phonological* transfer is very common, of course, and is a most difficult area in which to avoid interference (consider fluent adult speakers with 'horrible' accents). Equally, *prosodic* transfer – subtle differences in stress and intonation between languages, such that one's dominant variety influences the other – is also difficult to avoid. In Standard French the appropriate emphasis would be *il faut pas dire ça!* ('You mustn't say that!') but in Brussels French the emphasized word is *dire*, on the model of the Dutch *Ge moogt dat niet **zeggen***.

This brief discussion of interference and code-switching only scratches the surface, but it does reveal something of the variety of transference and, more importantly, the variability in terms of conscious intent. That is, bilingual speakers may *choose* to use *vogelpik*, and their choice may be determined by non-linguistic, social factors; syntactic and phonological interference, on the other hand, is presumably less subject to such factors or, more accurately perhaps, is less easily or directly influenced by them, necessitating more effort to remove it. In general one might roughly view interference phenomena as those determined by internal factors, and code-switching as more influenced by extralinguistic constraints; however this is only general, as even the few examples given here suggest.

However we divide the subject up, and whatever labels we apply – interference, code-switching, mixing, transference, etc. – it is clear that in all cases something is 'borrowed' from another language. Further, the degree to which the borrowed element is integrated (or can be integrated) into the other code may be of considerable interest for studies of group contact, of relative linguistic prestige, of the perceived or actual ease with which different languages deal with given topics, and so on. Borrowings may be on a 'nonce'basis or may represent more established practice, but the latter grows from the former and presumably reflects stronger and more widespread need. However, a further subdivision has been suggested for these established borrowings; some are indeed necessary – words filling lexical gaps in the other language, for example – but some are 'gratuitous' – there already exists the equivalent item. Why, then, the borrowing? The motivation here is most often perceived status and prestige. Common examples include the use of foreign words or phrases. To say that something is a *sine qua non* or, *mutatis mutandis*, might become *la crème de la crème* (*sensu bono*, of course) in terms of representing the *Zeitgeist*, is perhaps to reach the *Ultima Thule, poco a poco*, of prestige – but it can be overdone, *non è vero*? Four hundred years ago, du Bellay also had reservations:

> Among other things, let our poet take care not to use the Latin and Greek proper names, a thing as absurd really as if thou shouldst apply a piece of green velvet to a dress of red velvet. But would it not be an absurd thing to use in a Latin work the proper name of a man or other thing in French, as *Jan currit, Loyre fruit*, and other like words? Suit, then, such proper names, of whatever language they be, to the use of thy vulgar

tongue . . . say in French *Hercule, Thésée, Achille, Ulysse, Virgile, Ciceron, Horace*. Thou shouldst, however, in this use judgment and discretion, for there are many such names which cannot be appropriated into French: . . . I refer you to the judgment of your ear. As for the rest, use words purely French, not, however, too common, nor yet too rarely used.

At another level, one can observe the trendy status of English which seems to be growing around the world, even among those ignorant of it. It has been reported, for example, that shops in the re-emerging eastern European countries often find it easier to sell their products (when they have any) if they are labelled in English. No English competence is implied or required in either seller or buyer; simple recognition and cachet apparently do the trick. English is the international language, too, of pop music and culture (the coca-colonialism factor). As Michael Luszynski, a Polish singer, wryly noted recently, a phrase like *Słysze warkot pociagu nadjedzie na torze* does not have the same oomph as 'I hear the train a-coming, it's rolling down the line' – even to Polish speakers with no English. In Germany, teenagers wear *die Jeans*, in Moscow you can attend a *dzhazz-saission*, you can say *baj-baj* in many countries, and even the French grudgingly acknowledge the appeal of *le drugstore* and *le weekend*. In Japan, English has a social clout which, again, is underpinned by neither knowledge nor grammaticality. Tomato juice may be sold as 'red mix for city actives', a coffee-shop motto is 'world smell in cup, full', a soft drink is called 'Pocari sweat' and one can get advice on 'how to sex'. This omits the use of English words more fully integrated into Japanese, often in abbreviated form (e.g., *hamu tosuto* for a 'toasted ham sandwich', *apaato* for 'apartment' and many others in regular use).

Under the heading 'Pretentious diction', Orwell excoriated the use of many foreign words and expressions – *Weltanschauung, status quo, ancien régime* and all the rest – which he said are used to 'give an air of culture and elegance'. Some abbreviations – *e.g. i.e.*, and *etc.* – are useful, and Orwell thought that a few other terms might be necessary. He noted, though, that 'if we really need the word *café* . . . it should either be spelled "caffay" or pronounced "cayfe" '. He went on to say that 'bad writers, and especially scientific, political and sociological writers, are nearly always haunted by the notion that Latin or Greek words are grander than Saxon ones'; thus he also saw as unnecessary such terms as *ameliorate, deracinated* and *clandestine*. The avoidance of perfectly good English words, he felt, led to 'slovenliness and vagueness'. Finally, Orwell criticized phrases like *a not unjust final assumption* – which he thought should be laughed out of existence: 'One can cure oneself of the *not un-* formation by memorizing this sentence: *A not unblack dog was chasing a not unsmall rabbit across a not ungreen field.*' Well, there is a lot to all of this but, as elsewhere, Orwell's passion and generalization obliterate some useful elements along with many bad ones. I would not like to lose *clandestine*, for example, and phrases like *ancien régime* have resonances which one may quite appropriately wish to summon, and are not easily replaceable with concision.

In still other cases, borrowing may occur for what Weinreich (1966) lightly termed 'cacophemistic purposes'. Citing a study done in the 1930s, he observed that:

> the patois of French Switzerland have no morally favorable terms of German origin, but they swarm with German words for disreputable or badly dressed women, rudeness, coarseness, indolence, sloth [and] avarice, corresponding to the stereotyped ridicule

with which the French Swiss regards the German Swiss, his culture, and above all his language, of whose inferiority the former is deeply convinced.

This sort of borrowing is often, too, allied to the desire to produce a comic effect and both this and its unilingual counterpart – alteration of accents, say, within a joke – are well-understood and frequently used devices available to virtually all speakers.

It is interesting, in all of this, to recognize that attitudes towards code-switching are often negative, particularly on the part of monolinguals who are sometimes inclined to dismiss it as gibberish. Terms like *Tex-Mex, Franglais, Japlish* (and many others) are often used, and often meant pejoratively. Bilinguals, too, are wont to see their behaviour here as 'embarrassing', 'impure', 'lazy', even 'dangerous', but the reasons they give for the practice – fitting the word to the topic, finding a word with a nuance unavailable in the other variety, helping out a listener, strengthening intimacy, and so on – make a great deal of sense. If you have two languages to draw upon, why not maximize this happy circumstance as appropriate? The chimeras of impurity and laziness are exposed when we realize that, very often, switching involves the *repetition* – for emphasis, for intimacy – of the same idea in both languages. We see, then, speakers whose twin bowstrings allow them not only the style-shifting available to monolinguals but also full language-shifting. It is hard to imagine that this is anything but a valuable addition.

### Issues to consider

Exploring language interference patterns and code-switching is, of course, much easier if you are bilingual yourself. However, it is also possible to investigate code-switching when the codes concerned are at the level of accent or dialect. Many people switch their accent when on the telephone or when telling a joke or when reporting what someone else said. Most people are multi-dialectal, unless they have the misfortune to have the national standard language as their vernacular dialect. All of these can be investigated and the social motivations for switching points can be suggested.

Some practical project ideas follow.

❑  If you are planning a holiday in a different language area soon, collect newspapers, magazines, flyers and posters (especially ones that are local or not very professionally produced) and search then for examples of linguistic code-switching. Alternatively, let the data come to you by sitting at a computer and downloading email discussion groups and chatrooms used by young people in, say, Hong Kong, Singapore, Moscow, Tel Aviv, Berlin or Amsterdam.

❑  Take a passage from any text you can find and use an etymological dictionary to track the historical source of every borrowed word. More complexly, take a passage from several different genres (e.g. a piece of academic writing, a recipe, a child's poem, or a selection of different literary genres) and apply the same etymological analysis to see whether there are generic differences in word-choice.

❑  Many euphemisms for embarrassing, socially awkward, obscene or taboo notions use foreign language borrowing as a politeness disguise. For example, take as many words as you can think of to refer to a 'toilet' and track the source languages and literal meanings of each. Does a pattern emerge? Try the same analysis for other taboo concepts.

❑  Investigate the linguistic principles, borrowing and blending behind hybrid forms of language such as Franglais, Japlish, Tex-Mex, Wenglish, Thaiglish and others.

## THE SOCIOLINGUIST'S RESPONSIBILITY

More perhaps than in any other field of linguistics, sociolinguists have long been sensitive to the ethical dimensions of conducting research investigations into the language of ordinary people. Many scholars in the field also take the view that their expertise in sociolinguistics should be used in a way that is socially and politically engaged in society, rather than pursuing research in an ivory tower. Sociolinguists, in short, have a responsibility not only for scientific accuracy and thoroughness, but also towards the community and society of which they are a part.

The following article was written by Deborah Cameron in the late 1980s and was circulated amongst colleagues but never published. Many of the criticisms and dangers she identifies have since been addressed by many sociolinguists, largely in response to discussions like this one, and sociolinguistic fieldwork practice has moved on in a positive direction. However, the article is reproduced here in order to represent an important debate within the field and as a reminder to those new to the discipline of their ethical responsibilities.

The methods introduced and discussed throughout this book should be seen in the light of arguments like this (and especially the material treated in A5, B5 and C5).

### 'Respect, please!' Subjects and objects in sociolinguistics

**Deborah Cameron** (previously unpublished)

In the early part of 1985 I got a call from a youth worker at Charterhouse in Southwark. I knew her as a friend of a friend, and she knew I was a sociolinguist who enjoyed talking about my subject. She wondered if I could describe my work to a discussion group that met at Charterhouse.

The group consisted of about eight young people, mainly young women, between the ages of 18 and 22. It was not a closed group, but it so happened that all the core members at the time were Afro-Caribbean (Southwark is a run-down inner city area with a large ethnic minority population). There was a white full-time worker – my contact – and a Black part timer. Because of the circumstances, and although I am no expert (by sociolinguists' standards) on Black English, I decided to focus on topics of special interest to Afro-Caribbeans, i.e. racism in language and creole languages. I wanted to present my work to the group in a way they would see as relevant, and I also hoped to learn something useful from them about their experiences/attitudes.

As it turned out, this decision was a good one, in the sense that the topic generated so much enthusiasm, the group decided to go on exploring it. One evening with me turned into six weeks, and eventually we made a video about language and racism. The title for this video, chosen by the group, was significant: they called it *Respect, Please!*

They tried to design it to be shown to both Black and white audiences: for white viewers it depicts the everyday experience of racism, and demands that white people respect their Black compatriots, while for Black viewers it shows how the linguistic heritage of patois (creole) can be seen as a source of Black *self*-respect.

I want to explore the theme of respect, for it is closely bound up with my own feelings about the Southwark project, and my own work in general. What *Respect Please!* represents for me as a linguist is the possibility of doing democratic and accountable research which does not make its *subjects* — nonstandard speakers — into *objects*. This project to some extent enhanced the self-knowledge and understanding of those who participated, raising our consciousness in many different ways. It was politically as well as linguistically valuable, as I hope I can show later on in this report. [. . .]

*Towards democratic research methods*

Most fundamentally, it seems to me, linguists must bear in mind a principle like the following:

KNOWLEDGE IS NOT THE RESEARCHER'S PROPERTY. IT SHOULD SERVE THE NEEDS OF BOTH RESEARCHER AND RESEARCHED.

To observe this principle, I suggest we would need to conduct research in accordance with four maxims.

*MAXIM ONE: RELEVANCE.* WHEN YOU ARE RESEARCHING IN A PARTICULAR COMMUNITY, MAKE SURE YOU ASK QUESTIONS IN WHICH ITS MEMBERS ARE INTERESTED.

When a researcher goes into a community, clearly s/he has certain preconceptions and areas of interest. Often these are dictated by the state of the literature. Thus, I decided I wanted to make a video about patois. It soon became obvious however that this would not fully reflect the group's concerns. Unlike me, they did not distinguish between the question of patois and that of racism in language; both were instances of lack of respect. Attitudes to patois undervalue the language, and racist language undervalues those who speak it. For the group it was important to address both issues, and I revised my plans accordingly.

Another point which became important through the group's insistence was the differences between different islands in the West Indies. All books on British Black English stress its bias towards Jamaican even when spoken, say, by Bajans, and some suggest this reflects a general 'Black British' as opposed to 'specific island' identity among young people (especially those born in Britain). For this group any such sugges-tion is inaccurate, though: their roots in St Lucia or Dominica or Barbados are very important and we had interesting discussions of lexical and accent differences (and of the gulf between French and English creole speakers). If I had gone by my own inclin-ations, conditioned by reading standard texts, this question of inter-island variation would never have arisen.

*MAXIM TWO: ACCOUNTABILITY.* INVOLVE THE INFORMANTS IN THE PROCESS OF RESEARCH: DO NOT LIE TO THEM OR OTHERWISE VIOLATE THEIR TRUST. DISCUSS AND NEGOTIATE THE STEPS OF YOUR RESEARCH.

An atmosphere of trust was particularly important in a project where a white researcher worked with Black informants. I never recorded without permission, left the room when the group performed in patois for the video and did not try to elicit patois on other occasions (it is not the variety used in the youth club and certainly not where white members/workers are present). Another important part of my accountability was to acknowledge the racism of white people which was under discussion, including my own. I was not defensive where white people were criticised and did not attempt to dissociate myself, though this was often painful.

When I took part in a role-play, acting the part of a racist interviewer, I accepted their direction (telling me to be more racist) and was thus faithful to their experience rather than my own. The group dictated the style of the video as well as its content and from the beginning we negotiated what it was to be for, which meant me explaining the context of my work (teaching) in detail to them.

> MAXIM THREE: RESPECT FOR INFORMANTS' VIEWS. DO NOT ASSUME THESE CAN
> BE IGNORED OR SET ASIDE AS 'IGNORANT' AND 'NON-EXPERT'. SHOW
> RESPECT FOR INTERPRETATIONS AT ODDS WITH YOUR OWN.

One area where this was relevant was in discussing the attitudes of the group's parents to patois (usually pretty negative). I tried to present my own view as an alternative conditioned by my social position (I can afford to believe patois is a triumph of the human spirit under conditions of slavery, because I don't have to put up with the stigma of speaking it, which their parents did) and not as 'God's truth'. We considered why people (including their parents, linguists etc.) believe what they do without ascribing particular authority to certain beliefs *a priori*.

> MAXIM FOUR: ACCESSIBILITY. DO NOT WRITE UP RESEARCH JUST FOR LIN-
> GUISTS, IN A WAY THAT ENSURES YOUR INFORMANTS CAN NEVER READ IT.
> IF POSSIBLE, PRODUCE RESULTS IN A FORM THEY CAN MAKE USE OF, AND
> THROUGH A MEDIUM WITH WHICH THEY FEEL COMFORTABLE.

One of the most dispiriting experiences I had in Southwark was trying to find things on creoles that the group could read. This opened my eyes to the complexity of sociolinguistic writing even on the most entertaining subjects (e.g. Labov's paper on ritual insults which would have interested my informants could they have deciphered it) and to how little of a truly popular nature is written on the subject of language at all.

For younger people like the Southwark group, I feel that writing is not in any case the optimum means of communication. They do not have the habit of non-fiction reading or writing – it could be acquired, but they would not easily come to regard it as 'theirs' in the way TV and radio are. This is why we decided to make a video, though on the face of it language is a very unvisual topic. Video also has the advantage of requiring a highly collaborative effort with people using different skills. It allows a variety of approaches to a subject: role-play, discussion, information given straight to camera. It would not be ideal for every group (and given the scarcity of good equipment, the results are apt to be technically disappointing, as they were in this case) but for young people it is worth considering. The video we eventually produced is useful to me in teaching and to the group who plan to use it in a number of ways: to demonstrate points about racism and Black identity to club trustees with no direct experience, for instance, and to stimulate discussion of language among Black peers.

To sum up, democratic research in sociolinguistics requires at least four things:

(1) The research should be perceived as relevant by informants.
(2) The process of research should be accountable to them.
(3) The researcher should not present her/himself as an expert in all things whose views are unchallengeable.
(4) The end-product should be accessible and useful to all who took part.

There is one further point. In democratic research, the *process* should be considered as important as the *product*. I often wonder what happened to the Jets, the Thunderbirds and the Cobras after Labov and his workers left: were they the same, or were they changed? The Southwark group were changed, in their case consciously and with political goals in view. The knowledge they acquired and the questions they asked will last longer and be more valuable than the grainy and inexpert 20-minute tape we collectively produced, however useful it may be. Since sociolinguistic subjects are not rocks or molecules, to be measured objectively and then just walked away from, this is as it should be. We are dealing with people whose consciousness can be altered by what they experience in a research project; and furthermore, we are people ourselves, who have a lot more to learn from our informants than the height of their vowels.

### Issues to consider

The issues raised by Cameron should be considered throughout your work in socio-linguistics. Responsible data collection is not always an easy matter, however. For example, it can be difficult to collect naturalistic, unselfconscious examples of language use without violating the maxim of 'accountability'. The observer's paradox shows that informants who are aware their language is being recorded often alter their language as a result. Similarly, it can be a challenge to explain what you are interested in to a non-expert group, and also difficult to express your findings in ways which are scholarly and disciplined but also accessible and transparent. All of these considerations require greater imagination in method design and a more careful and considered style of investigation and writing.

Some specific issues for discussion follow.

❏ Can you apply Cameron's maxims to the readings and studies outlined in this book, in order to discover how many of them represent 'data-raids' on communities of people? Specifically, can you do a 'ethical audit' on each of the students' studies reported in section B? If you find faults, how would you have redesigned the methodologies along more positive ethical principles?
❏ How would you design a fieldwork study in the following areas, while trying to follow ethical principles in your research?

❏ an investigation of the transactional language of violent crack-cocaine dealers and their clients
❏ an account of the politeness strategies used by people passing through the connections desk of an airport or railway station

    ❑    a study of the accent patterns or dialectal choices of children in a school playground

    ❑    an outline of the natural casual conversational strategies of a group of professional sociolinguists.

❑    Do you agree with Cameron's maxims for ethical fieldwork research? Would you add any other considerations, or would you modify any of them? Can you imagine any circumstances in which you would have to choose between one maxim or another? Can you imagine any circumstances in which it would be legitimate to break the maxims?

---

# THE PROCESS OF STANDARDISATION

You will have realised through your reading of this book that sociolinguistics and the study of language change are very closely related. In many ways, sociolinguistics is the modern successor to the foundations of linguistic study in etymology and philology, which were mainly concerned in the nineteenth century with the historical development and influence of languages. In the following article, James Milroy re-evaluates the continuing legacy of earlier attitudes to language change in the light of sociolinguistic insights.

    This article has been included here in order to give you a taste of complex sociolinguistic theoretical argument. It uses many of the concepts and terms that you will have encountered in the course of this book, especially in the area of prestige and standardisation (A6, B6, C6 and also B5 and C5). I have found it one of those pieces that takes time to read carefully, but the effort is rewarded with an understanding of an elegant and precise logical discussion.

### Some new perspectives on sound change: sociolinguistics and the neogrammarians

**James Milroy** (reprinted from *Newcastle and Durham Working Papers in Linguistics* 1: 181–205 (1993.)

### *1 Introduction: sociolinguistics and Neogrammarian theory*

This paper is about a very traditional topic – the theory of sound change – and its purpose is to work towards an account of sound change that is more explicitly *socio-linguistic* than those that have been used to date. We have elsewhere been concerned chiefly with the social side of this enterprise discussing *speaker variables* such as social class and network (J. Milroy 1992a: 164–222; Milroy and Milroy 1992); in this paper, my main focus is on patterns of language, rather than society. I begin with some general comments.

Sound change is probably the most mysterious aspect of change in language, as it appears to have no obvious function or rational motivation. In a change from [eː] to [iː], for example (as in such items as *meet, need, keen* in the history of English), it is impossible to see any progress or benefit to the language or its speakers – the use of one vowel-sound rather than another is purely arbitrary: there is apparently no profit and no loss. Of all the theoretical questions about language variation that we might wish to address, the question of sound change seems to me the weightiest, and the greatest challenge to our powers of explanation.

The traditional apparatus for dealing with sound change is largely derived from, or related to, the late nineteenth-century Neogrammarian movement. Their basic axiom is that sound change is 'regular': sound 'laws' have no exceptions. Thus, when a sound is observed to have 'changed' in a particular lexical item, the regularity principle predicts that it should also have changed in the same way in all other relevant items: for example, items like (general) English *fat, cab, have* are believed to undergo same particular vowel-change (e.g., front-raising, as in New York City: Labov 1966) all at the same time. If there is an apparent exception, this will be accounted for by another regular change.

[. . .]

The Neogrammarians were also interested in how 'sound change', in the narrower sense outlined above (i.e., excluding analogy and borrowing), is implemented. One important Neogrammarian claim is that regular sound change is phonetically gradual but lexically abrupt. According to Bloomfield (1933), it proceeds by 'imperceptible degrees'. Thus, the change from Middle English /eː/ to later English /iː/ (in words of the type *meet, need, keen*) is assumed not to have been sudden: according to this view, speakers pronouncing these words did not make a sudden leap across phonetic space from [eː] to [iː], the change was so slow and so slight at any given time that it was not noticed by speakers. It is also assumed to have affected all relevant items in the same way at the same time: they all start off from [eː] and, after a slow progress, all reach [iː] at the same time. It will be clear in the remainder of this paper that I do not think that this is a plausible scenario for sound change. However, we must first notice that aside from their prominence in recent sociolinguistic discussion (with which I am mainly concerned here) the Neogrammarian axioms are still very much to the fore in several other branches of linguistic inquiry.

[. . .]

Phonetic gradualness appeared to be a feasible proposition to nineteenth century scholars because of their tendency to separate languages from their speakers and to focus on language as an object – often likening it to a living thing (for a discussion see J. Milroy 1992a: 22–3). When speakers are excluded in this way, it becomes easy to believe that linguistic change is language-internal, independent of speakers and imperceptible. For the Neogrammarians it proceeds 'with blind necessity' (*mit blinder Notwendigkeit*). It is obvious that sociolinguistic approaches, which necessarily deal with speakers, are not very likely to give support to the idea of 'blind necessity', and we shall return to this point below. First we consider the main general characteristics of the Neogrammarian axioms.

The Neogrammarian axioms have at least three characteristics that are worth noticing here:

(1)  They tend to be dichotomous;

(2)  They are non-social in character;

(3)  Although the Neogrammarians recognized the importance of listening to present-day dialects their main sources are written.

At various points I shall mention dichotomies relevant to sound change. It is the third characteristic, above, that I should like to consider first.

The Neogrammarians and nineteenth-to early twentieth-century scholars generally depended on documentary records of (often ancient) languages and could not adequately observe language in the community as we do today. Thus, patterns of linguistic change that they identified (by using the comparative method for the most part) consisted of completed or nearly completed changes in languages that were usually definable as discrete entities (Sanskrit, Gothic, Old Church Slavonic and so on): they could not identify change in progress at early stages and in localized varieties (such as New York City or Belfast). Thus, they did not actually *know* whether sound change was implemented in a phonetically gradual manner: phonetic gradualness was a hypothesis. For similar reasons, social explanations could not be used except in the most generalized ways, and as late as the mid-twentieth century, American structuralists were still assuming that social explanations were not usually feasible. Indeed, quite recently, Lass (1987: 34–5) has dismissed 'external' (i.e., socially or politically-based) explanations as inherently unsatisfactory. Thus, the orthodox non-social view of language change is still very much alive.

Present-day sociolinguistic research differs from the Neogrammarian position in a number of fundamental respects. These involve the data-base available for study and the methods used to study the data-base. For example, scholars now have access to bilingual and multilingual speech communities, in which cross-language patterns of variation can be studied. These approaches strongly question the principle that linguistic change is best studied by reference to monolingual states, as the Neogrammarians and others have assumed. Most relevant here, however, is research on social dialectology following the pattern set by Labov (1966) in New York City. Studies of this kind do not focus on whole languages, but on localized varieties in regional speech communities. It is in the localized variety, rather than in the 'language' (English, French, Spanish, etc) that they identify changes in progress. The contrast with orthodox historical methodology is quite evident here. In my own work, I have additionally tried to combine this type of research with a theory of language standardization (following Haugen, 1966 and others), to which I return below. Amongst other things I would like to know how changes originating in localized varieties of the kind studied in the 1960s and 1970s by Labov, Trudgill (1974) and others, succeed (or do not succeed) in entering supralocal or standard varieties of the kind studied by the Neogrammarians. In speech community researches, of course, we are not dealing with well-defined linguistic entities that can be regarded as uniform, but with highly variable states that do not have clearly defined boundaries. Much of our effort has been directed towards developing methods of analysing and describing these highly variable states. Thus, there are clearly great differences in data-base and method between Neogrammarian and sociolinguistic studies of sound change.

[. . .]

For these reasons it is quite illuminating to consider what we might have thought about sound change if recent studies of change in progress had been the first studies of sound change ever undertaken. Suppose that the Neogrammarians had never existed and their axioms about sound change had never been proposed, and suppose also that our knowledge of language change was based entirely on recent sociolinguistic studies of change in regional non-standard speech communities – would we then consider the Neogrammarian axioms to be fundamental in our enterprise? If we had never heard of them, would we ever think of them as primary principles – and would we follow out our argumentation in the Neogrammarian framework? I shall suggest that the answer to this is no – and, further, that the orthodox framework of argumentation is not capable of dealing adequately with the phenomena that we actually do observe.

Sociolinguistic findings have in effect laid the groundwork of a new kind of discourse about language change, in which some of the old axioms are no longer axiomatic and in which the questions that we ask about sound change are a new set of questions, overlapping with the old ones but in a different distribution. In this new perspective the question whether sound change is phonetically gradual or sudden is no longer fundamental. What *is* fundamental in sociolinguistic inquiries is how we define sound change itself and, further, how we locate a sound change when it is in progress.

[. . .]

## 2 Towards a sociolinguistic modelling of language change

My account here is based on a sociolinguistic approach to the study of language change that I have been developing over the years in collaboration with Lesley Milroy (J. and L. Milroy, 1985b; J. Milroy 1992a, 1993; L. and J. Milroy 1992), and which was partly motivated in the first place by my own dissatisfaction with well-known binary distinctions of types of language change ('blind' sound change *v* borrowing, conditioned *v* unconditional change, etc). This model is differentiated from other sociolinguistic models by its insistence on the methodological priority of the study of language *maintenance* over the study of language change. It is assumed that a linguistic change is embedded in a context of language (or dialect) *maintenance*. The degree to which change is admitted will depend on the degree of internal cohesion of the community (the extent to which it is bound by 'strong ties', which resist change), and change from outside will be admitted to the extent that there are large numbers of *weak ties* with outsiders. It also follows that if a change persists in the system, it has again to be *maintained* by social acceptance and social pressure; thus, we need to explain, not only how communities resist change, but also how a change is maintained in the system after it has been accepted.

[. . .]

### 2.1 Linguistic change as change in community norms

A second issue, which constitutes a sub-theme in this paper, is the place of *sound* change within more general patterns of language shift and language change. What we have traditionally called sound changes have usually been represented as taking place at the level of the classical phonemic segment – for example, the change from [eː] to [iː] in English cited above. In the words of Bloomfield (1933): 'phonemes change'. But we must consider the possibility that sound change is not actually triggered at this level: a sound change perceived by observers at the segmental level may be a secondary, and not a primary, phenomenon: although we can observe it at the micro-level (e.g., as a change from [eː] to [iː], it may be one of a number of a low-level manifestations of a change, or a shift, that originates at a more general level of language use. I have approached this point elsewhere by proposing that linguistic change in general is a result of changes in speaker-agreement on the *norms* of usage in speech communities (J. Milroy 1992a: 91), and there is plenty of anecdotal evidence that a whole 'dialect' can die out as another 'dialect' replaces it, leaving only a few traces behind (see below for some examples). It is fairly clear that the much greater access to spoken language that we now have gives us the opportunity to follow up such questions much more thoroughly than was possible for earlier scholars, and there is much scope for future research on this issue, using *inter alia* instrumental techniques and benefiting from advances in phonological theory.

### 3  Sound change in historical linguistics

In dealing with sound change of the traditional type, the first substantive point that we need to notice is that there is, in reality, no such thing. Speech 'sounds' do not physically change: what happens is that in the course of time one sound is substituted for another; speakers of a given dialect gradually and variably begin to use sound X in environments where speakers formerly used sound Y. Historical linguistic scholars then observe the result of this essentially social process and apply the term *sound change* to the phenomenon. As Andersen (1989) points out, what historical linguists actually observe in data from the past is not a sound change, but a 'diachronic correspondence' between language states at two or more points in time (formally this is precisely the same thing as a *synchronic* correspondence between two or more states of language at the same time). In effect, they use a system-based term (sound change) for a speaker-based event in time.

    [. . .]

### 4  Social aspects of sound change

We now turn to questions which seem to be more fundamental than the question whether the implementation of sound change is phonetically gradual or not. Among these questions the meaning of the term 'sound change' is crucial. We have argued elsewhere that it is not explainable as a wholly linguistic phenomenon: it is also inherently and necessarily a *social* phenomenon in that it comes about because speakers in conversation bring it about, speakers often have very strong feelings about it, and it is manifested in speaker-usage. It isn't languages that change – it is speakers who change languages. Such a view is obviously a very long distance away from the Neogrammarian notion that sound change is 'blind'. It does not make sense, from this perspective, to say that sound-change is phonetically gradual either. But it is definitely socially gradual: it passes from speaker to speaker and from group to group, and it is this *social* gradualness that sociolinguists attempt to trace by their quantitative methods.

It seems that scholars in the past may sometimes have equated phonetic gradualness with social gradualness; that is, when they have said that a change is phonetically gradual, they have 'really meant' that it spreads gradually in the social dimension – from speaker to speaker. On the other hand, as Ohala (1993: 266) points out, many have certainly believed in the imperceptibility of change – the idea that sound change takes place in phonetic steps that are too small for the ear to detect. It is surely clear now that this is a mystical view of change, more appropriate to a belief-system than to a science, for, as Ohala also points out, we must surely accept that sound change by definition is implemented in phonetic steps that are large enough to be detected. If this were not so, we could not detect it in progress, as Labov claims we can, nor could speakers imitate it. And if it is not detectable why should we call it a sound change anyway?

The principle of social gradualness supersedes the binary division between 'regular' sound change and lexical diffusion that Labov (1992) discusses. Both processes are socially gradual, both are abrupt replacement patterns, and both can be shown to be regular in some sense. The difference between them in terms of phonetic change now becomes one of greater or lesser phonetic distance between State A (before the change) and State B (after the change). What we have traditionally called gradual phonetic change differs from lexical diffusion (following Labov's account above) in that the new form differs only slightly from the older one, whereas in lexical diffusion (as studied so far) it differs markedly. Thus, from this perspective, the two kinds of sound change are not two *opposing* types, as Labov claims. In phonetic terms, they are two ends of a continuum, with slight phonetic difference at one end and gross phonetic difference at the other.

The axiomatic distinction between regular sound change and lexical diffusion is further undermined by the fact that, as my own work and that of other sociolinguists has amply demonstrated, there is no evidence to support the Neogrammarian assumption that in regular sound change all items in the affected set change at the same time. On the contrary, sound changes have normally been observed to spread gradually through the lexicon. If we had never heard of the Neogrammarians, it seems very unlikely that we would now propose these two categories as axiomatic opposites. As sociolinguists we may now be inclined to propose some sub-divisions of types of sound change – some new taxonomies – but they will presumably be socially-based and thus quite different from the traditional taxonomies. But we must be careful not to propose premature classifications, and I am therefore quite cautious here.

### 4.1 Varying patterns of change

I shall return below to social processes, but first I would like to observe that sound-change is not necessarily a unilinear process either, and this becomes especially clear if we take a socially- or speaker-oriented point of view. It isn't just a matter of A becoming B in a unidirectional way in the course of time. What Le Page and Tabouret-Keller (1985) have called focusing and diffusion and what I have sometimes called convergence and divergence, are also patterns of change. There are other patterns also: at a sub-phonemic level, sound-change can be manifested by reduction in the number of allophonic variants (as in outer-city *v* inner-city Belfast: J. Milroy 1982) – a trend towards simplification. At much more general levels there are patterns of dialect displacement – displacement of one dialect by another which is, for some reason, socially dominant at some particular time. For example, there is evidence from recordings of persons born around 1860 which can be interpreted as indicating that much New Zealand English in the nineteenth century was southern British in type (favoured by males), and that it was displaced by an Australasian type (favoured by females) with some effects of mixing and residue. The gradual displacement of heavily inflected West

Midand dialects of Middle English by weakly inflected East Midland dialects is another example (J. Milroy 1992b) – one which led to morphological simplification of the grammar of English more generally. Changes from more heterogeneous to more homogeneous states (including the process of standardization) are also patterns of linguistic change – even though they are seldom recognized as such in orthodox historical linguistics.

## 4.2 Changing norms of language

According to our social view, language is a normative phenomenon. The norms of language are maintained and enforced by social pressures. It is customary to think of these norms as standardizing norms – norms that are codified and legislated for, and enforced in an impersonal way by the institutions of society. But the fact that we can recognize different dialects of a language demonstrates that other norms exist apart from the standard ones, and that these norms are observed by speakers and maintained by communities often in opposition to standardizing norms. It is convenient to call these *community norms* or *vernacular norms*. I have tried to show (J. Milroy 1992a: 81–4) that these norms manifest themselves at different levels of generality. Some of them, for example, characterize the dialect as a whole and are recognized by outsiders as markers of that dialect. Others, however, are hardly accessible except by quantitative methods and may function within the community as markers of internal social differences, for example, gender-difference. We have elsewhere demonstrated stable markers of gender-difference in the community (L. Milroy 1982; J. Milroy 1981, 1992a), in which the pattern is maintained over both the generations studied. It follows from this that the stable speech community is not one in which everyone speaks the same way, but one in which there is consensus on a pattern of stable variation. Another way of putting it is to say that community norms can be variable norms – in contrast to standard norms, which are invariant.

All these observations suggest certain important modifications to orthodox views of the nature of linguistic change, and these ultimately have to do with the definition of what actually constitutes a sound change, as distinct from synchronic variation. Just as language stability depends on speaker-agreement on the (variable) norms of language, so linguistic change is brought about by changes in agreement on norms. In the solidary group, which agrees on a stable variation pattern, a linguistic change in progress will show up as a disturbance of this consensus pattern. Sometimes (when the direction of change has not yet been determined) this pattern may seem to be rather inconsistent and unpredictable: in Belfast we found in the outer city a number of patterns which did not seem to have much consistency to them. We interpret this kind of pattern as indicating the break-up of consensus norms of the kind we found in the inner city (see further J. Milroy 1992a: 105–109). At other times – presumably when the direction of change has been more clearly set – there will be a regular social pattern in terms of age, sex, social class and other social variables, and it is through this that we will recognize linguistic change in progress. It should also be noted that the starting point and the end-point of change are not necessarily uniform states. As I tried to show in a paper on /h/-dropping (J. Milroy 1983), a change can persist as a variable state for seven or eight centuries without ever going to 'completion' in the traditional sense.

[. . .]

### 4.3 Speaker-innovation and linguistic change

The distinction between innovation and change leads, as we have seen, to an associated distinction – the distinction between speaker innovation, on the one hand, and linguistic change, on the other. We have suggested (Milroy and Milroy 1985b) that the terms *innovation* and *change* should reflect a conceptual distinction: an innovation is an act of the speaker, whereas a change is manifested within the language system. It is speakers and not languages, that innovate. It should also be noted that an innovation, when it occurs, must be unstructured and 'irregular' and not describable by quantitative or statistical methods. It may be observable, but when observed, it is not known that it will lead to a change and is probably thought to be an error or defective usage of some kind (Trudgill 1986b, discusses such a case in Norwich – labio-dental /r/). It is also quite clear that this distinction between innovation and change has not been sufficiently carefully or consistently observed in historical linguistics, and that many discussions about linguistic change have been in reality about linguistic innovation. Indeed, partly as a result of this conceptual confusion, questions about how linguistic change is implemented have often appealed to phenomena that have to do with synchronic variability rather than change itself. The appearance of phonetic gradualness in the data (as discussed above) is a case in point.

From a speaker-based perspective, we can think of sound-change as moving gradually through a population of speakers, assuming a regular sociolinguistic pattern, rather than postulating gradual movement within the language system (e.g., phonetic gradualness). Quantitative statements do not show how innovations occur; however, they can be interpreted as manifesting the *socially* gradual diffusion of changes. Bloomfield's account of how change may come about through gradual favouring of new variants at the expense of older ones is consistent with this position: 'Historically, we picture phonetic change as a gradual favoring of some nondistinctive features and a disfavoring of others (1933: 365)'. Although he was defending the Neogrammarians, Bloomfield's position is in certain respects also consistent with that of lexical diffusionists, as it can be disputed whether the variants involved must always be 'non-distinctive'. Bloomfield's position does not require an assumption of phonetic gradualness: it can apply equally well regardless of whether the two phonetic variants involved are closely similar or grossly different from one another, i.e., whether they are represented as resulting from gradual phonetic movement or from abrupt replacement – it is still a gradual favouring of new variants. But this gradual favouring is a speaker-based social process, rather than an intralinguistic one. It must be speakers rather than languages who 'favour' the new variants. I shall return to this point.

It should also be noted that, although we sometimes say that sound-change can now be 'observed' in progress by sociolinguistic methods, this is a loose formulation which is not strictly accurate. Locating change in progress depends on extensive (normally quantitative) analysis of data that has been collected from a speech community, and the direction and patterning of a change in a monolingual community cannot usually be reliably determined until much careful analysis has been carried out. So we don't just 'observe' it in the community. However, as I have pointed out above and elsewhere (Milroy and Milroy 1985b), we cannot *successfully* observe innovations either. To put it more precisely, although we can in principle observe linguistic innovations, we do not know when we observe them whether they are innovations that will lead to changes.

It must be assumed that the vast majority of innovations are ephemeral and lead nowhere.

It is, however, clear that for a speaker-innovation to become a change, it must be adopted by some community. It must pass from one speaker to others. Thus, the adoption of a linguistic change depends at the speaker-level on a process of *borrowing*. It is appropriate therefore to consider more closely here the effect of our social approach on another Neogrammarian dichotomy – the distinction between sound change and borrowing.

### 4.4 Innovation, change and 'borrowing'

The sound change/borrowing distinction is sometimes formulated as a distinction between 'internally' and 'externally' motivated change. This dichotomy has certainly been prominent in the work of many scholars, and although it is a well motivated distinction in certain respects (in vocabulary replacement, for example), it can be problematic at the level of phonological/morphological structure (for an especially clear discussion of important difficulties see Dorian 1993). In sociolinguistic investigations, what we call 'sound changes' in progress are often traceable to borrowings from neighbouring dialects. Bloomfield himself, in his defence of the Neogrammarians, cites an example that happens to show very clearly the difficulty of drawing the distinction between sound change and borrowing as it relates to gradual and abrupt change.

> In various parts of Europe, for instance, the old tongue-tip trill [P] has been replaced . . . by a uvular trill. . . . Aside from its spread by borrowing, the new habit . . . could have originated only as a sudden replacement of one trill by another. A replacement of this sort is surely different from the gradual and imperceptible alterations of phonetic change (1933: 390).

From a sociolinguistic perspective, the difficulties with Bloomfield's assumptions here are very striking. First, the 'origin' of this abrupt change is equated with the change itself; that is, what Bloomfield calls a change is what I have called a speaker innovation, and what has to be explained (in Bloomfield's account) is the phonetic event of abrupt replacement, not the adoption of this replacement by a community. Second, it is assumed that the spread of the change is by 'borrowing' and implied that the spread therefore *does not involve* sudden replacement – this is said to be 'aside from its spread by borrowing'. But in fact, whether we are dealing with some original event or with a concatenation of 'borrowings', each single event is equally abrupt – 'a sudden replacement of one trill by another'. In other words, it is possible to argue that each single event of 'borrowing' into a new speech community is just as much an innovation as the presumed original event in the 'original' speech community (and even that some of these events are independent innovations). Furthermore, if we accept the Bloomfieldian distinction, we may be inclined to believe that we can locate the 'original' innovation in some specific community (perhaps Parisian French), when there can be no guarantee at all that this is the original 'sound change' – the *Urquelle* of all the 'borrowings'; we cannot be certain that it had not previously been imported from somewhere else where it was 'more original' – and so backwards ad infinitum with the origin continuously receding and eluding our grasp. In other words, the distinction on which Bloomfield depends here (true sound change v phonological borrowing) is poorly motivated.

It is also possible that abrupt events of the kind envisaged by Bloomfield can occur without ever having a long-term effect on the speech community. Thus, a speaker-innovation of uvular [ɾ] may happen again and again without resulting in a linguistic change in the speech community concerned. An innovation is not in itself a change, and it is linguistic *change*, not innovation, that we are trying to explain.

As I have noted above, many consonant alternations that have been studied are manifestly of this sudden replacement type: for example, alternation of alveolar with dental stops and alternation of dental fricatives with zero in inner-city Belfast (J. Milroy 1981, etc). In the work of Trudgill (1974), Mees (1990), Kingsmore (1995) and others, alternation of [t] with the glottal stop (intervocalically and word-finally) is a particularly clear example of sudden replacement and a very common one in British English. In recent years it has been noticed that this 'glottalling' (Wells 1982: 261) is spreading rapidly in British English, and we hope to investigate this further. The work that has so far been carried out, however, raises a number of issues about the origin, spread and social correlates of glottalling that are relevant to the question of speaker-innovation and linguistic change. Here I can only summarize the main points briefly.

According to Anderesen (1968, cited in Kingsmore 1995), the earliest references to the glottal stop are from central Scotland in the 1860s, where it was noticed by Alexander Graham Bell. Subsequently there are references to it in various parts of England, including the London area in the early 1900s. Therefore, it is suggested that from an origin in Central Scotland it spread rapidly to locations in England. This raises some obvious sociolinguistic questions, such as the following: Why should Central Scotland have the kind of 'prestige' required for this rapid spread to England? How could the glottal stop have become so stereotypical of London and East Anglian English in such a short time? Additionally, from the perspective of this paper, there are other questions to be asked. These are: 1) does the evidence show that the 'original' innovation was in Central Scotland? 2) does the evidence show that the glottal stop diffused by borrowing from Central Scotland to several other places in the period 1860–1900?

The answer to both of these questions must be no. There is no evidence to support a positive answer to either. When the phenomenon was noticed in Central Scotland, it was already a well-established variant that was socially salient. If it had been at a very early stage of development with no social salience, it would not have been noticed – not even by such an excellent observer as Bell. Therefore, the origin of the glottal stop is earlier than 1860. The fact that it is well established in the Ulster Scots of County Antrim suggests (but does not prove) that it may even pre-date the Plantation of Ulster in the seventeenth century. Taking all these matters into account, it seems most unlikely that it spread to other dialects (including London English) from Central Scots. There may be an ultimate common origin for the glottal stop in some variety of early Modern English, or there may be multiple origins. The point of primary innovation and the speaker-innovator are irrecoverable. However, as I have tried to show here, drawing a careful distinction between innovation and change makes a great difference to how we interpret these phenomena.

In many of the cases discussed (including some aspects of the spread of glottalling in modern English), the most immediate explanation for the changes observed is dialect contact – externally motivated change. For Bloomfield and the Neogrammarians, this is not sound-change proper: as we have seen they tended to equate soundchange with innovation internal to the 'dialect' concerned. If Bloomfield's view is accepted, it follows that much of our sociolinguistic research has not been about sound-change at all, but about the diffusion of changes through 'borrowing'. But as I have already pointed out, the logically prior distinction between speaker-innovation and linguistic change greatly alters our understanding of this Neogrammarian distinction.

The main implication of the innovation/change distinction here is that when an innovation is taken up by a speech community, the process involved is fundamentally a borrowing process, i.e. the implementation of a sound change depends on the 'borrowing' of an innovation: all sound change is implemented by being passed from speaker to speaker, and it is not a linguistic change until it has been adopted by more than one speaker. Indeed, perhaps we need a stronger requirement: a change is not a change until it has assumed a social pattern of some kind in a speech community. To put it in another way – all sound-change must be socially conditioned, simply because those so-called changes that arise spontaneously are not actually changes: they are *innovations*, and they do not become changes until they have assumed a social pattern in the community. If, as often happens, these innovations are not adopted by some community, then they do not become changes at all. It is obviously important to try to explain how spontaneous innovations arise (and much of our intralinguistic research has been in reality about innovations), but this is not the central question that we seek to answer, which is: how do we specify the conditions under which some of these innovations, and not others, are admitted into linguistic systems as linguistic changes? From this perspective, a linguistic change is by definition a sociolinguistic phenomenon (it has both linguistic and social aspects): it comes about for reasons of marking social identity, stylistic difference and so on. If it does not carry these social meanings, then it is not a linguistic change. Similarly, if we think in traditional terms about 'sound change' and 'borrowing', we must accept that all sound change depends on a process of borrowing. Change is negotiated between speakers, who 'borrow' new forms from one another.

I have discussed the innovation/change distinction more fully elsewhere (J. Milroy 1992a, b). Here, we need to recall that we have to determine whether and in what manner the innovation (say, a uvular [ʁ]) will feed into the system as a patterned change. As long as it occurs as a variant, it is possible for it to feed into the system in this way, but although there are billions of occasions on which this is possible, it may not happen at all – even when favourable structural conditions exist in the language. For the change to take place it is necessary for the social conditions to be favourable. Thus, if we explain the phonetic and other intra-linguistic conditions that lead to this possible change, we have not thereby explained why this particular change took place, and not some other change: what we have explained are the linguistic circumstances that made possible a speaker innovation. We have not explained why it entered the linguistic system at some particular time and place and in particular social circumstances. This, of course, is the actuation problem itself (why did it happen at this particular time and place, and not at some other time and place?). This is a problem that is not ever likely to be completely solved, but our empirical studies of language in speech communities have certainly enabled us to get considerably closer to it than was previously possible. From all this, we can reasonably conclude that, in micro-level studies of sound change, the traditional distinction between 'regular sound change' and 'borrowing' is otiose, and to apply it at this level simply leads to confusion.

We have also tried to specify elsewhere (Milroy and Milroy 1985b) what the social conditions for linguistic change are likely to be, arguing that as close social ties tend to maintain stability, a large number of weak ties must be present for linguistic changes to be communicated between people. I believe that the 'weak-tie' model of change can lead us to more satisfactory accounts of change in many traditional areas of interest than have been offered to date, for example in the history of English and in some aspects of Indo-European studies (and I had these things in mind when I embarked on empirical sociolinguistic research in the first place). Here my main point is that a linguistic change is a change in linguistic structure which necessarily has a social distribution. If it does not manifest such a distribution, it should not be counted as a linguistic change.

### 5 Some broader perspectives

[. . .]

It has become very clear that the historical linguistic tradition has itself been greatly influenced by the consequences of living in a standard language culture, and this has affected judgements on the implementation and diffusion of sound change. The main influence is what I have elsewhere called *the ideology of the standard language* (Milroy and Milroy 1985a). The principles of historical linguistics have been largely based on the study of uniform states and standard or near-standard languages. Therefore, changes have frequently been envisaged as originating in 'languages' (well-defined entities such as English and French) or in fairly widely spoken 'dialects' (i.e., in linguistic abstractions), rather than in speech communities.

[. . .]

From a sociolinguistic perspective, standard languages are not 'normal' languages. They are created by the imposition of political and military power; hence the sound-patterns in them and the changes that come about in these sound patterns do *not* come about *through blind necessity*, as the Neogrammarians argued, and they are not wholly explainable by reference to phenomena internal to the *structure* of language. These language states are planned by human beings and maintained through prescription (Milroy and Milroy 1985a). The idea that there are discrete languages that can be treated as if they were physical entities is in itself a consequence of standardization and literacy – discreteness of languages is not inherent in the nature of 'language' as a phenomenon. Standard languages are carefully constructed in order to appear as if they are discrete linguistic entities – and the ideology of standardization causes people to believe that they are indeed discrete physical entities – whereas dialects and languages that have not been standardized have fuzzy boundaries and are indeterminate. The idea that the sound changes differentiating these well-defined socially-constructed entities must always come about *blindly* and independently of socially-based human intervention is, on the face of it, absurd: it is another consequence of believing in the ideology of standardization. Standard languages are not merely the structural entities that linguists have believed them to be: they are also socio-political entities dependent on powerful ideologies which promote 'correctness' and uniformity of usage (it is likely that they are in some senses more regular than non-standard forms, but further empirical research is needed into this). Thus, although regularity of the Neogrammarian kind remains as part of the general picture, it can no longer provide an adequate backdrop for the study of the origins of sound changes in the variable language states that are found in real speech communities.

Another reason for this inadequacy is that whereas standard languages (being idealizations) provide the investigator with relatively 'clean' data which have already been largely normalized, the vernaculars that we actually encounter in the speech community are relatively intractable: the data we encounter is to a greater extent 'dirty' data. To the extent that the data-base of sociolinguistic investigations presents itself as irregular and chaotic, progress in understanding linguistic change will largely depend on our ability to cope with these 'dirty' data and expose the systematicity behind them. To the extent that traditional thinking has been affected by the 'standard ideology', it has supported the emphasis on the uniform, unilinear and normalized language histories which have dominated the tradition. Now we may be better able to understand these histories for what they actually are.

### Issues to consider

In general, standardisation and the ideology of standardisation are fascinating areas to investigate. Some standardisation is a result of official and quite explicit language planning by governments or other authorities. Certain dialects or individual features are adopted, codified and promoted, and others are proscribed as 'errors'. The consequences of such language planning is especially noticeable and important when it is applied oppressively by autocratic regimes and is resisted by local speech communities. In areas where language or dialect is especially regarded as a marker of ethnic identity, there will be interesting conflicts to be explored. Attempts in history to eradicate 'Scotticisms' in English writing, or the language of the Basques by Franco's fascist regime in Spain, or the promotion of modern Hebrew in Israel, or the non-recognition of African-American English as a grammatical code are all situations that would reward reading and research.

Some practical suggestions for exploration follow.

❑ Concrete evidence for historical language change is available even in the absence of a time-machine as a sociolinguistic tool. For example, documents from the past, whether literary, legal, ecclesiastical or practical, can make very useful comparisons with the equivalent modern texts. The modern English spelling system largely represents a medieval system of pronunciation. You could list as many words as you can think of which are no longer pronounced 'as seen', and use your reading to discover when their pronunciations changed.

❑ Milroy emphasises the innovations of speakers and communities of speakers as a major factor in linguistic change. The rate of influence and change depends on the degree of creativity of the individual and their range of social connections. Do you know someone who is linguistically creative or adept at telling jokes or stories or imitating voices, for example? Are their innovations likely to be taken up by others? You could also investigate the enormous amount of creative uses of language in everyday conversation, where puns, rhyme, impromptu jokes, poetic metaphor and other witticisms occur constantly. Alternatively, you could list the buzzwords that people have adopted this year in your area or community and trace where they come from.

❏ It is possible to investigate apparent change in time by comparing the language of old and young people from the same community. Select a particular dimension of language (an accent variation, the use of particular words or constructions, prevalence of certain idioms or proverbs, and so on) and devise a means of comparing a set of grandparents and their grandchildren.

## D7   MEN'S LANGUAGE

Many recent studies of genderlects and gendered practices in language use have moved away from looking at differences in word-choice and are instead exploring the different discursive strategies used by men and women, such as conversational principles or the patterns of narrative adopted by men and women in single-sex and mixed-sex conversations. Sociolinguistic work within a broadly feminist perspective has also in recent years turned its analytical focus on the discourse practices of men. In this extract from her book, *Men Talk*, for example, Jennifer Coates uses some real examples of male story-telling to draw out the characteristic patterns of narrative organisation.

Issues in language and gender which you studied in A7, B7 and C7 are developed here. You could also compare the data presented in B10, C10, and B11.

### The formal characteristics of male narrative

**Jennifer Coates** (reprinted from *Men Talk*, Oxford: Blackwell, 2003: 18–37).

(The chapter begins with two narratives, which Coates divides into numbered narrative clauses. Transcription conventions have been adapted to match C1 in this book.)

#### *Jonesy and the lion*

1    God that reminds me talking of lion cages d'you remember Jonesy?
2    ((friend replies)) oh yeah Jonesy yeah
3    well he lost his job at the um –
4    he worked at an army camp but lost his job there
5    (   )
6    but the one I was thinking of was when he was at er – he worked at the zoo
7    (   )
8    and somebody said that they needed some electrical sockets in the lion's cage
9    and they said that that would be his next task to put some electrical sockets in the
      – in the lion's cage
10   but – ((laughs)) but then ((laughs)) what he did

11    he just went and picked up the keys from the office one day

12    and he went *in* to the lion's cage ((laughs))

13    ((friend laughs))

14    and started drilling

15    and this lion. became sort of ((laughs)) quite aroused by the er – by this drilling

16    ((friend, laughing:)) OH NO

17    and he ended up being chased around the cage by the – by the lion

18    ((friend)) *oh no*

19    and then the

20    and well by this time there was quite a commotion in the zoo generally

21    ((friend, laughing)) *there would be*

22    so the um head or – the head keeper discovered what was going on

23    so he was outside the cage you know

24    doing um whatever er lion um tamers do to keep the lion away from this guy

25    and eventually they managed to get him out of the cage

26    so um –

27    ((friend:)) he wasn't hurt?

28    no he wasn't hurt

29    so there you go

30    he's just mad ((laughs))

31    and it's just a miracle really

32    that he's still alive

33    but um he's always ((laughs)) been mad like that

## *The area manager's call*

1    did I tell you about that time when um. the area manager phoned me up?

2    ((friend replies:)) no ((narrator laughs)) what, was it still JT?

3    yeah.

4    just. we got this bloke at our place that's called John

5    and his days off on a Tuesday

6    and I answered the phone

7    it was the ex-D line

8    so it's li – like staff phoning in,

9    said 'hello it's John'.

10    I said 'I tell you something mate.

11    it's fucking crap here today'

12    said 'you're not missing anything'.

13    said 'the customers are (stuffing) ( ). it's dead.

14    bollocks.

15    I wish I wasn't here' ((laughs))

16    and I wasn't getting a lot of feedback off him

17    so. 'I'm sorry

18    what was it you wanted anyway?'.

19    he goes 'I wanna speak to the manager.

20    it's John Taylor your area manager'.

21    'oh right. OK' ((speaks slowly as implication sinks in))

22    oh shit.

23    ((friend laughs:)) beaut

24    I thought 'oh shit.

25    if there's a hole I'd be digging myself deeper.' ((laughs))

26    yeah that's Rob Harrison

27    ((laughs)) I mean what a twat

### 'And he went in to the lion's cage': the narrative core

'Jonesy and the Lion' has a narrative core of eight narrative clauses which are listed below (verbs are underlined):

(1a)

8     and somebody <u>said</u> that they needed some electrical sockets in the lion's cage

9     and they <u>said</u> that that would be his next task to put some electrical sockets in the – in the lion's cage

11    he just <u>went</u> and <u>picked up</u> the keys from the office one day

12    and he <u>went</u> *in* to the lion's cage ((laughs))

14    and <u>started</u> drilling

17    and he <u>ended up</u> being chased around the cage by the – by the lion

22    so the um head or – the head keeper <u>discovered</u> what was going on

25    and eventually they <u>managed</u> to get him out of the cage

'The area manager's call' also has a narrative core of eight narrative clauses:

(2a)

6        and I <u>answered</u> the phone

9        <u>said</u> 'hello it's John'.

10–11    I <u>said</u> 'I tell you something mate. it's fucking crap here today'

12       <u>said</u> 'you're not missing anything'.

13–15    <u>said</u> 'the customers are (stuffing) ( ). it's dead. bollocks. I wish I wasn't here'

17–18    so. [I <u>said</u>] 'I'm sorry what was it you wanted anyway?'.

19–20    he <u>goes</u> 'I wanna speak to the manager. it's John Taylor your area manager'.

24–5     I <u>thought</u> 'oh shit. if there's a hole I'd be digging myself deeper.'

Each narrative clause in these two stories has a simple past tense verb, apart from line 19 in the second, where the narrator switches to the historic present. The main difference between these two stories is in the stylistic choice of whether or not to use direct speech. The narrator of 'Jonesy and the lion' chooses to tell his story without any direct speech to animate his characters; what people say is still foregrounded as significant (lines 8 and 9), but what is said is presented as indirect (reported) speech. For example, line 8 – 'and somebody said that they needed some electrical sockets in the lion's cage' – could have been produced as 'and somebody said "we need some electrical sockets in the lion's cage" '. The narrator of 'The area manager's call', by contrast, presents his story very dramatically, with seven of the eight narrative clauses involving direct speech (or the character's thoughts). This choice underlines the fact that this is a story involving the narrator himself; it is a significant episode in the continuing saga of his life, and he demonstrates his first-hand knowledge of the event by reproducing the words of the main characters. (Of course, his audience is not expected to believe that these were the actual words spoken.) Direct speech has a significant role to play in evaluation, that is, in getting the narrator's point across. So his choice of words for himself and the Area Manager can be assumed to embody important messages to his audience about how to take the story.

Another interesting point about the second story is the narrator's use of the historic present tense in line 19 (*goes*). This marks the climax of the story, the moment at which the point of this story becomes clear. Recent analysis of the conversational historic present has claimed that it is the switch from past to present (or from present to past) which is significant, rather than anything intrinsic to the present tense itself. So by making the switch at this dramatic moment, the narrator of this story signals to his audience that this is an important line. The final narrative clause reverts to the simple past tense.

### *'So he was outside the cage': narrative and non-narrative clauses*

Another characteristic of narrative which is illustrated by these two stories is that they do not consist solely of narrative clauses with verbs in the simple past tense. They also contain non-narrative clauses which involve other kinds of verb phrase. Non-narrative clauses differ from narrative clauses in having either stative verbs such as *be* and *have*, or more complex verb phrases. Wlliam Labov [1972a: 375] calls these two types of clause 'narrative clauses' and 'free clauses'; he uses the term 'free' to capture the fact that, whereas narrative clauses have to occur in a specific order to match the order of events being described, non-narrative clauses are not so restricted in their placement. Background material about who, where and when ('orientation' in Labov's terms), for example, may be given at the beginning of a story, or may be added at some later point. Livia Polanyi [1985: 17] opts for different terms: she refers to these two types of clause as 'event clauses' and 'state clauses'. This terminology captures an important distinction between the two types of clause: while event clauses refer to one single moment in the past, state clauses 'encode states of affairs which persist over some interval of time in the discourse world rather than occurring at one unique discrete instant'.

In each of the two stories, 'Jonesy and the lion' and 'The area manager's call', as we have seen, the core narrative consists of eight narrative clauses. The other clauses in these stories, the non-narrative clauses, provide background information or evaluate the story. Line 20 in 'Jonesy and the lion' is a good example of a non-narrative clause: 'and well by this time there was quite a commotion in the zoo generally'. The verb *was* is a stative verb and describes 'a state of affairs which persists over some interval of time', unlike the verbs in the lines that precede and follow it (*ended up; discovered*). This line enables the narrator to give us a fuller picture of the situation developing at the zoo, and to make an important evaluative move: the word *commotion* signals that the narrator intends us to read the scenario he has described as chaotic rather than orderly. As the story reaches its climax, we get a series of non-narrative clauses: 'so he was outside the cage you know, doing um whatever er lion um tamers do to keep the lion away from this guy'. Again we have a stative verb — *was* — in the main clause, followed by a non-finite clause introduced by *doing*, and this in turn has an embedded noun clause as object. The sequence is syntactically complex and contrasts markedly with the preceding simple narrative clauses. These two complex lines give us important background information about the head keeper but keep us in suspense about Jonesy's fate.

The opening of 'The area manager's call' involves several non-narrative clauses which give important background information (lines 4–8 are given in (2b) below):

(2b)

| | |
|---|---|
| 4 | just. we got this bloke at our place that's called John |
| 5 | and his days off on a Tuesday |
| 6 | <u>and I answered the phone</u> |
| 7 | it was the ex-D line |
| 8 | so it's li – like staff phoning in, |

Line 6 is the only narrative clause here, with the simple past tense verb *answered*. The verbs in the other clauses are *(have) got, is called, is, was, is, phoning*. None of them is a simple past tense verb: all these verbs refer to states rather than events, or to recurring events in the case of *phoning*. These lines are crucial in preparing the audience for the point of the story. It is vital if the story is to have its intended impact that story recipients understand that there is another John at the narrator's workplace who was off work that day and who therefore might have phoned in on the ex-directory line. Other non-narrative clauses are line 22 *Oh shit* and line 27 *I mean what a twat*. Both are evaluative: they signal the narrator's attitude to the events in the story and orient the audience to the narrative point. Note that both these fines are verbless (apart from the discourse marker *I mean*), which again distinguishes them from the lines which constitute the narrative core.

### 'He's just mad': breaching the canonical script

Besides having a narrative core, stories need to have tellability, that is, they need to have a point. What counts as 'having a point' will differ from culture to culture, but a fair generalization seems to be that stories involve 'deviations from expected norms'. Jerome Bruner (1991: 11) explains this in terms of the concept 'the canonical script'. A canonical script is the unmarked script of everyday life, the way we expect things to be. For a story to be tellable, it must involve a breach of the canonical script.

The story 'Jonesy and the lion' is a good example of breaching a canonical script. The story works – is tellable – because it is understood that in the canonical script you don't go into a lion's cage when the lion is there. The point of the story – *he's just mad* (line 30) – is irrefutable: anyone who breaches canonical scripts in this way can definitely be regarded as foolish, if not mad, and certainly Jonesy is lucky to be alive, as the narrator points out. The function of third-person stories like 'Jonesy and the lion' is to confirm group values and attitudes, and in this case to affirm the three friends as an in-group with Jonesy positioned as the outsider. This construction of 'otherness' plays an important part in our maintenance of our sense of self. We assert who we are by establishing who we are not.

In the case of 'The area manager's call', the canonical script would have the narrator answering the phone and enquiring politely what the caller wants. However, for reasons he makes clear, he assumes he is speaking to another John, the John whose day off is on Tuesday, John who is an equal not a superior. He therefore lets off steam about work. To discover that you have told the Area Manager that *it's fucking crap here today* is a definite breach of the canonical script. The laughter and appreciative comments (e.g. *beaut*) that greet the story demonstrate that its audience has no doubts about its tellability. The narrator's own final comment *I mean what a twat* evaluates the story and makes the point that that he had put his foot in it in a big way. The function of this story is more subtle than that of 'Jonesy and the lion'. At one level, the first-person narrator exposes his foolishness to his friends and declares himself to be *a twat*. At a more profound level, the story is a boast and fits a masculine tradition of stories involving achievement (even though the achievement here is 'laddish' rather than heroic). [. . .]

The stories in the conversations I've collected range from those which involve major breaches in the canonical script – cars breaking down, illness, fights – to those which deal more with the minutiae of life. But even when the events reported are less earth-shattering, even when the narrator is not saying 'this was terrifying, dangerous, weird, wild, crazy; or amusing, hilarious, wonderful', it is still necessary to make clear that what happened was unusual. Otherwise the narrator runs the risk of having their narrative perceived as pointless, as not tellable.

[. . .]

### 'Only twenty-five p': gender and story-telling

I do not think it is possible to read the stories discussed here without being aware of the gender of the narrators. They are men's stories, not stories in general. These narrators are doing many things simultaneously as they tell their stories. But one of the things they are doing is performing masculinity. Does this mean that their stories differ in structure from stories told by women?

The canonical story I have outlined in this chapter has been defined in relation to three criteria: first, it has a beginning, a middle and an end; secondly, it involves a narrative core consisting of a sequence of narrative clauses; and thirdly, it has a point (tellability). At first glance, analysis of a parallel corpus of all-female conversation suggests that all three criteria are met: stories told by women in conversation with other women have beginnings, middles and endings, contain a core series of narrative clauses, and make a point. Moreover, female narrators, like male narrators, bring their characters to life by using direct speech, position their characters in time and space, and communicate the tellability of their stories through evaluative devices of various kinds.

However, on closer inspection it seems that women's and men's notions of tellability might vary. Polanyi (1979: 207) observes that 'what stories can be about is, to a very significant degree, culturally constrained: stories . . . can have as their point only culturally salient material generally agreed upon by members of the producer's culture to be self-evidentiy important and true'. While both the men's and the women's narratives I've collected attest to membership of the culture which is Britain at the end of the twentieth century, some stories told by women suggest that women may have a different idea from men about what counts as culturally salient material.

Discussion of this aspect of story-telling has tended to be androcentric, with male norms interpreted as human norms. Labov, for example, talking about danger of death stories collected from Black male adolescents and pre-adolescents, asks why some stories are tellable and some are not. He argues that 'if the event [i.e. what the story is about] becomes common enough, it is no longer a violation of an expected rule of behaviour, and it is not reportable' (Labov 1972a: 370–71). He shows how narrators evaluate their narratives with adjectives such as 'terrifying, dangerous, weird' or 'funny' or 'unusual', not with adjectives like 'ordinary' or 'everyday'.

Yet women's stories are often precisely about the ordinary and the everyday. Women tell stories about seeing grain trains in the docks, about body hair, about forgetting to take a towel to school for PE, about buying a sundress, about comfortable shoes, about painting the ceiling. The following is a very short example, but one which makes the point well. The narrator is Pat: she is telling her friend Karen about her shopping spree that morning (Karen's contributions are indicated).

1   I went and bought some stupid things this morning in Boots.
2   twenty-five p. ((laughs))
3   for twenty-five p you could be as silly as you want to couldn't you?
4   silly aren't they?
5   ( )
6   oh what fun
7   silly green nonsense
8   children's bead ear-rings
9   ((Karen:)) you got green?
10  I've got a green jumper which I wear in the winter
11  ((Karen:)) yeah, that's fine
12  so I thought I would.
13  I'm – am very fond of my green jumper.
14  silly pair of green ear-rings to go with it.
15  ((Karen:)) why not?
16  it's a laugh
17  there was another lady there looking through all the stuff when I was
18  and she said to me, 'isn't it fun?' ((laughs))
19  and I said, 'yes. only twenty-five p' ((laughs))
20  absurd

The opening four lines operate as a kind of abstract, giving a summary of the story, which is that things were for sale at the ridiculous price of 25 pence. The middle section (lines 6–16) is more stream of consciousness than narrative: the narrator talks about the green ear-rings she has bought in the present tense. Only at line 17 does she revert to narrative proper, with an orientation clause introducing a new character (*another lady*), followed by two narrative clauses each introducing direct speech. The last line provides the evaluation: *absurd*. This evaluative adjective conforms to Labov's strictures on how a narrator presents their story as tellable – Pat's claim that her buying of a pair of ear-rings for 25p is 'absurd' demonstrates to her addressee that her story has a point. She implicitly appeals to a cananonical script in which ear-rings cost more than 25p.

My interest in this story, and stories like it, lies in the fact that the subject matter differs so enormously from the kind of subject matter that is normally regarded as 'tellable' in men's stories. Even with its claim to absurdity, I suspect this example would fail as a story if told to a male audience. Or at the very least it might be met with puzzlement. Where is the heroism? What contest has the protagonist entered and won? What skill has been demonstrated? These questions can only be answered satisfactorily by adopting a gendered world-view, where a story about buying something for very little can be regarded as tellable.

Narrative construction performs important gender work, and men and women are actively engaged in constructing and maintaining masculinity and femininity in their story-telling. Given that masculinity and femininity are relational constructs (that is, they can only be defined in relation to each other), it is hardly surprising that the norms of men's and women's story-telling differ in some respects. After all, in telling a story, a male speaker is, among other things, performing *not* being a woman (just as a female speaker is performing *not* being a man). Certain themes are typical of men's stories – heroism, conflict, achievement – but not of women's stories.

It is important not to ignore these gender differences. Research into oral narrative has often relied on data collected from male speakers, and norms have been established which are assumed to account for the whole speech community. In the field of literary narrative, assumptions about what is 'normal' stretch back hundreds of years, and given the dominance of men in terms of access to literacy, it is not surprising that themes of heroism and achievement, of lone protagonists making epic journeys or struggling with a variety of foes, are the norm. Because of the prestige of the written in Western cultures, these literary norms inevitably have an impact on what we expect to find in oral narrative. It seems that women's stories do not conform in every respect to these norms, but that does not mean they should be seen as deviant.

## Issues to consider

The inter-relationship of gender and power as social variables complicates all investigations into this area. In many societies across the world, feminism and economic changes in wealth and the workplace have either changed the social position of women and men or have at least made the issue one that is foregrounded and discussed. Ascribing a variation in the use of a linguistic feature to gender rather than power relations, or even distinguishing between the two, is not straightforward. All of this means that designing a data-elicitation methodology must involve a great deal of care and awareness.

Many studies guarantee easily comparable data by investigating situations which are highly marked for an asymmetry in power, such as doctor-patient dialogues, or court transcripts, for example. You can make life more difficult but more interesting for yourself by exploring situations where power is more evenly shared, but gender is still an issue, such as in conversations between students on the same course, or between male and female nurses, for example.

You are likely to have the most to discuss if you focus on the level of discourse or global strategies, rather than on individual word-choices (though accent variation by gender is also an interesting area for research). Exploring the performance of narratives, jokes, academic prose, casual conversation structure, arguments, or the pragmatics of politeness are all fruitful possibilities in terms of gender distinctions.

Some specific suggestions follow.

❑  There are examples in this book of both mixed-gender and single-gender conversations. In order to elicit easily comparable passages, both sets of speech concerned contentious discussions. You could record mixed and single-gender conversations in other genres, such as commentary on ongoing tasks like rewiring a plug or digging the garden, or a discussion of what to watch on TV or at the cinema, or how different genders give directions to someone who is lost, for example. Examine the apparent objectives of the speaker in designing their utterance.

❑  How responsive are men and women to their addressees? Are the word-choices, grammar and discourse strategies used by men and women determined mainly by the subject-matter or more by a consideration of who they are talking to? Design a study that could test these questions.

❑  You can use written material to investigate whether writing can be gendered. One experimental way of doing this is to get a group of boys to write an article for a specific girl's magazine, and a group of girls to do the same for a boy's magazine. They are likely to identify and exaggerate stereotypical features, which will give you an insight into their attitudes to genderlects. You can then use this to make notes on a discussion between the groups.

❑  You could try to replicate Coates' collections of men's and women's narratives to explore any differences in narrative organisation, and to see if similar patterns hold for your own community.

---

**THE ORIGINS OF PIDGINS AND CREOLES**

Since the birth and early development of new languages can be observed at first hand in pidgins and creoles, their study has become very important in sociolinguistics. In particular, theories of the origins of widely-used creoles have enormous consequences for different theories of language development, and debates amongst creolists reflect wider debates in linguistics in general. In this extract, Mark Sebba presents a case-study of Sranan Tongo ('Surinam Tongue') from the north coast of South America, and considers some of its features in relation to the degree of influence of the *substrate* (underlying) languages and the *superstrate* or *lexifier* languages. Sranan shows some West African language substrate evidence, with lexification from English and Dutch.

The passage builds on your study from A8, B8 and C8, and is also a development of material in A9, B9 and C9.

### Case-study: Sranan

**Mark Sebba** (reprinted from *Contact Languages: Pidgins and Creoles*, Basingstoke: Palgrave, 1997: 194–201.)

In this case study, we will look at two aspects of Sranan Tongo [. . .]. We examine *serial verb structures*, a relatively unusual syntactic feature found in a number of Creoles [and . . .] we will look at the *derivational processes* at work in the Sranan lexicon. In considering serial verbs, we will see that there are numerous similarities between Sranan and some African languages, which suggest a possible substrate explanation. In looking at lexical processes of derivation, we will see that Sranan possesses a range of strategies for enlarging the referential capacity of the lexicon, for which a substrate explanation is unnecessary.

### Serial verbs

While probably in most languages just one main verb per clause is the norm, some languages permit chains or series of finite verbs to be present in the same clause. Such structures are usually called *serial verb structures*. (See Sebba 1987 for a detailed cross-linguistic study of serial verbs; Lefebvre 1991 for more recent research developments). Example (1) from Sranan gives an idea of what such structures are like. They clearly do not correspond to any structures found in English or other European languages.

(1) **Rudy ben *tyari* den buku *kon* na ini a oso**
    Rudy PAST carry the-PL book come LOC in the house
    'Rudy had brought the books into the house'

In (1), *tyari* and *kon* are both finite verbs; in other words neither is an auxiliary or modal verb, and neither is dependent on the other in the way that *come* is dependent on *want* in a sentence like *I wanted to come into the house*. The tense marker *ben* occurs only once, before the first verb, but determines the tense of both verbs, because both actions have to be interpreted as simultaneous.

    Sentence (2) is from Akan (the name of a group of closely related Ghanaian languages which includes Ashanti, Fanti and Twi) from the Kwa language group of Niger-Congo.

(2) *ɔde* **poŋ** no *baae*
    3PERS-take-PAST table the come-PAST
    'S/he brought the table'

The structure of (2) is almost exactly the same as (1), with the difference that in Akan, both verbs are marked for tense; however, the tense must be the same for both verbs (one of the tense markers is thus redundant).

    The fact that serial verbs are an 'areal feature', confined to very specific geographical regions and language groups, suggests that they are sufficiently highly marked for the correspondence between (1) and (2) to be a 'striking similarity' which suggests substrate influence. The similarities become stronger when we look at the range of different types of serial verbs which are found in Sranan and in the Kwa language group.

### Directional serial verbs: 'go/come'

Sentences (1) and (2) are illustrations of this type, which indicate direction away from or towards a reference point.

### Other motion verb complements: 'fall down', 'come out', etc.

A number of other verbs can function as complements of motion verbs: (3) and (4) are examples.

(3)  **Sranan:**  **Kofi**  *fringi*  **a**  **tiki**  *fadon*
      Kofi      throw     the   stick    fall-down
      'Kofi threw down the stick'

(4)  **Yoruba:**  **Olu**  *ti*  **omo**  **naa**  *subu*
      Olu       push    child    the    fall
      'Olu pushed the child down'

### Instrumental serial verbs: 'take'

These indicate the means or instrument whereby something is done, and have the form *take X do Y*, e.g. (5) and (6):

(5)  **Sranan:**  **Mary**  *teki*  **a**  **aksi**  *fala*  **a**  **bon**
      Mary     take    the   axe     fell    the   tree
      'Mary felled the tree with an axe'

(6)  **Yoruba:**  **Mo**  *fi*  **ada**  *ge*  **igi**
      I        take   machete   cut    tree
      'I cut the tree with a machete'

### Goal-indicating verbs: 'hit', 'pierce', 'fall down', etc.

Like *go* and *come*, these are usually complements of motion verbs. The first verb may be transitive or intransitive. If it is transitive, the *object* of the first verb is *subject* of the second verb, e.g.

(7)  **Sranan:**  Mi  *fringi*  a  ston  *naki*  Amba
      I     throw    the   stone   hit    Amba
      'I threw a stone at Amba (and hit her)'

(8)  **Akan:**  **me***tow*  **bo**  **no**  **me***bɔɔ*  **Amma**
      I-throw-PAST   stone   the   I-pierce-PAST   Amma
      'I threw the stone at Amma (and hit her)'

Note that the English translation requires some clarification because in the Sranan and Akan sentences both verbs represent *completed* actions: hence the stone actually struck its victim rather than just going in the victim's direction.

### Lexical idioms

Often two verbs operating in tandem have an idiomatic meaning, i.e. one that is not transparent from the meanings of the separate verbs. This suggests that the combination should have the status of a single discontinuous lexical item. For example:

**Akan:**       *gye* 'accept' + *di* 'eat' = 'believe'
**Anyi-Baule:** *kâ* 'touch' + *kle* 'show' = 'say, tell'
**Yoruba:**     *la* 'cut open' + *ye* 'understand' = 'explain'

Lexical idiom serial verbs seem to be found in all the West African languages which have serial structures, but they are less easy to find in creoles. The Sranan examples that exist are certainly more transparent than their African counterparts:

Sranan: *bro* 'breathe, blow' + *kiri* 'kill' = 'blow out (candle)'

## Grammatical function: comparative constructions

A verb meaning 'pass' or 'surpass' may be used to form comparatives. In Sranan, either the verb *pasa* or the verb *moro*, 'surpass' (which can also function as an adverb meaning 'more'), may be used:

(9)  Sranan:  Anansi    koni      *pasa*    tigri
              Anansi    cunning   pass      tiger
        'Anansi is more cunning than tiger'

(10) Yoruba:  Omo       naa       gbon      ju        asarun
              child     the       clever    surpass   tsetse-fly
        'The child is cleverer than the tsetse fly'

We have now seen that serial verbs exist both in West African languages such as Akan, Yoruba and Anyi-Baule – all of which are known to have had speakers who were taken as slaves to the Caribbean – and in Sranan Tongo. Furthermore, for each different type of serial verb which can be found among the West African languages, Sranan has a more or less exactly corresponding construction. This is true even of the [. . .] constructions ('give', 'say' and 'surpass') which seem to have undergone grammaticalisation to varying degrees. Serial verb constructions are not widespread in the world's languages, but seem to be confined to a few geographical areas: they seem to be a good example of a marked syntactic construction.

However, the evidence for substrate influence is not unequivocal. Serial-like constructions have also been found in other creoles and creolising languages which have no African substratum. Bickerton (1981: 131) reports traces of serial-like constructions among the oldest Hawaiian Creole speakers, in particular the use of directional *come* and *go* after a main verb. Bickerton ridicules the suggestion that this is due to Chinese influence, but in fact it cannot be ruled out, as Chinese has exactly this kind of construction, and was one of the substrate languages in Hawaii. Harder to explain by reference to the substrate are instances of serialisation in Tok Pisin, reported by Sankoff (1984). Sankoff reports a range of 'verb chaining' structures some of which closely resemble the directional serial verbs of Sranan, e.g. *em i salim mi kam*, 'he sent me come = he sent me (here)'. There is no apparent substrate source for these.

Bickerton (1981) rejects substrate explanations and regards serial verbs as a consequence of the fact that rudimentary creoles lack categories which mark grammatical relations, such as prepositions and morphological casemarkers. According to him, 'verb serialisation is the only solution to the problem of marking cases in languages which have only N and V as major categories' – which he argues is the case with creoles, until such time as they develop other categories. Other languages, he says – like the West African serialising languages – have developed them as a response to the need for case-marking as existing prepositions have decayed.

This argument is not convincing if we bear in mind that most creole languages (as well as pidgins) do in fact have prepositions – though only a few of them. The fact that the category exists suggests that serial verbs are not simply a response to a need that prepositions can fulfil. It is also apparent from the range of functions which serial verbs in languages like Sranan perform, that case-marking is not the main purpose of serial verbs (though of course it may be their *original* purpose; once the construction is there, any language would probably tend to maximise the use of it). It also seems, on the basis of the available data, that serial verbs in Tok Pisin are not primarily used as case-markers (there are several well-documented prepositions which can do this).

Once again, we have to rely on some notion of markedness to tell us whether the serial verbs of Sranan are 'direct descendants' of the serial verbs of West Africa, The range of different functions seems to be the most significant factor in this. Both Hawaiian Creole English and Tok Pisin have serial verbs documented, but with a restricted range of functions (and low frequency in HCE). By contrast, Sranan serial verbs are frequent and widespread, and exactly mimic a range of uses found in West Africa.

### Derivation in the Sranan lexicon

If there seems to be some compelling evidence for substrate influence in a language like Sranan, does the substrate have to account for *all* the structural characteristics of the language? Could some of the structures be developed independently, without being based on the substrate? In order to begin to answer this question, in this section we will look at the expansion of the Sranan lexicon by studying the processes by which nouns are derived. Sranan, in common with many pidgins and creoles, has quite limited morphology. Also in keeping with other contact languages, the size of the Sranan lexicon is not great even now and the 'basic' lexicon at the time of the creole's formation was undoubtedly smaller. There is a need for productive morphological processes to increase the referential range. Sranan has two morphological processes which it uses to do this, *reduplication* and *compounding*, while *multifunctionality* is also important.

### Reduplication

Some of the oldest words in Sranan seem to be the names of animals, which have been formed by reduplicating the word from the lexifier language. We find **konkoni**, 'rabbit' (from obsolete English *coney*), and **puspusi**, 'cat' (English 'pussy'), as well as **moys-moysi**, 'mouse', from Dutch *muis*.

Another set of reduplicated words – presumably old, because of their meanings – refer to body parts: **gorogoro**, 'throat', *fokofoko*, 'lungs'. The origins of these words are not known with certainty.

The above examples show that reduplicated forms exist in Sranan, but they do not show that reduplication is productive. In fact, reduplication *is* productive and has several different functions.

We find that many words for *instruments* are derived from verbs by reduplication. For example: **ariari**, 'rake', from **ari** (verb: 'to rake'); **kankan**, 'comb', from **kan** (verb: 'to comb'); **nanay**, 'needle', from **nay** (verb: 'to sew') (from Dutch *naaien*).

Reduplication can also be used to create nouns from adjectives, for example **moy-moy**, 'finery', from Dutch *mooi*, 'beautiful'.

Reduplication of verbs may also produce a verb with an altered meaning, for example *wakawaka*, 'wander about', from *waka*, 'walk'; *takitaki*, 'chatter', from *taki*, 'talk'; *tantan*, 'stay intermittently', from *tan*, 'stay (English *stand*).

Reduplication can also be used to derive adjectives from nouns, e.g. *tiftiji*, 'cogged, indented', from *tifi*, 'tooth' (English *teeth*). Here *tiftifi* means 'toothed' in a figurative sense: it cannot be used to describe, say, an animal which has teeth. There are other examples of reduplicated adjectives (derived from adjectives in this case) with figurative meanings: *bakabaka*, 'underhand', from *baka*, 'back, behind', and *broko-broko* as in *brokobroko tongo*, 'broken language', from *broke*, 'broken'. A similar kind of figurative meaning seems to attach to some reduplicated adverbs, e.g. *afuafu*, 'moderately', from *afu*, 'half, and *wanwan*, 'one at a time', from *wan*, 'one'.

Reduplication of adjectives can also produce an intensive meaning, e.g. *bisibisi*, 'very busy', from *bisi*, 'busy'; *libilibi*, 'likely', from *libi*, 'living, alive'.

## Compounding

Compound nouns are common in Sranan. We find *noun + noun* compounds such as *Sranan + man*, 'Surinamese person', *adjective + noun* compounds like *bigi + futu*, 'big foot' = 'elephantiasis' (a disease which causes the leg to swell), and *verb + noun* compounds like *sidon + preysi*, 'sit-down place' = 'seat'. The nouns *ten*, 'time', *preysi*, 'place', *man*, 'person/man', *uma*, 'woman and *sani*, 'thing', combine freely with most nouns, verbs and adjectives to produce a compound noun with transparent meaning.

## Multifunctionality

Many Sranan nouns are derived from verbs without any change in form, e.g. *bro* (verb: 'blow, breathe'; noun: 'breath'). In other cases, reduplication may be involved (see above). *Abstract* nouns can be derived from any unreduplicated adjective which denotes a quality, e.g. *ogri* (adjective: 'ugly, bad'; verb: 'badness, evil'), *fri* (adjective: 'free'; verb: 'freedom') This process is completely productive, with the result that English and Dutch names for such abstract qualities are systematically absent from the lexicon of Sranan (Sebba 1981: 109). *Freyheti*, 'freedom', from Dutch *vrijheid*, is listed in Wullschlagel's dictionary (1856) as a word of Missionary origin. It seems to have dropped out of use altogether. Since Sranan *fri*, derived by a regular process, has the same meaning, borrowings like *freyheti* are redundant.

## Productivity and constraints

The observation that a borrowing from Dutch is redundant as Sranan has its own word-creation processes is an important reminder that creole languages have their own resources and are not dependent for all their linguistic needs on the lexifier or substrate languages. The Sranan lexicon has a complexity of its own. Part of this is the operation of constraints which prevent the formation of homophonous words by reduplication. For example, the noun *freyfrey*, 'fly', is one of the reduplicated animal names mentioned [above]. It might be expected that the verb *frey* 'to fly', would be reduplicated on the pattern of *nanay*, 'needle', to mean 'an instrument for flying', i.e. 'wing'. In fact, this does not happen; the word for 'wing' is the unreduplicated form *frey*. The reduplicated animal name *freyfrey* seems to 'block' the formation of any potential homophone. Possibly the same principle is at work in producing two non-homophonous derived nouns from the verb *tay*, 'tie': ***taytay***, 'bundle', and ***tetey***, 'string, rope, muscle' (i.e. 'instrument used for tying').

### *Commentary*

We have seen in this section two aspects of the grammar of Sranan: on the one hand, the syntactic phenomenon of verb serialisation, and on the other, the lexical processes of reduplication, compounding and multifunctionality. While in the case of serialisation, there seems to be a strong argument for seeing African substrate influence as responsible for establishing the patterns, in the case of the lexicon we can see that Sranan has its own resources for deriving new lexical items on the basis of words originally from English and Dutch. Even if these lexical processes could be shown to be patterned on existing ones found in West African languages – which so far has not been shown – the processes themselves are Sranan ones.

Thus while substrate influence may account for some aspects of the grammar of a creole language, it is necessary to keep this in perspective. As a pidgin or creole develops, it creates its own resources for further development. This has been documented for Tok Pisin by Mühlhäusler [1986], and is partly demonstrated above for Sranan. What this suggests is that while pidgins and creoles must be seen as the products of multilingual contact situations – because that they certainly are – they also have to be seen, at least once they have stabilised, as autonomous systems with their own pathways of development. It is probable that substrate influence is most significant when it confirms a tendency already present in the pidgin or creole grammar, or coincides with universal principles which are already pointing the language in the same direction.

### Issues to consider

You should consider your own response to the various theories of creolisation. Examine the logic of each of the approaches, and find examples of published studies that represent each one. You can then decide where you consider the weight of evidence to be. You should also consider the social consequences of 'buying into' any one of these theories. There are ideological and political implications, implications for our approach to language and linguistics, as well as consequences for educational policy that follow from the adoption of every one of these theories. You should consider what these are.

The issues of prestige and stigmatisation are also important in relation to pidgin and creole users. There are various means of exploring the relative prestige values attached to different varieties, depending on the range of factors introduced in A6.

Some practical suggestions follow.

❑   You can test the perceived prestige value of a particular pidgin or creole using Bell's criteria (A6). Before making any decisions on these dimensions, you will have to decide which variety of the creole you are focusing on, and you must also consider the context and environment of its usage: the prestige of a creole alters radically when considered in its original, native context as compared with the variety spoken by people who have emigrated to another country and live amongst a different speech community.

❑ You should look around your own region to see if any creole languages are spoken by communities that are accessible to you. Do they have a written form or are they taught locally either formally or informally? Is the creole recognised in your local school system?

❑ If you do not have the fortune to be planning a trip to the Caribbean, West Africa, Pacific Islands or Papua New Guinea in the near future, you can still explore a lot of creole data using the internet. University linguistics departments in these locations are especially good sources of interesting material, often with commentary included.

❑ Consider the use made of pidgins and creoles, and the representation of their speakers, in literature and film. You could compare the representation with what you can discover about the reality of the situation.

## WORLD ENGLISHES AND CONTACT LITERATURE

Many teachers of English as a second or foreign language use creative writing or the reading of literary texts as a teaching tool. In the article that follows, Braj Kachru demonstrates the creativity involved in the practice of bilingualism, and argues for an awareness of the processes involved in creating and reading 'contact literatures'. Sometimes literature is not seen as authentic sociolinguistic data, since it is in a sense 'artificial' rather than 'real'. However, I would argue that literature is a language event like any other and so is amenable to a sociolinguistic analysis.

The article develops concepts that were discussed in A9, B9 and C9, but it also touches upon issues of ethnicity and multilingualism (from A4 and C4).

### The bilingual's creativity: discoursal and stylistic strategies in contact literatures

**Braj Kachru** (reprinted from Larry Smith (ed.) *Discourse Across Cultures: Strategies in World Englishes,* New York: Prentice-Hall, 1987: 125–40.)

The bilingual's creativity in English on a global scale, and the issues concerning nativization of discourse patterns, discourse strategies and speech acts, are a natural consequence of the unprecedented world-wide uses of English, mainly since the early 1920s. The phenomenon of a language with fast-increasing diaspora varieties – and significantly more non-native users than native speakers – has naturally resulted in the pluricentricity of English. The sociolinguistic import of this pluricentricity is that the non-native users of English can choose to acquire a variety of English which may be distinct from the native varieties. As a result, two types of model of English have developed: native and institutionalized non-native (see Kachru 1982c). It is with reference to these models that the innovations, creativity and emerging literary traditions in English must be seen. Each model has its own linguistic and literary norms – or a tendency to develop such norms. This is the linguistic reality of English in its world context. Attitudinally, however, the way people react to this situation opens up an entirely different can of worms, not directly related to the discussion in this chapter.

The concept 'pluricentricity' of English is a useful beginning point for this chapter. I will address certain issues which, it seems to me, are related to both Western and non-Western pluricentricity of the English language. I will first raise a theoretical question concerning linguists' common perception of a speech community, particularly their understanding of the linguistic behaviour of the members of a speech community which alternately uses two, three or more languages depending on the situation and function. One might ask: How valid is a theory of grammar which treats monolingualism as the norm for description and analysis of the linguistic interaction of traditional multilingual societies? Yet in linguistic description – save a few exceptions – the dominant paradigms have considered monolingualism as the norm (i.e. judgements based on the ideal speaker–hearer). My second concern – not unrelated to the first point – is with description and methodology: Are the models proposed for discourse and text-analysis of monolinguals' linguistic interaction observationally, descriptively, and explanatorily adequate for the analysis of bilinguals' language use? My third aim is to discuss some underlying processes of nativization and innovations which characterize literariness (both formal and contextual) of selected texts manifesting the bilingual's creativity. The examples have been taken primarily from what has earlier been termed 'contact literature'. Finally, I shall refer to the issue of relationship between this creativity and underlying thought patterns of bilinguals.

I believe that the theoretical and methodological tracks followed to date in the study of contact literatures in English fail on several counts. The foremost limitation one detects in a majority of studies is that of using almost identical approaches for the description of the bilingual's and monolingual's creativity. Literary creativity in English has until now been studied within the Western Judeo-Christian heritage and its implications for understanding English literature. True, the English language shows typical characteristics of a 'mixed' language development in its layer after layer of borrowings, adaptations, and various levels of language contact. But even there, the earlier main intrusion has been essentially European and more or less consistent with the Hellenistic and Roman traditions.

However, the prolonged colonial period substantially changed that situation in the linguistic fabric of the English language, and extended its use as a medium for ethnic and regional literatures in the non-Western world (e.g. Indian English, West African English; see Kachru 1980). The extreme results of this extension can be observed in the 'Sanskritization' and 'Kannadaization' of Raja Rao's English, and in the 'Yorubaization' and 'Igboization' of Amos Tutuola and Chinua Achebe. The labels indicate that these authors have exploited two or more linguistic – and cultural – resources which do not fit into the paradigms of what Kaplan (1966) terms 'the Platonic-Aristotelian sequence' and the dominant Anglo-Saxon thought patterns of the native speakers of English. Recognition of this mixing of Western and non-Western resources has implications for our use of terms such as *cohesion* or *coherence*, and even *communicative competence*. We should also be cautious in suggesting typologies of culture-specific speech acts in various varieties of English (see Chishimba 1983 and Magura 1984).

In contact literature the bilingual's creativity introduces a nativized thought process (e.g. Sanskritic, Yoruba, Malaysian) which does not conform to the recognized canons of discourse types, text design, stylistic conventions, and traditional thematic range of the English language, as viewed from the major Judeo-Christian traditions of literary and linguistic creativity.

The linguistic realization of the underlying traditions and thought processes for a bilingual may then entail a *transfer* of discoursal patterns from one's other (perhaps more dominant) linguistic code(s) and cultural and literary traditions. That such organization of discourse strategies – conscious or unconscious – arises in different ways in different cultures has been shown in several studies on non-Western languages.

### 'Contact' in contact literatures

What does the term 'contact literatures' imply? The term refers to the literatures in English written by the users of English as a second language to delineate contexts which generally do not form part of what may be labelled the traditions of English literature (African, Malaysian, Indian and so on). Such literatures, as I have stated elsewhere, are 'a product of multicultural and multilingual speech communities' (Kachru 1982b: 330). Furthermore:

> The concept of 'contact literature' is an extension of 'contact language'. A language in contact is two-faced; it has its own face, and the face it acquires from the language with which it has contact. The degree of contact varies from lexical borrowing to intensive mixing of units. Contact literatures (for example, non-native English literatures of India, Nigeria or Ghana; the Francophone literatures; or the Indian-Persian literature) have certain formal and thematic characteristics which make the use of the term 'contact' appropriate (Kachru 1982b: 341).

It has already been shown that contact literatures have both a national identity and a linguistic distinctiveness (e.g., *Indianness, Africanness*). The 'linguistic realization' of such identities is achieved in several ways: the text may have both a surface and an underlying identity with the native varieties of English; it may show only partial identity with the native norms; or it may entail a culture-specific (e.g. African, Asian) identity both at the surface and the underlying levels and share nothing with the native variety. Thus contact literatures have several linguistic and cultural faces: they reveal a blend of two or more linguistic textures and literary traditions, and they provide the English language with extended contexts of situation within which such literatures may be interpreted and understood. In such literatures there is a range of discourse devices and cultural assumptions distinct from the ones associated with the native varieties of English. One must extend the scope of the historical dimension and cultural traditions from that of Judeo-Christian traditions to the different heritages of Africa and Asia. This kind of historical and cultural expansion results in a special type of linguistic and literary phenomenon: such texts demand a new literary sensibility and extended cultural awareness from a reader who is outside of the speech fellowship which identifies with the variety.

It is in this sense that English writing has become, to give an example, 'our national literature', and English 'our national language' in Nigeria as claimed by Nnamdi Azikiwe, the first President of Nigeria (quoted in Thumboo 1976: vii). The same is, of course, true of most of the former British and American colonies or areas of influence, such as India, Singapore, and the Philippines.

Thumboo (1976: ix) is making the same point in connection with Commonwealth writers in English when he says that

> language must serve, not overwhelm, if the Commonwealth writer is to succeed. Mastering it involves holding down and breaching a body of habitual English associations to secure that condition of verbal freedom cardinal to energetic, resourceful writing. In a sense the language is remade, where necessary, by adjusting the interior landscape of words in order to explore and mediate the permutations of another culture and environment.

And discussing the problems of such writers, Thumboo adds (xxxiv):

> The experience of peoples crossing over into a second language is not new, though the formalization of the move acts as a powerful rider. What amounts to the re-location of a sensibility nurtured by, and instructed in one culture, within another significantly different culture, is complicated in the outcome.

### Discoursal thought pattern and language design

The relationship between underlying thought patterns and language designs has been well illustrated by Achebe in a very convincing way. In his *Arrow of God*, Achebe (1969) provides two short texts as an illustration – one nativized (Africanized) and the other Englishized – and then gives reasons for choosing to use the former. In explaining his choice he says that it will '. . . give some idea of how I approach the use of English'. In the passage, the Chief Priest is telling one of his sons why it is necessary to send him to church. Achebe first gives the Africanized version:

> I want one of my sons to join these people and be my eyes there. If there is nothing in it you will come back. But if there is something then you will bring back my share. The world is like a mask, dancing. If you want to see it well, you do not stand in one place. My spirit tells me that those who do not befriend the white man today will be saying, 'had we known', tomorrow.

Achebe then asks, 'supposing I had put it another way. Like this for instance:

> I am sending you as my representative among those people – just to be on the safe side in case the new religion develops. One has to move with the times or else one is left behind. I have a hunch that those who fail to come to terms with the white man may well regret their lack of foresight.

And he rightly concludes: 'The material is the same. But the form of the one is in character and the other is not. It is largely a matter of instinct but judgement comes into it too.'

It is thus a combination of creative *instinct* and formal *judgement* which makes a text language- or culture-specific within a context of situation (e.g. Yoruba speech, Chicano English, Kannada influence, Punjabi English).

Furthermore, if we accept Kaplan's claim that the preferred dominant 'thought patterns' of English are essentially out of 'the Anglo-European cultural patterns' based on 'a Platonic-Aristotelian sequence', the logical next step is to recognize that in the case of, for example, Raja Rao or Mulk Raj Anand, the underlying thought patterns reflect the traditions of Sanskrit and the regional or national oral lore. And in the case of Amos Tutuola and Chinua Achebe they stem from Yoruba and Igbo traditions, respectively.

Raja Rao makes it clear that such transfer of tradition is part of his creativity.

> There is no village in India, however mean, that has not a rich *sthala-purana* or legendary history, of its own. . . . The *Puranas* are endless and innumerable. We have neither punctuation nor the treacherous 'ats' and 'ons' to bother us – we tell one interminable tale. Episode follows episode, and when our thoughts stop our breath stops, and we move on to another thought. This was and still is the ordinary style of our story telling. I have tried to follow it myself in this story [*Kanthapura*] (Rao 1963: vii–viii).

Raja Rao's narration of an 'interminable tale' results in breaking the Western norms of punctuation and prose rhythm, and he shares it, for example, with the writers on another continent, West Africa. Tutuola has a 'peculiar use of punctuation, resulting in an unending combination of sentences', which he 'owes to his Yoruba speech' (Taiwo 1976: 76).

> When he tried all his power for several times and failed and again at that moment the smell of the gun-powder of the enemies' guns which were shooting repeatedly was rushing to our noses by the breeze and this made us fear more, so my brother lifted me again a very short distance, but when I saw that he was falling several times, then I told him to leave me on the road and run away for his life perhaps he might be safe so that he would be taking care of our mother as she had no other sons more than both of us and I told him that if God saves my life too then we should meet again, but if God does not save my life we should meet in Heaven (*Bush of Ghosts*, p. 20; quoted in Taiwo 1976: 76).

In addition to this characteristic, Taiwo (1976: 111) argues that Tutuola and his compatriot Achebe 'exhibit in their writings features which may be described as uniquely Nigerian'. Taiwo further explains (1976: 75) that Tutuola 'has carried Yoruba speech habits into English and writes in English as he would speak in Yoruba. . . . He is basically speaking Yoruba but using English words.' And 'the peculiar rhythms of his English are the rhythms of Yoruba speech' (1976: 85). With regard to Achebe, Taiwo (1976: 116–117) observes that in the following scene which he quotes from *Things Fall Apart*, Achebe 'has had to rely heavily on the resources of Igbo language and culture to dramatise the interrelation between environment and character:'

> 'Umuofia kwenu!' shouted the leading *egwugwu*, pushing the air with his raffia arms. The elders of the clan replied. 'Yaa!'
>
> 'Umuofia kwenu!'
>
> 'Yaa!'
>
> 'Umuofia kwenu!'
>
> 'Yaa!'
>
> Evil Forest then thrust the pointed end of his rattling staff into the earth. And it began to shake and rattle, like something agitating with a metallic life. He took the first of the empty stools and the eight other *egwugwu* began to sit in order of seniority after him.

### The bilingual's grammar: some hypotheses

It seems to me that for understanding the bilingual's creativity one must begin with a distinct set of hypotheses for what has been termed 'the bilingual's grammar' (or multilingual's grammar). I am, of course, not using the term 'grammar' in a restricted sense: it refers to the productive linguistic processes at different linguistic levels (including discourse and style) which a bilingual uses for various linguistic functions.

The bilingual's grammar has to be captured in terms of what sociolinguists term 'verbal repertoire' or 'code repertoire', with specific reference to a speech community (or a speech fellowship). Such speech communities have a formally and functionally determined range of languages and/or dialects as part of their competence for linguistic interaction.

A characteristic of such competence is the faculty and ease of mixing and switching, and the adoption of stylistic and discoursal strategies from the total verbal repertoire available to a bilingual. One has to consider not only the blend of the formal features, but also the assumptions derived from various cultural norms, and the blending of these norms into a new linguistic configuration with a culturespecific meaning system. There are several salient characteristics of the creativity of such a person. I shall discuss some of these below.

First, the processes used in such creativity are based on multinorms of styles and strategies. We cannot judge such devices on the basis of one norm derived from one literary or cultural tradition (see Parthasarathy 1983).

Second, nativization and acculturation of text presupposes an altered context of situation for the language. Traditionally accepted literary norms with reference to a particular code (say, Hindi or English) seem to fail here. A description based on an approach which emphasizes the monolingual 'speaker-hearer' is naturally weak in terms of its descriptive and explanatory power.

Third, the bilingual's creativity results in the configuration of two or more codes. The resultant code, therefore, has to be contextualized in terms of the new uses of language.

Finally, such creativity is not to be seen merely as a formal combination of two or more underlying language designs, but also as a creation of cultural, aesthetic, societal and literary norms. In fact, such creativity has a distinct context of situation.

It is this distinctive characteristic which one might say on the one hand formally *limits* the text and on the other hand extends it, depending on how one looks at linguistic innovations. The creative processes used in such texts have a *limiting* effect because the conventional 'meaning system' of the code under use is altered, lexically, grammatically, or in terms of cohesion (see Y. Kachru 1983a, b). A reader-hearer 'outside' the shared or re-created meaning system has to familiarize himself or herself with the processes of the design and formal reorganization, the motivation for innovations, and the formal and contextual implications of such language use. In other words, to borrow Hallidayan terms (1973: 43) one has to see what a multilingual 'can say' and 'can mean'. The *range in saying* and the *levels of meaning* are distinct, and one has to establish 'renewal of connection' with the context of situation.

What is, then, inhibiting (limiting or unintelligible) in one sense may also be interpreted as an extension of the codes in terms of the new linguistic innovations, formal experimentation, cultural nuances, and addition of a new cultural perspective to the language. If the linguistic and cultural 'extension' of the code is missed, one also misses the interpretation at the linguistic, literary, socio-linguistic and cultural levels. One misses the relationship between *saying* and *meaning*, the core of literary creativity.

What does it take from a reader to interpret such creativity? It demands a lot: it almost demands an identification with the literary sensibility of the bilingual in tune with the ways of *saying* and the levels of new *meaning*.

### Linguistic realization of distinctiveness

This altered 'meaning system' of such English texts is the result of various linguistic processes, including nativization of context, of cohesion and cohesiveness, and of rhetorical strategies.

### Nativization of context

One first thinks of the most obvious and most elusive process which might be called *contextual* nativization of texts, in which cultural presuppositions overload a text and demand a serious cultural interpretation. In Raja Rao's *Kanthapura*, to take a not-so-extreme example, such contextualization of the following exemplary passage involves several levels.

> 'Today,' he says, 'it will be the story of Siva and Parvati.' And Parvati in penance becomes the country and Siva becomes heaven knows what! 'Siva is the three-eyed,' he says, 'and Swaraj too is three-eyed: Self-purification, Hindu-Moslem unity, Khaddar.' And then he talks of Damayanthi and Sakunthala and Yasodha and everywhere there is something about our country and something about Swaraj. Never had we heard *Hari-kathas* like this. And he can sing too, can Jayaramachar. He can keep us in tears for hours together. But the *Harikatha* he did, which I can never forget in this life and in all lives to come, is about the birth of Gandhiji. 'What a title for a *Harikatha*!' cried out old Venkatalakshamma, the mother of the Postmaster.
>
> 'It is neither about Rama nor Krishna.' – 'But,' said her son, who too has been to the city, 'but, Mother, the Mahatma is a saint, a holy man.' – 'Holy man or lover of a widow, what does it matter to me? When I go to the temple I want to hear about Rama and Krishna and Mahadeva and not all this city nonsense,' said she. And being an obedient son, he was silent. But the old woman came along that evening. She could never stay away from a *Harikatha*. And sitting beside us, how she wept! . . . (Rao 1963: 10).

In this passage it is not so much that the underlying narrative technique is different or collocational relationships are different, but the 'historical' and 'cultural' presuppositions are different from what has been traditionally the 'expected' historical and cultural milieu for English literature. One has to explain Siva and Parvati with reference to the multitude of the pantheon of Hindu gods, and in that context then *three-eyed* (Sanskrit *trinetra*) makes sense: it refers to Lord Siva's particular manifestation when he opens his 'third eye', located on his forehead, spitting fire and destroying the creation. Damayanthi [Damayantī], Sakunthala [Sakuntalā], and Yasodha [Yasodā] bring forth the epic tradition of Indian classics: Damayanthi, the wife of Nala; Sakunthala, who was later immortalized in Kalidasa's [Kālīdāsa: 5th century AD?] play of the same name; and Yasodha, the mother of Krishna, the major character of the epic *Mahābhārata*. The contemporariness of the passage is in reference to Gandhi (1869–1948), and the political implications of Hindu-Muslim unity and *khaddar* (handspun cloth). The *Harikatha* man is the traditional religious storyteller who has woven all this in a fabric of story.

Now, this is not unique: this is in fact characteristic of context-specific texts in general. But that argument does not lessen the *interpretive* difficulties of such texts. Here the presupposition of discourse interpretation is at a level which is not grammatical. It is of a special lexical and contextual nature. It extends the cultural load of English lexis from conventional Greek and Roman allusions to Asian and African myths, folklore, and traditions. It universalizes English, and one might say 'de-Englishizes' it in terms of the accepted literary and cultural norms of the language.

### Nativization of cohesion and cohesiveness

The second process involves the alteration of the native users' concept of *cohesion* and *cohesiveness*: these concepts are to be redefined in each institutionalized variety within the appropriate universe of discourse (see Y. Kachru 1983a, b). This is particularly true of types of lexicalization, collocational extension and the use or frequency of grammatical forms. A number of such examples are given in my earlier studies.

The lexical *shift*, if I might use that term, is used for various stylistic and attitudinal reasons. The lexicalization involves not only direct lexical transfer but also entails other devices, too, such as hybridization and loan translation. Such English lexical items have more than one interpretive context: they have a surface 'meaning' of the second language (English) and an underlying 'meaning' of the first (or dominant) language. The discoursal interpretation of such lexicalization depends on the meaning of the underlying language – say Yoruba, Kannada, Punjabi, Malay, etc.

### Nativization of rhetorical strategies

The third process is the nativization of rhetorical strategies in close approximation to the devices a bilingual uses in his or her other code(s). These include consciously or unconsciously devised strategies according to the patterns of interaction in the native culture, which are transferred to English.

A number of such strategies are enumerated below. First, one has to choose a style with reference to the stylistic norms appropriate to the concepts of 'high culture' and 'popular culture'. In India, traditionally, high culture entails Sanskritization, and in certain contexts in the north, Persianization. We see such transfer in the much-discussed and controversial work of Raja Rao, *The Serpent and the Rope*. On the other hand, in *Kanthapura*, Rao uses what may be called a 'vernacular style' of English. His other work, *The Cat and Shakespeare*, introduces an entirely new style. In devising these three styles for Indian English, Rao has certainly demonstrated a delicate sense for appropriate style, but such experimentation has its limitations, too. These innovations make his style linguistically 'deviant' from a native speaker's perspective, and culturally it introduces into English a dimension alien to the canons of English literature.

In the expansion of the style range, the African situation is not different from the South Asian. In Achebe we find that 'he has developed not one prose style but several, and in each novel he is careful to select the style or styles that will best suit his subject'

(Lindfors 1973: 74). It is for this reason that, as Lindfors says, 'Achebe has devised an African vernacular style' (74).

Once the choice of the style is made, the next step is to provide authenticity (e.g. *Africanness, Indianness*) to the speech acts, or to the discourse types. How is this accomplished? It is achieved by 'linguistic realization' of the following types:

(1)   the use of native similes and metaphors (e.g. Yoruba, Kannada, Malay) which linguistically result in collocational deviation;
(2)   the transfer of rhetorical devices for 'personalizing' speech interaction;
(3)   the translation ('transcreation') of proverbs, idioms, etc.;
(4)   the use of culturally dependent speech styles; and
(5)   the use of syntactic devices.

Let me now illustrate these five points one by one. First the use of native similes and metaphors. It is through such similes that Achebe, for example, is able to evoke the cultural milieu in which the action takes place (Lindfors 1973: 75). Examples of such similes are: *like a bush-fire in the harmattan, like a yam tendril in the rainy season, like a lizard fallen from an iroko tree, like pouring grains of corn into a bag full of holes* (also see B. Kachru 1965 [1983: 131 ff.]).

Second, the transfer of rhetorical devices for contextualizing and authenticating speech interaction. Such devices provide, as it were, the 'ancestral sanction' to the interaction, a very important strategy in some African and Asian societies. It is one way of giving 'cultural roots' to English in African and Asian contexts, particularly to its 'vernacular style'. One might say it is a device to link the past with the present. Onuora Nzekwu (*Wand of Noble Wood*) accomplishes this by the use of what may be called 'speech initiators' which appear 'empty' to one who does not share the cultural and linguistic presuppositions. But for contextualizing the text, these are essential. Consider among others the following: *our people have a saying; as our people say; it was our fathers who said; the elders have said.* Stylistically this also preserves the 'orality' of the discourse.

A third strategy is that of 'transcreating' proverbs and idioms from an African or Asian language into English. The culture-embeddedness of such linguistic items is well recognized and, as Achebe says, they are 'the palm-oil with which words are eaten' (1964: viii). The function of such expression is to universalize a specific incident and to reduce the harshness of an utterance. Achebe's use of proverbs, in Lindfors' view (1973: 77), sharpens characterization, clarifies conflict, and focuses on the values of the society. In other words, to use Herskovits' term (1958), the use of such a device provides a 'grammar of values'. Consider, for example, the use of the following proverbs by Achebe: *I cannot live on the bank of the river and wash my hand with the spittle; if a child washed his hands he could eat with kings*, and *a person who chased two rats at a time would lose one*. It is through the proverbs and word play that the wit and wisdom of the ancestors is passed on to new generations. I have shown earlier (B. Kachru 1965, 1966) how this device is used to nativize speech functions such as abuses, curses, blessings, and flattery.

A fourth characteristic is to give the narrative and the discourse a 'naive tall-tale style' typical of the earthy folk style (Lindfors 1973: 57). This is typical of Tutuola, or of

Raja Rao's *Kanthapura*. This, as Jolaoso observes (quoted by Lindfors 1973: 57), 'reminds one very forcibly of the rambling old grandmother telling her tale of spirits in the ghostly light of the moon' (see also Afolayan 1971 and Abrahams 1983: 21–39).

The fifth strategy is the use of particular syntactic devices. An example is the enhancement of the above folk style by using the device of a traditional native village storyteller and occasionally putting questions to the audience for participation. This assures a reader's involvement. Tutuola makes frequent use of asking direct questions, or asking rhetorical questions in the narration. In Raja Rao's case the Harikathaman or the grandmother uses the same devices, very effective indeed for passing on the cultural tradition to new generations and for entertaining other age groups.

One might ask here: Is there evidence that the discourse of Indians reflects features which according to Lannoy represent a 'culture of sound'? (1971: 275) Would one agree with him that one consequence of belonging to such a culture is 'the widespread tendency of Indians to use language as a form of incantation and exuberant rhetorical flourish on public occasions. Orators rend the air with verbose declamations more for the pleasure of the sound than for the ideas and facts they may more vaguely desire to express'? (176). One wonders, is Babu English (see Widdowson 1979: 202–211) a manifestation of such 'culture of sound' in the written mode?

[. . .]

## Conclusion

The study of the bilingual's creativity has serious implications for linguistic theory, and for our understanding of culture-specific communicative competence. It is of special interest for the study and analysis of the expanding body of the non-native literatures in English and of the uses of English in different cultures.

The universalization of English may be a blessing in that it provides a tool for crosscultural communication. But it is a double-edged tool and makes several types of demands: a new theoretical perspective is essential for describing the functions of English across cultures. In other words, the use of English is to be seen as an integral part of the socio-cultural reality of those societies which have begun using it during the colonial period and, more important, have retained it and increased its use in various functions in the post-colonial era.

In recent years many such proposals for a theoretical reorientation have been made, not necessarily with reference to international uses of English, by Gumperz (1964), Halliday (1973), Hymes (1967) and Labov (1972b), among others. And in 1956, when Firth suggested (in Palmer 1968: 96–7) that 'in view of the almost universal use of English, an Englishman must de-anglicize himself', he was, of course, referring to the implications of such universalization of the language. In his view, this de-Anglicization was much more than a matter of the readjustment of linguistic attitudes by the Englishmen; it entailed linguistic pragmatism in the use of English across cultures.

The diaspora varieties of English are initiating various types of changes in the English language. More important is the decanonization of the traditionally recognized literary conventions and genres of English. This change further extends to the introduction of new Asian and African cultural dimensions to the underlying cultural assumptions traditionally associated with the social, cultural, and literary history of English. The shared conventions and literary milieu between the creator of the text and the reader of English can no more be taken for granted. A text thus has a unique context. English is unique in another sense too: it has developed both national English literatures, which are specific and *context-bound*, and certain types of *context-free* international varieties. The national varieties show more localized organizational schemes in their texture, which may be 'alien' for those who do not share the canons of literary creativity and the traditions of underlying culture which are manifest in such varieties.

The national English literatures are excellent resources for culture learning through literature, a topic which has attracted considerable attention in recent years. However, for such use of these texts one has to acquire the appropriate interpretive methodology and framework for identifying and contextualizing the literary creativity in English, especially that of its non-native bilingual users. It is only by incorporating such pragmatic contexts, as has been recently shown, for example in Chishimba (1983), that the functional meaning and communicative appropriateness of the new discourse strategies and discourse patterns will be understood and appreciated.

### Issues to consider

Kachru raises large issues that are at the heart of linguistics. Do you agree that there is a link between stylistic expression and particular cultural views or thoughts? This would mean that – as several of his quoted sources imply – certain world-views could only be expressed in the appropriate language. What do you think of this link between language and thought?

You might also consider the place of literature in this area of bilingual linguistics. Is there a trade-off between the authenticity of the language and the accessibility of the text to a wider audience? Universality is often suggested as a feature of literature, but the specific nature of 'contact literature' might not share this feature. You could also consider which cultural knowledge is assumed by a specific text, and which pieces of knowledge are provided by the text for readers who do not have access to the source culture. Obviously, the main way into this area is to read some 'contact literature' and investigate its sociolinguistic aspects.

Some suggestions follow.

- ❏ If you examine a literary text which arises out of a language-contact situation, can you discern a stylistic distinctiveness that indicates its origins? Is this distinctiveness at the level of word-choice, metaphor construction, syntax, or other interference patterns at the level of discourse organisation? Essentially you will be investigating the stylistic representation of characterisation, whether it is through the speech and thought of actual characters in the novel or the through the 'voice' of the narrator. You might evaluate how successful the text is as a piece of literature.

- ❏ Using a descriptive linguistic account of the source language, you could evaluate the degree of 'authenticity' in Kachru's terms. It is likely in a literary text that the author has selected certain features of the source language and culture rather than trying to represent its detail exactly. What can you surmise from the selection process and what image does it give you of the stereotypes involved?

❏ You could try to copy the creative process yourself. If you have a competence in another language, you might try to write a brief narrative which represents your own native culture in that language. You could also try to do this using another dialect of your own language to represent your own local culture. This is actually quite difficult, and so you should also consider why it is not easy.

---

## THE POLITICS OF TALK

Brown and Levinson's (1987) classic account of politeness universals has been a very productive framework in pragmatics and sociolinguistics, but it has in recent years attracted criticism especially from the perspective of gender studies. In particular, it does not seem to account very well for examples of impoliteness or deliberate power struggle, and its reliance on the older notion of 'face' results in a scheme that is not complex enough for analysing a rich sociolinguistic setting. In the extracts from the following paper, Louise Mullany takes an approach based on the notion of a *community of practice*. Briefly, this defines politeness phenomena socially rather than (only) psychologically and individually. A set of people constitute a CofP if they are mutually engaged in various behavioural, social and linguistic practices; CofPs can be well-established or very transient; they can have central and peripheral members. A performed social role such as gender is enacted within a CofP, which in turn then seems to offer a richer way of understanding social politeness.

### 'I don't think you want me to get a word in edgeways do you John?' Re-assessing (im)politeness, language and gender in political broadcast interviews

**Louise Mullany** (reprinted from the special issue of *English Working Papers on the Web* 3, 'Linguistic Politeness and Context', 2002: http://www.shu.ac.uk/wpw/politeness/index.htm)

### *Introduction*

The topic of politeness has proved to be a popular line of enquiry for language and gender researchers in recent years, with interest originating with Lakoff's (1975) anecdotal assertions that women are more linguistically polite than their male counterparts. Similar conclusions have been drawn by Brown (1980) and Holmes (1995) who offer empirical evidence to justify their arguments. At its time of publication, Holmes' (1995) work offered a detailed analysis of linguistic politeness and gender, drawing on her own and others' research in a variety of contexts. As Crawford (1997: 428) argues, Holmes manages to incorporate a large amount of material 'under her politeness umbrella', including critical reviews of influential language and gender studies conducted by Zimmerman and West (1975), P. Fishman (1978, 1980) and Tannen (1984, 1992). Holmes concludes that the multitude of evidence she has collected over a number of years clearly demonstrates that women are more linguistically polite than their male counterparts.

However, researchers including Cameron (1995a, 1995b, 1996, 1997) and Bergvall, Bing and Freed (1996) have questioned assertions such as those made by Holmes and others, where men and women are seen as having distinctive speech styles. They argue that viewing men and women in a dichotomised way results in a gross oversimplification of the complexity of language and gender. It not only ignores the diversity of speech within groups of women and groups of men, it also ignores cultural differences, and differences that may result from other social variables such as class, age and ethnicity. As Freed (1996: 55) points out, whilst 'people generally persist in believing that . . . women are more polite than men', research which continues to address such questions is both 'misguided and naive'. She argues that researchers need to abandon frequently asked questions such as 'what differences exist between men's and women's speech?' (1996: 55), as this serves only to perpetuate stereotypes about male and female discourse.

Cameron (1995b) argues that the problem lies in the persistence of both the power/dominance and culture/difference approaches to language and gender. Both approaches assume that there is a pre-existing difference between male and female speech patterns. Power/dominance theorists believe that this stems from the considerable amount of economic, social and political power men have over women in society, whilst the culture/difference researchers believe that speech differences are implemented during the socialisation process. Cameron (1995b: 39) accuses the dominance approach of becoming 'obsolete', and the difference approach of being 'reactionary'. Both frameworks result in the formulation of inaccurate over-generalisations such as women are more linguistically polite than their male counterparts.

Theorists, including Freed (1996), Bergvall (1996) and Cameron (1997), have turned to the notion of gender as a performative social construct, following Butler's (1990) work, as a way of avoiding gender polarisation in language and gender studies. Butler believes that masculinity and femininity are not traits that we inherently possess, rather they are effects that are produced by the activities we engage in. She argues that 'gender is always a doing', and as there is 'no gender identity behind the expressions of gender . . . identity is performatively constituted by the very "expressions" that are said to be its results' (1990: 25). Freed (1996), Bergvall (1996, 1999) and Mills (2006) argue that as well as adapting the notion of gender as a performative social construct, language and gender research also needs to adopt Eckert and McConnell-Ginet's (1992 a, b) Community of Practice (CofP) approach. Bergvall (1999: 282) argues that the CofP framework enables the 'performative construction and achievement of gendered identity' to be examined, thus focusing 'much needed attention on the social construction of gender' (1999: 273).

In [this paper, . . . ] the CofP framework will be [. . .] applied to the institutional context of political interviews, with the aim of demonstrating how viewing them as a CofP can bring insights into how notions of gender and impoliteness can be conceived.

[. . .]

### Impoliteness and political interviews

If Brown and Levinson's (1987) model is applied to a study of political interview discourse, the FTAs uttered by participants without redressive action would be regarded as impolite by implication. However, in political interviews it is not in the interests of participants to pay mutual attention to each other's face needs. The centrality of the preservation of face needs to Brown and Levinson's theory means that it does not appear to account for confrontational discourse where not paying attention to the addressees' face needs and attacking their position is a frequent and expected occurrence. Failure to pay attention to the face needs of fellow interlocutors does not result in conversational breakdown in political interviews, as would be predicted by Brown and Levinson's theory.

Unlike Brown and Levinson's approach, the CofP framework enables a more fluid and dynamic approach to be taken to a definition of politeness, which accounts for impoliteness as part of the overall concept of politeness. It draws attention away from a search for politeness universals, and leads instead to a detailed examination of what politeness means in specific contexts. Adopting the CofP approach means that it is the participants themselves who define what is polite and impolite behaviour against the norms they have for the specific communities in which their discourse practices take place. In a specific concentration on the CofP approach and impoliteness, Mills (2006) argues:

> Impoliteness is only classified as such by certain, usually dominant community members, and/or when it leads to a breakdown in relations.

For impoliteness to be evident, either the interviewer or the interviewee would need to highlight this themselves. However, [. . .] conversational breakdown rarely occurs in political interviews, and it is notable that only one example of impoliteness, as defined through the CofP approach, can be found in my database. Before analysing this example, and the potential implications it has for language and gender studies on politeness, I wish to focus on Mills's definition that it is usually the 'dominant' member of the CofP who will classify impoliteness in discourse as this raises interesting issues of power operating at both a micro and macro level in the [Synthetic] CofP of political interviews [that is, a CofP that is artificially and temporarily constructed].

At a local level of discourse management, it is the interviewers who appear to control the encounter [. . .]. However, it is often the case that the interviewees will hold a much more dominant position in wider society [. . .]. As Winter (1993) points out, this is noticeable through the non-reciprocal use of address terms, which is also observable in all the interviews in my database. The interviewees use FN to refer to their interviewers, whereas the interviewers will use T only, TLN, TFNLN or FNLN to refer to their interviewees, signalling the distinction between their positions of power in society as a whole. As a consequence of the discrepancy between power at local and global levels, the identification of the most dominant participant in the interaction can become blurred, and on certain occasions, interviewees can stipulate which topics they will talk about, either during the interview or beforehand, thus limiting the amount of local power interviewers have over the encounter. It thus appears that as the identification of the most dominant participant can become indistinct, both the interviewers and the interviewees could, on occasions, perceive that impolite linguistic behaviour has occurred in the interview.

The only example of impoliteness found in my database of 20 encounters occurs in a M-F interview between John Humphrys (JH) and Hilary Armstrong (HA), broadcast on the 2nd December 1997. It is the female interviewee who accuses her male interviewer of impolite behaviour towards her by marking his linguistic behaviour as inappropriate using metalanguage and by posing a question to him, thus reversing the expectation of whose role it is to initiate the question-answer sequences. In the [Synthetic] CofP of political interviews, the interviewer and interviewee should mutually engage with one another through a process of joint negotiation in order to produce discourse for the overhearing audience. However, HA accuses JH of not allowing her to respond to his questions. The accusation by HA therefore shows that the norms of the [Synthetic] CofP, as far as she is concerned, are not being adhered to by the male interviewer.

I intend to demonstrate that impolite behaviour, as classified by the participant herself, is something that emerges at a discourse level, rather than at the level of a single speech act. HA does not judge JH's behaviour as impolite due to a single speech act that he performs; rather it is his interactional behaviour over a stretch of talk during the interview that leads her to accuse him of not letting her have the conversational floor when she is entitled to it.

The topic of the interview is the Government's announcement of a settlement which will determine the amount of money local authorities are to be given towards the cost of providing services. This issue has been highlighted on the news bulletin that took place fifteen minutes before JH and HA's interview. Immediately preceding their encounter is a F-M interview with Anna Ford and a Liberal Democrat MP who argues that by sticking to Conservative spending plans, the Government will be unable to provide more finance as council tax bills will not be allowed to increase. The extract below shows JH questioning HA about the fairness of the settlement:

Example 7

| 1 | JH | if it er if it were truly a fair settlement then it would take full allowance |
|---|---|---|
| 2 | | wouldn't it make full allowance for inflation the cost of pay increases the |
| 3 | | cost of providing services for the growing number of old people and |
| 4 | | the children in school the extra fifty thousand fifty five thousand people |
| 5 | | we've just been hearing pupils we've just been hearing about if it were fair. |
| 6 | | it would take account of all that wouldn't it? |
| 7 | HA | well the settle [ment                    ] the settlement has taken account |
| 8 | JH | [but it won't will it?] |
| 9 | HA | [of the increase in                                    ] |
| 10 | JH | [how can it when it's less than the rate of inflation?] |

11  HA  h – the settlement has taken into account of the changes in pupil
          numbers. er
12        and so on and so [forth       ]
13  JH                      [not all th ]ose other things [there listed]
14  HA                                                    [no it hasn't] taken
15        acc   [ount of ] all that [because          ]
16  JH        [OH     ]            [and that's what ] Frank Dobson ATTACKED
17        this the last government for doing precisely a year ago=
18  HA                                                    =well er I was
19        doing the rounds in the studios as well then John and we weren't
20        saying [precisely what you're saying]
21  JH          [well I'll quote you          ] will the Secretary of State
22        confirm that his figures make [no allowance for inflation      ].
23  HA                                   [I don't think you want me to  ]
24  JH  [the cost of pay increases. that no no no no no but but but          ]
25  HA  [I don't think you want me to get a word in edgeways do you John?]
26      [((laughs))    ]
27  JH  [but you say  ] that you didn't say that I've just quoted to you the exact
28        words that Frank Dobson used not just in the studios in the House of
29        COMMONS will the Secretary of State confirm that his figures make
30        no allowance for inflation the cost of pay increases the cost of
31        providing extra services and so on. precise words
32  HA  well [the           ]
33  JH        [out of Hansard  ]
34  HA  the this this year's settlement takes as much allowance for those as
35        we've been possibly able to do. and I think when you see the
36        settlement this afternoon you will see that we have worked very
37        hard within what are tight guidelines and tight budgets. to make
38        sure that local government gets a fairer settlement and we have
39        tried to make sure that we re-distribute the money in a more fair way,
40        but it is true that local government spends a quarter of the whole
41        of public finance it is an enormous amount and no government that
42        is responsible within six months can come in and wave a magic
43        wand

All of the questions posed by John Humphrys in this section are defined as antagonistic
in nature. Following Holmes' (1992) definition, antagonistic questions are aggressively
critical assertions, which function to attack the interviewee's position and demonstrate
that it is wrong. They occur frequently in political interviews. Antagonistic questions
in this extract take either the syntactic form of a question (lines 1–6, 8, 10) or appear
in the form of a declarative which has the pragmatic function of a question (lines 13,
16–17, 21–22, 27–31, 33).

In lines 1–6, JH's antagonistic question accuses the Government's settlement of
being unfair, thus challenging HA's position and attempting to demonstrate that it is
wrong. HA begins to respond to this, but JH successfully interrupts her answer with
another antagonistic question 'but it won't be will it?' HA precedes to answer the

question by repeating her initial utterance 'the settlement', but JH successfully inter-rupts again with another antagonistic question (line 10). For the third time HA precedes to answer the initial question commencing yet again with the repetition of 'the settle-ment'. On this occasion she is allowed to proceed (lines 11–12), but JH successfully interrupts her again with the declarative 'not all those other things there listed' (line 13).

HA responds to JH's declarative, successfully interrupting his utterance to agree with him (line 14). JH show his surprise by interrupting with 'OH'. As HA attempts to explain why all of the things listed haven't been taken into account commencing with 'because' (line 15), JH interrupts once more to declare that this is what [her colleague] Frank Dobson attacked the Tory government for doing, thus accusing HA of hypocrisy. She responds to this, accusing JH of not presenting a correct version of the facts (lines 18–20).

He interrupts her again in an attempt to demonstrate that her position is wrong (line 21), by quoting directly from Hansard [the official record of Parliament]. It is during this declarative utterance that HA accuses JH of not allowing her to answer his questions, thus accusing him of being impolite because, as far as she is concerned, he has broken the norms of the political interview. Her initial interruption attempt to do this is unsuccessful (line 23). However, she then proceeds to accuse JH of not wanting her to respond to the questions he is posing, interrupting him, though he does not concede the floor to her. In her accusation she reverses the expectation that the interviewer initiates the question-answer sequence by asking him an antagonistic question of her own: 'I don't think you want me to get a word in edgeways do you John?' He denies that this is the case in his response which he repeats four times (line 24), but after he has completed his utterance he does allow HA to have a turn in the discourse without disruptively interrupting her (lines 34–42).

It is important to note that HA's accusation is mitigated. She hedges the initial part of her utterance 'I don't think', followed by a conventional metaphorical expression 'get a word in edgeways', and then laughs when she has completed her utterance (line 26). The joking tone adopted lessens the force of the antagonistic question, and ironically focuses on their respective roles of interviewer and interviewee, i.e. that the interviewee is expected to take up the majority of turn-taking time when responding to the interviewer's questions. An unmitigated accusation could have led to conversational breakdown. This would be damaging both for HA and the Labour Party she represents if she is perceived to be unable to cope with JH's aggressive style. HA thus avoids potential conversational breakdown by implicitly classifying her fellow interlocutor's linguistic behaviour as being impolite, using metalanguage and reversing the role expectations of who should be the questioner in political interviews. JH is thus being impolite as he is not allowing HA to mutually engage with him in the joint enterprise of producing discourse for an overhearing audience.

In terms of gender, a potential explanation that could be suggested for JH's behaviour by the culture difference/approach is that as a male speaker he will not pay attention to conventions of linguistic politeness and thus disruptively interrupts his female interlocutor on numerous occasions. The power/dominance approach could explain JH's behaviour towards HA as yet another example of male domination, with the male interrupting the female on far more occasions in mixed-sex interaction.

However, it is the female speaker who accuses her male interlocutor of displaying impolite behaviour towards her. Although her accusation is mitigated to avoid potential conversational breakdown, she nevertheless displays dominant behaviour by uttering an antagonistic question of her own which subverts the expected interviewer-interviewee power relationship at a local level of discourse management. Both the power/ dominance and the culture/difference approaches would have difficulty in explaining this example of a female not paying close attention to the face needs of her male interlocutor, implicitly accusing him of inappropriate behaviour.

The CofP approach emphasises that gender is just one aspect of social identity that is being enacted in a CofP. In political broadcast interviews, the interviewers and interviewees, as well as enacting their gender identity, are also enacting other parts of their social identity, such as their age, class and ethnicity. Furthermore, because the discourse takes place in an institutional context, they are also enacting their professional identities as either politicians or journalists, which is influenced by factors such as what political party they belong to or what broadcast network they appear on, what position they have within their party or within their broadcast network, and how long they have been an MP or a political interviewer. All of these aspects of identity can be expected to affect the discourse strategies male and female journalists and politicians use in political interviews.

### Conclusion

By focusing on the institutional context of political broadcast interviews, it is hoped that the benefit of focusing studies of politeness on discourse in institutional settings has been emphasised. The neglect of impoliteness by previous linguistic politeness researchers has been overcome by using the CofP framework to theorise how notions of both politeness and impoliteness can be conceived. Instead of applying an alleged set of politeness universals to individual speech acts, the CofP approach demonstrates that politeness and impoliteness have different functions for different individuals depending on what kind of community they are interacting in.

The CofP approach also redefines the manner in which the relationship between language and gender should be conceived. Instead of treating men and women as monolithic categories, the focus on local practices enables language and gender researchers to stop searching for differences between male and female speech patterns and instead consider that gender may not be the only aspect of identity that is influencing linguistic behaviour in specific communities of practice.

However, this is not to suggest that gender as a variable is not significant. Although Freed (1996) points out that gender may not always be the most salient feature which affects speech patterns on all occasions, she argues that inspiration for language and gender studies should lie in the fact that, due to deeply embedded gender stereotypes that continue to operate in society, 'there are a well-organized set of social expectations about who, women or men, will convey which social meanings' (1996: 70) and, as a consequence, women and men have different access to specific social roles and activities.

[. . .]

Adopting the CofP approach has highlighted that gender is not the only variable which affects linguistic behaviour. Instead gender should be seen as 'a sex-based way of experiencing other social attributes like class, ethnicity and age' (Eckert and

McConnell-Ginet 1992a: 91), and also as a sex-based way of experiencing other aspects of identity, such as professional identity that are enacted when interaction takes place in an institutional context. [. . .]

## Issues to consider

The intersection between sociolinguistics and the public discourses of politicians, social commentators and celebrities is a rich area for investigation. Social variables which have a correlation with the dimension of power are obvious fields for exploration: for example, how speakers in an interview or panel behave linguistically as an apparent consequence of their gender, age, wealth, celebrity status, second language fluency, and so on. Since these linguistic events take place in the media, it is a very easy matter to gain access to recordings and make your own transcripts. Furthermore, because the discourse setting by definition is public, observed and recorded, you have no problem as far as the observer's paradox is concerned. Of course, you do then have to remember that any conclusions you draw can only safely be applied to public discourse and only tentatively extended to take account of the principles at work in private conversations.

Some practical suggestions follow.

❑  With a friend, collect your own transcript of an argumentative and disruptive conversation, such as a political interview on radio or television. In order to determine which is the best approach to such discourse, you should analyse the transcript from the perspective of politeness theory based on *face*, and your friend could analyse the same transcript from the perspective of the CofP model. Which account seems most satisfactory to you? Are there things that one framework allows you to see and describe that the other one does not? Can you find problems with both approaches that you might want to repair by challenging parts of each model?

❑  Politeness frameworks are usually applied to spoken discourse. However, you might want to explore the politeness strategies used in written texts, such as advertising copy, local government leaflets, election flyers, or literary fiction. How far do the politeness features used in these texts assume or even construct a certain sort of reader?

❑  Given the richness of a social setting as presumed by the CofP approach, how can you decide which particular social factors are more or less important? In other words, if you treat a social group as a holistic rich network, how is it possible to control the social variables to isolate whether, for example, the group's most important defining factor is gender, or politics, or geography, or occupation, or age, and so on. Is it, in fact, possible at all to apply this sort of controlled *variationism* to a notion like the CofP, or are they fundamentally at odds in principle? One way of answering this for yourself is to take the description and data from a variationist study and try to re-account for it using a CofP approach, or equally of course the other way round.

**D**

## CLOSING TURNS

Emanuel Schegloff and Harvey Sacks produced one of the most influential frameworks for the analysis of conversational structure in terms of 'turn-taking'. In the following reading, their article on conversational closure develops their framework in a systematic way.

The passage builds on concepts introduced in A11, B11 and C11, and also B10. It can usefully be explored in relation to the extracts given in B7, B10 and C10.

### Opening up closings

**Emanuel Schegloff and Harvey Sacks** (reprinted from *Semiotica* 7: 289–327, (1973).)

Our aim in this paper is to report in a preliminary fashion on analyses we have been developing of closings of conversation. Although it may be apparent to intuition that the unit 'a single conversation' does not simply end, but is brought to a close, our initial task is to develop a technical basis for a closing problem. This we try to derive from a consideration of some features of the most basic sequential organization of conversation we know of – the organization of speaker turns.

[. . .]

This project is part of a program of work undertaken several years ago [this paper was first delivered to the American Sociological Association in 1969] to explore the possibility of achieving a naturalistic observational discipline that could deal with the details of social action(s) rigorously, empirically, and formally. For a variety of reasons that need not be spelled out here, our attention has focused on conversational materials; suffice it to say that this is not because of a special interest in language, or any theoretical primacy we accord conversation. Nonetheless, the character of our materials as conversational has attracted our attention to the study of conversation as an activity in its own right, and thereby to the ways in which any actions accomplished in conversation require reference to the properties and organization of conversation for their understanding and analysis, both by participants and by professional investigators. This last phrase requires emphasis and explication.

We have proceeded under the assumption (an assumption borne out by our research) that insofar as the materials we worked with exhibited orderliness, they did so not only for us, indeed not in the first place for us, but for the co-participants who had produced them. If the materials (records of natural conversations) were orderly, they were so because they had been methodically produced by members of the society for one another, and it was a feature of the conversations that we treated as data that they were produced so as to allow the display by the coparticipants to each other of their orderliness, and to allow the participants to display to each other their analysis, appreciation, and use of that orderliness. Accordingly, our analysis has sought to explicate the ways in which the materials are produced by members in orderly ways that exhibit their orderliness, have their orderliness appreciated and used, and have that appreciation displayed and treated as the basis for subsequent action.

In the ensuing discussion, therefore, it should be clearly understood that the 'closing problem' we are discussing is proposed as a problem for conversationalists; we are not interested in it as a problem for analysts except insofar as, and in the ways, it is a problem for participants. (By 'problem' we do not intend puzzle, in the sense that participants need to ponder the matter of how to close a conversation. We mean that closings are to be seen as achievements, as solutions to certain problems of conversational organization.) [. . .]

The materials with which we have worked are audiotapes and transcripts of naturally occurring interactions (i.e., ones not produced by research intervention such as experiment or interview) with differing numbers of participants and different combinations of participant attributes. There is a danger attending this way of characterizing our materials, namely, that we be heard as proposing the assured relevance of numbers, attributes of participants, etc., to the way the data are produced, interpreted, or analyzed by investigators or by the participants themselves. Such a view carries considerable plausibility, but for precisely that reason it should be treated with extreme caution, and be introduced only where warrant can be offered for the relevance of such characterizations of the data from the data themselves.

[. . .]

It seems useful to begin by formulating the problem of closing technically in terms of the more fundamental order of organization, that of turns. Two basic features of conversation are proposed to be: (1) at least, and no more than, one party speaks at a time in a single conversation; and (2) speaker change recurs. The achievement of these features singly, and especially the achievement of their cooccurrence, is accomplished by co-conversationalists through the use of a 'machinery' for ordering speaker turns sequentially in conversation. The turn-taking machinery includes as one component a set of procedures for organizing the selection of 'next speakers', and, as another, a set of procedures for locating the occasions on which transition to a next speaker may or should occur. The turn-taking machinery operates utterance by utterance. That is to say [. . .] it is within any current utterance that possible next speaker selection is accomplished, and upon possible completion of any current utterance that such selection takes effect and transition to a next speaker becomes relevant. We shall speak of this as the 'transition relevance' of possible utterance completion. [. . .] Whereas these basic features [. . .] deal with a conversation's ongoing orderliness, they make no provision for the closing of conversation. A machinery that includes the transition relevance of possible utterance completion recurrently for any utterance in the conversation generates an indefinitely extendable string of turns to talk. Then, an initial problem concerning closings may be formulated: *how to organize the simultaneous arrival of the co-conversationalists at a point where one speaker's completion will not occasion another speaker's talk, and that will not be heard as some speaker's silence.* The last qualification is necessary to differentiate closings from other places in conversation where one speaker's completion is not followed by a possible next speaker's talk, but where, given the continuing relevance of the basic features and the turn-taking machinery, what is heard is not termination but attributable silence, a pause in the last speaker's utterance, etc. It should suggest why simply to stop talking is not a solution to the closing problem: any first prospective speaker to do so would be hearable as 'being silent' in terms of the turn-taking machinery, rather than as having suspended its relevance. [. . .]

How is the transition relevance of possible utterance completion lifted? A proximate solution involves the use of a 'terminal exchange' composed of conventional parts, e.g., an exchange of 'good-byes'. [. . .] We note first that the terminal exchange is a case of a class of utterance sequences which we have been studying for some years, namely, the utterance pair, or, as we shall refer to it, the adjacency pair. [. . .] Briefly, adjacency pairs consist of sequences which properly have the following features: (1) two utterance length, (2) adjacent positioning of component utterances, (3) different speakers producing each utterance. The component utterances of such sequences have an achieved relatedness beyond that which may otherwise obtain between adjacent utterances. That relatedness is partially the product of the operation of a typology in the speakers' production of the sequences. The typology operates in two ways: it partitions utterance types into 'first pair parts' (i.e., first parts of pairs) and second pair parts; and it affiliates a first pair part and a second pair part to form a 'pair type'. 'Question-answer', 'greeting-greeting', 'offer-acceptance/refusal' are instances of pair types. [. . .] Adjacency pair sequences, then, exhibit the further features (4) relative ordering of parts (i.e. first pair parts precede second pair parts) and (5) discriminative relations (i.e., the pair type of which a first pair part is a member is relevant to the selection among second pair parts). [. . .]

In the case of that type of organization which we are calling 'overall structural organization', it may be noted that at least initial sequences (e.g., greeting exchanges), and ending sequences (i.e., terminal exchanges) employ adjacency pair formats. It is the recurrent, institutionalized use of adjacency pairs for such types of organization problems that suggests that these problems have, in part, a common character, and that adjacency pair organization [. . .] is specially fitted to the solution of problems of that character. [. . .]

But it may be wondered, why are two utterances required for either opening or closing? [. . .] What two utterances produced by different speakers can do that one utterance cannot do it: by an adjacently positioned second, a speaker can show that he understood what a prior aimed at, and that he is willing to go along with that. Also, by virtue of the occurrence of an adjacently produced second, the doer of a first can see that what he intended was indeed understood, and that it was or was not accepted. [. . .]

We are then proposing: If *where* transition relevance is to be lifted is a systematic problem, an adjacency pair solution can work because: by providing that transition relevance is to be lifted after the second pair part's occurrence, the occurrence of the second pair part can then reveal an appreciation of, and agreement to, the intention of closing *now* which a first part of a terminal exchange reveals its speaker to propose. Given the institutionalization of that solution, a range of ways of assuring that it be employed have been developed, which make drastic difference between one party saying 'good-bye' and not leaving a slot for the other to reply, and one party saying 'good-bye' and leaving a slot for the other to reply. The former becomes a distinct sort of activity, expressing anger, brusqueness, and the like, and available to such a use by contrast with the latter, it is this consequentiality of alternatives that is the hallmark of an institutionalized solution. [. . .]

In referring to the components of terminal exchanges, we have so far employed 'good-bye' as an exclusive instance. But, it plainly is not exclusively used. Such other components as 'ok', 'see you', 'thank you', 'you're welcome', and the like are also used. Since the latter items are used in other ways as well, the mere fact of their use does not mark them as unequivocal parts of terminal exchanges. [. . .]

The adjacency pair is one kind of 'local', i.e., utterance, organization. It does *not* appear that *first* parts of terminal exchanges are placed by reference to that order of organization. While they, of course, occur after some utterance, they are not placed by reference to a location that might be formulated as 'next' after some 'last' utterance or class of utterances. Rather, their placement seems to be organized by reference to a properly initiated closing *section*.

The [relevant] aspect of overall conversational organization concerns the organization of topic talk. [. . .] If we may refer to what gets talked about in a conversation as 'mentionables', then we can note that there are considerations relevant for conversationalists in ordering and distributing their talk about mentionables in a single conversation. There is, for example, a position in a single conversation for 'first topic'. We intend to mark by this term not the simple serial fact that some topic gets talked about temporally prior to others, for some temporally prior topics such as, for example, ones prefaced by 'First, I just want to say . . .', or topics that are minor developments by the receiver of the conversational opening of 'how are you' inquiries, are not heard or treated as 'first topic' is to accord it to a certain special status in the conversation. Thus, for example, to make a topic 'first topic' may provide for its analyzability (by coparticipants) as 'the reason for' the conversation, that being, furthermore, a preservable and reportable feature of the conversation. In addition, making a topic 'first topic' may accord it a special importance on the part of its initiator [. . .].

These features of 'first topics' may pose a problem for conversationalists who may not wish to have special importance accorded some 'mentionable', and who may not want it preserved as 'the reason for the conversation'. It is by reference to such problems affiliated with the use of first topic position that we may appreciate such exchanges at the beginnings of conversations in which news *is* later reported, as:

A: what's up
B: not much. what's up with you?
A: nothing

Conversationalists, then, can have mentionables they do not want to put in first topic position, and there are ways of talking past first topic position without putting them in.

A further feature of the organization of topic talk seems to involve 'fitting' as a preferred procedure. That is, it appears that a preferred way of getting mentionables mentioned is to employ the resources of the local organization of utterances in the course of the conversation. That involves holding off the mention of a mentionable until it can 'occur naturally', that is, until it can be fitted to another conversationalist's prior utterance [. . .]

There is, however, no guarantee that the course of the conversation will provide the occasion for any particular mentionable to 'come up naturally'. This being the case, it would appear that an important virtue for a closing structure designed for this kind of topical structure would involve the provision for placement of hitherto unmentioned mentionables. The terminal exchange by itself makes no such provision. By exploiting the close organization resource of adjacency pairs, it provides for an immediate (i.e., next turn) closing of the conversation. That this close-ordering technique for terminating not exclude the possibility of inserting unmentioned mentionables can be achieved by placement restrictions on the first part of terminal exchanges, for example, by requiring 'advance note' or some form of foreshadowing.

[. . .]

The first proper way of initiating a closing section that we will discuss is one kind of (what we will call) 'pre-closing'. The kind of pre-closing we have in mind takes one of the following forms, 'We-ell . . .', 'O.K . . .', 'So-oo', etc. (with downward intonation contours), these forms constituting the entire utterance. These pre-closings should properly be called '*possible* pre-closing', because providing the relevance of the initiation of a closing section is only one of the uses they have. One feature of their operation is that they occupy the floor for a speaker's turn without using it to produce either a topically coherent utterance or the initiation of a new topic. With them a speaker takes a turn whose business seems to be to 'pass', i.e., to indicate that he has not now anything more or new to say, and also to give a 'free' turn to the next, who, because such an utterance can be treated as having broken with any prior topic, can without violating topical coherence take the occasion to introduce a new topic [. . .] When this opportunity is exploited [. . .] then the local organization otherwise operative in conversation, including the fitting of topical talk, allows the same possibilities which obtain in any topical talk. The opening [. . .] may thus result in much more ensuing talk than the initial mentionable that is inserted [. . .] The extendability of conversation to great lengths past a possible pre-closing is not a sign of the latter's defects with respect to initiating closings, but of its virtues in providing opportunities for further topic talk that is fitted to the topical structure of conversation.

[. . .] The other possibility is that co-conversationalists decline an opportunity to insert unmentioned mentionables. In that circumstance, the pre-closing may be answered with an acknowledgement, a return 'pass' yielding a sequence such as:

A: O.K.
B: O.K.

thereby setting up the relevance of further collaborating on a closing section. When the possible pre-closing is responded to in this manner, it may constitute the first part of the closing section.

[. . .]

Clearly, utterances such as 'O.K.', 'We-ell', etc. (where those forms are the whole of the utterance), occur in conversation in capacities other than that of 'pre-closing'. It is only on some occasions of use that these utterances are treated as pre-closings. [. . .]

[They] operate as possible pre-closings when placed at the analyzable (once again, *to participants*) end of a topic.

[. . .] Not all topics have an analyzable end. One procedure whereby talk moves off a topic might be called 'topic shading', in that it involves no specific attention to ending a topic at all, but rather the fitting of differently focused but related talk to some last utterance in a topic's development. But co-conversationalists may specifically attend to accomplishing a topic boundary, and there are various mechanisms for doing so; these may yield 'analyzable ends', their analyzability to participants being displayed in the effective collaboration required to achieve them.

For example, there is a technique for 'closing down a topic' that seems to be a formal technique for a class of topic types, in the sense that for topics that are of the types that are members of the class, the technique operates without regard to what the particular topic is. [. . .] We have in mind such exchanges as:

A: okay?
B: alright

Such an exchange can serve, if completed, to accomplish a collaboration on the shutting down of a topic, and may thus mark the next slot in the conversational sequence as one in which, if an utterance of the form 'We-ell', 'O.K.', etc. should occur, it may be heard as a possible pre-closing.

Another 'topic-bounding' technique involves one party's offering of a proverbial or aphoristic formulation of conventional wisdom which can be heard as the 'moral' or 'lesson' of the topic being thereby possibly closed. Such formulations are 'agreeable with'. When such a formulation is offered by one party and agreed to by another, a topic may be seen (by them) to have been brought to a close. Again, an immediately following 'We-ell' or 'O.K.' may be analyzed by its placement as doing the alternative tasks a possible pre-closing can do.

(1)   Dorrinne: uh-you know. it's just like bringin the – blood up
      Theresa: yeah well. THINGS UH ALWAYS WORK OUT FOR  THE
                                                        [BEST      ]
      Dorrinne:                                         [oh certainly.]
                  alright Tess.
      Theresa: oh huh.
      Theresa: okay.
      Dorrinne: g'bye.
      Theresa: goodnight
(2)   Johnson: and uh. uh we're gonna see if we can't uh tie in our plans a little better.
      Baldwin: okay – fine.
      Johnson: ALRIGHT?
      Baldwin: RIGHT.
      Johnson: okay boy.
      Baldwin: okay
      Johnson: bye. bye
      Baldwin: g'night

[. . .]

What the preceding discussion suggests is that a closing section is initiated, i.e., turns out to have begun, when none of the parties to a conversation care or choose to continue it. Now that is a *warrant* for closing the conversation, and we may now be in a position to appreciate that the issue of placement, for the initiation of closing sections as for terminal exchanges, is the issue of warranting the placement of such items as will initiate the closing at some 'here and now' in the conversation. The kind of possible pre-closing we have been discussing – 'O.K.', 'We-ell', etc. – is a way of establishing one kind of warrant for undertaking to close a conversation. Its effectiveness can be seen in the feature noted above, that if the floor offering is declined, if the 'O.K.' is answered by another, then together these two utterances can constitute not a possible, but an actual first exchange of the closing section. The pre-closing ceases to be 'pre-' if accepted, for the acceptance establishes the warrant for undertaking a closing of the conversation at some 'here'.

We may now examine other kinds of pre-closings and the kinds of warrants they may invoke for initiating the beginning of a closing section. The floor-offeringexchange device [above] is one that can be initiated by any party to a conversation. In contrast to this, there are some [. . .] devices whose use is restricted to particular parties. We can offer some observations about telephone contacts, where the formulation of the parties can be specified in terms of the specific conversation, i.e., caller – called. What we find is that there are, so to speak, 'caller's techniques' and 'called's techniques' for inviting the initiation of closing sections. [. . .]

One feature that many of them have in common [is] that they employ as their warrant for initiating the closing the interests of the other party. It is in the specification of those interests that the techniques become assigned to one or another party. Thus, the following invitation to a closing is caller-specific and makes reference to the interests of the other.

A discussion about a possible luncheon has been proceeding:

A: uhm livers 'n an gizzards 'n stuff like that makes it real yummy. makes it too rich for
    me but: makes it yummy

A: well I'll letchu go. I don't wanna tie up your phone

And, on the other hand, there are such called-specific techniques, also making reference to the other's interests, as

A: this is costing you a lot of money

There are, of course, devices usable by either party which do not make reference to the other's interests, most familiarly, 'I gotta go'.

[. . .]

The 'routine' questions employed at the beginnings of conversations, e.g., 'what are you doing?', 'where are you going?', 'how are you feeling?', etc., can elicit those kinds of materials that will have a use at the ending of the conversation in warranting its closing, e.g., 'Well, I'll let you get back to your books', 'why don't you lie down and take a nap?', etc. By contrast with our earlier discussion of such possible pre-closings as 'O.K.' or 'We-ell', which may be said to accomplish or embody a warrant for closing, these may be said to announce it. That they do so may be related to the possible places in which they may be used.

[. . .]

It is the import of some of the preceding discussion that there are slots in conversation 'ripe' for the initiation of closing, such that utterances inserted there may be inspected for their closing relevance. To cite an example, 'why don't you lie down and take a nap' properly placed will be heard as an initiation of a closing section, not as a question to be answered with a 'Because [. . .]' (although, of course, a coparticipant can seek to decline the closing offering by treating it as a question). To cite actual data:

B has called to invite C, but has been told C is going out to dinner:

B: yeah. well get on your clothes and get out and collect some of that free food and
    we'll make it some other time Judy then
C: okay then Jack
B: bye bye
C: bye bye

While B's initial utterance in this excerpt might be grammatically characterized as an imperative or a command, and C's 'Okay' as a submission or accession to it, in no sense but a technical syntactic one would those be anything but whimsical characterizations. While B's utterance has certain imperative aspects in its language form, those are not ones that count; his utterance is a closing initiation; and C's utterance agrees not to a command to get dressed (nor would she be inconsistent if she failed to get dressed after the conversation), but to an invitation to close the conversation. The point is that no analysis – grammatical, semantic, pragmatic, etc. – of these utterances taken singly and out of sequence, will yield their import in use, will show what coparticipants might make of them and do about them. That B's utterance here accomplishes a form of closing initiation, and C's accepts the closing form and not what seems to be proposed in it, turns on the placement of these utterances in the conversation. Investigations which fail to attend to such considerations are bound to be misled. [Schegloff and Sacks go on to discuss 'pre-topic closing offerings', utterances like 'Did I wake you up?', which offer listeners a means of moving into a closing section.]

[. . .]

Once properly initiated, a closing section may contain nothing but a terminal exchange and accomplish a proper closing thereby. Thus, a proper closing can be accomplished by:

A: O.K.
B: O.K.
A: bye bye
B: bye

Closing sections may, however, include much more. There is a collection of possible component parts for closing sections which we cannot describe in the space available here. Among others, closings may include 'making arrangements', with varieties such as giving directions, arranging later meetings, invitations, and the like; reinvocation of certain sorts of materials talked of earlier in the conversation, in particular, reinvocations of earlier-made arrangements (e.g., 'See you Wednesday') and reinvocations of the reason for initiating the conversation (e.g., 'Well, I just wanted to find out how

Bob was'), not to repeat here the earlier discussion of materials from earlier parts of the conversation to do possible preclosings; and components that seem to give a 'signature' of sorts to the type of conversation, using the closing section as a place where recognition of the type of conversation can be displayed (e.g., 'Thank you'). Collections of these and other components can be combined to yield extended closing sections, of which the following is but a modest example:

> B: well that's why I said I'm not gonna say anything. I'm not making any comments about anybody
> C: hmh
> C: ehyeah
> B: yeah
> C: yeah
> B: alrighty. well I'll give you a call before we decide to come down. O.K.?
> C: O.K.
> B: alrighty
> C: O.K.
> B: we'll see you then
> C: O.K.
> B: bye bye
> C: bye

However extensive the collection of components that are introduced, the two crucial components (*for the achievement of proper closing*; other components may be important for other reasons, but not for closing *per se*) are the terminal exchange which achieves the collaborative termination of the transition rule, and the proper initiation of the closing section which warrants the undertaking of the routine whose termination in the terminal exchange properly closes the conversation.

[. . .]

To capture the phenomenon of closings, one cannot treat it as the natural history of some particular conversation; one cannot treat it as a routine to be run through, inevitable in its course once initiated. Rather, it must be viewed, as much conversation as a whole, as a set of prospective possibilities opening up at various points in the conversation's course; there are possibilities throughout a closing, including the moments after a 'final' good-bye, for reopening the conversation. Getting to a termination, therefore, involves work at various points in the course of the conversation and of the closing section; it requires accomplishing. For the analyst, it requires a description of the prospects and possibilities available at the various points, how they work, what the resources are, etc., from which the participants produce what turns out to be the finally accomplished closing.

[. . .]

## Issues to consider

Recent advances in recording technology have enormously improved our ability to investigate conversation, especially in its natural setting rather than in the experimental context of a classroom or interview room. This means you can undertake your own studies with relative ease.

Perhaps the first difference you will notice between many transcriptions of speech and real examples is the number and extent of silences and long pauses in normal conversational exchanges. Since these are obviously a prominent feature of spoken discourse, you might want to think of ways of categorising different types of silence.

A framework for conversational analysis often assumes both an orderliness in the structure and 'recipient design': that is, an assumption that speakers tailor their utterance for optimal communicativeness for the addressee. Schegloff and Sacks make this assumption in their article. However, how would you deal analytically with different situations: when someone is being wilfully obscure; or has a very idiosyncratic style of speech that seems more like a monologue; or is engaged in argument and domination? What about the conversational structure of small children, especially when talking to adults? And how are the patterns of conversational structure exploited in absurdist drama?

Some other suggestions follow.

❑ Many conversations, especially those involving older people, often conclude with the citation of an idiom or proverbial saying. There are two connected hypotheses here: some conversations end with idioms; and the practice is dying out, using the age distinction as an apparent change over time. How would you design a study that would test whether these hypotheses were the case?

❑ In addition to the non-normative situations of dialogue mentioned above, how would you adapt the Schegloff and Sacks framework to analyse conversations in which one person is desperate to leave and the other wants to prolong the conversation?

❑ Though Schegloff and Sacks acknowledge the social context in conversation, theirs is more a pragmatic model than a sociolinguistic one, in the sense that it focuses on intentions and meanings rather than the social factors of the speakers. Consider the effect of the different social variables that might attach to speakers in a conversation, and how this would affect the structure and language choices in the dialogue.

## LINGUISTIC DETECTION                                                          D12

The linguistic analysis of naturally occurring language data is the central methodological principle in sociolinguistics, and this book has taken a broad view of the range of sociolinguistics as a discipline. As part of the application of sociolinguistic techniques as a means of addressing and solving real-world problems, the discipline of **forensic linguistics** has grown substantially in recent years. This has involved using the tools of linguistics to assist in matters such as disputed authorship, identifying speakers in criminal cases by their accent or writing style, deciding whether transcribed evidence has been falsified or distorted, and determining what exactly was meant in court cases. A key figure in the field is Malcolm Coulthard.

In the following extract, Coulthard shows how ambiguity lay at the centre of the evidence in one of the last cases of murder which led to an execution in Britain.

## Hidden voices in monologue

**Malcolm Coulthard** (reprinted from ' "... and then ..." Language description and author attribution', the final Sinclair Open Lecture, 2006.)

In November 1952 two teenagers, Derek Bentley aged 19 and Chris Craig aged 16, were seen climbing up onto the roof of a London warehouse. The police surrounded the building and three unarmed officers went up onto the roof to arrest them. Bentley immediately surrendered; Craig started shooting, wounding one policeman and killing a second. Bentley was jointly charged with his murder, even though he had been under arrest for some time when the officer was killed. The trial, which lasted only two days, took place five weeks later and both were found guilty. Craig, because he was legally a minor, was sentenced to life imprisonment; Bentley was sentenced to death and executed shortly afterwards. Bentley's family fought tenaciously to overturn the guilty verdict and were eventually successful 46 years later, in the summer of 1998. (The feature film *Let Him Have It, Chris*, released in 1991, gives a mainly accurate account.) The evidence which was the basis for both Bentley's conviction and the subsequent successful appeal was in large part linguistic.

In the original trial the problem for the Prosecution, in making the case against Bentley, was to demonstrate that he could indeed be guilty of murder despite being under arrest when the murder was committed. At this point it would be useful to read the statement which, it was claimed, Bentley dictated shortly after his arrest. It is presented in full below; the only changes I have introduced are the numbering of sentences for ease of reference and the highlighting, by underlining and bold, of items to which I will later refer.

### *Derek Bentley's statement*

(1) I have known Craig since I went to school. (2) We were stopped by our parents going out together, but we still continued going out with each other – I mean **we have not gone out** together until tonight. (3) I was watching television tonight (2 November 1952) and between 8 p.m. and 9 p.m. Craig called for me. (4) My mother answered the door and I heard her say that I was out. (5) I had been out earlier to the pictures and got home just after 7 p.m. (6) A little later Norman Parsley and Frank Fasey called. (7) **I did not answer the door or speak to them**. (8) My mother told me that they had called and I then ran out after them. (9) I walked up the road with them to the paper shop where I saw Craig standing. (10) We all talked together and then Norman Parsley and Frank Fazey left. (11) Chris Craig and I then caught a bus to Croydon. (12) We got off at West Croydon and then walked down the road where the toilets are – I think it is Tamworth Road.

(13) When we came to the place where you found me, Chris looked in the

window. (14) There was a little iron gate at the side. (15) Chris then jumped over and I followed. (16) Chris then climbed up the drainpipe to the roof and I followed. (17) Up to then **Chris had not said anything**. (18) We both got out on to the flat roof at the top. (19) Then someone in a garden on the opposite side shone a torch up towards us. (20) Chris said: 'It's a copper, hide behind here.' (21) We hid behind a shelter arrangement on the roof. (22) We were there waiting for about ten minutes. (23) **I did not know** he was going to use the gun. (24) A plain clothes man climbed up the drainpipe and on to the roof. (25) The man said: 'I am a police officer – the place is surrounded.' (26) He caught hold of me and as we walked away Chris fired. (27) **There was nobody else** there at the time. (28) The policeman and I then went round a corner by a door. (29) A little later the door opened and a policeman in uniform came out. (30) Chris fired again then and this policeman fell down. (31) I could see that he was hurt as a lot of blood came from his forehead just above his nose. (32) The policeman dragged him round the corner behind the brickwork entrance to the door. (33) I remember I shouted something but I forgot what it was. (34) **I could not see** Chris when I shouted to him – he was behind a wall. (35) I heard some more policemen behind the door and the policeman with me said: **'I don't think** he has many more bullets left.' (36) Chris shouted 'Oh yes I have' and he fired again. (37) I think I heard him fire three times altogether. (38) The policeman then pushed me down the stairs and **I did not see** any more. (39) I knew we were going to break into the place. (40) **I did not know** what we were going to get – just anything that was going. (41**) I did not have** a gun and **I did not know** Chris had one until he shot. (42) I now know that the policeman in uniform that was shot is dead. (43) I should have mentioned that after the plain clothes policeman got up the drainpipe and arrested me, another policeman in uniform followed and I heard someone call him 'Mac'. (44) He was with us when the other policeman was killed.

Bentley's barrister spelled out for the jury the two necessary pre-conditions for them to convict: they must be 'satisfied and sure',

i)   that [Bentley] knew Craig had a gun and
ii)  that he instigated or incited Craig to use it. [Trow 1992: 179]

The evidence adduced by the Prosecution to satisfy the jury on both points was linguistic. For point i) it was observed that in his statement, which purported to give his unaided account of the night's events, Bentley had said 'I did not know he was going to use the gun', (sentence 23). In his summing up, the judge who, because of the importance of the case was the Lord Chief Justice, made great play with this sentence, telling the jury that its positioning in the narrative of events, before the time when there was a single policeman on the roof, combined with the choice of '*the* gun' (as opposed to 'a gun') must imply that Bentley knew that Craig had a gun well before it was used. In other words 'the gun', given its position in the statement, must be taken to mean 'the gun I already knew that Craig had'.

The evidence used to support point ii), that Bentley had instigated Craig to shoot, was from the police officers. In their written statements and in their verbal evidence in court, they asserted that Bentley had uttered the words 'Let him have it, Chris' immediately before Craig had shot and killed the policeman. As the judge emphasised, the strength of the linguistic evidence depended essentially on the credibility of the police officers who had remembered it, recorded it, written it down later and then sworn to its accuracy. When the case came to Appeal in 1998, one of the defence strategies was to challenge the reliability of Bentley's statement. If they could throw doubt on the veracity of the police, they could mitigate the incriminating force of both the statement and the phrase 'Let him have it', which Bentley, supported by Craig, had vehemently denied uttering.

At the time of Bentley's arrest the police were allowed to collect verbal evidence from those accused of a crime in two ways: either *by interview*, when they were supposed to record contemporaneously, verbatim and in longhand, both their own questions and the replies they elicited, or *by statement*, when the accused was invited to write down, or, if s/he preferred, to dictate to a police officer, their version of events. During statement-taking the police officers were supposed not to ask substantive questions. At trial three police officers swore on oath that Bentley's statement was the product of unaided monologue dictation, whereas Bentley asserted that it was, in part at least, the product of dialogue, and that police questions and his replies to them had been reported as monologue. There is no doubt that this procedure was sometimes used for producing statements. A senior police officer, involved in another murder case a year later, explained to the Court how he had himself elicited a statement from another accused in exactly this way:

> I would say 'Do you say on that Sunday you wore your shoes?' and he would say 'Yes' and it would go down as 'On that Sunday I wore my shoes'

There are many linguistic features which suggest that Bentley's statement is not, as claimed by the police, a verbatim record, see Coulthard (1993) for a detailed discussion; here we will focus only on evidence that the statement was indeed, at least in part, dialogue converted into monologue. Firstly, the final four sentences of the statement

> (39) I knew we were going to break into the place. (40) I did not know what we were going to get – just anything that was going. (41) I did not have a gun and I did not know Chris had one until he shot. (42) I now know that the policeman in uniform that was shot is dead.

form some kind of meta-narrative whose presence and form are most easily explained as the result of a series of clarificatory questions about Bentley's knowledge at particular points in the narrative. In searching for evidence of multiple voices elsewhere in the statement we must realise that there will always be some transformations of Q-A which will be indistinguishable from authentic dictated monologue. In the [policeman's] example quoted above, had we not been told that 'On that Sunday I wore my shoes' was a reduction from a Q-A, we would have had some difficulty in deducing it, although the preposed adverbial 'On that Sunday' is certainly a little odd.

We can begin our search for clues with the initial observation that narratives, particularly narratives of murder, are essentially accounts of what happened and to a lesser extent what was known or perceived by the narrator and thus reports of what did *not* happen or was *not* known are rare and special. There is, after all, an infinite number of things that did not happen and thus the teller needs to have some special justification for reporting any of them to the listener, in other words there must be some evident or stated reason for them being newsworthy. [. . . In general], positive finite clauses [are] 8 times more likely to occur than negative clauses.

We can see typical examples of 'normal' usage of negative reports in the sentences below which are taken from a crucial confession statement in another famous case, that of the Bridgewater Four [another murder case in 1979 . . .]:

i)   Micky dumped the property but **I didn't know where**.
ii)  Micky Hickey drove the van away, **I don't know where he went** to
iii) **We didn't all go together**, me and Vinny walked down first.

(Molloy's Statement)

In examples, i) and ii) the second negative clause functions as a *denial* of an inference which the listener could have reasonably derived from the first clause. Example iii) is similar, but this time it is a denial of an inference which the narrator guesses the listener might have made, as there is no textual basis for the inference. In other words such negatives are an integral part of the ongoing narrative. We find examples of negatives being used in a similar way in Bentley's statement

(6)     A little later Norman Parsley and Frank Fasey called.
(7)     **I did not answer the door or speak to them**

When Bentley reported that his friends had called, the listener would reasonably expect him to have at least talked to them and therefore this is a very natural denial of a reasonable expectation.

However, there are some negatives in Bentley's statement which have no such narrative justification, like sentence (17) below:

(16)    Chris then climbed up the drainpipe to the roof and I followed.
(17)    Up to then **Chris had not said anything**.
(18)    We both got out on to the flat roof at the top.

Chris is not reported as beginning to talk once they have got out onto the roof, nor is his silence contrasted with anyone else's talking, nor is it made significant in any other way later in the narrative. A similarly unwarranted negative is:

(26)    He caught hold of me and as we walked away Chris fired.
(27)    **There was nobody else** there at the time.
(28)    The policeman and I then went round a corner by a door.

None of the possible inferences from this denial seem to make narrative sense here – i.e. that as a result of there being no one else there a) it must be the policeman that Craig was firing at, or b) that it must be Craig who was doing the firing, or c) that immediately afterwards there would be more people on the roof. So, the most reasonable explanation for the negatives in these two examples is that, at this point in the statement-taking process, a policeman asked a clarificatory question to which the answer was negative and the whole sequence was then recoded and recorded as a negative statement by Bentley. The fact that some of the statement may have been elicited in this way is of crucial importance in sentence (23):

(23)    **I did not know** he was going to use the gun

This is the one singled out by the judge as incriminating. This sentence would only make narrative sense if it were linked backwards or forwards to the use of a gun – in other words if it has been placed immediately preceding or following the report of a shot. However, the actual context is:

(22)   We were there waiting for about ten minutes.

(23)   **I did not know** he was going to use the gun.

(24)   A plain clothes man climbed up the drainpipe and on to the roof.

If it is accepted that there were question/answer sequences underlying Bentley's statement, it follows that the logic and the sequencing of the information were not under his direct control. Thus the placing of the reporting of some of the events must depend on a decision by the police questioner to ask his question at that point, rather than on Bentley's unaided reconstruction of the narrative sequence. Therefore, and crucially, this means that the inference drawn by the judge in his summing up about Bentley's prior knowledge of Craig's gun was totally unjustified – if the sentence is the product of a response to a question, with its placing determined by the interrogating police officers, there is no longer any conflict with Bentley's later denial 'I did not know Chris had one [a gun] until he shot'. Nor is there any significance either to be attached to Bentley saying 'the gun'. All interaction uses language loosely and co-operatively and so, if the policeman had asked Bentley about 'the gun', Bentley would have assumed they both knew which gun they were talking about. In that context the sensible interpretation would be 'the gun that had been used earlier that evening' and not 'the gun that was going to be used later' in the sequence of events that made up Bentley's own narrative of the evening.

### Using corpus evidence

One of the marked features of Derek Bentley's confession is the frequent use of the word 'then' in its temporal meaning – 11 occurrences in 588 words. This may not, at first, seem at all remarkable given that Bentley is reporting a series of sequential events and that one of the obvious requirements of a witness statement is accuracy about time. However, a cursory glance at a series of other witness statements showed that Bentley's usage of 'then' was at the very least atypical, and thus a potential intrusion of a specific feature of policeman register deriving from a professional concern with the accurate recording of temporal sequence.

Two small corpora were used to test this hypothesis, the first composed of three ordinary witness statements, one from a woman involved in the Bentley case itself and two from men involved in another unrelated case, totalling some 930 words of text, the second composed of statements by three police officers, two of whom were involved in the Bentley case, the third in another unrelated case, totalling some 2,270 words. The comparative results were startling: whereas in the ordinary witness statements there is only one occurrence, 'then' occurs 29 times in the police officers' statements, that is an average of once every 78 words. Thus, Bentley's usage of temporal 'then', once every 53 words, groups his statement firmly with those produced by the police officers. In this case it was possible to check the findings from the 'ordinary witness' data against a reference corpus, the Corpus of Spoken English, a subset of the COBUILD Bank of English, which, at that time, consisted of some 1.5 million words. 'Then' in all its meanings proved to occur a mere 3,164 times, that is only once every 500 words, which supported the representativeness of the witness data and the claimed specialness of the data from the police and Bentley, (see Fox 1993).

What was perhaps even more striking about the Bentley statement was the frequent post-positioning of the 'thens', as can be seen in the two sample sentences below, selected from a total of 7:

> Chris **then** jumped over and I followed.
> Chris **then** climbed up the drainpipe to the roof and I followed.

The opening phrases have an odd feel, because not only do ordinary speakers use 'then' much less frequently than policemen, they also use it in a structurally different way. For instance, in the COBUILD spoken data 'then I' occurred ten times more frequently than 'I then'; indeed the structure 'I then' occurred a mere 9 times, in other words only once every 165,000 words. By contrast the phrase occurs 3 times in Bentley's short statement, once every 194 words, a frequency almost a thousand times greater. In addition, while the 'I then' structure, as one might predict from the corpus data, did not occur at all in any of the three witness statements, there were 9 occurrences in one single 980 word police statement, as many as in the entire 1.5 million word spoken corpus. Thus, the structure 'I then' does appear to be a feature of policeman's (written) register.

When we turn to look at yet another corpus, the shorthand verbatim record of the oral evidence given in court during the trial of Bentley and Craig, and choose one of the police officers at random, we find him using the structure twice in successive sentences, 'shot him *then* between the eyes' and 'he was *then* charged'. In Bentley's oral evidence there are also two occurrences of 'then', but this time the 'thens' occur in the normal preposed position: 'and *then* the other people moved off", 'and *then* we came back up'. Even Mr. Cassels, one of the defence barristers, who might conceivably have been influenced by police reporting style, says '*Then* you'. Thus these examples, embedded in Bentley's statement, of the language of the police officers who had recorded it, added support to Bentley's claim that it was a jointly authored document and so both removed the incriminating significance of the phrase 'I didn't know he was going to use the gun' and undermined the credibility of the police officers on whose word depended the evidential value of the claimed-to-be remembered utterance 'Let him have it Chris'.

In August 1998, 46 years after the event, the then Lord Chief Justice, sitting with two senior colleagues, criticised his predecessor's summing-up and allowed the Appeal against conviction.

## Issues to consider

This passage draws on **corpus linguistics** as an investigative tool: this is the collection of large amounts of natural language data in electronic form, so that it is searchable. Searches can involve looking for specific words, as above, or different versions of words, or the language used in comparable situations. Transcription data is often annotated or 'tagged' to give some indication of the social setting and social factors related to the speakers. Clearly, large language corpora are becoming increasingly important in sociolinguistic research, and indeed they can be seen as an equally important technical innovation in the discipline as the invention of the portable tape-recorder.

You might consider making use of corpus linguistic techniques in your own sociolinguistic studies. There are numerous corpora that you can access either on the internet or through your own college or university; or you could even consider setting up your own modest corpus of language (see Kennedy 1998 and McEnery and Wilson 1996).

Some practical suggestions follow.

❑   It is a relatively easy matter to find two different accounts of the same event by buying two different newspapers on the same day and comparing the reports of the same news story. It is important to remember that neither version can be treated as the 'undistorted' truth: both versions involve numerous linguistic choices which can be traced back to the social positioning of the newspaper or writer in question. Where you only have a single version of an event, you can still explore the ideological choices made by the writer by asking yourself at every point in the text what were the other linguistic possibilities available that the writer chose not to take.

❑   You could investigate the assumptions about language and society that are made in 'official' documents in the education system of your country. How far is your knowledge of sociolinguistics in accord with or at odds with the viewpoint expressed in such documents? How have the policies that you find been implemented in the classroom? Do you think they have been successful or not? Do you agree with the basis of the policy? How might you design a sociolinguistically-informed study to investigate these matters?

❑   What ideological assumptions are made in works within sociolinguistics? Even though I have been presenting the discipline as having a 'toolkit' and a set of principles, these tools and concepts also have an ideological dimension, and represent the writer's world-view and position. You could take a famous socio-linguistic study, and attempt to explain its data by some means other than that offered by the original writer. Or you could undertake a replication study to see if the same results are obtained. If the results vary, you will have to think about the reasons for this: it is possible that the interpretation of the original researcher is open to analysis in its own right.

# FURTHER READING

## 1 Sociolinguistic methods and techniques
A key text for further explorations in sociolinguistics is *The Routledge Companion to Sociolinguistics* (Llamas *et al.* 2007), which sets out basic techniques and includes chapters by key figures in the field. Other good introductions to sociolinguistics include Montgomery (1995), Hudson (1996) Spolsky (1998), Romaine (2000), Trudgill (2000), Holmes (2001) and Wardhaugh (2005). More detailed surveys of the field can be found in Chambers (2003), Milroy and Gordon (2003) and Mesthrie (2001). Extended collections of key readings can be found in Bratt-Paulston and Tucker (2003), and the two volumes of Trudgill and Cheshire (1998) and Cheshire and Trudgill (1998). For a good practical introduction to beginning a linguistics project, see Wray and Bloomer (2006). To learn statistics in sociolinguistics, Bell (2005) and Healey (2006) are accessible; Healey (2004) is more comprehensive; and Oakes (1998) is specifically for corpus linguistic techniques. Johnstone (2000) and Wengraf (2001) are good surveys of qualitative methods.

## 2 Accent and dialect
Accent and dialect studies are the foundation of sociolinguistics, so there is a mass of material in almost every sociolinguistics book. The classic accounts of accent varieties are the three volumes of Wells (1982), Foulkes and Docherty (1999) and Trudgill and Hannah (2002); see also Lippi-Green (1997 and D2). On dialects, see Davis (1983, 1990), Petyt (1980), Francis (1983), Downes (1984), Trudgill (1986a, 1990), Chambers and Trudgill (1998), Hughes *et al.* (2005), Auer *et al.* (2005), Britain (2006) and Wolfram and Schilling-Estes (2006). Milroy (1991) and Watts and Trudgill (2002) are good sociolinguistic histories. The original studies of attitude to accent are: Addington (1968), Ellis (1967), Giles (1970), Hopper and Williams (1973), Giles and Powesland (1975), Lambert *et al.* (1966), Seligman *et al.* (1972) and Eiser (1984). The area has been revisited by Andersson and Trudgill (1990), Edwards (1989) and Giles and Coupland (1991).

## 3 Register and style
Style in sociolinguistics is addressed in Eckert and Rickford (2001), and register in Ventola (1987), Swales (1990) Biber and Finegan (1994). The original work of Bernstein (1971, 1977, 1996) and his associates, and more educational linguistics, is discussed by Stubbs (1976, 1980, 1983, 1986), Trudgill (1975) and Perera (1984). Bernstein (1990) is a re-evaluation. Useful discussions on language and education appear in Carter (1990, 1995, 1997), Carter and McRae (1996), Bain *et al.* (1992), and McCarthy and Carter (1994). Literacy and multiliteracy is treated in Barton (1994) and Cope and Kalantzis (2000). Identity and attitudes to language are addressed in

Ryan and Giles (1982) and Joseph (2004). Critical Discourse Analysis receives its theoretical foundations from Fairclough (1995a, 1995b, 1995b, 2001, see D3), and examples can be seen in the reader edited by Caldas-Coulthard and Coulthard (1996). Chilton's (1986) article appears in revised form in Chilton (1988), and his work on nuclear discourse appears in Chilton (1985). Examples of critical linguistics appear in Fowler (1981, 1986, 1991), Fowler *et al.* (1979), Kress and Hodge (1983) and Hodge and Kress (1988), and is evaluated by Pateman (1981) and Richardson (1987). Renkema (2004) and Fairclough (2003) are good introductions to discourse analysis.

### 4 Ethnicity and multilingualism

J. Edwards (1995) and V. Edwards (2004) are both recommended for discussion of multilingualism, and Zentella (1997) for bilingualism. On pronoun usage and terms of address, see Mühlhäusler and Harré (1990), Braun (1988) and Adler (1978). The classic works on bilingualism and code-switching are J. Fishman (1972, 1974, 1978), Beardsmore (1982), Heller (1988), Romaine (1989), Myers-Scotton (1993a, 1993b), Milroy and Muysken (1995) and Rampton (1995). The classic case-studies can be found in the following collections: J. Fishman (1968), Whiteley (1971), Gumperz and Hymes (1972), Giglioli (1972), and Pride and Holmes (1972). Ethnography and identity are covered in J. Fishman (1999) and Saville-Troike (2003).

### 5 Variation and change

The classic method in sociolinguistics is exemplified by Labov (1966, 1972a, 1972b, 1994, 2001), and Trudgill (1972, 1974, 1984, 1988). A critique of the classic 'variation-ist' paradigm in sociolinguistics has been made by Cameron (1990, 1992), Coates (1993), Fasold (1990), Bickerton (1981, 1990), and Chambers (2003). Key work in variation and change is represented by Fasold and Schiffrin (1989), Chambers *et al.* (2003), Coulmas (2005) and Tagliamonte (2006). Age is discussed in Coupland *et al.* (1991), class in Reid (1989) and social networks in Milroy (1987b). Historical change from a sociolinguistic persepctive is handled by McMahon (1994) and Fennell (2000).

### 6 Standardisation

There is a great deal of work on RP, Standard English, their prestige values and people's attitudes to speakers of these and more stigmatised varieties. Peter Trudgill (1974, 1975, 1978, 1983, 1984, 1986a, 1990 and 2000) is a major figure. See also Honey (1989), Giles and Powesland (1975), Giles and Coupland (1991), Wilkinson (1995), and Bex and Watts (1999). Bell (1976) and Hymes (1974) remain useful sources. Joseph (1987) and Milroy and Milroy (1993, 1997) address the whole issue of 'correctness' in dialect: see also Crowley (1989). Discussion of Estuary English and related accent shifts in Britain can be found in Rosewarne (1994, 1996), Coggle (1993), Wells (1994, 1997), and Mugglestone (2003). Language change in general is addressed by Aitchison (1991), Hock (1986) and Labov (1994). Further to the reading given for thread 5 above, the historical development of English is also described in the classic texts by McCrum *et al.*, (1992), Baugh and Cable (2002), Pyles and Algeo

(1993), Graddol, Leith and Swann (1996), and from a social perspective by Leith (1997). Minority languages are discussed in Fase *et al.* (1992).

## 7 Gender

The classic work in sociolinguistics from a feminist perspective is in Cameron (1990, 1992 and 1995a). See also Coates (1993, 1998, 2004), Coates and Cameron (1986), Graddol and Swann (1989), Tannen (1992), Crawford (1995) and the introduction by Talbot (1998). Work that also addresses men's language can be found in Connell (1995), Johnson and Meinhof (1997), Macaulay (2005) and Cameron and Kulick (2003). The construction of gender can be found in Hall and Bucholtz (1995) and Bucholtz *et al.* (1999). Older studies include Thorne and Henley (1975), Thorne (1983), Poynton (1985), Spender (1985), and the original study by Lakoff (1975), updated in Lakoff (1990). With specific reference to the educational and classroom context, see Mahony (1985) and Mahony and Jones (1989). For a perspective from sociolinguistics into literature and narrative, see Mills (1995a) and Thornborrow and Coates (2005). Holmes and Meyerhoff (2003) is a handbook of the area.

## 8 Pidgins and creoles

There is an enormous amount of literature on pidgins, creoles, and post-creole forms of English, including Todd (1974), Bickerton (1981), Romaine (1988), Aitchison (1991), Morgan (1994), Holm (1988, 1989), Sebba (1997) and the *Journal of Pidgin and Creole Languages*. The place of creole studies in work on language birth, evolution and death is discussed in Crystal (2000), Chaudenson (2001), DeGraff (2001), and Mufwene (2001). Crystal (2003) discusses English as a global language. Edwards (1986) and Sutcliffe (1982) remain the classic accounts of British Black English, supported by Sutcliffe and Wong (1986) and Sutcliffe and Figueroa (1992). Wells (1973), Hewitt (1986) and Sebba (1993) record Jamaican English in London. There is an *International Journal of Bilingual Education and Bilingualism*, and a handbook edited by Kouwenberg and Singler (2005). Thomason (2001) is a good introduction.

## 9 New Englishes

The features and sociopolitical situation of Singaporean English are described by Crewe (1977), Platt and Weber (1980), Fraser-Gupta (1991, 1992), Pakir (1994), and in the articles in Foley *et al.* (1998). More generally, there is a mass of work on the formation and status of the New Englishes, including Kachru (1983, 1988, 1992), Smith (1983, 1987), Bailey and Gorlach (1984), Platt *et al.* (1984), Quirk and Widdowson (1985), Ashcroft *et al.* (1989), Sajavaara *et al.* (1991), Cheshire (1991), Mohanan (1992), Pennycook (1994), Crystal (1995) and McArthur (1998). Books on the dangers to minority languages are represented by Heller (1999), Nettle and Romaine (2000) and J. Fishman (2001). Recent work in world Englishes includes Brutt-Griffler (2002), Hickey (2004), Trudgill (2004) and of course Jenkins (2003) in this Routledge English Language Introductions series.

## 10 Pragmatics and politeness

On politeness norms and the address system see the original research by Brown and Gilman (1960), and also Adler (1978), Brown and Levinson (1987), Braun (1988),

Mühlhäusler and Harré (1990) and Watts *et al.* (1999). Eelen (2001) takes issue with these classic accounts. Mills (2003) also critically examines gender and politeness: see also Mills (1995b), Crawford (1995) and Wodak (1997). Locher (2004) focuses on arguments. Watts (2003) is a good overview. Institutional talk is discussed in Holmes and Stubbe (2003) and Thornborrow (2002). Key texts in pragmatics include Leech (1983), Levinson (1983) and Grundy (2000). Communities of practice discussions can be found in Wenger (1998). See also Garrett, Coupland and Williams (2003).

## 11 Conversation

The area of conversation analysis is growing rapidly. Classic models for the analysis of discourse include the 'turn-taking' model of Sacks *et al.* (1974 and see D11), Sacks (1992), Ochs *et al.* (1996) and the initially classroom-based discourse analysis model of Sinclair and Coulthard (1975), developed by Stenström (1994). See also Schiffrin (1987, 1994), Burton (1980), Boden and Zimmerman (1991), Hoey (1983), Sinclair, Hoey and Fox (1993), McCarthy (1991, 1998), Psathas (1995) and Pridham (2001). Wooffitt (2005) is a good overview and Eggins and Slade (2004) is a key text. Corpus linguistics is also a fast developing field: see Barnbrook (1996), Greenbaum (1996), Stubbs (1996), Biber *et al.* (1998), Aston and Burnard (1998), Biber *et al.* (1999), Tognini-Bonelli (2001), Meyer (2002), and Hunston (2002).

## 12 Ideology

Further to the reading listed for thread 3 above, critical discourse analysis is further represented in Birch (1989), Chilton *et al.* (1998), Meinhof and Richardson (1994), Richardson and Meinhof (1999), Wodak (1996), Wodak and Chilton (2005a, 2005b) and Fairclough (2003). Identity and contemporary literacy are addressed in Kress and van Leeuwen (2001), Androutsopoulos (2003) and Jewitt and Kress (2003): see also Gee (1996) and Ball (2005). On language policy and language planning, see Cooper (1989), Wright (2004), and Ricento (2005). For forensic linguistics, see Gibbons (1994), Cotterill (2002) and the journal *Forensic Linguistics*.

# REFERENCES

Abrahams, R.D. (1983) *The Man-of-Words in the West Indies: Performance and the Emergence of Creole Culture*, Baltimore: Johns Hopkins University Press.

Achebe, C. (1964) 'Foreword', in W.H. Whitley (ed.) *A Selection of African Prose*, Oxford: Clarendon Press.

Achebe, C. (1969) *Arrow of God*, New York: Doubleday.

Addington, D.W. (1968) 'The relationship of selected vocal characteristics to personality perception', *Speech Monographs* 25: 492–503.

Adler, M.K. (1978) *Naming and Addressing: A Sociolinguistic Study*, Hamburg: Helmut Buske.

Afolayan, A. (1971) 'Language and sources of Amos Tutuola', in C. Heywood (ed.) *Perspectives on African Literature*, London: Heinemann.

Aitchison, J. (1991) *Language Change: Progress or Decay?* (2nd edition), Cambridge: Cambridge University Press.

American Civil Liberties Union (1996) 'Briefing paper', http://www.aclu.org/library/pbp20.html

Andersen, H. (1989) 'Understanding linguistic innovations', in L. Breivik and E.H. Jahr (eds) *Language Change: Contributions to the Study of its Causes*, Berlin: Mouton de Gruyter, pp. 56–83.

Andersson, L. and Trudgill, P. (1990) *Bad Language*, Oxford: Basil Blackwell.

Androutsopoulos, J.K. (ed.) (2003) *Discourse Constructions of Youth Identities*, Philadelphia: Benjamins.

Ashcroft, B., Griffiths, G. and Tiffin, H. (1989) *The Empire Writes Back: Theory and Practice in Post-Colonial Literatures*, London: Routledge.

Aston, G. and Burnard, L. (1998) *The BNC Handbook: Exploring the British National Corpus with SARA*, Edinburgh: Edinburgh University Press.

Auer, P., Hinskens, F. and Kerswill, P. (eds) (2005) *Dialect Change: Convergence and Divergence in European Languages*, Cambridge: Cambridge University Press.

Bailey, R.W. and Görlach, M. (eds) (1984) *English as a World Language*, Ann Arbor: University of Michigan Press.

Bain, R., Fitzgerald, B. and Taylor, M. (eds) (1992) *Looking into Language: Classroom Approaches to Knowledge about Language*, London: Hodder & Stoughton.

Ball, M.J. (ed.) (2005) *Clinical Sociolinguistics*, Oxford: Blackwell.

Barber, C. (1976) *Early Modern English*, Edinburgh: Edinburgh University Press.

Barnbrook, G. (1996) *Language and Computers: A Practical Introduction to the Computer Analysis of Language*, Edinburgh: Edinburgh University Press.

Barton, D. (1994) *Literacy: An Introduction to the Ecology of Written Language*, Oxford: Blackwell.

Baugh, A.C. and Cable, T. (1978) *A History of the English Language* (1st edition), London: Routledge & Kegan Paul.

Baugh, A.C. and Cable, T. (2002) *A History of the English Language* (5th edition), London: Routledge.

Beardsmore, H.B. (1982) *Bilingualism: Basic Principles*, Clevedon: Tieto.

Bell, J. (2005) *Doing Your Research Project: A Guide for First-Time Researchers in Education, Health and Social Science* (4th edition), Milton Keynes: Open University Press.

Bell, R.T. (1976) *Sociolinguistics: Goals, Approaches and Problems*, London: Batsford.

Bergvall, V. (1996) 'Constructed and enacting gender through discourse: negotiating multiple roles as female engineering students', in V. Bergvall, J. Bing and A. Freed (eds), *Rethinking Language and Gender Research: Theory and Practice*, New York: Longman, pp. 173–201.

Bergvall, V. (1999) 'Towards a comprehensive theory of language and gender', *Language in Society* 28: 273–93.

Bergvall, V., Bing J. and Freed, A. (eds) (1996) *Rethinking Language and Gender Research: Theory and Practice*, New York: Longman.

Bernstein, B. (1971) *Class, Codes and Control, Vol. 1*, London: Routledge and Kegan Paul.

Bernstein, B. (1977) *Class, Codes and Control, Vol. 3*, London: Routledge and Kegan Paul.

Bernstein, B. (1990) *The Structuring of Pedagogic Discourse: Class, Codes and Control Volume 4*, London: Routledge.

Bernstein, B. (1996) *Pedagogy, Symbolic Control and Identity: Theory, Research, Critique*, London: Taylor and Francis.

Bex, A.R. and Watts, R. (eds) (1999) *Standard English: The Widening Debate*, London: Routledge.

Biber, D., Conrad, S. and Reppen, R. (1998) *Corpus Linguistics: Investigating Language Structure and Use*, Cambridge: Cambridge University Press.

Biber, D. and Finegan, E. (eds) (1994) *Sociolinguistic Perspectives on Register*, Oxford: Oxford University Press.

Biber, D., Johanssen, S., Leech, G., Conrad, S. and Finegan, E. (1999) *The Longman Grammar of Spoken and Written English*, London: Longman.

Bickerton, D. (1977) 'Pidginization and creolization: language acquisition and language universals', in A. Valdman (ed.) *Pidgin and Creole Linguistics*, Bloomington: Indiana University Press, pp. 66–83.

Bickerton, D. (1981) *Roots of Language*, Ann Arbor: Karoma.

Bickerton, D. (1983) 'Creole languages', *Scientific American* 249 (1): 116–22.

Bickerton, D. (1990) *Language and Species*, Chicago: University of Chicago Press.

Birch, D. (1989) *Language, Literature and Critical Practice: Ways of Analysing Text*, London: Routledge.

Bloomfield, L. (1933) *Language*, London: Allen and Unwin.

Boden, D. and Zimmerman, D. (eds) (1991) *Talk and Social Structure*, Oxford: Polity Press.

Bratt-Paulston, C. and Tucker R. (2003) *Sociolinguistics: The Essential Readings*, Oxford: Blackwell.

Braun, F. (1988) *Terms of Address*, Berlin: Mouton de Gruyter.

Britain, D. (ed.) (2006) *Language in the British Isles* (2nd edition), Cambridge: Cambridge University Press.

Brown, Penelope, (1980) 'How and why some women are more polite: some evidence from a Mayan community', in S. McConnell-Ginet, R. Borker and N. Furman (eds) *Women and Language and Literature in Society*, New York: Prager, pp. 111–36.

Brown, P. and Levinson, S. (1979) 'Social structure, groups and interaction', in K.R. Scherer and H. Giles (eds) *Social Markers in Speech*, Cambridge: Cambridge University Press, pp. 76–98.

Brown, P. and Levinson, S. (1987) *Politeness: Some Universals of Language Use*, Cambridge: Cambridge University Press.

Brown, R. and Gilman, A. (1960) 'The pronouns of power and solidarity', in T.A. Sebeok (ed.) *Style in Language*, New York: John Wiley, pp. 58–71.

Bruck, P.A. (ed.) (1989) *A Proxy for Knowledge: The News Media as Agents for Arms Control and Verification*, Ottawa: Norman Paterson School of International Affairs.

Bruner, J. (1991) 'The narrative construction of reality', *Critical Inquiry* 18 (1): 1–21.

Brutt-Griffler, J. (2002) *World English: A Study of its Development*, Clevedon: Multilingual Matters.

Bucholtz, M., Liang, A.C. and Sutton, L. (eds) (1999) *Reinventing Identities: the Gendered Self in Discourse*, Oxford: Oxford University Press.

Burton, D. (1980) *Dialogue and Discourse*, London: Routledge & Kegan Paul.

Butler, J. (1990) *Gender Trouble*, New York: Routledge.

Caldas-Coulthard, C.R. and Coulthard, M. (eds) (1996) *Texts and Practices: Readings in Critical Discourse Analysis*, London: Routledge.

Cameron, D. (ed.) (1990) *The Feminist Critique of Language: A Reader*, London: Routledge.

Cameron, D. (1992) *Feminism and Linguistic Theory* (2nd edition), London: Macmillan.

Cameron, D. (1995a) *Verbal Hygiene*, London: Routledge.

Cameron, D. (1995b) 'Rethinking language and gender studies: some issues for the 1990s', in S. Mills (ed.) *Language and Gender: Interdisciplinary Perspectives*, New York: Longman, pp. 31–44.

Cameron, D. (1996) 'The language-gender interface: challenging co-optation', in V. Bergvall, J. Bing and A. Freed (eds) *Rethinking Language and Gender Research: Theory and Practice*, New York: Longman, pp. 31–53.

Cameron, D. (1997) 'Performing gender identity: young men's talk and the construction of heterosexual masculinity', in S. Johnson and U.H. Meinhof (eds) *Language and Masculinity*, Oxford: Blackwell, pp. 47–64.

Cameron, D. and Kulick, D. (2003) *Language and Sexuality*, Cambridge: Cambridge University Press.

Carter, R.A. (ed.) (1990) *Knowledge about Language and the Curriculum*, London: Hodder & Stoughton.

Carter, R.A. (1995) *Keywords in Language and Literacy*, London: Routledge.

Carter, R.A. (1997) *Investigating English Discourse: Language, Literacy, Literature*, London: Routledge.

Carter, R.A. and McRae, J. (eds) (1996) *Language, Literature and the Learner: Creative Classroom Practice*, London: Longman.

Cassidy, F.G. and Le Page, R.B. (eds) (1980) *Dictionary of Jamaican English* (2nd edition), Cambridge: Cambridge University Press.

Chambers, J.K. (2003) *Sociolinguistic Theory: Linguistic Variation and its Social Significance* (2nd edition), Oxford: Blackwell.

Chambers, J.K. and Trudgill, P. (1998) *Dialectology* (2nd edition), Cambridge: Cambridge University Press.

Chambers, J.K., Trudgill, P. and Schilling-Estes, N. (eds) (2003) *The Handbook of Language Variation and Change* (2nd edition), Oxford: Blackwell.

Chaudenson, R. (2001) *Creolization of Language and Culture*, London: Routledge.

Cheshire, J. (1978) 'Present tense verbs in Reading English', in P. Trudgill (ed.) *Sociolinguistic Patterns in British English*, London: Edward Arnold, pp. 45–55.

Cheshire, J. (ed.) (1991) *English Around the World: Sociolinguistic Perspectives*, Cambridge: Cambridge University Press.

Cheshire J. and Trudgill P. (eds) (1998) *The Sociolinguistics Reader, Vol 2: Gender and Discourse*, London: Arnold.

Chilton, P. (ed.) (1985) *Language and the Nuclear Arms Debate*, London: Pinter.

Chilton, P. (1986) 'Metaphor, euphemism, and the militarization of language'. Paper presented at the Biannual Meeting of the International Peace Research Association, Sussex.

Chilton, P. (1988) *Orwellian Language and the Media*, London: Pluto Press.

Chilton, P. (1996) *Security Metaphors: Cold War Discourse from Containment to Common House*, New York: Peter Lang.

Chilton, P. (2003) *Analysing Political Discourse: Theory and Practice*, London: Routledge.

Chilton, P., Ilyin, M.V. and Mey, J.L. (eds) (1998) *Political Discourse in Transition in Europe, 1989–1991*, Amsterdam: Benjamins.

Chishimba, M. (1983) 'African varieties of English: text in context', Unpublished doctoral dissertation, University of Illinois.

Christy, C. (1983) *Uniformitarianism in Linguistics*, Amsterdam: John Benjamins.

Coates, J. (1993) *Women, Men and Language* (2nd edition), London: Longman.

Coates, J. (1996) *Women Talk: Conversation Between Women Friends*, Oxford: Blackwell.

Coates, J. (ed.) (1998) *Language and Gender: A Reader*, Oxford: Blackwell.

Coates, J. (2004) *Women, Men and Language* (3rd edition), London: Longman.

Coates, J. and Cameron, D. (eds) (1986) *Women in Their Speech Communities*, London: Longman.

Coggle, P. (1993) *Do You Speak Estuary?* London: Bloomsbury.

Connell, R.W. (1995) *Masculinities*, Cambridge: Polity Press.

Cooper, R. (1989) *Language Planning and Social Change*, Cambridge: Cambridge University Press.

Cope, B. and Kalantzis, M. (eds) (2000) *Multiliteracies: Literacy Learning and the Design of Social Futures*, London, Routledge.

Cotterill, J. (ed.) (2002) *Language in the Legal Process*, Basingstoke: Palgrave.

Coulmas, F. (2005) *Sociolinguistics: The Study of Speakers' Choices*, Cambridge: Cambridge University Press.

Coulthard, M. (1993) 'Beginning the study of forensic texts: corpus, concordance, collocation', in M.P. Hoey (ed.) *Data Description Discourse*, London: Harper-Collins, pp. 86–97.

Coupland, N., Coupland, J. and Giles, H. (1991) *Language, Society and the Elderly: Discourse, Identity and Ageing*, Oxford: Blackwell.

Crawford, M. (1995) *Talking Difference: On Gender and Language*, London: Sage.

Crawford, M. (1997) 'Review of Holmes' *Women, Men and Politeness*', *Language in Society* 26: 426–9.

Crewe, W. (ed.) (1977) *The English Language in Singapore*, Singapore: Eastern Universities Press.

Crowley, T. (1989) *The Politics of Discourse*, London: Macmillan.

Crystal, D. (1995) *The Cambridge Encyclopedia of the English Language*, Cambridge: Cambridge University Press.

Crystal, D. (2000) *Language Death*, Cambridge: Cambridge University Press.

Crystal, D. (2003) *English as a Global Language* (2nd edition), Cambridge: Cambridge University Press.

Davis, L.M. (1983) *English Dialectology: An Introduction*, Tuscaloosa: University of Alabama Press.

Davis, L.M. (1990) *Statistics in Dialectology*, Tuscaloosa: University of Alabama Press.

DeGraff, M. (ed.) (2001) *Language Creation and Language Change: Creolization, Diachrony, and Development*, Cambridge, Mass: MIT Press.

Dobson, E.J. (1968) *English Pronunciation 1500–1700* (Volume 1, 2nd edition), Oxford: Oxford University Press.

Dorian, N. (1993) 'Internally and externally motivated change in language contact settings: doubts about dichotomy', in C. Jones (ed.) *Historical Linguistics: Problems and Perspectives*, London: Longman, pp. 131–89.

Downes, W. (1984) *Language and Society*, London: Fontana.

Dyer, J. (2007) 'Language and identity', in C. Llamas, L. Mullany and P. Stockwell (eds) *The Routledge Companion to Sociolinguistics*, London: Routledge, pp. 101–8.

Eckert, P. and Rickford, J.R. (eds) (2001) *Style and Sociolinguistic Variation*, New York: Cambridge University Press.

Eckert, P. and McConnell-Ginet, S. (1992a) 'Communities of Practice: where language, gender and power all live', in K. Hall, M. Bucholtz and B. Moonwomon (eds) *Locating Power: Proceedings of the Second Berkeley Women and Language Conference*, Berkeley: Berkeley Women and Language Group, pp. 89–99.

Eckert, P. and McConnell-Ginet, S. (1992b) 'Think practically and look locally: language and gender as community-based practice', *Annual Review of Anthropology* 21: 461–90.

Eckert, P. and McConnell-Ginet, S. (1995) 'Constructing meaning, constructing selves', in K. Hall and M. Bucholtz (eds) *Gender Articulated: Language and the Socially-Constructed Self*, New York: Routledge, pp. 469–507.

Eckert, P. and McConnell-Ginet, S. (1999) 'New generalizations and explanations in language and gender research', *Language in Society* 28: 185–201.

Edwards, J. (1989) *Language and Disadvantage* (2nd edition), London: Cole and Whurr.

Edwards, J. (1995) *Multilingualism*, Harmondsworth: Penguin.

Edwards, V. (1986) *Language in a Black Community*, Clevedon: Multilingual Matters.

Edwards, V. (2004) *Multilingualism in the English-Speaking World*, Oxford: Blackwell.

Eelen, G. (2001) *A Critique of Politeness Theories*, Manchester: St Jerome.

Eggins, S. and Slade, D. (2004) *Analysing Casual Conversation*, London: Equinox.

Eiser, J.R. (ed.) (1984) *Attitudinal Judgement*, New York: Springer-Verlag.

Ellis, D.S. (1967) 'Speech and social status in America', *Social Forces* 45: 431–7.

Fairclough, N. (1991) *Discourse and Social Change*, Cambridge: Polity.

Fairclough, N. (1995a) *Critical Discourse Analysis: The Critical Study of Language*, London: Longman.

Fairclough, N. (1995b) *Media Discourse*, London: Edward Arnold.

Fairclough, N. (2001) *Language and Power* (2nd edition), London: Longman.

Fairclough, N. (2003) *Analysing Discourse: Textual Analysis for Social Research*, London: Routledge.

Fase, W., Jaspaert, K. and Kroon, S. (eds) (1992) *Maintenance and Loss of Minority Languages*, Amsterdam: Benjamins.

Fasold, R. (1990) *The Sociolinguistics of Language*, Oxford: Basil Blackwell.

Fasold, R.W. and Schiffrin, D. (eds) (1989) *Language Change and Variation*, Amsterdam: Benjamins.

Fennell, B. (2000) *A History of English: A Sociolinguistic Approach*, Oxford: Blackwell.

Ferguson, C.A and Heath, S.B. (eds) (1981) *Language in the USA*, Cambridge and New York: Cambridge University Press.

Ferguson, C.A. (1964) 'Diglossia', in D.H. Hymes (ed.) *Language in Culture and Society: A Reader in Linguistics and Anthropology*, New York: Harper & Row, pp. 423–38.

Fishman, J. (ed.) (1968) *Readings in the Sociology of Language*, The Hague: Mouton.

Fishman, J. (1972) *The Sociology of Language: An Interdisciplinary Social Science Approach to Language in Society*, Rowley: Newbury House.

Fishman, J. (1974) *Advances in Language Planning*, The Hague: Mouton.

Fishman, J. (ed.) (1978) *Advances in the Study of Societal Multilingualism*, The Hague: Mouton.

Fishman, J. (ed.) (1999) *Handbook of Language and Ethnic Identity*, Oxford: Oxford University Press.

Fishman, J. (2001) *Can Threatened Languages Be Saved?* Clevedon: Multilingual Matters.

Fishman, P. (1978) 'Interaction: the work women do', *Social Problems* 26: 397–406.

Fishman, P. (1980) 'Conversational insecurity', in H. Giles, P. Robinson and P. Smith (eds) *Language: Social Psychological Perspectives*, Oxford: Pergamon Press, pp. 127–32.

Foley, J.A., Kandiah, T., Zhiming, B., Fraser-Gupta, A., Alsagoff, L., Ho, C.L., Wee, L., Talib, I.S. and Bokhorst-Heng, W. (eds) (1998) *English in New Cultural Contexts: Reflections from Singapore*, Singapore: Oxford University Press.

Foulkes, P. and Docherty, G. (eds) (1999), *Urban Voices: Variation and Change in British Accents*, London: Arnold.

Fowler, R. (1981) *Literature as Social Discourse*, London: Batsford.

Fowler, R. (1986) *Linguistic Criticism*, Oxford: Oxford University Press.

Fowler, R. (1991) *Language in the News: Discourse and Ideology in the Press*, London: Routledge.

Fowler, R., Hodge, R., Kress, G. and Trew, T. (eds) (1979) *Language and Control*, London: Routledge & Kegan Paul.

Fox, G. (1993) 'A comparison of "policespeak" and "normalspeak": a preliminary study', in J.M. Sinclair, M.P. Hoey, and G. Fox (eds) *Techniques of Description: Spoken and Written Discourse*, London: Routledge, pp. 183–95.

Francis, W.N. (1983) *Dialectology*, Harlow: Longman.

Fraser-Gupta, A. (1991) 'Acquisition of diglossia in Singapore English', in A. Kwan-Terry (ed.) *Child Language Development in Singapore and Malaysia*, Singapore: Singapore University Press, pp. 119–60.

Fraser-Gupta, A. (1992) 'The pragmatic particles of Singapore colloquial English', *Journal of Pragmatics* 17(3): 39–65.

Freed, A. (1996) 'Language and gender in an experimental setting', in V. Bergvall, J. Bing and A. Freed (eds) *Rethinking Language and Gender Research: Theory and Practice*, New York: Longman, pp. 54–76.

Garrett, P., Coupland, N. and Williams, A. (2003) *Investigating Language Attitudes: Social Meanings of Dialect, Ethnicity and Performance*, Cardiff: University of Wales Press.

Gee, J.P. (1996) *Social Linguistics and Literacies: Ideology in Discourses* (2nd edition), London: Taylor and Francis.

Gibbons, J. (ed.) (1994) *Language and the Law*, London: Longman.

Giglioli, P.P. (ed.) (1972) *Language and Social Context: Selected Readings*, Harmondsworth: Penguin.

Giles, H. (1970) 'Evaluative reactions to accents', *Educational Review* 22: 211–27.

Giles, H. and Coupland, N. (1991) *Language: Contexts and Consequences*, Milton Keynes: Open University Press.

Giles, H. and Powesland, P.F. (1975) *Speech Style and Social Evaluation*, London: Academic Press.

Graddol, D. and Swann, J. (1989) *Gender Voices*, Oxford: Blackwell.

Graddol, D., Leith, D. and Swann, J. (1996) *English: History, Diversity and Change*, Milton Keynes: Open University Press.

Greenbaum, S. (ed.) (1996) *Comparing English World-wide: The International Corpus of English*, Oxford: Oxford University Press.

Grimes, M.F. (ed.) (1992) *Ethnologue: Languages of the World*, http://www-ala.doc.ic.ac.uk/~rap/Ethnologue

Grundy, P. (2000) *Doing Pragmatics* (2nd edition), London: Arnold.

Gumperz, J.J. (1964) 'Linguistic and social interaction in two communities', in J.J. Gumperz and D. Hymes (eds) *The Ethnography of Communication* (special edition, *American Anthropologist* 66(2): 137–53).

Gumperz, J.J. (1982) *Discourse Strategies*, Cambridge: Cambridge University Press.

Gumperz, J.J. and Hymes, D.H. (eds) (1972) *Directions in Sociolinguistics: The Ethnography of Communication*, New York: Holt, Rinehart and Winston.

Hall, K. and Bucholtz, M. (eds) (1995) *Gender Articulated: Language and the Socially Constructed Self*, London: Routledge.

Halliday, M.A.K. (1973) *Explorations in the Functions of Language*, London: Edward Arnold.

Halliday, M.A.K. (2003) *An Introduction to Functional Grammar* (3rd edition), London: Edward Arnold.

Haugen, E. (1966) 'Dialect, language, nation', *American Anthropologist* 68: 922–35.

Healey, J.F. (2004) *Statistics: A Tool for Social Research* (7th edition), London: Wadsworth.

Healey, J.F. (2006) *The Essentials of Statistics: A Tool for Social Research*, London: Wadsworth.

Heller, M. (ed.) (1988) *Codeswitching*, Berlin: Mouton de Gruyter.

Heller, M. (1999) *Linguistic Minorities and Modernity: A Sociolinguistic Ethnography*, London: Longman.

Herskovits, M.J. (1958) *Dahomean Narrative*, Evanston: Northwestern University Press.

Hewitt, R. (1986) *White Talk, Black Talk: Interracial Friendship and Communication Amongst Adolescents*, Cambridge: Cambridge University Press.

Hickey, R. (2004) *Legacies of Colonial English. Studies in Transported Dialects*, Cambridge: Cambridge University Press.

Hildebrandt, H.W. (1977) *A Treatise of Schemes and Tropes (1550) by Richard Sherry: A Facsimile Reproduction*, New York: Scholars' Facsimiles and Reprints.

Hock, H.H. (1986) *Principles of Historical Linguistics*, Berlin: Mouton de Gruyter.

Hodge, R. and Kress, G. (1988) *Social Semiotics*, Cambridge: Polity Press.

Hoey, M. (1983) *On the Surface of Discourse*, London: Allen & Unwin.

Holm, J. (1988, 1989) *Pidgins and Creoles* (2 vols), Cambridge: Cambridge University Press.

Holmes, J. (1992) 'Women's talk in public contexts' *Discourse and Society* 3: 131–50.

Holmes, J. (1995) *Women, Men and Politeness*, New York: Longman.

Holmes, J. (2001) *An Introduction to Sociolinguistics* (2nd edition), Harlow: Addison Wesley Longman.

Holmes, J. and Meyerhoff, M. (eds) (2003) *The Handbook of Language and Gender*, Oxford: Blackwell.

Holmes, J. and Stubbe, M. (2003) *Power and Politeness in the Workplace: A Sociolinguistic Analysis of Talk at Work*, London: Longman.

Honey, J. (1989) *Does Accent Matter? The Pygmalion Factor*, London: Faber and Faber.

Hopper, R. and Williams, F. (1973) 'Speech characteristics and employability', *Speech Monographs* 46: 296–302.

Hudson, R.A. (1996) *Sociolinguistics* (2nd edition), Cambridge: Cambridge University Press.

Hughes, A., Trudgill, P. and Watt, D. (2005) *English Accents and Dialects: An Introduction to Social and Regional Varieties of English in the British Isles* (4th edition), London: Edward Arnold.

Hunston, S. (2002) *Corpora in Applied Linguistics*, Cambridge: Cambridge University Press.

Hymes, D.H. (1967) 'Models of the interaction of language and social setting', *Journal of Social Issues* 23(2): 8–28.

Hymes, D.H. (1974) *Foundations in Sociolinguistics: An Ethnographic Approach*, Philadelphia: University of Pennsylvania Press.

James, B. and Savile-Smith, K. (1989) *Gender, Culture and Power: Challenging New Zealand's Gendered Culture*, Auckland: Oxford University Press.

Jenkins, J. (2003) *World Englishes: A Resource Book for Students*, London: Routledge.

Jespersen, O. (1922) *Language: Its Nature, Development and Origin*, New York: W.W. Norton.

Jewitt, C. and Kress, G. (eds) (2003) *Multimodal Literacy*, New York: Peter Lang.

Johnson, S. and Meinhof, U.H. (eds) (1997) *Language and Masculinity*, Oxford: Blackwell.

Johnstone, B. (2000) *Qualitative Methods in Sociolinguistics*, New York: Oxford University Press.

Joseph, J. (1987) *Eloquence and Power*, London: Pinter.

Joseph, J. (2004) *Language and Identity*, Basingstoke: Palgrave.

Kachru, B.B. (1965) 'The *Indianness* in Indian English', *Word* 21: 391–410.

Kachru, B.B. (1966) 'Indian English: a study in contextualization', in C.E. Bazell (ed.) *In Memory of J.R. Firth*, London: Longman.

Kachru, B.B. (1980) 'The new Englishes and old dictionaries: directions in lexicographical research on non-native varieties of English', in L. Zgusta (ed.) *Theory and Method in Lexicography: A Western and Non-Western Perspective*, London: Hornbeam Press.

Kachru, B.B. (1982a) 'The bilingual's linguistic repertoire', in B. Hardford (ed.) *Issues in International Bilingual Education: The Role of the Vernacular*, New York and London: Plenum Press.

Kachru, B.B. (ed.) (1982b) *The Other Tongue: English Across Cultures* (1st edition), Urbana: University of Illinois Press.

Kachru, B.B. (1982c) 'Models for non-native Englishes', in B.B. Kachru (ed.) *The Other Tongue: English Across Cultures* (1st edition), Urbana: University of Illinois Press.

Kachru, B.B. (1983) *The Indianization of English*, Delhi: Oxford University Press.

Kachru, B.B. (1988) *The Alchemy of English: The Spread, Functions and Models of Non-Native Englishes*, Oxford: Pergamon.

Kachru, B.B. (1992) *The Other Tongue: English Across Cultures* (2nd edition), Chicago: University of Chicago Press.

Kachru, Y. (1983a) 'Cross-cultural texts, discourse strategies and discourse interpretation', paper presented at the Conference on English as an International Language: Discourse Patterns Across Cultures, East-West Center, Honolulu.

Kachru, Y. (1983b) 'Linguistics and written discourse in particular languages: contrastive studies: English and Hindi', in R. Kaplan (ed.) *Annual Review of Applied Linguistics*, Rowley: Newbury House.

Kaplan, R.B. (1966) 'Cultural thought patterns in intercultural education', *Language Learning* 16: 1–20.

Kennedy, G. (1998) *An Introduction to Corpus Linguistics*, London: Longman.

Kingsmore, R. (1995) *Ulster Scots Speech: A Sociolinguistic Study*, Tuscaloosa: University of Alabama Press.

Kouwenberg, S. and Singler, J.V. (eds) (2005) *The Handbook of Pidgin and Creole Studies*, Malden: Blackwell.

Kress, G. and Hodge, R. (1993) *Language as Ideology* (2nd edition), London: Routledge & Kegan Paul.

Kress, G. and van Leeuwen, T. (2001) *Multimodal Discourse: The Modes and Media of Contemporary Communication*, London: Arnold.

Labov, W. (1963) 'The social motivation of a sound change', *Word* 19: 273–309 (also reprinted in Labov 1972b).

Labov, W. (1966) *The Social Stratification of English in New York City*, Washington, DC: Center for Applied Linguistics.

Labov, W. (1972a) *Language in the Inner City: Studies in the Black English Vernacular*, Philadelphia: University of Pennsylvania Press.

Labov, W. (1972b) *Sociolinguistic Patterns*, Philadelphia: University of Pennsylvania Press.

Labov, W. (1992) 'Evidence for regular sound change in English dialect geography', in M. Rissanen (ed.) *History of Englishes: New Methods and Interpretations in Historical Linguistics*, Berlin: Mouton de Gruyter, pp. 42–71.

Labov, W. (1994) *Principles of Linguistic Change, vol. 1: Internal Factors*, Oxford: Basil Blackwell.

Labov, W. (2001) *Principles of Linguistic Change, vol. 2: Social Factors*, Oxford: Blackwell.

Lakoff, R. (1975) *Language and Woman's Place*, New York: Harper & Row.

Lakoff, R. (1990) *Talking Power*, New York: Basic Books.

Lambert, W.E., Frankel, H. and Tucker, G.R. (1966) 'Judging personality through speech: a French-Canadian example', *Journal of Communication* 16: 305–21.

Lannoy, R. (1971) *The Speaking Tree: A Study of Indian Culture and Society*, New York: Oxford University Press.

Lass, R. (1987) *The Frame of English*, London: Dent.

Laver, J. (1975) 'Communicative functions of phatic communion', in A. Kendon, R.M. Harris and M.R. Key (eds) *Communication in Face to Face Interaction*, Berlin: Mouton, pp. 73–92.

Lawton, D. (1968) *Social Class, Language and Education*, London: Routledge & Kegan Paul.

Le Page, R. and Tabouret-Keller, A. (1985) *Acts of Identity*, Oxford: Blackwell.

Lee, C-R. (1995) *Native Speaker*, New York: Riverhead Books.

Lee, D. (1992) *Competing Discourses: Perspective and Ideology in Language*, London: Longman.

Leech, G.N. (1983) *Principles of Pragmatics*, London: Longman.

Lefebvre, C. (ed.) (1991) *Serial Verbs*, Amsterdam: Benjamins.

Leith, D. (1997) *A Social History of English* (3rd edition), London: Routledge.

Levinson, S. (1983) *Pragmatics*, Cambridge: Cambridge University Press.

Linde, C. (1993) *Life Stories: The Creation of Coherence*, New York and Oxford: Oxford University Press.

Lindfors, B. (1973) *Folklore in Nigerian Literature*, New York: Africana.

Lippi-Green, R. (1997) *English with an Accent: Language, Ideology and Discrimination in the United States*, London: Routledge.

Llamas, C., Mullany, L. and Stockwell, P. (eds) (2007) *The Routledge Companion to Sociolinguistics*, London: Routledge.

Locher, M., (2004) *Power and Politeness in Action: Disagreements in Oral Communication*, Berlin: Mouton de Gruyter.

Macaulay, R.K.S. (2005) *Talk that Counts. Age, Gender and Social Class Differences in Discourse*, Oxford: Oxford University Press.

Magura, B. (1984) 'Style and meaning in African English: a sociolinguistic study', Unpublished PhD dissertation, University of Illinois.

Mahony, P. (1985) *Schools for the Boys? Co-education Reassessed*, London: Hutchinson.

Mahony, P. and Jones, C. (eds) (1989) *Learning our Lines: Sexuality and Social Control in Education*, London: Women's Press.

Makkai, A. (1972) *Idiom Structure in English*, The Hague: Mouton.

McArthur, T. (1998) *The English Languages*, Cambridge: Cambridge University Press.

McCarthy, M. (1991) *Discourse Analysis for Language Teachers*, Cambridge: Cambridge University Press.

McCarthy, M. (1998) *Spoken Language and Applied Linguistics*, Cambridge: Cambridge University Press.

McCarthy, M. and Carter, R.A. (1994) *Language as Discourse: Perspectives for Language Teaching*, London: Longman.

McCrum, R., Cran, R. and MacNeil, R. (eds) (1992) *The Story of English* (revised edition), London: Faber and Faber.

McEnery, A. and Wilson, A. (1996) *Corpus Linguistics*, Edinburgh: Edinburgh University Press.

McMahon, A.M.S. (1994) *Understanding Language Change*, Cambridge: Cambridge University Press.

McWhorter, J.H. (1995) 'The scarcity of Spanish-based creoles explained', *Language in Society* 24: 213–44.

Mees, I. (1990) 'Patterns of sociophonetic variation in the speech of Cardiff schoolchildren', in N. Coupland (ed.) *English in Wales: Diversity, Conflict and Change*, Clevedon: Multilingual Matters, pp. 167–94.

Meinhof, U. and Richardson, K. (1994) *Text, Discourse and Context: Representations of Poverty in Britain*, London: Longman.

Mesthrie, R. (ed.) (2001) *Concise Encyclopedia of Sociolinguistics*, Oxford: Elsevier.

Meyer, C. (2002) *English Corpus Linguistics: An Introduction*, Cambridge: Cambridge University Press.

Mills, S. (1995a) *Feminist Stylistics*, London: Routledge.

Mills, S. (1995b) *Language and Gender*, London: Longman.

Mills, S. (2003) *Gender and Politeness*, Cambridge: Cambridge University Press.

Mills, S. (2006) 'Rethinking politeness, impoliteness and gender identity', in L. Litosseliti and J. Sutherland (eds) *Discourse Analysis and Gender Identity*, Amsterdam: John Benjamins.

Milroy, J. (1981) *Regional Accents of English: Belfast*, Belfast: Blackstaff.

Milroy, J. (1982) 'Probing under the tip of the iceberg: phonological normalisation and the shape of speech communities', in S. Romaine (ed.) *Sociolinguistic Variation in Speech Communities*, London: Edward Arnold, pp. 35–47.

Milroy, J. (1983) 'On the sociolinguistic history of /h/-dropping in English', in M. Davenport, E. Hansen and H.F. Nielsen (eds) *Current Topics in English Historical Linguistics*, Odense: Odense University Press, pp. 37–53.

Milroy, J. (1991) *Linguistic Variation and Change: On the Historical Sociolinguistics of English*, Oxford: Blackwell.

Milroy, J. (1992a) *Linguistic Variation and Change*, Oxford: Blackwell.

Milroy, J. (1992b) 'Middle English dialectology', in N. Blake (ed.) *The Cambridge History of the English Language* (volume 2), Cambridge: Cambridge University Press, pp. 156–206.

Milroy, J. (1993) 'On the social origins of language change', in C. Jones (ed.) *Historical Linguistics: Problems and Perspectives*, London: Longman, pp. 215–36.

Milroy, J. and Milroy, L. (1985a) *Authority in Language* (1st edition), London: Routledge.

Milroy, J. and Milroy, L. (1985b) 'Linguistic change, social network and speaker innovation', *Journal of Linguistics* 21: 339–84.

Milroy, J. and Milroy, L. (1992) 'Social network and social class: toward an integrated sociolinguistic model', *Language in Society* 21: 1–26.

Milroy, J. and Milroy, L. (eds) (1993) *Real English: The Grammar of English Dialects in the British Isles*, London: Longman.

Milroy, J. and Milroy, L. (1997) *Authority in Language: Investigating Standard English* (3rd edition), London: Routledge.

Milroy, L. (1978a) 'Belfast: change and variation in an urban vernacular', in P. Trudgill (ed.) *Sociolinguistic Patterns in British English*, London: Arnold, pp. 7–34.

Milroy, L. (1987b) *Language and Social Networks* (2nd edition), Oxford: Basil Blackwell.

Milroy, L. (1987c) *Observing and Analysing Natural Language*, Oxford: Basil Blackwell.

Milroy, L. and Gordon, M. (2003) *Sociolinguistics: Method and Interpretation*, Oxford: Blackwell.

Milroy, L. and Muysken, P. (eds) (1995) *One Speaker, Two Languages: Cross-Disciplinary Perspectives on Code-Switching*, Cambridge: Cambridge University Press.

Mohanen, K.P. (1992) 'Describing the phonology of non-native varieties of a language', *World Englishes* 2 (3): 111–28.

Montgomery, M. (1995) *An Introduction to Language and Society* (2nd edition), London: Routledge.

Morgan, M. (ed.) (1994) *Language and the Social Construction of Identity in Creole Situations*, Los Angeles: Center for Afro-American Studies, UCLA.

Mufwene, S.S. (2001) *The Ecology of Language Evolution*, Cambridge: Cambridge University Press.

Mugglestone, L. (2003) *'Talking Proper'. The Rise of Accent as Social Symbol* (2nd edition), Oxford: Clarendon Press.

Mühlhäusler, P. (1986) *Pidgin and Creole Linguistics*, Oxford: Blackwell.

Mühlhäusler, P. and Harré, R. (1990) *Pronouns and People*, Oxford: Basil Blackwell.

Myers-Scotton, C. (1993a) *Duelling Languages: Grammatical Structure in Code-Switching*, Oxford: Clarendon.

Myers-Scotton, C. (1993b) *Social Motivation for Code-Switching*, Oxford: Clarendon.

Nettle, D. and Romaine, S. (2000) *Vanishing Voices: The Extinction of the World's Languages*, Oxford: Oxford University Press.

Oakes, M.P. (1998) *Statistics for Corpus Linguistics*, Edinburgh: Edinburgh University Press.

Ochs, E., Schegloff, E. and Thompson, S. (eds) (1996) *Interaction and Grammar*, Cambridge: Cambridge University Press.

Ohala, J. (1993) 'The phonetics of sound change', in C. Jones (ed.) *Historical Linguistics: Problems and Perspectives*, London: Longman, pp. 237–78.

Ortony, A. (ed.) (1993) *Metaphor and Thought* (2nd edition), Cambridge: Cambridge University Press.

Pakir, A. (1994) 'English in Singapore: the codification of competing norms', in S. Gopinathan, A. Pakir, H.W. Kam and S. Vanithamani (eds) *Language and Education in Singapore: Issues and Trends*, Singapore: Times Academic Press, pp. 221–34.

Palmer, F.R. (ed.) (1968) *Selected Papers of J.R. Firth, 1952–59*, Bloomington: Indiana University Press.

Parthasarathy, R. (1983) 'South Asian literature in English: culture and discourse', paper presented at the Conference on English as an International Language: Discourse Patterns Across Cultures, East-West Center, Honolulu.

Pateman, T. (1981) 'Linguistics as a branch of critical theory', *UEA Papers in Linguistics* 14/15: 1–29.

Penfield, J. and Ornstein-Galicia, J.L. (1985) *Chicano English: An Ethnic Contact Dialect*, Amsterdam and Philadelphia: John Benjamins.

Pennycook, A. (1994) *The Cultural Politics of English as an International Language*, London: Longman.

Perera, K. (1984) *Children's Writing and Reading*, Oxford: Blackwell.

Pettit, A. (1980) *Images of the Mexican-American in Fiction and Film*, College Station: Texas A&M University Press.

Petyt, K.M. (1980) *The Study of Dialect: An Introduction to Dialectology*, London: André Deutsch.

Platt, J.T. and Platt, H.K. (1975) *The Social Significance of Speech: An Introduction to and Workbook in Sociolinguistics*, Amsterdam: North-Holland.

Platt, J.T. and Weber, H. (1980) *English in Singapore and Malaysia: Status, Features, Function*, Kuala Lumpur: Oxford University Press.

Platt, J.T., Weber, H. and Ho, M.L. (1984) *The New Englishes*, London: Routledge & Kegan Paul.

Polanyi, L. (1979) 'So what's the point?' *Semiotica* 25 (3–4): 207–41.

Polanyi, L. (1985) *Telling the American Story: A Structural and Cultural Analysis of Conversational Storytelling*, Norwood: Ablex.

Poynton, C. (1985) *Language and Gender: Making the Difference*, New York: Deakin University Press.

Pride, J.B. and Holmes, J. (eds) (1972) *Sociolinguistics: Selected Readings*, Harmondsworth: Penguin.

Pridham, F. (2001) *The Language of Conversation*, London: Routledge.

Psathas, G. (1995) *Conversation Analysis: The Study of Talk-in-Interaction*, Thousand Oaks: Sage.

Pyles, T. and Algeo, J. (1993) *The Origins and Development of the English Language* (4th edition), London: Harcourt Brace Jovanovich.

Quirk, R. and Widdowson, H. (eds) (1985) *English in the World*, Cambridge: Cambridge University Press.

Rampton, B. (1995) *Crossing*, London: Longman.

Rao, R. (1963) *Kanthapura*, New York: New Dimensions.

Reid, I. (1989) *Social Class Differences in Britain* (3rd edition), London: Fontana.

Renkema, J. (2004) *Introduction to Discourse Studies*, Philadelphia: Benjamins.

Ricento, T. (ed.) (2005) *An Introduction to Language Policy*, Oxford: Blackwell.

Richardson, K. (1987) 'Critical linguistics and textual diagnosis', *Text* 7 (2): 145–63.

Richardson, K. and Meinhof, U. (1999) *Worlds in Common? Television Discourse in a Changing Europe*, London: Routledge.

Romaine, S. (1988) *Pidgin and Creole Languages*, London: Longman.

Romaine, S. (1989) *Bilingualism*, Oxford: Blackwell.

Romaine, S. (2000) *Language in Society: An Introduction to Sociolinguistics* (2nd edition), Oxford: Oxford University Press.

Rosewarne, D. (1994) 'Estuary English – tomorrow's RP?' *English Today* 10 (1): 3–8.

Rosewarne, D. (1996) 'Estuary as a world language', *Modern English Teacher* 5: 13–17.

Rubin, J. (1968) *National Bilingualism in Paraguay*, The Hague: Mouton.

Ryan, E.B. and Giles, H. (eds) (1982) *Attitudes towards Language Variation*, London: Edward Arnold.

Sacks, H. (1992) *Lectures on Conversation*, Oxford: Blackwell.

Sacks, H., Schegloff, E. and Jefferson, G. (1974) 'A simplest systematics for the organization of turn-taking for conversation', *Language* 50: 696–735.

Sajavaara, K., Marsh, D. and Keto, T. (eds) (1991) *Communication and Discourse across Cultures and Languages*, Jyväskyla: University of Jyväskyla Press.

Sankoff, G. (1984) 'A sociolinguistic perspective on substrate: the case of Tok Pisin verb chaining'. Paper presented at Sociolinguistics Symposium 5, Liverpool.

Saville-Troike, M. (2003) *The Ethnography of Communication* (3rd edition), Oxford: Blackwell.

Schiffrin, D. (1987) *Discourse Markers*, Cambridge: Cambridge University Press.

Schiffrin, D. (1994) *Approaches to Discourse*, Oxford: Basil Blackwell.

Sebba, M. (1981) 'Derivational regularities in a creole lexicon: the case of Sranan', *Linguistics* 19: 101–17.

Sebba, M. (1987) *The Syntax of Serial Verbs*, Amsterdam: Benjamins.

Sebba, M. (1993) *London Jamaican: A Case Study in Language Contact*, London: Longman.

Sebba, M. (1997) *Contact Languages: Pidgins and Creoles*, London: Macmillan.

Seligman, C.R., Tucker, G.R. and Lambert, W.E. (1972) 'The effects of speech style and other attributes on teachers' attitudes towards pupils', *Language in Society* 1: 131–42.

Simmen, E. (ed.) (1971) *The Chicano: From Caricature to Self-Portrait*, New York: Mentor Books.

Sinclair, J. (ed.) (1992) *Collins COBUILD English Usage*, London and Birmingham: Collins COBUILD and University of Birmingham Press.

Sinclair, J.M. and Coulthard, M. (1975) *Towards an Analysis of Discourse: The English Used by Teachers and Pupils*, Oxford: Oxford University Press.

Sinclair, J.M., Hoey, M. and Fox, G. (eds) (1993) *Techniques of Description: Spoken and Written Discourse*, London: Routledge.

Smith, L.E. (ed.) (1983) *Readings in English as an International Language*, Oxford: Pergamon Press.

Smith, L.E. (ed.) (1987) *Discourse Across Cultures: Strategies in World Englishes*, London: Prentice-Hall.

Spender, D. (1985) *Man Made Language*, London: Routledge & Kegan Paul.

Spolsky, E. (1998) *Sociolinguistics*, Oxford: Oxford University Press.

Stenström, A.B. (1994) *An Introduction to Spoken Interaction*, London: Longman.

Strang, B. (1970) *A History of English*, London: Methuen.

Stubbs, M. (1976) *Language, Schools and Classrooms*, London: Methuen.

Stubbs, M. (1980) *Language and Literacy*, London: Routledge & Kegan Paul.

Stubbs, M. (1983) *Discourse Analysis: The Sociolinguistic Analysis of Natural Language*, Oxford: Basil Blackwell.

Stubbs, M. (1986) *Educational Linguistics*, Oxford: Blackwell.

Stubbs, M. (1996) *Text and Corpus Analysis*, Oxford: Blackwell.

Sutcliffe, D. (1982) *British Black English*, Oxford: Blackwell.

Sutcliffe, D. and Figueroa, J. (1992) *System in Black Language*, Clevedon: Multilingual Matters.

Sutcliffe, D. and Wong, A. (1986) *The Language of the Black Experience: Cultural Expression through Word and Sound in the Caribbean and Black Britain*, Oxford: Blackwell.

Swales, J.M. (1990) *Genre Analysis*, Cambridge: Cambridge University Press.

Tagliamonte, S. (2006) *Analysing Sociolinguistic Variation*, Cambridge, Cambridge University Press.

Taiwo, O. (1976) *Culture and the Nigerian Novel*, New York: St Martin's Press.

Talbot, M. (1998) *Language and Gender: An Introduction*, Cambridge: Polity Press.

Tannen, D. (1984) *Conversational Style: Analyzing Talk Among Friends*, Norwood: Ablex.

Tannen, D. (1992) *You Just Don't Understand: Women and Men in Conversation*, London: Virago.

Thomas, L., Wareing, S., Singh, I., Stilwell Peccei, J., Thornborrow, J. and Jones, J. (2004) *Language, Society and Power*, London: Routledge.

Thomason, S.G. (2001) *Language Contact: An Introduction*, Washington, DC: Georgetown University Press.

Thornborrow, J. (2002) *Power Talk: Language and Interaction in Institutional Discourse*, London: Longman.

Thornborrow, J. and Coates, J. (eds) (2005) *The Sociolinguistics of Narrative*, Amsterdam: Benjamins.

Thorne, B. (1983) *Language, Gender and Society*, London: Newbury House.

Thorne, B. and Henley, N. (eds) (1975) *Language and Sex: Difference and Dominance*, London: Newbury House.

Thumboo, E. (1976) *The Second Tongue: An Anthology of Poetry from Malaysia and Singapore*, Singapore: Heinemann Educational Books.

Todd, L. (1974) *Pidgins and Creoles*, London: Routledge & Kegan Paul.

Tognini-Bonelli, E. (2001) *Corpus Linguistics at Work*, Amsterdam: John Benjamins.

Trow, M.J. (1992) *'Let Him Have It, Chris'*, London: HarperCollins.

Trudgill, P. (1972) 'Sex, covert prestige and linguistic change in the urban British English of Norwich', *Language and Society* 1: 179–95.

Trudgill, P. (1974) *The Social Differentiation of English in Norwich*, Cambridge: Cambridge University Press.

Trudgill, P. (1975) *Accent, Dialect and the School*, London: Edward Arnold.

Trudgill, P. (ed.) (1978) *Sociolinguistic Patterns in British English*, London: Edward Arnold.

Trudgill, P. (1983) *On Dialect: Social and Geographical Perspectives*, Oxford: Basil Blackwell.

Trudgill, P. (ed.) (1984) *Language in the British Isles*, Cambridge: Cambridge University Press.

Trudgill, P. (1986a) *Dialects in Contact*, Oxford: Basil Blackwell.

Trudgill, P. (1986b) 'The apparent time paradigm: Norwich revisited', paper presented to the Sociolinguistics Symposium VI, University of Newcastle upon Tyne.

Trudgill, P. (1988) 'Norwich revisited: recent linguistic changes in an English urban dialect', *English World-Wide* 9: 33–49.

Trudgill, P. (1990) *The Dialects of England*, Oxford: Basil Blackwell.

Trudgill, P. (1998) 'Standard English: what it isn't'. Paper presented to Poetics and Linguistics Association Conference, University of Bern.

Trudgill, P. (2000) *Sociolinguistics: An Introduction to Language and Society* (2nd edition), Harmondsworth: Penguin.

Trudgill, P. (2004) *New Dialect Formation: The Inevitability of Colonial Englishes*, Edinburgh: Edinburgh University Press.

Trudgill, P. and Cheshire, J. (eds) (1998) *The Sociolinguistics Reader, Vol I: Multilingualism and Variation*, London: Arnold.

Trudgill, P. and Hannah, J. (2002) *International English: A Guide to Varieties of Standard English* (4th edition), London: Edward Arnold.

United States Census Bureau (1990) *Social and Economic Characteristics: Metropolitan Areas*, Washington, DC: USCB.

United States Census Bureau (1994) *1990 Census of Population and Housing* (revised edition), Washington, DC: USCB.

Valdés, G. (1988) 'The language situation of Mexican Americans', in S.L. McKay and S-L.C. Wong (eds), *Language Diversity: Problem or Resource? A Social and Educational Perspective on Language Minorities in the United States*, Boston: Heinle & Heinle, pp. 111–39.

Veltman, C. (1983) 'Anglicization in the United States: language environment and language practice of American adolescents', *International Journal of the Sociology of Language* 44: 99–114.

Ventola, E. (1987) *The Structure of Social Interaction*, London: Frances Pinter.

Wardhaugh, R. (2005) *Sociolinguistics: An Introduction* (5th edition), Oxford: Blackwell.

Watts, R. (2003) *Politeness*, Cambridge: Cambridge University Press.

Watts, R. and Trudgill, P. (eds) (2002) *Alternative Histories of English*, London: Routledge.

Watts, R., Ide, S. and Ehlich, K. (eds) (1999) *Politeness in Language: Studies in its History, Theory and Practice*, Berlin: Mouton de Gruyter.

Weedon, C. (1987) *Feminist Practice and Poststructuralist Theory*, Oxford: Basil Blackwell.

Weinreich, U. (1966) *Languages in Contact*, The Hague: Mouton.

Wells, J.C. (1973) *Jamaican Pronunciation in London*, Oxford: Blackwell.

Wells, J.C. (1982) *Accents of English*, Cambridge: Cambridge University Press.

Wells, J.C. (1994) 'What is Estuary English?' *English Teaching Professional* 3 (April): 46–7.

Wells, J.C. (1997) 'Transcribing Estuary English', *Speech Hearing and Language* 8: 261–7.

Wenger, E. (1998) *Communities of Practice*, Cambridge: Cambridge University Press.

Wengraf, T. (2001) *Qualitative Social Interviewing: Biographic Narrative and Semi-Structured Methods*, London: Sage.

Whiteley, W.H. (ed.) (1971) *Language Use and Social Change: Problems of Multilingualism with Special Reference to Eastern Africa*, London: Oxford University Press.

Widdowson, H. (1979) *Pidgin and Babu: Explorations in Applied Linguistics*, London: Oxford University Press.

Wilkinson, A. (1965) 'Spoken English', *Educational Review* 6: 17.

Wilkinson, J. (1995) *Introducing Standard English*, Harmondsworth: Penguin.

Winter, Joanne, (1993) 'Gender and the political interview in an Australian context', *Journal of Pragmatics* 20: 117–39.

Wodak, R. (ed.) (1990) *Language, Power and Ideology: Studies in Political Discourse*, Amsterdam and Philadelphia: John Benjamins.

Wodak, R. (1996) *Disorders of Discourse*, London: Longman.

Wodak, R. (ed.) (1997) *Gender and Discourse*, London: Sage.

Wodak, R. and Chilton, P. (2005a) *Methods of Critical Discourse Analysis*, London: Sage.

Wodak, R. and Chilton, P. (2005b) *New Agenda in (Critical) Discourse Analysis*, Amsterdam: Benjamins.

Wolfram, W. and Schilling-Estes, N. (2006) *American English: Dialects and Variation* (2nd edition), Oxford: Blackwell.

Wood, F.T. and Hill, R.J. (1989) *Dictionary of English Colloquial Idioms*, London: Macmillan.

Wooffitt, R. (2005) *Conversation Analysis and Discourse Analysis: A Comparative and Critical Introduction*, London: Sage.

Wray, A. and Bloomer, A. (2006) *Projects in Linguistics: A Practical Guide to Researching Language*, London: Arnold.

Wright, S. (2004) *Language Policy and Language Planning: From Nationalism to Globalisation*, Basingstoke: Palgrave.

Zentella, A.C. (1988) 'The Language situation of Puerto Ricans', in S.L. McKay and S.L.C. Wong (eds) *Language Diversity: Problem or Resource?* Boston: Heinle and Heinle, pp. 140–65.

Zentella, A.C. (1996) 'The "Chiquitafication" of US Latinos and their languages, or why we need an anthropological linguistics', *SALSA III* (Proceedings of the Third Annual Symposium about Language and Society), Austin: University of Texas, pp. 1–18.

Zentella, A.C. (1997) *Growing up Bilingual*, Oxford: Blackwell.

Zimmerman, D. and West, C. (1975) 'Sex roles, interruptions and silences in conversation' in B. Thorne, C. Kramarae and N. Henley (eds) *Language, Gender and Society*, Rowley: Newbury House, pp. 89–101.

# GLOSSARIAL INDEX

Keywords (which are in **bold** throughout this book) are indicated here where a definition is provided or the term is used in a context which makes its meaning clear. Other page references are to places in the book where the term is also used.

accent **4**–8, 11–12, 13, 16, 19, 25, 28, 29, 33, 34, 41–3, 52–7, 62, 64, 66, 74, 76–7, 80, 81–5, 122, 127, 132, 133–45, 156, 158, 160, 162, 175, 183, 219
acceptance **18**, 166
accommodation 23, **29**–30, 34, 67, 106, 131
acrolect **24**, 61, 64
act 28, 44, **54**
act sequence **54**
active competence **10**
address 10, **27**–9, 49, 74, 111, 113–14, 122, 124, 182, 204
adjacency pair **30**–31, 211–13
advanced RP **55**
African-American English 19, 61, 64
Afrikaans 13, 23–4
age **3**–4, 7, 15–16, 50
Air-Traffic Control English 23
American English 7, 18, 19, 23, 25, 56, 96–7, 112, 133–45
Appalachian English 27
apparent time hypothesis **15**, 175, 209, 218
applied linguistics **32**
Arabic 13, 23, 51
asymmetrical T/V usage **28**, 49–50
Australian English 24–5, 56
autonomy **17**, 99
auxiliary language **22**–3

backchannel 21, **31**, 32, 56, 67, 113
Ballymena accent 16
basilect **24**, 61, 64
Basque 3, 12, 102

Bengali 22
bilingual **12**, 38, 47–8, 94, 100–102, 140, 142–3, 153, 156, 158, 165, 191–201
Black Country 8
borrowing 21, 57, 62–3, 108, 153–9, 164, 166, 170–73, 189, 192–3
Business English 23

Canadian English 7, 25
Cantonese 11, 93–4
careful speech 3, **14**, 82
casual speech 3, 10, 11, **14**, 43, 55, 61, 82, 129, 162, 183
casualisation **56**
Catalan 102
categorical rule **15**
centralisation **16**
circularity 2, **80**
class 4, 7, **13**, 14, 16, 18, 20, 23, 25, 29, 34, 41, 45–6, 52, 55, 56, 60, 67, 79–80, 90–92, 127, 129–30, 132, 138, 143, 163, 169, 202, 207–8
cline **10**, 21, 94
closings 67, 71–2, 114, 209–19
code **11**, 13, 17, 18, 25, 38, 43–51, 53, 55, 56, 64, 77, 79–80, 86, 87, 92, 94, 103, 107, 119, 124, 143, 145, 153–8, 192, 195–6, 198
code-loyalty 38, **48**
code-mixing **12**
code-switching **11**–12, 38, 48–51, 56, 77, 87, 94, 107, 124, 143, 153–8
codification 17, **18**, 35, 54, 57, 100, 107, 132, 169, 175
common gender **59**

community of practice 201–9
competence **10**, 12, 53–4, 88, 145, 157,
    192, 195, 200, 201
compound bilingual **12**
congruent order of discourse **73**, 146–53
conservative RP **55**
contact language **22**–3, 30, 57, 64, 107,
    153–8, 172, 184–201
control **4**, 41, 51, 60–61, 79, 81, 209
convergence **29**–30, 168
conversation 3, 9, 12, 14, 21, 29, 30–32, 34,
    48, 56, 61, 66–72, 74, 76, 82–3, 87, 88,
    112–18, 148, 162, 167, 175, 176–84,
    203–19
conversationalisation **73**
co-ordinate bilingual **12**
copying 21, 57, 62–3, 108, 153–9, 164,
    166, 170–73, 189, 192–3
Cornish 17, 99
corpus linguistics 8, 44, 116, 181, 223–**25**
covert observation 3, 52, 71, 82, 114
covert prestige **14**, 15, 20, 24, 43, 55
creole 17, **21**–**4**, 38, 61–3, 77, 107–9, 135,
    159–61, 184–90
creole continuum **24**, 61, 64
critical discourse analysis (CDA) **33**, 72,
    122–4
critical discourse moment (CDM) **44**
critical linguistics **33**, **72**, 126

data-driven **38**
decreolisation **24**
deficit **20**
dense network **52**–3
dependent variable **4**, 13–16, 79
deprivation theory **46**
descriptivism 19, 58, 72, **73**, 191, 196, 201,
    209
diachronic **15**–16, 127, 163–75
diacritics **6**–7
dialect 3–6, **7**, 8, 9, 11, 12, 17, 18, 21–3, 25,
    27, 30, 33–5, 43, 50, 53, 54, 56–8, 64–5,
    77, 81–4, 92, 94, 96, 99–101, 102–3, 120,
    127, 129, 131–2, 137, 143–5, 158,
    163–75
dialect chain **8**
dialect contact **30**
dialect continuum 101

dialectology **7**–**8**, 165
diatype **8**–9
diglossia **12**–**13**, 38, 50–51
diphthong **6**–7
discourse 20–21, 33–4, 44–5, 72, **73**, 74,
    118–22, 146–53, 183, 191–201
discursive practice 66, 68, **72**, 149, 176
divergence 13, **29**, 51, 168
domain **11**–13, 48–51, 53, 61, 66, 119
dominance **20**
Dublin accent 16, 27
Dutch 8, 18
Dyirbal 11

elaborated code **45**–7, 90, 92
elaboration **18**
elicitation technique 3, 14, 30–31, 39, 41,
    43, 50–51, 80, 81–2, 90, 160, 183, 216,
    221, 223
ends **54**
English for Special Purposes (ESP) **23**
escapable conversation 71–2
Esperanto 23
Estuary English 43, **55**–6
ethics **3**, 33, 45, 71, 80, 114, 151, 159, 162
ethnicity 9, **11**–13, 16, 34, 63, 133, 139–40,
    145, 159, 175, 191–2, 202, 207–8
ethnography 34, 92–4
euphemism 20, 43–7, **73**, 146, 152, 158
evaluation 19, 41, 47, 60–61, 74, 103, 136,
    151, 178, 192
expanding circle 26
extraterritorial English **24**

face **28**–9, 44, 88, 113–14, 124, 202, 203–9
face-threatening act (FTA) **28**–9, **44**,
    203–9
feedback **30**–31, 56
femininity **21**, 192, 203
field **9**, 10
fieldwork 38–40, 76, 159, 162
Finnish 17
forensic linguistics **219**–25
formal style 11, 14, 73, 129
French 7, 12, 13, 19, 21, 22, 23, 27–8, 43,
    51
frequency 4, **15**, 20, 45, 59–60, 129, 155,
    188, 198, 203, 224

Frisian 21, 103

Galician 102
gender **3**, 4, 7, 14, 16, 19–21, 29, 34, 38, 41,
   45, 49, 56, 59–61, 66–70, 103–7, 127,
   169, 176–94, 201–9
genderlect **20**, 21, 29, 59–61, 176, 183
general RP **55**
genre 9, **55**, 86, 151, 158, 183, 200
geography **3**, 15, 16, 60, 209
German 8, 13, 18, 27, 48–9
glide 6–7, 62
graded variable 15
grapheme **5**
Greek 13, 17, 21, 22, 27
group means **81**

Hebrew 17, 95
High German 13
high rising terminal **56**
Hindi 22
historical paradox **57**
historicity **17**, 99
Hokkien 3, 11, 65
Hong Kong Mix 18, 93–4
Hungarian 97–8
H-variety **13**, 50–51
hybridity **22**, 23, 43, 158, 198
hypercorrection **14**, 20, **43**, 129
hypothesis 15, **39**

ideational metafunction **72**
identity 11, 16, **34**, 124, 151, 160–61, 173,
   175, 193, 203, 207–8
ideology 15, 33–5, 44–5, **72**–4, 80, 123,
   132, 140–41, 144, 145–53, 174–5, 190,
   225
idiom **71**, 76, 94, 96, 97–9, 111–12, 119,
   175, 196, 198–9, 218
independent variable **4**, 13–16, 79
index **79**, 92
Indian English 18, 22, 25, 26, 85, 110–11
indicator **19**
inner circle 24
insertion sequence **31**
interference patterns 3, 22, 24, **25**, 26, 61,
   64–5, 94, 112, 145, 153–8, 201
international language **22**

International Phonetic Alphabet (IPA)
   **4–6**, 76, 83, 84
interpersonal metafunction **72**
intersentential switch **48**, 154–5
interventionism 35, **73**, 105, 210
interview technique 3, 29, 39, 82
intrasentential switch **48**, 154
Irish Gaelic 11, 13, 101
Irish (Hiberno) English 3, 7, 19, 85
isogloss **8, 53**
Italian 12, 13, 21, 22, 27, 43

Jamaican English 24, 61–3
Jamaican Patwa 3, 23, 61–3, 107
Japanese 30, 57, 111–12
jargon **9**, 46, **88**

key **55**
Korean 28
Krio 23

L1 12, 25, 26
L2 12, 25, 26, 94, 101, 112, 136
language **7**
language change 14, **15**, 16, 18–19, 21–4,
   50–51, 54–8, 126–33, 163–75
language death **103**
language loyalty **16–17**, 24, 38, 42, 48,
   52–3, 99
language planning 35, 45, 66, 72, 132, 145,
   175
latching **31**, 32
Latin 6, 17, 21, 27, 43, 96
lexicogrammar **8**–10, 26, 43, 53, 62, 73
lexifier **23**, 184, 188–9
lexis 20, **21**, 23, 25–6, 43, 61–3, 64, 66, 74,
   83, 107, 109, 124, 154–6, 160, 164,
   167–8, 170, 184–90, 193, 196–8
lingua franca **22**
linguistic variable **3**–4, 13–16, 32, 51, 61,
   129–30, 163
liquid 6
literacy 19, 24, 33, **34**, 45–6, 51, 64, 131–2,
   174, 183
Liverpool Scouse 7, 8, 17, 27, 43, 55, 65
London Cockney 8, 19, 43, 52, 56, 84–5
longitudinal study **15**
Low German 13

Luxembourgeois 102
L-variety **13**, 51

Malay 64–5
Mancunian 43, 55
Mandarin 12, 66
manner of articulation 4, **6**
Manx 17
Marathi 11
marker 18, **19**, 26, 27, 48, 55, 63, 67, 71,
    77, 97, 133, 139, 143, 169, 175
Martha's Vineyard 15–16
masculinities **21**, 176–84, 203
matched guise technique **41**
mesolect **24**, 64
metafunctions 72
metalanguage **32**, 205
metaphor 12, 43–5, 66, 73, 77, 97, 108,
    145–53, 175, 199, 201, 207
metaphorical code-switching **12**
metaphorical order of discourse **73**,
    145–53
metonymy **43**
minimal pair **14**, 82–3
minority language 48, 99–103, 133–45
mixture **17**, 99
mode **9**–10, 119, 122, 200
monolingual 11, 48, 101, 128–9, 133, 140,
    158, 165, 170, 192, 196
monophthong **6**–7
multilingual 11, **12**, 13, 38, 47–51, 102,
    133–45, 153–9, 165, 190, 191–202
multiplex network **52**

naming 27–9, 32–3, 46–7, 74, 114, 122,
    124, 146, 150–51
naturalise 45, **73**
negative face **28**, 44
negative politeness **29**
network **29**, 51–4, 61, 107, 163, 209
network strength score **52**
neutral phatic token **70**
Newcastle Geordie 7, 8, 17, 19, 43
New English **24**–6, 38, 64–6, 110–12
New London Voice **55**
New York accent 13–14
nonce-spelling **84**, 156
non-escapable conversation **71**–2

non-prevocalic /r/ **7**
norm 14, 17, 20, 25, 28–9, 30, 34, 38, 46,
    52–3, **55**, 56, 59, 61, 71, 99, 112, 133,
    141, 153, 166–7, 169, 180–81, 183,
    191–3, 195–6, 198, 204, 206–7
Norwich accent 14–15, 19, 20
number **27**

observer's paradox **3**, **29**, 57, **90**, 114, 162,
    209
occupation **3**, 9, 16, 86–8, 209
other-oriented phatic token **70**
outer circle 24–6

Parisian French 3
participant observation **48**, **52**
participants **54**
particularistic code **46**–7
passive competence **10**, 12
perceived value **53**
Persian 22
person-oriented family type **46**
phatic tokens **70**–71, 113
phatics 70–72, 112–13, 115–18, 119
phoneme **5**, 23, 166, 168
pidgin 21–2, **23**, 24, 38, 107, 184–91
pilot study 13, **39**
place of articulation 4, **6**
Polish 12
politeness 9, 20, 26, **27**–30, 32–4, 38,
    66–70, 71, 76, 112–18, 158, 162, 183,
    202–9
Portuguese 22
positional family type **46**
positive face **29**
positive politeness **29**
post-creole speech continuum **24**, 61
power 13, 15, **21**, 27–32, 50, 71, 183,
    202–9
preferred response **30**
prescriptivism 18, 54, **58**, 105, 132, 133,
    174
prestige 13–15, 17–21, 29, 42–3, 46, 51,
    54–8, 60–61, 85, 92–4, 99–103, 127, 130,
    133, 156, 163, 172, 183, 190
Punjabi 11, 13

qualitative **4**, 21, 47, 50, 60

quantitative **4**, 8, **34**, 50, 167, 169–70

rank 9, **27**
Reading dialect 15
reading style **14**, 41, 81–2
real time study **15**
Received Pronunciation (RP) **6**, 8, 9, 25, 41–3, **54**–6, 64, 92–3, 127
recipient design **27**, **30**, 219
reduction **17**, 99
reduplication 65, 188–90
reduplication 65, 188–90
register 3, **8**–10, 11, 28–9, 33, 39, 43–7, 53, 54, 59, 65, 67, 73, 86–92, 98, 111–12, 114, 121, 124, 145, 146–53, 224–5
relations **74**, 152, 187
repair 67, 70
replication study **41**–3, 226
research question **39**
restricted code **45**–7, 90–92, 119
rhoticity **7**, 13–14, 16, 19, 26, 57, 62, 130
Russian 27, 57

sampling method **3**, 78, 80
scene **54**
Scots English 7, 17, 19, 25, 85, 99
Scots Gaelic 11, 101
Sea-Speak 23
segmentary structure 53
selection **18**
self-consciousness 10, 14
self-oriented phatic token **70**
self-report **3**
semantic non-equivalence **59**
setting **54**
shibboleth **95**
Shona 13
side-sequence **31**
Singaporean English 11, 12, 18, 64–6, 92–3
Singlish 12, 24, 64–6
situational code-switching **12**
skip-connecting **31**, 121
social class 4, 7, **13**–16, 18, 20, 23, 25, 29, 34, 41, 45–6, 52, 55–6, 60, 67, 79–80, 90, 92, 127, 129–32, 138, 143, 163, 169, 203, 208
social constructionism **21**, 203

social meaning **34**, 173, 208
social network **29**, 51–4, 61, 107, 163, 209
social rank 9, **27**
social variable **3**–4, 13–16, 32–3, 51, 79, 169, 183, 203, 208–9, 219
sociolect **9**, 53
solidarity **27**, 43, 50, 53, 61, 65, 94
South African English 13
Spanish 11, 12, 13, 18, 21, 22, 23
speech repertoire 11–12, **53**, 143, 145
Sranan Tongo 184–91
standard deviation **81**
standard Englishes 7–8, 12, 17–19, **24**–6, 54, 61, 64, 81, 96, 99, 101, 109, 126–33, 134
standardisation 16, **17**, 18–19, 23, 25–6, 35, 43, 46, 50–52, 54, 56–8, 66, 81, 99, 103, 107, 126–33
stereotype **19**, 41–3, 52–3, 60, 65, 85
style 3, 8–**10** 11, 14, 29, 32, 43, 46, 54–5, 68, 73, 106, 114, 129–30, 141, 143, 145–53, 158, 196, 198–200, 203, 220, 225
subjunctive mood 19, **97**
Swahili 22
Swedish 17, 27
Swiss German 13, 49
synchronic **15**, 167–70
systemic-functional grammar **72**

taboo 43–5, 158
tag-switching (see also code-switching) **48**, 154
Tamil 64
Teesside 7, 8
tenor **9**–10
textual metafunction **72**
theory-driven **38**, 77
Toccharian 17
Tok Pisin 23, 107–9
trade language **22**, 64
transcription 2, 46, 60–61, 68, 73–4, **76**–7, 105–7, 114–18, 176–8, 183, 209, 211, 219, 220, 225
turn 21, **30**–32, 67, 76, 207, 210–19
turn-taking 21, **31**–2, 46, 77, 121, 207, 210–19
T/V system 27–8, 49–50

uniformitarian principle **57**
universalistic code **45**, 47
unofficial norms **17**, 99
unvoiced **6**, 62
upspeak/uptalk **56**
urban dialectology **8**
Urdu 11
utterance incompletor **32**, 67

variable **3**–4, 13–16, 32–3, 51, 61, 79,
    129–30, 163–76, 183, 203, 208–9,
    219
variable rule **15**
variationism **13**–16, 21, 51, 60, 209

verbal repertoire **53**, 11–12, 143, 145, 196
vernacular **12**–13, 15, 17, 23, 25, 43, 49,
    52–6, 61, 63, 97, 99, 101–3, 158, 169,
    175, 198–9
vitality **17**, 99
voiced **6**
Vorarlberg Austrian German 50
vowel **6**–7, 13–14, 16, 29, 52, 61–2, 107,
    129, 162, 164

Welsh English 11, 13, 100–1
word-list style **14**, 61

x-isation **24**–**5**, **53**, 56–7, 64

eBooks – at www.eBookstore.tandf.co.uk

## A library at your fingertips!

eBooks are electronic versions of printed books. You can store them on your PC/laptop or browse them online.

They have advantages for anyone needing rapid access to a wide variety of published, copyright information.

eBooks can help your research by enabling you to bookmark chapters, annotate text and use instant searches to find specific words or phrases. Several eBook files would fit on even a small laptop or PDA.

**NEW:** Save money by eSubscribing: cheap, online access to any eBook for as long as you need it.

### Annual subscription packages

We now offer special low-cost bulk subscriptions to packages of eBooks in certain subject areas. These are available to libraries or to individuals.

For more information please contact webmaster.ebooks@tandf.co.uk

We're continually developing the eBook concept, so keep up to date by visiting the website.

## www.eBookstore.tandf.co.uk